ECONOMICS OF EDUCATION

About the Editor

Dr. Mujibul Hasan Siddiqui, M.A. (Economics), M.Ed., M.Phil. (Education), Ph.D. (Education), PGDHE, PGDDE, MADE, CCCA, CCPALA is working as Associate Professor in the Department of Education, Aligarh Muslim University, Aligarh-202002, Uttar Pradesh, India. He has also worked as Acting Chairperson of the Department of Education, Aligarh Muslim University, Aligarh. He has authored and edited several books, encyclopaedias in the area of education, research and innovative teaching, published more than fifty research papers, reviewed eighty national and international research papers. He has attended several national and international seminars, workshops, conferences in India. He is a member of Scientific Advisory Committee of International Conferences, USA IISTE Journal of Education and Practice, IISTE International Institute of Science Technology and Education, Accelerating Global Knowledge, Creation and Sharing IISTE USA P.O. Box 5934, New York, NY 10016 USA and Institute of Knowledge, Sri Lanka and India. He is a member of editorial board of several national and international journals of research. He has guided several Ph.D. research scholars and research projects of M.Ed. students in the area of curriculum, Planning, ICT, Models of Teaching, Higher Education, Management of Education, Educational Psychology, Philosophy etc. He has guided Research Projects of the students of Indira Gandhi National Open University, India. He is the foreign examiner of Ph.D. research scholars and M.Ed. Students and evaluated Ph.D. theses and Dissertations in faculty of education of the University of South Africa (UNISA) and University of Zululand, South Africa. He has received many academic and research excellence awards in India like Life Time Education Achievement Award, Bharat Gaurav Ratan Award, Best Educationist Award, Bharat Shiksha Ratan Award, Eminent Educationist Award, Rashtriya Vidya Saraswati Puraskar. He has visited Lootah Groups of Companies as Educational Advisor, Dubai, UAE. He is the life member of several research and educational organisations in India like All India Association of Muslim Social Scientists, India; All India Association of Educational Research, India; All India Federation of Educational Associations, India. All India Association of Teacher Educators, New Delhi, Member in the International Panel of the Board of Research Advisors North Carolina, U.S.A. Vice-President of Commonwealth Association for Educational Administration and Management, Uttar Pradesh. He is Editor-in-Chief and Publisher of Five International Journals: 1. Excellence International Journal of Education and Research ISSN 2322-0147 (Online Journal), 2. Excellence International Journal of Education and Research ISSN 2349-8838 (Print Journal), 3. Excellence International Journal of Scientific Research ISSN 2394-4242 (Print Journal), 4. Excellence International Journal of Islamic Studies and Theological Research ISSN 2394-6830 (Print Journal), and 5. Excellence International Journal of Psychological and Mental Health Research ISSN 2395-5643 (Print Journal).

ECONOMICS OF EDUCATION

Edited by
Mujibul Hasan Siddiqui
Associate Professor
Department of Education
Aligarh Muslim University
Aligarh

CONCEPT PUBLISHING COMPANY PVT. LTD.
NEW DELHI-110059

ISBN: 978-93-5439-013-5

First Published 2021

Published and Printed by

Concept Publishing Company Pvt. Ltd.
A/15-16, Commercial Block, Mohan Garden
New Delhi-110059 (India)
T : 91 11 41101460, 91 11 25351460, 91 11 25351794
E : publishing@conceptpub.com, *W*: www.conceptpub.com

Cataloging in Publication Data--Courtesy: D.K. Agencies (P) Ltd. <docinfo@dkagencies.com>

Economics of education / edited by Mujibul Hasan Siddiqui.
pages cm
Contributed articles.
Includes bibliographical references and index.
ISBN 9789354390135

1. Education—Economic aspects—India. 2. Economic development—India. 3. Human capital—India. 4. Education and state—India. I. Siddiqui, Mujibul Hasan, editor.

LCC LC67.I5E26 2021 | DDC 370.954 23

Preface

> "*An investment in knowledge pays the best interest.*"
> —Benjamin Franklin

Though rather nascent, the economics of education is a rapidly growing and evolving field that applies a diverse array of economic theories, models, and quantitative methodologies to understand, analyse, and improve the performance of education systems. Economic theories, such as the theory of human capital, economic models, such as the input-output based model of educational production, and rigorous experimental and quasi-experimental designs that seek to establish causal relationships have been developed and used by economists to put light on a host of substantive issues that span education sectors, from formal to informal, and education levels, from early childhood education to higher education. Some of the most prominent issues in education that economists currently research include school choice, teacher accountability, and filling growing achievement gaps.

Obviously knowledge and skills acquired through educational investments increase human productivity. With each investment, one may incur costs in the form of out-of-pocket expenses, foregone earnings, and psychic costs associated with the pressure of studying and examinations. Benefits accrue later in life through enhanced earnings in the labour market, access to better jobs, a higher likelihood of being employed, and better health. Simultaneously, there are also psychic benefits from enhanced social status and the prestige associated with higher levels of education. Although individuals' motivation for pursuing schooling may differ, and the psychic costs and benefits may be quite varied depending on personality, expectations of returns, and other traits, economists hypothesize that, other things equal, the more the education acquired, the higher the earnings achieved after the schooling is completed.

In fact, economics of education is the study of economic issues relating to education, including the demand for education, the financing and provision of education, and the comparative efficiency of various educational programmes and policies. From early works on the relationship between schooling and labour market outcomes for individuals, the field of the economics of education has grown rapidly to cover virtually all areas with linkages to education.

The present volume is the compilation of scholarly research articles and papers contributed by the budding as well as seasoned scholars/researchers in the field of education. The major themes, given elaborate treatment herein are—role of principal in institutional planning, model educational planning, education and development, role of education in development of education, developing economics of value-based education, economic development in India through education, education and economic development, education and economic growth in India, progress of secondary education in India under five year plans, changing nature of higher education, education as an investment, legal perspective of government policy of education, human capital formation, HRM and HRD, human development index, costs of education, cost-benefit analysis in education, investment in education, economic approaches to education, manpower planning approach, role of education in human capital, supply of education, economic dimension of investment in human capital, return from education, and approaches of planning in education, etc.

Supported by facts and figures, the information furnished in this book will prove useful to students, researchers, teachers, teacher-trainers, teacher-trainees, policy-makers and educationists.

It is pertinent to note here that the real credit for this endeavour goes to contributors of different papers contained herein. I express my gratitude to all of them for sharing the fruits of their research findings and erudition. I am also grateful to my seniors, colleagues and friends for their cooperation, moral support and all possible help to successful execution of this volume. I am thankful to my kith and kin for their direct/indirect involvement in my academic pursuits. Last but not the least, I am deeply beholden to Shri Ashok Kumar Mittal, Managing Director, Concept Publishing Company Pvt. Ltd., New Delhi for undertaking publication of this volume and materialising it meticulously in elegant manner.

Definitely, we will feel amply rewarded if this serves the purpose of all those for whom this is meant.

—Mujibul Hasan Siddiqui
Editor

Contents

UNIT 3

Economic Approaches of Education

UNIT 4

Education and Human Development

Contributors

Dr. Afshan, Ex-Research Scholar, Department of West Asian Studies and North African Studies, Aligarh Muslim University, Aligarh-202002, Uttar Pradesh, India. *Email:* afsanirshad@gmail.com

Dr. Ahmad Mahmoud Ali Alghzawi, Ex-Research Scholar Department of Education, Aligarh Muslim University, Aligarh-202002, Uttar Pradesh, India. *Email:* ali07781473197@gmail.com

Dr. Chetna Trivedi, Research Scholar, Centre for Political Studies, Jawaharlal Nehru University, New Delhi. *Email:* trivedichetna93@gmail.com

Dr. D. Anita, M.A. (Philosophy), M.A. (Hindi)., M.A. (English), M.Ed., M.Phil., Ph.D. Vikas B.Ed. College, Chilkur, Ranga Reddy, Telangana. *Email:* anitaphd2014@gmail.com

Dr. Deepti Sharma, Research Assistant, Department of Psychology, Aligarh Muslim University, Aligarh. *Email:* deeptisharmaamu@gmail.com

Prof. Kartar Singh, Research Scholar, Faculty of Education (IASE), Jamia Millia Islamia, New Delhi. *Email:* kartar2030@yahoo.com

Kiran Arora, Research Scholar, Faculty of Education, Jamia Millia Islamia, New Delhi. *Email:* kiran.arora.id@gmail.com

Kounsar Jabeen, Research Scholar, Department of Education, Aligarh Muslim University, Aligarh. *Email:* kysarmohd002@gmail.com

Dr. M.P. Tripathi, Associate Professor, Department of Teacher Education and Research, R.R.P.G. College, Amethi-227405, UP, India. *Email*: msprv62@gmail.com

Maliha Batool, Research Scholar, Department of Economics, University of Jammu, *Email:* malihamughal1991@gmail.com

Dr. Mujibul Hasan Siddiqui, Associate Professor, Department of Education, Aligarh Muslim University, Aligarh, *Email*: mhsiddiqui50@gmail.com

Dr. Muqowim, M.A., Faculty of Tarbiyah and Teacher Training, State Islamic University (SIU), Sunan Kalijaga Yogyakarta, Indonesia. *Email*: muqowimk@gmail.com

Smt. Naipali, Assistant Professor, Law Department, Shri Varshney College, Aligarh. *Email:* vaishalilahri@gmail.com

Nazia Hassan, Research Scholar, Faculty of Education Jamia Millia Islamia, New Delhi. *Email:* kartar2030@yahoo.com

Dr. Qudsia Hafeez, School of Education, Osmania University, Hyderabad, Telangana. *E-mail*: qudsiahafeez@rocketmail.com

Md. Rajesh Ali, Research Scholar, Department of Education, Aligarh Muslim University, Aligarh-202002, UP, India. *Email:* rajeshali.alig@gmail.com/ creationzindadill@gmail.com

Dr. Rajni Bala, Assistant Professor, Shah Satnam Ji College of Education, Sirsa, Haryana. *E-mail*: balarajni1112@gmail.com

Dr. Rambat Nur Sasongko, Professor, Department of Education, Faculty of Education, University of Bengkulu, Indonesia.
E-mail: rambatnur@yahoo.com

Dr. Reena Trivedi, Assistant Professor and Head, Department of Economics, R.R.P.G. College, Amethi, U.P., India. *Email:* reenatrivedi28@gmail.com

Dr. S.R. Khalid, Associate Professor, S.V. College, Aligarh.
Email: srksvc70@gmail.com

Dr. Shazia Mansoori, Assistant Professor, Department of Education, Aligarh Muslim University, Aligarh. *Email:* shazia.ed@amu.ac.in

Dr. Tamara Nije Tawfiq Dawoud, Ex-Research Scholar, Department of Education, Aligarh Muslim University, Aligtarh, Uttar Pradesh, India.
Email: dawoudtamara235@gmail.com

Dr. Umme Salma, Assistant Professor, Department of Education, MANUU.
Email: us_mirza@yahoo.com

Y. Asha, M.A. English, M.Ed., Resource Person, Gowtham Model Schools.
Email: ashabharthi123456@gmail.com

Zainab Musheer, Research Scholar, Department of Education, Aligarh Muslim University, Aligarh. *Email:* zainab2509@gmail.com

Zubair Ahmad Parray, Research Scholar, BGSB University, Rajouri, Jammu & Kashmir, *Email*: zubairh24@gmail.com

Unit 1

Educational Planning

1
Institutional Planning: A Role of Principal

Mujibul Hasan Siddiqui

Concept of Institutional Planning

> "Institutional planning is a programme of development and improvement prepared by an educational institution on the basis of its felt needs and the resources available or likely to be available, with a view to improving the school programme and school practices. It is based on the principle of optimum utilisation of the resources available in the school and the community."
>
> — *M.B. Buch*

Planning is a purposeful action.

Objectives of Institutional Planning

1. To make quantitative and qualitative improvement.
2. To provide more amenities like teachers, students and community.
3. Reducing incidence of wastage and stagnation.
4. Develop a love for manual work.
5. Cultivate a good feeling of gardening, craft, interior and exterior decoration.
6. Promoting better relationship between the pupils and the teachers on the one hand, the teachers and the parents on the other.
7. Inspiring the teachers to give their best to the pupils in particular and the school in general.
8. Developing a taste in the pupils in dramatics, athletics and hobbies.

9. Reducing the cost of education per pupil by making the optimum utilisation of existing resources.
10. Tapping all the economic resources of the local community.
11. Procuring all possible plans and non-plans, recurring and non-recurring grants from the government agencies.
12. Receiving all possible help from the philanthropic associations in the form of scholarships for the pupils, book aid and amenities like the water cooler, the public address instruments etc.
13. On the social side it should aim at social development and enlightenment.
14. National integration for making the whole society strong.
15. Cultural and emotional integration.
16. But if it is an old and established one, the main objective would be to review and if need be, to redefine the philosophy.
17. On the political side it should aim at developing democratic attitudes in the teachers and the pupils.
18. Improvement of Instruction.
19. Improvement of library equipment and facilities in school.
20. Optimum utilization of existing resources.
21. Harnessing community resources and goodwill to improve and develop the school.
22. Providing an opportunity to the local community, school staff and student to join hands and improve the school.
23. Developing co-curricular programmes in the school like work experience, social service and adult educational programmes, and youth service which will make the school a community centre.

Institutional Planning—Steps

The principal of college should keep following steps in mind while making institutional plan:

1. Identifying the needs of the institution.
2. Pooling together the resources available.
3. Preparing a plan of action.
4. Implementing the plan.
5. Evaluating and taking corrective actions.

School Plant

The term school plant includes the site, building, furniture and equipment.

The Site

- The criteria to be observed in selecting a school site.
- It should be within the easy reach of the pupils.
- It should have public transportation facilities.
- It should not be too near to bus stand, railway station, factories, cinema theatres, liquor shops or cremation grounds.
- It should be free from disturbing noises.
- It should be located in a healthy environment.
- It should provide safe and healthy conditions to the pupils.
- It should be sufficient to meet all the educational requirements of the pupils, including play ground.

The School Building

- It should be beautiful and strong.
- It should meet all the educational requirements.
- It must provide all facilities for curricular and co-curricular activities.
- It should safeguard the health and safety of the pupils and teachers.
- Each unit of the school building should be designed to suit the purpose, but it should have a satisfactory co-ordinatlon with other units.
- It should be adaptable to the changing requirements of education.

Design of Classroom

- Apart from the regular classrooms there should be special rooms for laboratory, store room for science equipments and materials, libraries, a school hall, teachers' room, headmaster's room, office room, dining hall, waiting room for girls, visitors room, auditorium, toilets etc.
- While planning, rooms for special subjects should be located close to each other.
- Science room and laboratory should be adjacent.

- Library should be in central place.
- Headmaster's room should be so placed that he could have an overall view of the whole school campus from his room.
- There should be separate toilets for teachers, boys and girls.

Classroom

While planning classrooms, the following requirements should be ensured:

- *Size:* A classroom should be large enough to accommodate 40 to 45 pupils. The dimension may be 7m × 7m.
- *Lighting:* Every room should be well-lighted.
- *Windows:* Windows should admit enough light and air into the classroom. The window area should not be less than one-fifth of the floor area.
- *Ventilation:* Ventilation can be ensured by two method—natural or artificially produced by use of fan.
- *Blackboard:* Easel blackboard is better than wall blackboard because Easel blackboard can be moved from one place to another and their angle can be changed to suit the light.
- *Cleaning:* The classrooms must be cleaned daily.

Furniture and Equipment

- Lack of good furniture might result in poor postures of children, which in turn can affect their health, efficiency and even attitude.
- The seats and other furniture should suit the age and body measurement of pupils.
- While arranging the furniture, the following points must be in mind:
  - The desks should be arranged at right angles to the window walls.
  - Each student should be allowed at least 45 cms of space with enough moving space in between group of desks, and between desk and walls.
    - The teacher must be able to move freely among these in order to give individual attention to pupils.
    - There should not be more than six rows of desks.
    - There should be sufficient blackboards in each classroom.
    - There should be shelves and almirahs for keeping the books of pupils and for storing equipments.

Library

"A good library is one that keeps books on every subject—but selected books; where the librarian is a true devotee, devote of ulterior seeking, from pride in the mere loading of shelves, capable of discriminating rejection."

—Rabindranath Tagore

- Library is the store house of books.
- No system of education can succeed without a well stocked library.
- The efficient running of the library depends upon the factors—Role of Librarian, Role of Teachers, Location of the Library room, Quality of Books.
- The books for the school library should be selected with reference to the educational needs, vocational needs and recreational needs of the pupils.
- Reference books and encyclopaedias should be readily made available for teachers and pupils.
- Adequate copies of important books should be secured.
- There should be supply of current periodicals and newspapers, in the library which would be useful to pupils and teachers.

Purpose of School Library

- It provides self-study and self-education.
- It supplements classwork of students and increase pupil vocabulary.
- It broadens the outlook of students by placing before a vast store of useful information.
- It develops new interest in children and motivates them to write poems, stories, essays and plays.
- It helps pupil to improve their performance in debates.
- It gives them pleasure in leisure hours.
- It helps children to maintain good discipline in their life.
- It imparts training to pupils in comprehension, note-making and keeping books clean.
- It imparts training in punctuality by borrowing and returning books in time.
- It develops the habit of silent reading.

Organization of School Library

- Location of the library.
- Quality of books.
- Suitability of books.
- Librarian.
- Arrangement of the books.
- Issue of books.
- Class library.
- Reading rooms.
- How to encourage pupil to use the school library?
- Each student should be asked to maintain a library notebook.
- Periods for library work should be provided in the time-table.
- Class library system should be encouraged.
- Teachers should give talk on the importance of extra readings.
- Book lovers club should be formed.

Laboratory

- Laboratory provides help in making activity dominated teaching more successful.
- Interest is created in the subjects of study.
- In addition to a big room where experiments are performed, a lecture hall and a store room also be provided.
- The size of their rooms should be determined according to the number of students, so that at least 3 square metres of space is available for work of each student.

Equipments for Physics Laboratory

- Table for experiments.
- Proper arrangements for gas, gas burners and spirit lamps.
- Wall almirahs and cupboards for keeping apparatus safely.
- Fixed tables, preferably of stones, along the wall for keeping physical balance in a manner that students can work on them easily.
- Apparatus and materials related to different experiments.
- Proper arrangement of water-sink and tap.

Equipments for Chemistry Laboratory

- Table for keeping equipments. There should be ample arrangements for drawers, gas, gas burners, water taps and sinks attached to every table.
- Arrangements for fresh air.
- Glass cases for keeping chemical balances.
- Adequate provision of wall cupboards and almirahs for keeping chemicals and apparatus.
- Arrangements for preparing distilled water.
- Apparatus and materials for different experiments.
- Adequate number of microscopes.

Equipments for a Biology Laboratory

- Tables for experiments. In these water taps, drawers and shelves should be provided.
- Specimens of different creatures, charts, models and slide showing their life cycle.
- Instruments for dissecting and handling of creatures and plants.
- Almirahs for keeping different materials and apparatus.
- Aquarium for keeping fish and water plants.
- Arrangements for keeping plants outside the laboratory.
- An epidiascope and slide projector.
- Specimen book for plants, flowers and leaves.

Office

- There should be a well-equipped office in school in order to ensure effective administration of the school.
- The office room should have filing cabinets and racks for keeping files in orderly manner.
- Steel almirahs for keeping confidential papers and a small steel safe for keeping cash is also necessary.

Maintenance of Records

- **Maintenance of records is very important for school administration.**

The important records, that are maintained in school, are:

- Admission records
- Attendance register
- Fee registers
- Time-table records
- Examination records
- Corresponding records
- Stock registers
- Purchase register
- Registers regarding parents
- Progress records
- Visitors book
- Log book
- School calendar.

Curricular and Co-curricular Activities

Experience has shown that achieving all-round development of the learner is not possible with curricular activities alone.

The pupils have to provide with certain dynamic activities meant for all-round development of the learner is called co-curricular activities.

Co-curricular activities are not directly part of the regular studies in the classrooms but at the same time they supplement the curricular experience.

Objectives of Co-curricular Activities

- To promote physical and mental health.
- To develop team spirit and social cohesion.
- To inculcate love and a sense of dignity of work.
- To develop aesthetic tastes.
- To promote discipline.
- To supplement academic work.
- To develop positive attitude and value system.

Classification of Co-curricular Activities

Category I: Literary, Cultural and Club Activities

These provide the pupils opportunities for creative expression and for nurturing their specific innate talents and interests.

- Library activity
- Debate
- Creative writing
- Elocution
- Manuscript magazine
- Cultural activity
- Drama
- Music
- Dance
- Drawing and Painting
- Sculpturing
- Artistic embroidery
- Club activity
- Science club
- Social science club
- Mathematics club
- Young farmer's club
- Natural club
- Environmental club
- Philatelic club
- Health club

Category II: Outdoor Activities

- Games
- Sports
- Gymnastics
- Yoga
- Swimming
- Scouts
- N.C.C.
- Work experience
- Gardening
- First Aid
- Junior Red Cross
- National Service Scheme
- Organization of Co-curricular Activities
- Planning

- Implementing
- Evaluating

Time-table

- Time-table is the detailed plan showing the schedule of time allotment to various subjects and academic activities.
- Usually time-table is prepared for a week, to be repeated.
- All the work is carried out systematically in tune with the time-table.
- The successful working of the school depends on a suitable time-table.

Need for a Timetable

- Timetable is necessary for the proper management of the affairs of a school.
- Through this the headmaster knows the work of every class and every teacher.
- The time-table will help the headmaster in carrying out the work of the school effectively.
- Headmaster will be able to arrange extra work for teachers if required.

Importance of Timetable

- Timetable ensures orderly work. It assigns proper persons for particular classes during appropriate periods in a proper manner.
- It saves the time and energy of teachers and pupils by preventing duplication and overlapping.
- It ensures right allocation of time for different subjects and activities, by giving proper weightage according to needs.
- It ensures proper distribution of work among teachers.
- It makes the work-load of teachers balanced and equitable.
- It inculcates habit of orderliness, steadiness, regularity and alertness among the teachers and pupils.
- It helps to maintain discipline and order.

Content of Time-table

- Time of beginning and ending of the school day.

- Time of beginning and ending of each period.
- Subjects and activities assigned a specific period.
- Days on which and time during which each subject and each activity is to be handled.
- Name of the teachers engaging each subject and each activity during respective periods.
- Name of the teachers in charge of each division of each standard.
- Room in which each class meets.
- Details regarding the recess periods.

Types of Time-table

- Class time-table.
- Teacher's time-table.
- Master time-table.
- Teacher's vacant period time-table.
- Activities timetable (timetable for each school activity).
- Room time-table showing the work, the class and the teacher in relation to each room.

Time-table Construction

The first thing is to be decided in framing of a time-table is to determine the number of working days in a week and duration of school hours.

All these are determined by Department of Education and also prescribes number of periods for each subject.

Time-table also depends on the type of school. Timetable in a basic school, or in a double shift school will be different from that in ordinary school.

Principles of Time-table Construction

Principle of Fatigue

Each pupil has a warming-up stage, full-working stage and a falling-off stage, everyday.

During first period happens warming-up, the second and third period full-working stage, the fourth period is falling-off period.

In the same manner, first period of the afternoon happens warming-up, second period is full-working-stage, and third period happens falling-off.

The best period for fatigue creating subject (subject like Mathematics and English) are the second and third periods in the morning and second period in the afternoon.

Mother tongue and other subjects do not cause much fatigue, the first and fourth periods in the forenoon and the fourth and third periods in the afternoon can be set for these.

Principle of Variety

- Students will feel bored and dull if they are taught the same subject for a number of periods continuously.
- It is better not to have the same subject for two consecutive periods.
- There should be a alternation of mental and physical tasks also.

Principle of Justice

- Work among the members of the staff should be equally distributed.
- Unequal distribution of work may cause frustration.
- Leisure periods should be judiciously distributed.
- No teacher should be asked to teach a subject for which he is not qualified.

Principle of Rest and Recreation

Rest and recreation are essential for children. Hence, provision should be made for that.

Principle of Flexibility

- The time-table should be flexible, and not rigid.
- It should be a faithful servant and not a tyrant master.
- Student's Council
- Student's Council is formerly constituted body of students.
- New educational ideas give ample opportunities for students to actively take part in various curricular and co-curricular activities of the school.
- Student's council can help teachers and school administrators in conducting literary activities, cultural functions, and sports.

- Student's council can affectively take up the responsibilities of maintaining discipline in school.
- By actively participating in the activities of student's council, students will get training to be a democratic citizen of the country.

School Complex

- Clustering of 8-10 institutions in a vicinity for the purpose of sharing resources is what we call a school complex.
- There institutions can reinforce each other by exchanging resources, personnel, materials, teaching aids etc.
- The expertise of teachers can be shared among the institution belonging to the school complex.
- A complex can prepare and standardize achievement tests and conduct common examinations for all schools in the complex.
- Sharing of resources will help not only to reduce the expenditure but also rise the academic standards of the students.

2
Approaches of Planning in Education

Deepti Sharma and *Zainab Musheer*

Introduction

The word 'planning' is directed towards the objectives, that is supposed to achieve. It is not a single term rather it is a process which amalgamate in itself various steps and decisions beforehand. Its main purpose is to chalk out exactly what is to be done in a given situation with proper strategy and by whom the task is supposed to get done. Hence, it develops courses of action with maximum utilization of resources available. Therefore, planning is the most crucial for running any institution smoothly. As planning is a process it involves various steps, as we all know, it starts when we recognize the need of any action to be taken. Thus regarding that the first step is, to set goals that any organization wishes to achieve, corresponding to it the second step is to develop premises and assumptions that are made on previous knowledge in relation to present plans, third is to find alternatives available for better results, as fourth step is to select the better alternatives from the perspective of different approaches and select the best one as per the objectives of organization, among step fifth is to make a proper plan and strategy with supportive plans that actually prepare for stimulating the main plan, sixth step is to implement the plan, and seventh is to monitor the plan for its proper functioning. In order to better understand these steps look at the Fig. 2.1 of planning process.

The great philosopher Aristotle defines education as a "process of training man to fulfil his aim by exercising all the faculties to the fullest extent as a member of society." Hence, education is a deliberate effort for bringing out the best from an individual which is already exited in

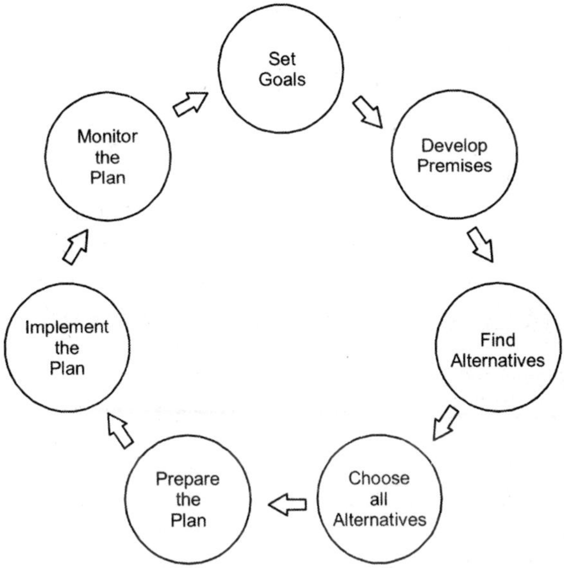

Fig. 2.1: Process of Planning.

him with rigorous training. Education always has a goal of improving knowledge and enhancing skills among learners that are all related to physical, mental, social and moral. Thus, it is development of all-round personality of a child.

In this way, we can see that education desperately need a proper planning in order to realize its goal. As education is always goal directed which needs some serious steps to take. Therefore, educational planning is of great significance.

Educational Planning

Educational planning is a procedure of making bunch of decisions related to the aims of an educational institution so that targets can be realized in the future with acknowledging the accessible assistance. It is mainly concerned with the strategy to utilize the human and material resources available properly for which rhetorical questions like where to go and how to do so is the best to start any process of planning. In order to better understanding in term of educational planning for instance educational planning is supposed to be done for school organization then its aims must develop for the development of the school organization with the consideration of future prospect. Now, the question arises where to go thus the planner must do extensive review regarding this and after that for, how to do that, we need manpower, and sound fund, i.e. money. Then planning is needed for applying fund from government or any organization that will need smart manpower approach. And planning is also necessary to keep an eye on the goals whether we are going in a correct direction. In the words of Okunamiri (2003), the motivation behind educational planning is for ensuring the successful achievement of objectives through a proper strategy which involves a series of activities directed towards the main goal of any institution. Hence, educational planning works on rational and creative thinking that ensures that productive educational outcomes. It includes anticipating the eventful future of educational prerequisite with the consideration of making satisfactory arrangement for them.

In this way, educational planning is an activity which involves collecting and analysing data and interpret them to make projection for future educational improvement specially estimates of manpower, material, and economical resources expected to accomplish targets (Fadipe and Adepoju, 2006).

Definitions of Educational Planning

According to P.H. Coomb (1970), "Educational planning, in its broadest generic sense, is the application of rational, systematic analysis to the process of educational development with the aim of making education more effective and efficient in responding to the needs and goals of its students and society."

According to J.I. Nwankwo (1981), "Educational planning is a process of preparing a set of decisions about educational enterprise in such a way that the goals and purposes of education will be sufficiently realized in future with the available resources."

According to R.S. Longe (1987), "Educational planning forms an integral part of development planning which involved attempt to solve the problem of scarce resources relative to the growing heads of the national development."

Importance of Educational Planning

1. Planning in education prepare the organization and its members goal oriented.

2. The aim of educational planning is to increase the effectiveness and efficiency of any programme in each aspect. Hence, before doing any task a well-structured plan saves time, energy and money of any institution and its members too.
3. By keeping in mind each and every step of any programme that is to be manifested, will increase the chances of great success for any educational institution.
4. By preparing a blue print of any task under the educational planning proves as a sound strategy for tackling any problem of educational institution. A proper planning assists in staying away from the experimentation techniques for getting things done.
5. As wastage and stagnations are the two critical impediments in the success of any educational institution hence by embracing a proper educational planning, the administrative functions of any institution can go in a longer run.
6. Planning in education makes the best use of available resources in education system and provides different opportunities for the further benefits of its institution.
7. As harmony is required for the smooth functioning of any institution. By making proper planning in education, balance can be created among its different approaches—social, political, economic and technological.
8. Educational planning encourage rational and creative thinking among the teachers, educational experts and administrators and make them more disciplined.
9. Through proper educational planning, the value and cultural system of a given society can be preserved and transmitted among the large group of talented citizen of a country.
10. A proper planning in education facilitates any nation in realizing the universal aims of education. Its development in every aspect can be done by making the ahead plan before time by proper analysing and research on time.

Major Approaches of Educational Planning

There are three major approaches that are social demand approach, cost benefit approach and manpower approach of educational planning which are discussed below.

Social Demand Approach

As per this approach educational planning should be done by taking care of demand from society. It is aimed to pacify the demand of all level education, hence its main focus is on quantitative planning. This approach for educational planning alludes that education should make accessible for all who are interested, qualified for getting it and have desire to get any sort or level of schooling.

Fundamentally, social demand approach endeavours to estimate the public demand for education at different times in future. The factors among the term 'demand' comes the size of the young populace, per captia salary, and the appropriation of the population by intellectual capacity. Thus, his approach is approximate to demand and supply formula as this method views education like any other services that are accessible to all. Hence, in this direction it is considered as a process of making assumption and forecasting the demand and aim to do planning for providing enough seats in educational institutions for satisfying the emerging demands.

According to Azunwena and Uchenna (2011) while doing the educational planning by using the lenses of social demand approach, type of education, levels of education and demographic data needs to take into consideration because it will increase the rate of literacy and will fulfil the requirement of the public by encouraging equal opportunities to all without any discrimination. It also facilitates the process of income redistribution.

Because of its appealing nature politicians in developing countries take this approach into consideration. There are few things that a planner of social demand approach must keep in mind while doing educational planning:

1. Evaluate the extent of students finishing the schooling and are probably going to attend higher education.
2. To measure the exact proportion of these effective school pass-outs and would really going to apply for admission in colleges.
3. Now the critical step of any planning comes that: taking decision, i.e. decide what number of candidates ought to be offered admission in higher education.
4. Make a judgement about the length and span of the study.

There are many factors that may influence this particular approach.

As this approach work on demand and supply system hence, cost of education is one of the factors. If it is very high consequently enrolment will be low and one thing also take into consideration that the return rate of education it also affects this approach if it is beneficial to society and nation in general government would invest more or *vice versa*. Cultural factors, quality of teachers and distance of school are the other factors that may influence the social demand approach.

Advantages of Social Demand Approach

1. The most important advantage of this approach is future oriented. Thus, it will let to know how many students are needed in demand and how many schools should be open for the benefit of society.
2. It is more beneficial to educational planner as it is more practical than theoretical. In this approach planners seek to satisfy the demand by kind of quantity of education which will serve greatest good to greatest demand.

Disadvantages of Social Demand Approach

1. This approach does not have any control over monetary system of education.
2. This approach only talks about the demand and supply and to satisfy them but does not provide guidance as how effectively these can be met.

Cost-Benefit Approach

Cost-benefit is an instrument which is adopted by analysts before undertaking any sort of financial operation or any commercial activity. The main purpose of such analysis is to make more as compared to the costs for the organization in order to survive and prosper. It is done to determine how well or poorly planned action turns out to be. Cost-Benefit Analysis can be traced back to the nineteenth century by Jules Dupuit, a French economist and engineer. This approach is based upon the accepted social principle based on individual preference. Adesina (1981) illustrated that the cost-benefit approach looks at each level of education as an investment in man with a purpose that it will return by improving the economy of the nation. The salaries received by the workers reflect the differences in the productivity, variation in the productivity are the result of educational status of the worker. It is a mode of analysis of current relationship between education and income. Education is perceived by the cost-benefit approach from two angles—the social rates of return and the private rates of return.

1. *The Social Rates of Return:* This focuses on the benefit to be delivered by the state of investing at a particular form of education. The cost of education is usually borne by the society as a whole. It can be calculated by equating the total present value earnings of an average educated person before tax with benefits to be gained from alternative investments in physical capital.

Social Rate of Return to training then again, is the advantage that gathers to the society when all is said done. Count of social advantages makes a difference the legislature in contrasting the advantages (rate of return) of other elective types of social speculation and accordingly to outline the future instructive strategy moreover. Additionally, social rate of return count in one specific sort or level of training is valuable to contrast it and the paces of come back to different kinds and levels of training which gives the data as to the degree of monetary productivity of instructive use by the state. For the most part these rates of return are marginal rates of return to marginal levels of schooling. These marginal rates of return are estimated concerning the costs in question peripheral degree of tutoring and the income (advantage) related with the specific level.

2. *The Private Rates of Return:* This is the investment by private individual and the expected benefits for acquiring a particular type of education. This is calculated by equating the direct costs of students plus earning foregone by them while studying, to the present value of earning after tax. Private Rate of Return is the advantage that accumulates to the individual or his family straightforwardly. This advantage empowers him to know the value of his cash interest in his instruction as far as expanding his future gaining limit when contrasted with the advantages of other elective ventures. Along these lines private rate of return helps the person in picking the best type of speculation.

Advantages of Cost-Benefit Approach

1. It is possible to calculate the increase in productivity of an educated person by looking at the age structure of an educated man.

2. The Cost-Benefit Approach suggests the direction in which the education system in a society should expand in order to minimize the earning capacity of their products.
3. It shows the relation between the cost of gaining more education and the increment in salaries due to additional knowledge.

Disadvantages of Cost-Benefit Approach

1. Many nations consider it as a wrong assumption that salaries reflect productivity.
2. Measuring the benefits derived from investing in any sort of education is difficult.
3. Many studies claim that primary education gives the highest return to the society.
4. Economic variable plays a dominant role rather than productivity in influencing the salaries of civil servants.
5. Financial return from education has been inflated in many under developed countries by scarcity of people with particular type and level of education.

Manpower Approach

Manpower approach entails analysis of demand and supply of manpower. It is an educational planning approach that considers human resource in every field. Education planning should be skilled based on the demand and supply principle making it need based. This approach focuses on the manpower need of the economy. This approach focuses on the three elements—specification of the composition of manpower need at some future date, specification of manpower availabilities and specification which reconciles former specification with later. It is the coordination of labour arrangements, practices and procedures in order to accomplish the right job at the right time. Comprehensively, manpower planning refers to an investment in individuals. It includes a wide spectrum of exercises, for example, instruction and instructive organizations, logical, specialized and professional establishments, general well-being, work, the business capability of work and business offices or what have called exercises that influence the nature of human resources. Manpower planning is a significant perspective in respect with ideal use of physical capital. Due to specific examinations and technological enhancements, the production phenomena turns out to be very complex. To adapt up to such perplexing creation methods it requires skilled labour force, which cannot be made accessible in a limited span of time.

Advantages of Manpower Approach

1. This approach does not need elaborate statistical studies. Manpower could call for attention to extreme gaps and imbalance in the education output pattern.
2. It gives guidance on how educational qualification of the labour force ought to be developed in the future. The proportion of people who would have primary, secondary and tertiary training.
3. Unemployment resulted from overemphasis on manpower approach making it a challenge to move towards right kind of education which may be development oriented.

Disadvantages of Manpower Approach

1. Limited guidance is provided to the educational planner regarding the benefit of right kind of education for each job.
2. The approach does not focuses on primary education which is the foundation of every education. It suggests curbing of primary education till the nation is rich enough to expand it.
3. Because of economic and technological uncertainties, it is not possible to make reliable forecast of manpower approach.

Conclusion

In this chapter, the process of planning is discussed which involves a rigorous cycle to follow for realizing the specific objectives. As education is always goal directed and it is always directed towards the benefit of the societies in general and nation in particular. Hence, educational planning is of great significance as it save time, money and labour and for the maximum benefit of the individuals, it also analyses the process from time to time. There are various resources available but to use them for the optimum output planning should be done with some approach in mind that should be used as per the need and ideology of the nation. Therefore, in this chapter three different approaches of educational planning are given—social demand approach, cost benefit approach and manpower approach that should be selected as per the requirement having in mind the objectives of that institution.

REFERENCES

Adesina, S. (1981). *What is Educational Planning? Introduction to Educational Planning.* Ili–Ife; University of Ife Press.

Azunwena, R.N. and Uchenna, N.G. (2011). "Educational Planning and Policy". In S.U. Bassey and U.U. Bassey (Eds), *Management of Higher Education in Africa*, Uyo: Abaam Publishers.

Coombs, P.H. (1970). *What is Educational Planning?* UNESCO IIEP.

Fadipe, J.O. and Adepoju, T.L. (2006). Planning for Educational Reforms and Innovation in J.B. Babalola, A.O. Ayeni, S.O. Aderdeji, A.A. Suleiman & M.O. Arikewuyo (Eds.) *Educational Management Thoughts and Practice.* Ibadan: Codat Publications.

Longe, R.S. (1987). *Fundamentals of Educational Planning.* Akure: Fagbamigbe Publishers.

Nwankwo, J.I. (1981). *Fundamentals of Management Information Systems.* Ibadan: Associated Book-Makers (Nig.) Ltd.

Okunamiri, P.O. (2003). *Resourcing and Guidance for Educational Finance in Tertiary Institutions in Nigeria Okigwe*: Fasmen Communication.

3

Analysis of Five Year Plans with Reference to Progress of Secondary Education in India

Shazia Mansoori

Introduction

Education and national development are closely related, with the nation's growth and development, education too progresses. As qualitative and quantitative improvement takes place in education, so does the nation prospers to greater heights. Each five year plan in India sets specific tasks and forecasts the planned development of the nation in desirable manner. After every five years, Government of India makes enormous efforts, undertakes tedious surveys, and analysis to generate a plan for successful growth and development. The various five year plans have helped in the successful development of education both quantitatively and qualitatively by appropriately allocating the resources and budget in a judicious manner. Secondary education, in India, has seen tremendous growth and changes, both quantitatively and qualitatively, over the period of time. Since Independence, the facilities of secondary schools, training of teachers, number of enrolment, ratio of boys and girls, quality improvement, schemes of development etc. have been introduced with a view to promote secondary education. In this chapter, the progress and status of secondary education in each of the five year plans of India are discussed explicitly. A critical analysis is done of the then prevailing status and the changes proposed in secondary education system during those five year plans.

In the Indian system of education, secondary education occupies a place between elementary and higher education. A student at this stage generally lies within the age range from 14-18 years. Secondary education prepares the students who are aiming towards university education or the higher education. The period of secondary stage is an important phase in the life of a child as these are the years of transition. The changes in the body physique, mental and emotional transformations, behaviour etc. are characerised with the onset of adolescence. Adolescence is the stage of (NCERT, India):

(a) "Intense physical change and formation of identity.
(b) Emergence of abstract reasoning and logical thinking.
(c) Intense vibrancy and energy.
(d) Emotional transformation and maturity that swings between joy and trauma.
(e) Stage of transition to work."

Educational planning is a well thought process of achieving the set targets and movimg towards growth and development of the country. Planning is a sequence of events which involves setting up of aims and objectives, follow-up of the achievement of the stated goals, and using feedback to determine further plans. Planning means assessment of the resources which are available and those needed to achieve the targets. Educational planning asks questions "What? When? Where? By whom? How?" Certain steps or methodology have to be followed for successful implementation of planning process and to obtain the desired results. During planning process, there are various concerns and issues which may rise according to the prevailing situation and thus the changes are accordingly developed. The five year plans beginning from 1951 onwards have placed emphasis on all sectors of the country's development. Educational problems and measures have been thoroughly worked upon, in these five year plans. After every five years, a document in the form of a Five Year Plan is prepared which details the growth and development achieved in the previous years, the present status and the future plans for the upcoming 5 years. The Five Year Plans are developed, executed and monitored by Planning Commission of India (now NITI Aayog). NITI Aayog, an acronym for National Institution for Transforming India, is a premier policy 'think tank' of the Government of India, established on January 1, 2015, to achieve sustainable development goals. The Planning Commission (established in 1950) of India was replaced by NITI Aayog.

Planning of education in India primarily has both quantitative and qualitative goals of the education system. This may include formal, non-formal and other modes of learning. The objective is to help the citizens acquire literacy, numeracy, computational skills, environmental education, life skills, understanding of the local community etc.

The secondary education serves to the age group 14-18 years, by bridging elementary education and higher education. The students at this level are preparing for entry into higher education. "The percentage distribution of students at the secondary level in government schools is 57.2 per cent males and 62.5 per cent females." (NSS 75th Round)

In this chapter, I have reviewed all the five year plans of India with respect to secondary education.

The status, growth rate, planning, and measures for improvement of secondary education under each five year plan were studied extensively. The original reports and documents of the five year plans starting from the First Five Year Plan were used to collect and assimilate the content for the chapter. In the upcoming section, the planning of secondary education under each five year plan is discussed thoroughly.

First Five Year Plan (1951-1956)

The First Five Year Plan was proposed for the period 1951-1956. Based on the Harrod-Domar model, the emphasis of the plan was on the growth of agricultural sector of India. During the plan period, a Commission was set up by Government of India, to examine the condition and status of secondary education. The Commission popularly known as Mudaliar Commission or Secondary Education Commission (1952) was formed to enquire and prepare a report on the then current position of the secondary education in India. In the First Five Year Plan, the following objectives were set for secondary education:

1. Secondary education was to be designed in such a manner that it is closely linked to the psychological needs of the growing children.
2. In view of the economic and social progress of the nation, several schemes were to be encouraged to help the youth for work so as to improve the existing socio-economic situation. This could be achieved by promoting vocationalisation of secondary education.
3. The methods of teaching and curriculum have to be reviewed keeping in mind the need of the secondary education system.
4. A close association of primary education especially basic education with secondary education was to be built.
5. Multilateral or unilateral schools offering parallel courses need

to be strengthened. Provision of guidance for those students who leave the education system after primary schooling was to be encouraged.

6. A joint financial assistance both by the State and the local people was to be provided. The assistance can also be in the form of land, free labour in the construction of buildings etc.

The objectives were set with the existing situation in India soon after Independence. The condition of secondary education required tremendous changes and appropriate steps were required to help in the growth of the education system. Keeping in mind the objectives that were rolled out in this plan, efforts were made both by Central and State Governments to implement suitable measures for improvement of secondary education. Several schemes were proposed which included—

1. Establishment of new secondary schools, occupational schools and a pilot school in each state with funding from Centre to act as a multi-lateral high school.
2. Introduction of technical education, commerce, agriculture, physical education, military training, gardening and agriculture, music etc. in the schools. Appropriate training of teachers in the subjects was required.
3. Schemes for construction and provision of physical facilities like buildings, playgrounds, equipment, staff and upgradation of schools.
4. Problems of secondary education to be studied as research questions at higher level.
5. Scholarships of merit for eligible poor students was to be provided.

The Secondary Education Commission presented its document in 1953 stating the problems of secondary education. It reported that curriculum, methods of teaching, were not appropriate to build students personality, more emphasis on English language study etc. Emphasis was placed on diversification of school courses, introduction of reforms, and a complete re-orientation of secondary education. Even the changes in the structural pattern of schooling period was proposed. This structure of school education comprised a period of four or five years as primary or junior basic education, a middle or senior basic or junior secondary stage of three years and a higher secondary stage of four years. Setting up of multilateral schools, technical schools, and agricultural courses in the rural areas was strongly proposed by the Commission (1952). It was also recommended that adoption of courses in Languages, General Science, Social Studies and a Craft as a common core in all secondary schools.

In the First Five Year Plan, about Rs. 169 crore were provided for the development of education—Rs. 44 crore at the Centre and Rs. 125 crore in the States.

Second Five Year Plan (1956-1961)

The Second Five Year Plan was proposed for the period 1956-1961. Formed on the P.C. Mahalanobis Model, this plan focused on the industrial development of the country. The Second Five Year Plan laid emphasis on the diversification of secondary education. The recommendations of Secondary Education Commission (1952) were the foundation of Second Five Year Plan, as a result of which various schemes and programmes were proposed. The Plan defined measures to fulfil the needs of the increasing number of students entering the secondary education. It was believed that economic development of the nation necessitates improvements in secondary education, in order to help the youth for future employment.

The proposed scheme of introduction of vocational courses, technical education etc. required trained teachers and experts in the specific vocations. Similar to the First Five Year Plan, the diversification of courses and introduction of crafts at secondary stage was emphasised. According to the abilities and aptitudes of the students, guidance for choosing the vocations and training was recommended. Establishment of multi-purpose schools and junior technical schools were focused. These technical schools were set-up to enable students for taking up some occupations as semi-skilled workers or starting their own small businesses on completion of secondary stage education. It was highlighted that boys in the age group 14-17 years will receive education (both general and technical) and also workshop training for three years. The growth in the establishment of multi-purpose schools can be observed as they numbered 250 in the First Plan and 1187 in the Second Plan. Lack of trained teachers was a major hindrance to fulfil the objective of providing skilled training to students. The Plan emphasised on focused training of teachers and the essential qualifications required in these schools. Special schemes for girl education, improved libraries, upgradation of high schools into higher secondary schools, better laboratories, improving teaching standards and teachers' salaries etc. for the reorientation of secondary education were required. Teaching of Hindi and other regional languages need to be taught and so, trained teachers and appropriate funds were needed. Establishment of a Central Bureau of Educational and Vocational Guidance, State Bureau of Educational and Vocational Guidance in 12 States, which carried out courses of training as counsellors, construction of required tests and providing guidance services to schools.

In the Second Five Year Plan, Rs. 307 crore were provided—Rs. 95 crore at the Centre and Rs. 212 crore in the States.

Third Five Year Plan (1961-1966)

The Third Five Year Plan was made for the period 1961 to 1966. Also known as 'Gadgil Yojana'. Economic independence of the population was the target of this Plan. With respect to secondary education, huge demands were placed to improve the system. The aim of secondary education is to fulfil the educational needs of the students. Keeping in mind the diverse requirements of students in the workfield, a number of courses related to administration, rural development, commerce, industry and training in manpower development were proposed at the school level.

The recommendations of Secondary Education Commission were taken as reference points in this Plan. The reorganisation of secondary education system with respect to increase in the number of schools, improvements in curriculum, diversified curricula, improvements in conditions of teachers, merit scholarships for the needy students, schemes for girl students etc. was still underway.

- The Third Five Year Plan focused on strengthening the entire programme of the secondary school reorganisation, especially the qualitative aspects.
- Establishment of multi-purpose schools, offering a variety of skill-based courses along with other school subjects, so as to present a variety of options to choose from, for the students, according to their abilities and interests.
- Special programmes of education for gifted students were also emphasised.
- State Education Departments to organise nationwide in-service and pre-service teacher education programmes were proposed. Increase in the establishment of training colleges was an

important step in this Plan. Extension centres were already built during the previous plans, which carried out an exhaustive programme of in-service training, including seminars, workshops and conferences, audio-visual, library, guidance services and publications. Each centre provided extension service to a number of schools in the area allotted to it. These centres were to be made an integral part of every training college, in this Plan.

- Emphasis on science education for enhancing the scientific attitude and in turn development of the country. General science as a compulsory or elective subject was introduced so that the students attain basic quantum of scientific knowledge. Curricular modifications in science syllabi were also necessary. There was lack of laboratories, equipments, text-books and handbooks, and even less number of teachers with expertise to teach science. Establishment of science clubs as proposed in the Second Five Year Plan was encouraged. In order to coordinate, guide and direct the entire programme of science teaching as well as the training of key personnel, a central organisation for science education was proposed to be set-up in the Third Plan. A scheme of science talent search is to be introduced with the aim to identify promising talent at the secondary stage and providing opportunities for the development.
- Increase in educational and vocational programmes so as to reach a large group of students. In the proposed Third Plan, the State Bureau needed to be strengthened so as to improve and develop the guidance programme in as many secondary schools as possible.
- The increase in girls enrolment in the schools was also followed during this plan period.
- In the Third Plan, teaching of crafts was given due importance as part of secondary as well as vocational education.
- The establishment and improvement of libraries in the First and Second Plans led to further enrichment of the library facilities. Similarly, in the Third Plan, proposal to establish few model school libraries was given, which will act as standards for the organisation and running of libraries. These libraries were to be set-up in demonstration schools which were linked to training colleges, where they acted as training centres for teacher librarians.

Annual Year Plans (1966-1969)

The period from 1966 to 1969 was devoid of any Five Year Plan. However, annual or yearly plans were proposed during this duration. Sometimes, also known as Plan Holiday. This was because the Third Plan failed and also due to the Indo-Pakistan War. During this Plan, equal priority was given to agriculture, its allied sectors and the industry sector.

Fourth Five Year Plan (1969-1974)

The duration of Fourth Five Year Plan was from 1969 to 1974. Growth with stability and progressive achievement of self-reliance were the main objectives of this plan. The slogan of "Garibi Hatao" was given by Indira Gandhi, during this period. With respect to education, major emphasis was on improvement in teacher education, increasing the number of trained teachers at the secondary stage and providing better training facilities. Training of untrained teachers through correspondence was to be initiated by the Central Institute of Education, Delhi and the four Regional Colleges of Education. In-service education and training was to be provided to mathematics and science teachers. The provision of funds to University Grants Commission with the goal of upgrading the Departments of Education in the universities by providing adequate facilities. The training colleges were also to be improved so as to benefit the professional competence of the teachers. National Council of Educational Research and Training, State Institutes of Education and State Institutes of Science Education will coordinate these programmes accordingly.

"During the Fourth Plan, the programmes already initiated in the fields of evaluation and guidance, curriculum construction, extension, text-book production, educational research and science education will be expanded. A number of pilot projects were to be worked out through these organisations. An important area of investigation and experimentation was the reduction of wastage and stagnation at the secondary stage. Training programmes for teacher educators will be continued. A Committee was appointed to review and evaluate the activities and programmes of NCERT. In the light of its recommendations, the departments of the National Institute of Education have been reorganised. Also suitable changes are being made in the working of the Regional Colleges of Education so that they may provide leadership in the field of teacher education."

Fifth Five Year Plan (1974-1979)

Beginning from 1974 to 1979, the Fifth Five Year Plan laid emphasis on agriculture, industry and mines. The success of the Plan could be seen from the fact that growth of 4.8 per cent was achieved in this Plan as against the target of 4.4 per cent. Initially, draft preparation and implementation was done by D.P. Dhar.

With reference to secondary education, an increase in enrolment was observable. New pattern of Education led to bringing about appropriate provisions. The number of teachers at the secondary stage were considered adequate, however, there was a need to expand the training facilities. Training of the teachers was to be undertaken by CIE, Delhi, RIEs, State Institute of Education, and NCERT. NCERT functioning was reviewed and evaluation done by an Expert Committee. During this Plan, the programmes already initiated in the fields of evaluation and guidance, curriculum construction, extension, text-book production, educational research and science education were to be expanded.

For vocationalisation at the secondary stage, steps were underway and selected regions were covered in the programme of vocationalisation for a period of two years. The Fifth Five Year Plan was terminated in 1978.

Rolling Plan: This plan was an annual plan for 1978-79 and was a continuation of the terminated Fifth-Five Year Plan.

Sixth Five Year Plan (1980-1985)

The period of Sixth Five Year Plan was from 1980 to 1985. Eradication of poverty and technological self-reliance were the main objectives of this Plan. The Plan was on the model of investment yojna, infrastructural changes and growth. In order to fulfil the ever-increasing demands in education system, expansion of the base, i.e. primary and secondary education was essential. Special attention to the qualitative aspects of secondary education was highlighted. Updating the curriculum, changes and modifications in the methods of teaching, improved text-books, teaching materials and awareness of technologies, and advancements in science around the world in various fields was the main focus. Curriculum and teaching of science, mathematics required special efforts, supply of science kits which were specially designed for secondary education, as well as training of teachers for these subjects was proposed strongly during this plan. Special courses were recommended for satisfying the needs of the exceptionally talented children so as to provide them opportunities suited to their talents and strengths. Vocationalistion was another important aspect in the secondary education. The growing need of the country for providing human resource and manpower development, was targeted. The potentials of the youth and the workforce demands have to be balanced accordingly. Appropriate skills in varying occupations needed to be taught to the students to prepare them for career and professional development. For this, several measures were taken to impart skills and promote learning by doing, with the support of experienced craftsmen and practitioners of the vocation. The agencies of vocational training like Krishi Udyog and Van Vikas Kendras will also be involved. Rural areas were to be focused upon with regard to this aspect of secondary education. During the Sixth Plan, computer literacy was to be introduced in secondary schools. The computer literacy included programme of computer appreciation and applications.

Seventh Five Year Plan (1985-1990)

The Seventh Five Year Plan was proposed for the period from 1985 to 1990. Self-sufficient economy along with provision of productive employment opportunities were the main goals in this Plan. Private sector was emphasised more than public sector in this Plan.

- Secondary education observed growth both in quantitative and qualitative aspects. But the prevailing conditions still necessitated improvements at various levels. Educational planning directed the best possible utilization of resources already available in the schools.
- Facilities for open/distance learning were recommended.
- Unplanned growth of high/higher secondary schools needed regulation. Certain norms and standards have to be followed by the schools to check the educationally inefficient institutions.
- Girls education to be made free up to higher secondary level.
- Underprivileged/backward sections of the society to be focused and special provisions to be made for the same.
- Teaching of science and mathematics, facilities of laboratories, modernisation of science curriculum, setting up of libraries in schools, in-service training programmes for science teachers for quality were emphasized.
- Another important aspect to be included in science education is Environmental education.

- To develop positive attitude towards work ethics, and socially useful productive work (SUPW) or work experience course to be integrated in the school programme. This programme involved participation of the community and using vocational education system to derive development, training, management, and supervision for use.
- Vocationalisation at higher secondary stage to be given more importance, and vocational education to cover fields in agriculture, industry, trade and commerce, and services. In order to cater to employment opportunities, adequate and appropriate skills have to be imparted.
- Flexibility in choosing vocational/career courses and their introduction in educational institutions to be ensured.
- In order to grow the programme of vocationalisation and meet the manpower requirements of economy, an Expert Committee was set up to recommend ways and measures in this aspect, which will be further used as guidelines for development.
- Provisions to make use of media in education, production of audio-video educational materials and software for broadcasting and telecasting need to be increased for quality education.
- An effective mechanism of in-service training of teachers for quality teaching, training in the use of Information and communication technologies and computers in education were given high priority. NCERT, India took effective steps towards this direction in starting programmes for the training purpose.
- Education for promotion of values like understanding, sense of togetherness, harmony, and national integration, in the school programme for curricular and co-curricular activities, and revision of text-books etc. needed consideration.

Annual Plans: Because of the tense political situation in India, the Eighth Five Year Plan was not formed. So two annual programmes were generated in 1990-91 and 1991-92.

Eighth Five Year Plan (1992-1997)

The Eighth Five Year Plan was prepared for the period 1992 to 1997. In this Plan, employment, education, and public health were given greater emphasis. During this Plan, Narasimha Rao Government launched the "New Economic Policy" of India.

Education in general, and secondary education in specific, received great impetus during this Plan. Enormous measures were proposed in this Plan for developing the secondary education, with provisions for both quantitative and qualitative aspects at this stage:

- The aim of this Plan was to bring improvement, regulated expansion of better facilities for marginalised and deprived sections of the society especially girls, SCs & STs, and in rural regions.
- National and State Open Schools catered to fulfil the needs of those learners out of formal system of education. Various provisions like multi-media packages and contact centres were to be utilized in these schools.
- Vocational education becomes an essential component of secondary education.
- Recommendations to provide assistance from Centre in order to devise measures for subjects like science, mathematics and computer literacy.

Some statistics (Planning Commission Report) with respect to the abovementioned points are:

- During the Eighth Plan, an increase in the number of secondary schools and enrolment was observed. The percentage of girls was 36.2 in 1996-97.
- Statistics related to the number of training colleges (697) and enrolment in these institutions for the year 1996-97 was 1.16 lakh out of which girls constituted 43 per cent.
- The programme of vocationalisation has shown improvements with respect to schools intake reaching 9.35 lakh students, which equalled 11.5 per cent against a target of 4.8 per cent at the end of 1995-96. Pre-vocational training programme was implemented in 1993-94.
- Funds were provided for improvement of libraries (in 14,734 secondary schools) and laboratories (in 15,775 schools).
- A total of Rs. 146 crore was provided for maintaining the scheme of Computer Literacy and Studies in Schools (CLASS) which covered 1,598 schools. However, it will reach out to include 2,290 more schools.
- The number of study centres through National Open School

increased to 666 in 1996-97, out of which105 were vocational study centres.

Ninth Five Year Plan (1997-2002)

The duration of Ninth Five Year Plan was from 1997 to 2002. This Plan focused on "*growth with justice and equity*". It was launched in the 50th year of India's Independence.

Education was identified as an important aspect for the nation's development in the Ninth Five Year Plan. The growth in number and improvement in the social infrastructure of education was recognised as critical in the Prime Minister's Special Action Plan (SAP).

Status of Secondary Education

- A large number of differences were observed in access to education between various regions, i.e. the urban, rural and tribal areas.
- Gender differences existed in enrolment.
- Curricular revisions in the subjects taught and vocationalisation were required.
- Scholarships, incentives, etc. for girls and deprived sections needed attention. To ensure equalisation of educational access, provision of compensatory education was accepted.
- There will be provisions of pre-vocational and hands-on training for secondary level, expansion of open learning system, training reorganisation of pre-service and in-service teachers, and application of ICT.

Critical Issues and Measures for Secondary Education

The concerning issues in secondary education and their remedial measures proposed in the Ninth Plan are as follows:

(i) Vocationalisation of Secondary Education

The scheme of Vocationalisation was important for students who aspire for self-employment or wage-employment (almost 25% of the students was the target). This also regulated entry to higher education level. The programme could not get success over the period of time because of academic and logistic hindrances.

To overcome the difficulties of vocationalisation of education, it was proposed that meaningful coordination between government, industry and trade was needed which will constitute an Empowered Committee. This will also help in promoting vocational courses which are associated with industries.

(ii) Open and Distance Education

Open learning system or distance education developed in the country to fulfil the growing demands of secondary education. The demand for secondary education increased as a result of tremendous enrolment in elementary education. The challenge was met by widening the responsibilities of NIOS and the State Open Schools (SOSs). Information Technology (IT) was another approach to be used in the education system.

(iii) Quality Improvements in Teaching

The previous plans emphasised on teaching of science, mathematics and computer education in schools and raising the quality of teaching in these subjects. However, the quality of teaching science and mathematics turned out to lag behind which may affect higher education.

- Effective measures were framed to devise new reference books at the secondary level. A Science Talent Research Scheme will be encouraged.
- Time-bound measures need to be implemented for computer education in accordance with the proposal of the Task Force on Computer Education
- The learning especially science and mathematics in the schools need to be linked to the local environment of the learners.

(iv) Education of Minorities

Although innumerous facilities have increased at the secondary stage but the students from minority groups were still far away from access.

The recommendations with reference to this aspect suggested the Scheme of Modernisation of Madarasas, for improving access to education. Another important point raised was to increase the allocation of budget for educationally backward minorities by a procedure like Area Intensive Programme.

(v) Integrated Education for the Disabled

Disability Act of 1995 was enacted to legalise education of the disabled up to 18 years of age. Educational facilities have to be made available to the special groups. Trained teachers were required for special learners. Several approaches need to be adopted in which more regions will be covered under this scheme, like composite area approach.

(vi) Curriculum

Curricular areas needed to be modified at the secondary education stage. The Ninth Plan proposed following changes (as documented by Planning Commission):

(a) "National Council of Educational Research and Training (NCERT) in collaboration with State Councils of Educational Research and Training (SCERTs) will revise curriculum and a National Draft will be prepared for discussion and adoption thereafter. New areas of concern will be included in the curriculum. After the draft is adopted, the same organisations will upgrade the text-books so as to keep pace with international standards.

(b) Simultaneously, NCERT and SCERTs will review the training needs of in-service teachers and take steps to meet the new challenges.

(c) National Council for Teacher Education will prepare a framework for pre-service teacher education, so that quality standards are upgraded across the nation."

(vii) Girl Education

The Ninth Plan proposed hostel facilities for girl students in secondary schools who were residing in remote and tribal areas. The programmes of MHRD, India will collaborate with the Ministry of Welfare to provide for the same.

Tenth Five Year Plan (2002-2007)

The period of Tenth Five Year Plan ranged from year 2002 to 2007. To double the per capita income of India in the next 10 years, was the main target. This Plan aimed for quality education and excellence at all levels of education system.

In the context of secondary education, the Tenth Five Year Plan focused on—

- Provision of educational access and bridging the gap between the different sections of the society. This was done through establishment of Common School System, wherein students from low income families were allowed admission by making it compulsory for the schools to do so.
- Revision of curriculum was another key element in this Plan, laying emphasis on vocational education, skill-based courses, expanding the environment of distance learning, reorganisation of training of teachers and enhanced application of new ICTs.
- Opening of new secondary schools was also a key point in this Plan, in order to accommodate the students at the secondary stage. The existing schools also increased their capacity through shifts, upgradation of primary schools in backward and remote areas, taking advantage of open schooling system etc. was also put to action.
- The KVS (Kendriya Vidyalaya Sangathan) to establish 150 Kendriya Vidyalayas (KVs) in partenrship with voluntary agencies. Navodaya Vidyalayas were proposed to set schools in those districts which were devoid of them, and provision of facilities in these schools. More schools were to be established for children of Tibetan refugees under Central Tibetan School Administration (CTSA), which already runs about 70 schools. A number of trusts, societies and non-profit organisations like the R.K. Mission, the Jesuits, the DAV Trust, were encouraged to start more schools in the country.
- CBSE and ICSE were the main bodies which conducted end examinations of Classes X and XII. Open schooling system for the underprivileged was also focused in this Plan. National Open School (NOS), another important nation-wide examination conducting body, played an important role in strengthening the affiliated schools/centres which adopted curriculum of different Boards, also offered NOS curriculum. Scheme to offer admissions and examinations in mid-session was made possible through 'On-Demand Admissions' and 'On-Demand Examinations'.

- A number of schemes at the secondary level, to enhance the enrolment of girl child were encouraged like provision of hostel for girls, incentives and financial assistance.
- NCERT was given the task to modernise and revise the curriculum, update courses, diversification of the syllabus etc. One step taken by NCERT was to initiate a country-wide Seventh All India Educational Survey. A fifth Regional Institute of Education for the North-Eastern Region at Shillong will be started by the Council.

The various schemes in this plan are as follows:

1. ***"Quality Improvement in Schools:*** This comprised the centrally sponsored schemes of Promotion of Science Laboratories, Environmental Orientation to School Education, Promotion of Yoga, as well as the central sector schemes of Population Education Project, International Mathematics/Science Olympiad.
2. ***Information and Communication Technologies (ICT):*** This included the centrally sponsored schemes—Computer Education and Literacy in Schools (CLASS) and Educational Technology (ET)—which seek to familiarise students with IT. State Governments would prepare Computer Education Plans (CEPs) for computer literacy and education. The components of the merged scheme ICT in Schools would include (a) funding support for CEPs; (b) strengthening and reorientation of the staff of the State Institutes of Education and Training (SIETs); (c) Digitalisation of SIETs' video and audio cassettes in partnership with NGOs; (d) web/internet-based education to be managed by the SIETs.
3. ***Access and Equity:*** This scheme comprised the ongoing scheme of Strengthening of Hostel/Boarding Facilities for Girl students.
4. ***Integrated Education for Disabled Children (IEDC):*** Inclusive education became an important aspect of school education for the educational needs of special groups. The scheme focused on: convergence with the Integrated Child Development Services (ICDS) scheme for early interventions; with the DPEP and Sarva Shiksha Abhiyan for education of the mentally and physically challenged up to the elementary level; with the special schools under the Ministry of Social Justice and Empowerment. Other

components of the scheme will be inclusive pedagogy and curriculum, training of teachers and preparation of teaching learning material; research and development (R&D), advocacy and evaluation; and funding through the PTAs/VECs/ management committees of the schools.

5. ***Environmental Orientation to School Education:*** The scheme is being run entirely by the NGOs, with three agencies identified as the 'nodal agencies'. Resource Centres have been set up at Almora, Ahmedabad and Chennai by the 3 designated nodal agencies, i.e. Uttarakhand Paryavaran Siksha Sansthan, Almora, Centre for Environmental Education, Ahmedabad and CPR Environmental Education Centre, Chennai respectively" (Report of Tenth Five Year Plan, India).

Eleventh Five Year Plan (2007-2012)

The Eleventh Plan came into existence for a period which ranged from 2007 to 2012. It was prepared by C. Rangarajan. The theme of Eleventh Five Year Plan was "faster and more inclusive growth".

In the context of secondary education, the Eleventh Plan aimed to: "(i) raise the minimum level of education to class X and accordingly universalize access to secondary education; (ii) ensure good quality secondary education with focus on Science, Mathematics, and English; and (iii) aim towards major reduction in gender, social, and regional gaps in enrolments, drop-outs, and school retention. The norm will be to provide a secondary school within 5 km and a higher secondary school within 7-8 km of every habitation. A target to increase GER at secondary stage was also mentioned. The action plan in the Eleventh Plan has been discussed under some very important schemes of secondary education:

1. "*Scheme for Universal Access and Quality at the Secondary Stage (SUCCESS):* Several schemes, namely ICT in schools, girl child incentive, IEDC, VE, etc. will be subsumed under the name 'SUCCESS'. The principal objectives of SUCCESS will be (i) universalizing access with major reduction in gender, social, and regional gaps in enrolment, drop-out, and retention, and (ii) improving quality with focus on Science and Maths.
2. Specific interventions will include setting up 6,000 high quality Model Schools at block level to serve as benchmark for

excellence in secondary schooling. These schools will be set-up in EBBs and in those areas to promote geographical, demographic, gender, and social equity. Upgradation of primary schools to secondary schools, increasing the capacity of the schools, improving the infrastructure of classrooms and intake of teachers, revamped ICT in secondary and higher secondary schools were other concerns in the Plan" (Planning Commission Report, 2007).

3. *Substantial Improvement in Quality of Secondary Education:* An increased emphasis on adoption of National Curriculum Framework (2005), adoption of NET/SET of NCERT/CBSE/SCERT/State Boards to enable recruitment of quality teaching faculty; long pending institutional reforms in school management, and ensuring accountability at all levels.
4. *ICT in Schools:* During the Eleventh Plan period, facilities of ICT will be provided in the government and government-aided secondary and senior secondary schools. An amount of Rs. 5,000 crore is being provided during this Plan for providing ICT infrastructure in schools. Under this programme, each school will be provided with ICT infrastructure consisting of a networked computer lab with at least ten computers, a server, a printer connected on Local Area Network and Broadband Internet connectivity of 2 Mbps. Every school will also have a technology classroom, with audio-visual equipment for enhancing the learning. A dedicated programme for content creation as per the curricula will be undertaken as an integral part of this initiative. In addition, educational content on CDs for embellishing classroom teaching will also be made available. Training of teachers in the use of computers and teaching through computers will be another important component of this initiative. This revamped scheme of ICT in schools will be implemented in partnership with the States and private providers. This will be a sub-Mission of the National Mission of ICT of MHRD.
5. *Girl Education:* In this direction, a scheme of Girl Child Incentive will be launched on a pilot basis in the selected EBBs (Educationally Backward Blocks) and later it will be expanded. Also, incentives, fellowships, schemes for girls education recieved importance in this Plan period.
6. *Bridging Social Disparities:* The differences in society based on caste, religion, gender etc. were addressed through

(i) upgradation of elementary schools to secondary schools in geographic concentration areas of relevant social groups, (ii) supply of free uniforms, text-books, footwear, (iii) supply of bicycle/wheelchairs, (iv) hostels for boys and girls, (v) stipends to the deserving children, (vi) support to all Madrasas for adoption of general curriculum of States, (vii) pre-matric and post-matric scholarships, (viii) special remedial coaching for needy students within/outside school, and (ix) an approach like area-intensive along with participation of the local community.

7. *Education of the Disabled:* Providing secondary schooling in an inclusive and enabling environment and training of teachers for educating children with disabilities, was the main focus of IEDSS (Inclusive Education for the Disabled at the Secondary Stage).
8. *Fee Structure:* Provision of scholarships for those students especially girl child who cannot afford school fees and can drop-out because of insufficient resources was recommended in this Plan.
9. *Open Learning System through National Institute of Open Schooling (NIOS) in the following manner:* "(i) Developing NIOS as a potential Resource Organization in Open Schooling at the national and international level, besides offering courses of study, (ii) up-scaling programmes of the existing 10 State Open Schools (SOSs), and (iii) setting up SOSs in the remaining 19 States. In order to ensure quality in Open Schooling, there will be a full-time coordinator with ancillary staff on contract basis in each Study Centre under the Open Schooling system. During the Eleventh Plan, 1000 Accredited Vocational Institutes (AVIs) will be set-up as a part of the Skill Development Mission (SDM).
10. *Vocational Education:* The schemes like National Skill Development Mission, Vocational Education programmes, and training, ICT training, clear strategies for encouraging access to Vocational Education and Training (VET) for marginalized groups, including SCs, STs, OBCs, minorities, girls, street children, working children and differently abled children will be adopted, a National Vocational Qualification (NVQ) system under which modular competency based vocational courses will be offered along with a mechanism of testing skills, an integrated

institutional mechanism for effective implementation of vocational programmes, with quality checks at the state, district, and block levels could be established as a distinct wing of the existing institutional arrangements of SCERT, DIETs, and BRCs" (Eleventh Plan Document).

Twelfth Five Year Plan (2012-2017)

The duration of Twelfth Five Year Plan was from 2012 to 2017. Its main theme was "Faster, More Inclusive and Sustainable Growth".

The Twelfth Plan goals for secondary education stage have been summed as follows (MHRD Report, India):

1. "Achieve near-universal enrolment in secondary education, with the GER exceeding 90 per cent by 2017;
2. Raise the GER at the higher secondary level to 65 per cent by 2017;
3. Reduce Drop-out rate to less than 25 per cent by 2017;
4. Ensure quality secondary education with relevant skills including basic competency in mathematics, science, languages and communication;
5. Implement common curricula and syllabi of nationally acceptable standards for Science, Mathematics and English in all schools in the country.
6. Develop life skills including skills of critical and constructive thinking, use of ICT, organisation and leadership, and community services" (Planning Commission Report).

Several important schemes during the Twelfth Plan are:

1. Rashtriya Madhyamik Shiksha Abhiyan (RMSA),
2. Model Schools Scheme,
3. Girls Hostel Scheme,
4. ICT @ Schools,
5. Inclusive Education for Disabled at Secondary Stage,
6. Scheme of Vocational Education,
7. National Means-*cum*-Merit Scholarship Scheme,
8. National Incentive to Girls,
9. Appointment of Language Teachers, and
10. Appointment of additional Physical Education Teachers (PETs).

Planning Commission Document of Twelfth Plan reports about these various schemes:

- *Rashtriya Madhyamik Shiksha Abhiyan (RMSA)* will cover several Centrally sponsored schemes that benefit secondary school students of different categories and background. They are *ICT@Schools, Inclusive Education for Disabled at Secondary Stage (IEDSS) Scheme, Girls' Hostel for Students of Secondary and Higher Secondary Schools, and Scheme of Vocational Education.*
- *Sector Skill Councils (SSCs)* will define the vocational courses, which should meet the standards and competencies required in the occupations. *Ministry of Labour through Industrial Training Centres and National Skills Development Corporation (NSDC)* will provide skill training by organising training programmes.
- It was proposed to start around 2,500 Model Schools in non-educationally backward blocks in a phased manner. This will occur during the first three years of the Twelfth Plan and in PPP mode. The role of these schools was to act as standard for other schools in those regions. These schools also carried out programmes and activities which will be practised by government schools in those areas.
- *Schools under Central Government:* The Twelfth Plan will work towards shaping KVs and JNVs into pace setting schools with specific activities like acting as Smart Schools. "An additional 500KVs and 378 JNVs, including 27 for uncovered districts and 2 special NVs in Manipur, will be set-up. The intake capacity will be expanded from 80 to 160 students per class and 10 Science Magnet schools will be set-up within or in close proximity to the institutions of higher education and other scientific research institutions.
- *Neighbouring school children* will be allowed enrolment in NCC/NSS/Scouts and Guides/Judo/Karate/Yoga/Archery in Kendriya Vidyalayas/Navodaya Vidyalayas. These schools will be centres for the National Physical Fitness Programme to be launched during the Twelfth Plan with 100 per cent Central Assistance. All facilities, provisions, and quality initiatives stipulated for Jawahar Navodaya Vidyalayas shall be made available to Eklavya and Sainik Schools, which are residential schools. The Plan will strengthen the infrastructure facilities for

NIOS and 16 State Open Schools (SOS) under RMSA in order to improve the outreach of open schooling programmes with special focus on skill development and vocationalisation, particularly in the educationally backward districts of the country." (Planning Commission, India).

- *Research, monitoring and evaluation:* A school-based Annual Information System, called SEMIS, which collected data on physical infrastructure and facilities, availability of teachers, enrolment and academic performance of students, professional development of teachers, will also be strengthened. Quality indicators for educational status of each State, increasing planning at micro-level and framing annual work plans whether for district/State is important. *Unified System of Data Collection for School Education Statistics* will be initiated in Twelfth Plan.
- *National Merit-cum-Means Scholarship:* This scheme was continued in the Twelfth Plan to award 1,00,000 scholarships each year, at class IX stage.
- *Technology Use and Education*: Mission Mode Project (MMP) on School Education, under the National e-Governance Plan (NeGP), would enable comprehensive technology in the school education. It will include:
    1. "Developing ICT skills of all heads of schools, teachers, non-teaching staff and students;
    2. Creating a repository of quality-assured digital contents in English, Hindi and regional languages in all subjects especially in science and mathematics;
    3. Training and encouraging teachers to develop and use e-content;
    4. Creating provisions for ICT in classrooms or portable facilities like a netbook/laptop/iPad and a projector with rechargeable battery, and implement ICT-integrated education; and
    5. Enabling provision of ICT-integrated examination and e-governance at the institutional and systemic level including setting up of education portal(s)."
- *Quality Improvement in Teaching:* Several measures were taken to improve the standards of teachers and teaching. The concerns of teacher education were explicitly expressed in Twelfth Plan and a number of changes were proposed for development of teaching and increase in the number of quality teachers. These are as follows:

(i) A *National Mission on Teachers and Teaching* was proposed.
(ii) Research in teacher education curriculum, pedagogy, assessment and evaluation, training etc. will be conducted in the universities wherein 30 Schools of Education will be established.
(iii) Degree programmes either in the form of full-time or distance mode contact under capacity building scheme for teachers need to be conducted. These are essential for professional development of teachers.
(iv) TETs to be made compulsory for entry into teaching field.
(v) Academicians and practitioners in the work field i.e. schools and the NGOs along with teacher education institutes like DIETs, IASEs, & CTEs need to coordinate and develop teacher education programme.
(vi) A quality indicator called as *Teacher Education Index* to be utilised to assess the teacher education institutions. This has to be measured after every five years.

Conclusion

Secondary Education in India has seen highs and lows over the years. The system of secondary education has grown continuously both in terms of quantity and quality. However, challenges did arise in the development, management and implementation of several programmes and schemes in secondary education. In all the five year plans, a common pattern of development schemes were introduced and adopted for the growth of secondary education. The number of secondary schools increased and Model Schools, JNVs, KVs etc. acted as benchmarks. Since the First Five Year Plan, the scheme of vocational education was encouraged and additional skill-based programmes were attached to it. Information and Communication technologies were integrated in the education system to make it more effective. Schemes promoting girl education, education of the disabled, minorities, and deprived sections of the society were also introduced. Emphasis was laid on qualitative improvement of teachers (professional development) by initiating teacher's training programmes and providing adequate facilities. Teaching of science, mathematics and computer education were strengthened. Institutes of academic and technical training were brought together and coordinated so as to balance the requirements of the education system, for instance MHRD, NCERT,

NCTE, NIOS, industrial units etc. Education of the special need category was given a boost during the various five year plans. Scholarships, fellowships, incentives etc. were generated for those in need, and also based on the merit of the students. Examination system, evaluation and monitoring approaches were developed and utilised to improve regulatory mechanisms in the education system. As a whole, the planned development in these five year plans helped in giving impetus to secondary education to meet the needs of the nation.

REFERENCES

Government of India, Ministry of Human Resource Development.

J.B.G. Tilak and Bhatt (1992). *Educational Planning at Grassroots*, New Delhi: Ashish Publishing House, New Delhi.

National Council of Educational Research and Training (NCERT), India.

Five Year Plan Documents, Planning Commission, Government of India.

Rashtriya Madhyamik Shiksha Abhiyan (RMSA), MHRD, India.

Report of the Secondary Education Commission: 1952-53, Ministry of Education, Government of India, 1953, New Delhi.

m.jagranjosh.com

mhrd.gov.in

planningcommission.gov.in

www.scribd.com

www.slideshare.net

yojana.gov.in

4

Government Policy of Education

A Legal Perspective

S.R. Khalid

History

Education in India has a rich and interesting history. In the ancient days, education was imparted orally by sages and scholars and thus, information passed on from one generation to the other. Later, the *Gurukul System* of education, which set up the traditional Hindu residential schools of learning came into existence and flourished. It is in these *gurukuls* that children from all strata in society studied ranging from Princes of States to their subjects.

The first university in the World was established at Takshila in 700BC and thereafter, higher education flourished at Nalanda, Ujjain and Vikramshila Universities. As per the writings of British historians and educationists, education flourished in India in the 18th century, with a school in every temple or mosque in the villages in most regions of the country. The main subjects were art, architecture, painting, logic, grammar, philosophy, astronomy, literature, Buddhism, Hinduism, Arthashastra, law and medicine.

The present system of education, having Western style and content, was introduced and founded by the British rule in the 20th century, at the recommendations of Lord Macaulay.

India has always laid great importance to education. From the time of Independence, the expansion and advancement of education have been a priority of India's development agenda. Several commissions and policies have been moulded from time to time to take initiatives required to increase accessibility to education, encourage further participation, and improve educational quality.

One of the prominent policies on education is the National Policy on Education which was framed in 1986 and modified in 1992. The policy conceived a democratic system of education which implies that "up to a given level, all students, irrespective of caste, creed, location or sex, have access to education of a comparative quality" (NPE, 1986). Since its formulation, the National Policy on Education has focused on refining the quality of education at all stages, inculcating moral and social values, scientific and technological advancement, and to link education with people's life. Developing a sense of commonality among people, promoting national progress, and fortifying national integrity have been the cornerstone of the National Policy on Education.

Present Indian Education System

The Indian Education System, considered as one of the largest in the world, is divided into two major segments of core and non-core businesses. While, schools and higher education for the core group, the non-core business consists of pre-schools, vocational training and coaching classes.

The education sector in India is also considered as one of the major areas for investment as the entire education system is going through a process of overhaul, according to a report 'Emerging Opportunities for Private and Foreign Participants in Higher Education'.

The Indian Education System, like everywhere else in the world, is divided into stages starting from Nursery, Primary, Secondary, to Higher Secondary, Graduation and Post Graduation. The Pre-Primary or Nursery has Lower Kindergarten and Upper Kindergarten, where basic reading and writing skills are taught and developed. The Primary School has children between the ages of six and eleven. It has organized classes from one to five where basic knowledge of languages, calculations and reading and writing skills are enhanced to make the child well-versed with the language.

The Secondary School has children between the ages of eleven and fifteen and the classes are organized from six to ten and whereas, the Higher Secondary school has students between the ages of sixteen and eighteen and the classes are organized as eleventh and twelfth, respectively. In some States, the classes between six and eight are also referred as the Middle School and those between eight and ten are referred as the High School. Higher Secondary School plays a pivotal role in laying the foundation of the future course of discipline a child may want to adopt. It provides education to specialize in a field and there are different streams available for the same.

Perspectives of Education Policy

It may be attractive and convenient to be able to offer short and succinct definitions of the concepts being analysed but this is seldom possible or helpful, and a discussion of policy is no exception. The range of conceptual issues embraced by the term policy are too broad to be confined to a single, pithy definitions—rather it is necessary to develop an understanding of policy that reflects the breadth and complexity that the reality of policy analysis entails. One common approach is to conceptualize policy as a programme of action, or a set of guidelines that determine how one should proceed given a particular set of circumstances. This presents a definition of policies as "...aims or goals, or statements of what ought to happen". This distinction between objectives and 'statements of what ought to happen' echoes a similar distinction identified by between policies as statements of intent, and those that represent plans or programmes of work.

For Harman, therefore, it is important to recognize that policy is systematic rather than random. It is goal-oriented and it is complex—it is the coordination of several courses of action, and not one discrete activity. However, in both Blakemore's and Harman's argument the emphasis is on policy as a product—as an outcome. The limitation of seeing policy only as a product is that it disconnects it from policy as a process—there is a failure to see policy as both product and process. Furthermore, this conceptualization of policy is de-coupled from the context from which it is taken—what is the purpose of the policy? What is it trying to achieve? The notion of policy as the pursuit of fundamentally political objectives is recognized in Kogan's study of educational policy making in which he refers to policies as the 'operational statements of values'—the 'authoritative allocation of values' and this helpfully locates policy within a context of wider fundamental questions that have already been identified—what is education for? Who is education for? Who decides?

The service that Kogan provides is to place values at the centre of understanding policy. Kogan identified four key values that underpin and inform educational policy—educational, social, economic and institutional values. In his study he distinguishes between basic and secondary values with educational, social and economic values being considered as instrumental, or basic, and institutional values being considered as consequential or secondary. Kogan asserted that a basic value is one that 'requires no further defence than that it is held to be right by those who believe it' (1975: 53). Secondary, or instrumental, values are justified by the extent to which they support, or further, the advancement of basic values. The basic values are self-justificatory oughts. The secondary values are concepts that carry the argument into the zone of consequences and instruments and institutions."

Kogan's highly authoritative study of the policy-making process in England and Wales presents a thoroughly researched study of the development of education policy in a period characterized largely by cross-party consensus and a commitment to the expansion of educational provision. This was a period of social and political consensus in which an accommodation between capital and labour, the emergence of Keynesian economic management and the development of a substantial welfare sector provided the basis for a social democratic settlement. This phase of broad political consensus was, therefore, effectively a period of values consensus in which it was argued that the development of welfarism had presaged a new era of citizenship based on the developments of new social rights. As a result of this consensus, studies of policy such as Kogan's, viewed the values underpinning policy as largely unproblematic. Policies were presented in terms of achieving objectives, or solving problems—negotiation and compromise through the policy process would result in a coalescing of views and values. The process was both technical and rational. The corollary of this analysis was a largely linear view of policy development whereby problems were identified, solutions developed and strategies and interventions then implemented. Such an approach to policy-making is located within the pluralist tradition that sees the role of political institutions as reconciling the competing demands and expectations of different interest groups.

Childhood Care and Education: The Foundation of Learning

The learning process for a child commences immediately at birth. Evidence from neuroscience shows that over 85 per cent of a child's cumulative brain development occurs prior to the age of 6, indicating the critical importance of developmentally appropriate care and stimulation of the brain in a child's early years to promote sustained and healthy brain development and growth. Indeed, analysis of brain scans of children who encountered various levels of neglect or deprivation in their early years revealed unfortunate deficiencies in the development of critical areas of the brain, and corresponding adverse effects on cognitive and emotional processing. Excellent care, nurture, nutrition, physical activity, psycho-social environment, and cognitive and emotional stimulation during a child's first six years are thus considered extremely critical for ensuring proper brain development and, consequently, desired learning curves over a person's lifetime.

This evidence from cognitive science is fully borne out by numerous national and international studies on the learning outcomes of children having various levels of Early Childhood Care and Education (ECCE). A study conducted by the National Council of Educational Research and Training (NCERT) titled "The impact of pre-school education on retention in primary grades" (1992) on 30,000 children illustrated strong and direct correlations between exposure to pre-school education and retention rates, attendance rates, and most significantly learning outcomes in primary school and beyond. Various global studies have also revealed longer-term impacts: quality pre-school education is strongly correlated with higher incomes and rates of home ownership, and lower rates of unemployment, crime, and arrest. In terms of the growth of the national economy, it has been estimated that the development of a strong ECCE programme is among the very best investments that India could make, with an expected return of 10 or more for every 1 invested. It is recognized that investment in ECCE gives the best chance for children to grow up into good, moral, thoughtful, creative, empathetic, and productive human beings.

Studies tracking student learning outcomes clearly demonstrate that children who start out behind tend to stay behind throughout their school years. At the current time, there is a severe learning crisis in India, where children are enrolled in primary school but are failing to attain even basic skills such as foundational literacy and numeracy. A major part of this crisis appears to be occurring well before children even enter Grade 1. Far too many 6+ year olds are entering Grade 1 with very limited ECCE. Furthermore, far too many children are enrolling in Grade 1 before the age of 6, due to a lack of any suitable preprimary options; these are often the children that remain the most behind in primary school and beyond. In fact, during the academic year 2016-17, over 70 lakh children were enrolled in Grade 1 prior to the age of 6.

This tragic deficiency in grade school-preparedness is particularly marked between advantaged and disadvantaged groups. This is because students from more advantaged families have greater access to role models, print awareness, language fluency in the school language, and strong learning environments at home, in addition to better nutrition, healthcare, and of course access to pre-school education. Investment in ECCE has the potential to give all young children such access in an engaging and holistic way, thereby allowing all children to participate and flourish in the educational system throughout their lives. ECCE is perhaps the greatest and most powerful equalizer.

For all these reasons from brain development to school-preparedness, improved learning outcomes, equality and justice, employability, and the prosperity and economic growth of the country–India absolutely must invest in accessible and quality ECCE for all children.

From 3 to 6 years of age, ECCE includes continued healthcare and nutrition, but also crucially self-help skills (such as "getting ready on one's own"), motor skills, cleanliness, the handling of separation anxiety, being comfortable around one's peers, moral development (such as knowing the difference between "right" and "wrong"), physical development through movement and exercise, expressing and communicating thoughts and feelings to parents and others, sitting for longer periods of time in order to work on and complete a task, and generally forming all-round good habits.

Supervised play-based education, in groups and individually, is considered particularly important during this age range to naturally build up the child's innate abilities and all-important lifelong skills of cooperation, teamwork, social interaction, compassion, equity, inclusiveness, communication, cultural appreciation, playfulness, curiosity, creativity, as well as the ability to successfully and respectfully interact with teachers, fellow students, staff, and others. ECCE during these years also entails learning about alphabets, languages, numbers, counting, colours, shapes, drawing/painting, indoor and outdoor play, puzzles and logical thinking, visual art, craft, drama, puppetry, music, and movement.

Education of Children from Urban Poor Families

There are nearly 1 crore children from urban poor families, and this number seems to continue to increase (though it is hoped that measures may be taken soon to reverse this trajectory). About half of all urban poor children are severely malnourished, while nearly three-quarters are illiterate. The parents of these children have often left their hometowns in other States to make a new living in an urban area in a new State, often rendering their children unacquainted with both their home State's culture as well as life in the city. As a result, the generational divide between parents and children is often particularly stark among the urban poor. This, coupled with the lack of literacy and proper schooling and playing opportunities, often leads children and adolescents into unfortunate and harmful activities, including petty crime and drugs; an estimated one-third of street children are dealing with substance abuse.

Providing children from urban poor families with quality education is the only way to rescue so many of these children and enable them to become happy and productive members of society.

Education of Children with Special Needs

The Policy recognizes the importance of providing Children With Special Needs (CWSN) the same opportunities of obtaining quality education as any other child. The RTE Amendment Act, which came into force with effect from the 1st of August, 2012, provides for the inclusion of CWSN as contained in the Persons with Disabilities Act, 2005 and the National Trust Act, under the purview of the Right of Children to Free and Compulsory Education Act, 2009 (RTE) Act, thereby providing CWSN free and compulsory education; in fact, the RTE Act ensures CWSN free and compulsory education either until the completion of the elementary stage of school education or till the age of 18 years. Further, the RTE Act also provides to parents of children with severe and profound disabilities, the right to opt for home-based education. The Policy points indicated in Section 6.1 are all important in the context of Children With Special Needs (CWSN) as well.

An integrated yet Flexible Approach to Education

The present Policy begins with viewing early childhood care and education (ECCE) as a part of the Foundational stage of school education (three years of pre-primary education and Grades 1 and 2), a single curricular and pedagogical phase of play- and discovery-based learning for very young children, between the ages of 3-8 years. The Eighty-sixth Constitutional Amendment in 2002 extended the provision of ECCE to children from age 3 onwards and this commitment has been honoured. The Policy takes cognizance of the differences in the development of cognitive abilities in children. The flexibility in the first five years will enable equalising of the multiple cognitive abilities of children. This is followed by a Preparatory phase consisting of three years (Grades 3, 4 and 5) of basic education incorporating some textbooks as well as aspects of more formal classroom learning. The next three years of Middle school education (Grades 6, 7 and 8) would involve developing more abstract thinking and subject teaching leading up to a Secondary education phase of four years (Grades 9, 10, 11 and 12). This last phase of four years of secondary school education will facilitate multidisciplinary studies with appropriate exit options besides preparing for the next phase of undergraduate programme of study, including early introduction to Liberal Arts education.

The concept of interconnectedness also provides for preparation of the students for further studies at higher levels through proper orientation, coming from early efforts at broad-based liberal education that will be introduced at the Secondary stage of education. A strong base of Liberal Arts education and provision for vocational education at different levels are all part of undergraduate education. A fourth year of undergraduate education can also seamlessly integrate itself to education at the Masters and Doctoral levels. In the long run, this integrated concept should also lead to bringing professional education into mainstream undergraduate education, thereby creating an overarching integrated approach to education, embodying the spirit of the Policy in totality.

A New Curricular and Pedagogical Structure for School Education

One of the most well-known legacies of the National Policy on Education 1968 is the "10+2" structure of the school education system–an extremely important and influential recommendation for the time which helped to standardise and uniformise the structure of school education across the country. In many parts of the country, the 12 years of the 10+2 system have been referred to as Grades/Classes 1-12, with Grades 1-5 the primary stage, Grades 6-8 the upper primary stage, Grades 9-10 the secondary stage, and Grades 11-12 the higher secondary, pre-university, intermediate, or junior college stage.

While the 10+2 system of school education has served the country well over the past 50 years and has been an important step forward in uniformising the school education structure in India–modern times and needs with respect to employment and beyond, together with advances and discoveries in cognitive science, have also made clear that a new structure for the educational system is required in order to deliver the vision of education enunciated in this Policy and to prepare our students optimally in the twenty-first century.

The restructuring of school education mentioned in this Policy is based, in particular, on the cognitive importance of play-based ECCE starting at the age 3, together with the modern necessity of providing free and compulsory education for all students through Grade 12–as was already discussed in the first three chapters. Furthermore, within this school-age range of 3 to 18 years, there must be periodic changes in curricular and pedagogical delivery and styles, designed to be in sync with a child's natural cognitive, emotional, and physical development. Studies in cognitive science demonstrate that children prior to the age of 8 learn best through play-based, activity-based, and discovery-based multilevel flexible styles of learning and interaction, whereas around the age of 8 children naturally begin to adapt to a more prescripted style of learning, indicating that teaching-learning processes in Grade 3 may also begin to transition to a more formal style of learning, e.g. by incorporating some basic textbooks, while still maintaining a strong play and discovery-based approach.

Meanwhile, by the age of 11, children begin to develop the capacity for abstraction. At this stage, i.e., around Grade 6, it therefore becomes beneficial for students to begin to have specialised subject teachers in the classroom, where students' discussion of higher-level concepts within each subject area becomes possible and indeed desirable. By the age of 14, i.e., Grade 9, adolescents begin to think about their life plans; schooling at this stage must therefore build on the styles of previous stages, while also incorporating preparation for university, for the world of work, and for life. Students at this stage must have flexibility of subject options for their differing talents, interests, goals, and ambitions, including access to vocational and arts courses. A semester-based system, which allows exposure to a multitude of subjects at differing levels, can be of great benefit to students at this stage.

Reduce Curriculum Content to Enhance Essential Learning and Critical Thinking

The Policy recognises, from inputs of teachers, students, scientists, and educators, that the curriculum content is currently severely overloaded. Both the 1993 MHRD Yashpal Committee Report 1993 "Learning Without Burden" and the NCF 2005 highlighted the great need for reducing our overcrowded curriculum content load in favour of a more engaging, holistic, experiential, and analysis-based form of learning. Those well-researched recommendations have never been more relevant than today. Indeed, today, the rush in classrooms to finish and rush through all the mandated curricular material *via* rote memorisation continues to prevent opportunities for critical thinking and discovery-based, discussion-based, and analysis-based learning–and thus true understanding–from taking place.

Empower Students Through Flexibility in Course Choices

Reducing the curriculum content load–in addition to allowing greater room for nuanced understanding, analysis, and discussion in mandated curriculum—will also enable students to explore subjects beyond the current usual curriculum. Learners must be empowered to have more flexibility in the courses that they take, especially in secondary school, so that they may make the best use of their time in school; in particular, they must be given the time and the options to experiment with different subjects in a more hands-on and experiential way in order to decide what they enjoy, and so that they can gradually assess what they may want to do with their lives. Specialisation should be delayed, so that students' choices are not dictated simply by parents or society, but rather via their own experiences, interests, and self-reflections.

All fields of human endeavour, including arts, crafts, and sports, are valuable to both human and societal advancement, and so should be actively pursued by students in their curricula to achieve holistic development. In particular, there should be no extra-curricular and co-curricular activities; all such activities must also be considered curricular. A holistic approach to education must come hand-in-hand with student empowerment and choice, and all subjects should carry importance within the curriculum for each student according to his/her choices and inclinations.

Curricular Integration of Essential Subjects and Skills

While students must have a large amount of flexibility in choosing their individual curricula, at the same time this Policy envisions that certain subjects and skills should be learned by all students in order to become good, successful, innovative, adaptable, and productive human beings in today's rapidly changing world. In addition to proficiency in languages, these skills include: scientific temper; sense of aesthetics and art; languages; communication; ethical reasoning; digital literacy; knowledge of India; and knowledge of critical issues facing local communities, States, the country, and the world.

Scientific Temper

Inculcate Scientific Temper and encourage evidence-based thinking throughout the curriculum: Evidence-based reasoning and the scientific method will be incorporated throughout the school curriculum--in science as well as in traditionally "non-science" subjects–in order to encourage rational, analytical, logical, and quantitative thinking in all aspects of the curriculum.

For example, in history, one could ask, "What are the possible historical scenarios consistent with the known archaeological and literary evidences?" In music/physics, one could ask, "What frequencies of notes should be used in musical scales, given that notes with resonant frequencies are the ones that sound good together to the ear?" In ethics, one could ask, "What are the positive benefits to society if every individual always acts according to certain ethical principles?"

Evidence-based and scientific thinking throughout the curriculum will lead naturally to rational, ethical, and compassionate individuals who can make good, logical, and sound decisions throughout their lives. Evidence-based thinking and a scientific temper is also considered a key ingredient in teaching students to "learn how to learn", to adapt to new situations, and to establish themselves as lifelong learners.

Oral and Written Communication

Communication skills–both verbal and written–have become increasingly important in the modern world. People spend much of their daily lives communicating messages, requests, questions, opinions, feedback, anecdotes, and more–both in person and in written or digital form. Numerous surveys of employers around the world reveal that verbal communication skills are ranked first among potential job candidate's "must-have" skills and qualities. The ability to speak, listen, question, discuss, and write with clarity and conciseness—and with confidence, eloquence, friendliness, and open-mindedness–is considered a truly essential skill for all managers and leaders.

The Policy, therefore, recognises the importance of schooling systems developing excellent communicators. As students learn languages, they must have regular practice in using these languages to speak, write, and communicate with their teachers and their peers. A core principle here will be that every student must have the opportunity to speak freely and creatively in front of their peers on topics of interest to them for at least a few minutes every week, starting in the very foundational years.

Physical Education, Wellness, and Sports

Physical education is important for both physical and mental health and development. It helps improve a child's muscular and cardiovascular strength, flexibility, endurance, motor skills, and mind-body connection and wellness. It gives children the opportunity to set and strive for personal and achievable goals. Moreover, playing sports also helps students develop the qualities of teamwork, cooperation, problem-solving, discipline, perseverance, and responsibility. In general, physical activity is well established to be among the best releases for tension and anxiety, and facilitates emotional stability and resilience. All of these qualities and benefits are also relevant to success in the classroom; studies show that students who stay physically active are more successful with other school work as well. Finally, people who are physically active as young people tend to stay more fit as adults as well, leading them to lead longer, healthier, and more productive lives.

Vocational Exposure and Skills

Vocational education is extremely vital for our country to run efficiently and properly, and thus it is beneficial to increasingly incorporate elements of vocational education into the school curriculum to expose children to its utility and its value as art. Indeed, some exposure to practical vocational-style training is always fun for young students, and for many students it may offer a glimpse of future professions while for others it would at the very least help teach and reinforce the dignity of all labour.

Vocational exposure: The importance of and a basic knowledge of various livelihoods and life-skills (such as gardening, pottery, wood-work, electric work, and many others) will be taught at the Foundational and Elementary level, as early as the safety of children allows, so that students are well aware of, and may become interested in, these professions well before finishing high school. Some vocational arts, such as gardening or work with clay, will even be introduced in the foundational years (ages 3-8), so that experiential learning through working with one's hands is completely integrated.

Schools may choose a subset of livelihoods and related skills that are of value to the local community. Artisans and practitioners will be hired as tutors by schools or school complexes for teaching each of these skills, and tutors may be shared across multiple schools in the school complex as needed.

Transforming Assessment for Student Development

The changes in curriculum described in Section 4.2–Section 4.8 must be accompanied by parallel changes in assessment procedures and mechanisms. The very aim of assessment in the culture of our schooling system must shift from one that primarily tests rote memorisation skills to one that is more formative, promotes learning and development for our students, and tests higher-order skills such as analysis, critical thinking, and conceptual clarity. The primary purpose of assessment should indeed be for learning–it should help the teacher and student—and the entire schooling system–continuously revise teaching-learning processes in order to optimize learning and development for all students.

The approach must be to focus on formative and developmental assessment throughout the school years. Learning assessment must shift towards testing only the understanding of core concepts and knowledge, along with higher order capacities such as critical thinking, analysis, and application; this approach must be used throughout the educational system and throughout all subjects, including on school examinations, Board Examinations, entrance examinations for universities, university examinations, and examinations for employment.

Unfortunately, the current nature of examinations–and the resulting coaching culture of today–are doing much harm, especially at the secondary school level, replacing valuable time for true learning with excessive examination coaching and preparation.

Responsibility for the Education of all Children within the Education Ministry

Realization of the equal right of every child to education without discrimination requires that the responsibility for education of every child must rest with ministries of education. However, in some countries mainstream schooling and special education are still managed under different administrations, with primary responsibility for disability, including education, often resting within ministries of social welfare. This has resulted in the exclusion of children with disabilities from mainstream education legislation, policy, planning and resourcing, and a lack of overarching and coherent structures in place to support inclusive education. This separation of responsibilities can lead to a number of serious obstacles to inclusive education, resulting in children with disabilities not only being segregated from other children, but also receiving a poorer quality of education.

- Barriers to accessing the mainstream curriculum.
- Inability to enter national examinations.
- Teacher training failing to address teaching methodologies to support inclusive classrooms.
- Design and development of new schools failing to address the need for accessibility.
- Lower levels of investment per capita in education of children with disabilities.
- Lack of integrated data collection on enrolment, retention and attainment to provide evidence of progress in realizing the right to education for children with disabilities.

Although many governments have now recognized the imperative for bringing responsibility for the education of all children under the umbrella of ministries of education, it is not yet universal. For example, in both India and Bangladesh the education of special schools remains the responsibility of the Ministry of Social Welfare. Basically, where the education of children with disabilities is managed by a different, non-education department, children with disabilities will always end up marginalized. They will not be taken into account in planning and monitoring of education goals, and will invariably be denied equal chances to achieve.

Effective education policies require collaboration with a number of ministries beyond education. Without coordinated action across all relevant government ministries, it is not possible to build and support a consistent culture of inclusion. If possible, governments need to develop a national plan of action within which all relevant ministries are expected to have a common understanding of commitment to inclusive education. Given the challenges in many countries of cross-departmental working, it is important to identify a lead agency with a nominated focal point to provide leadership to the process. This will enable them to achieve an integrated and holistic approach where they are working collaboratively towards a shared agenda.

Constitutional Provisions

The Constitution of India has clearly stated in its Preamble that everyone has the right of equality of status and of opportunity. The Directive

Principles of the State Policy further stress in Article 41 the right to work, to educate and to public assistance in certain cases including disablement. In addition to Article 45, the Constitution lays down that free, compulsory and universal primary education should be provided to all children up to 14 years of age. Article 46 of the Constitution of India commits the State to promote educational and economic interests of Scheduled Castes, Scheduled Tribes and Weaker Sections. Thus, you will notice that all these Articles and their implementation aim at providing quality education to all including different disadvantaged groups. Even today, after more than 70 years of independence, India is struggling to fight against all kinds of biases of caste, religions, ideology, gender etc. Education can play a significant role to minimising and finally, eliminating these differences by providing equality of access to quality education and opportunity. Equality of opportunity means that every individual will receive suitable education at a pace and through methods suitable to her/ him and therefore, children from the disadvantaged and socially discriminated groups also suffering specific challenges must be paid special attention.

Recommendations for the New National Policy on Education

Although the present government aims to enhance the quality of education and eliminate disparities, and has put forward its plan of action through its documents and manuals, not much has been stated with regard to education of minorities and girl education. The previous Education Policy of 1986 and 1992 had clearly stated that, "it will lay special emphasis on the removal of disparities and to equalize educational opportunity by attending to the specific needs of those who have been denied equality so far." However, this goal is yet to be achieved to its fullest. Following recommendations would prove to be helpful to the present government to formulate the New National Policy on Education keeping in view the needs of the minorities and girls and their upliftment through education.

Conclusion

Initiatives undertaken by the Government of India cover a wide range of policies, plans, programmes, schemes and legal enactments related persons in the country. Although the Government of India has attempted to create numerous policies that are inclusive for people since the country's Independence in 1947, their implementation efforts have not resulted in an inclusive system of education, nor have they reached their goal of "Education for All" across the country. Still, at present, the policies governing the education system are inclusive but, the problem is with implementation. The Government of India needs to bridge the gaps in their education system to build a strong system of inclusive education in India.

India's tremendous economic and technical development calls for a major shift in efforts to expand and enhance the education system taking into consideration the achievements of the previous policies and commissions and promote quality and inclusiveness in education at all levels. It is highly anticipated that the New National Policy on Education would prove to be a foundation stone in accomplishing this vision.

A healthy and fair competition needs to begin from a single start line, with every individual standing beside each other, not behind each other. This can only happen when certain incentives and concessions are made available to the deprived groups so that they are uplifted and made competent enough to step on the road to success. The deprived group includes people belonging to the Minorities, particularly Muslims, the SCs, and the STs. A fair step needs to be taken for them to ensure accessibility to and equity in education. They should be given special preference not as a separate religious group, but as people of our country who are economically and socially deprived.

REFERENCES

Annual Report 2013-14. Higher Education in India, University Grants Commission, New Delhi, http://mhrd.gov.in/annual report 2013-14. Accessed September, 2016.

Bindal S. and Sharma S. (2010). "Inclusive Education in Indian Context." *Journal of Indian Education*; *35*(4): 34-45.

Census of India. Government of India. Retrieved from http://censusindia. gov.in/., 2011.

Distribution of Population by Religion Drop in Article: Census of India 2011. http://censusindia.gov.in/Ad Campaign/drop in articles/04 Distribution_by_ Religion.pdf. Accessed September, 2016.

Educational Statistics at a Glance. Bureau of Planning, Monitoring and Statistics, Ministry of Human (2014) http://mhrd.gov.in/sites/upload_files/mhrd/files/ statistics/EAG2014_0.pdf. Resource Development Government of India. New Delhi. Accessed April, 2020.

Harman, G. (1984). "Conceptual and Theoretical Issues", In J.R. Hough (ed.) *Educational Policy: An International Survey*, London: Groom Helm.

Higher Education in India. Issues Related to Expansion, Inclusiveness, Quality and Finance. University Grants Commission, (2008). New Delhi.

Human Development Reports. (2016). "Expenditure on Education Public (%)". United Nations Development http://hdf.undp.org/eu/content/expenditure education publicado. Accessed September 2016.

Kingdon, G.G. (2007). *The Progress of School Education in India Economic and Social Research Council.* Global Poverty Research Group.

Kogan, M. (1975). *Educational Policy-Making: A Study on Interest Groups and Parliament*, London: George Allen and Unwin Ltd.

Marshall, T.H. (1950). *Citizenship and Social Class, and Other Essays*, London: Cambridge University Press.

National Policy for Persons with Disabilities. Ministry of Social Justice and Empowerment, Government of India, 2006. Retrieved from http://www.social justice.nic.in/nppde.php

National Policy on Education 1986 (As modified in 1992) with National Policy on Education 1968. Department of Education, Ministry of Human Resource Development, Government of India, New Delhi. (1998).

National Report on the Development of Education (India), 47th Session of the International Conference on Education, India, September 2004.

Press Information Bureau. *Education to Minorities*, Ministry of Human Resource Development, Government of India. (March 5th 2015).

Simon (1991). *Education and the Social Order 1940-1990*, London: Lawrence and Wishart.

Taylor, S., Rizvi, F., Lingard, B. and Henry, M. (1997). *Educational Policy and the Politics of Change*, London: Routledge.

UNESCO (1994). *The Salamanca Statement and Framework for Action on Special Needs Education.* UNESCO. Retrieved from http://www.unesco.org/education/eduprog/sne/salamanc/stntme. html.

World Bank. (2007) *People with Disabilities in India: From Commitments to Outcomes.* Human Development Unit, South Asia Region. Retrieved from http://www.worldbank. org/INDIAEXT, 2007.

5
Model Educational Planning in India

Mujibul Hasan Siddiqui and *Md. Rajesh Ali*

Introduction

Planning plays a pivotal role. For democratic decisions, the plan is very essential. It must be well organized so that the goals must be achieved within a specific time. That is why the steps of planning have greater importance here. Educational planning is a systematic design of action for the realization of educational aims and objectives for individual and as well as social development through maximum utilization of available resources. From a practical perspective, educational planning is defined as a process utilized by an administrator while performing the role of a leader, decision-maker, and change-agent, and so on. Various educational models like interactional-rational, technicists, consensual, and political act as producing agents of good outcomes to the institution or nation. The national progress and national growth are dependable on its educational model.

Planning

Meaning of Planning

The concept of planning is old enough. Planning was advocated by Confucius almost 2500 years ago. He said, "A man who does not think and plan long ahead will find trouble right at his door." There is a saying that if there is a will there is a way. The will of a man comes into the picture after thinking which can be done through planning at the mental level. The term planning is the major guideline for the development of any institution, organization, individual, and society in every respect.

India is a democratic, dynamic, and developing one marching to become a country of a superpower by 2020 A.D. Behind this target there is systematic and deliberate planning. Planning means looking ahead and chalking out future courses of action to be followed. It is rightly said, "*Well plan is half done*". Planning deals with the future and involves forecasting. But mere forecasting is not planning. Planning requires assessing the future and providing resources for it.

Definition of Planning

According to the *Oxford English Dictionary*, "Planning is to design some action to be done before hand".

Adesina (1990) holds that "a way projecting our intentions, that is, a method of deciding what we want to accomplish."

Ejiogu (1990) defines planning as, "to plan, means to project, forecast, design or make or chart out course."

A plan is a detailed programme or method, the scheme worked out beforehand to achieve a set objective. There are three basic elements of a plan, it deals with the future involved action and identifies who is to implement the future action. It bridges the gap between where a person is and where he wants to be.

From the above definitions, it can be concluded that planning is an act of deciding in advance what is to be done, how and when to do it, where, and who is to do it to achieve the goals or objectives of the system.

Nature and Characteristics of Planning

Planning is concerned with the establishment of objectives of an enterprise and finding out the way of realization of those objectives. However, without setting the objectives there is nothing to organize, direct, or control. Therefore, every organization is required to specify what it wants to achieve. Planning is related to this aspect (Fig. 5.1).

The nature and characteristics of planning may be stated as follows:

1. *Intellectual Process*: Planning is an intellectual (thinking before doing) as well as a rational process. It is a mental exercise. Sound judgment comes through good imagination and insightfulness. Planning requires a mental disposition of thinking before acting in the light of facts rather than guess. The quality of planning depends upon the abilities of the managers who are required to collect all relevant facts, analyse and interpret them in a correct way. Therefore, a planner goes through an

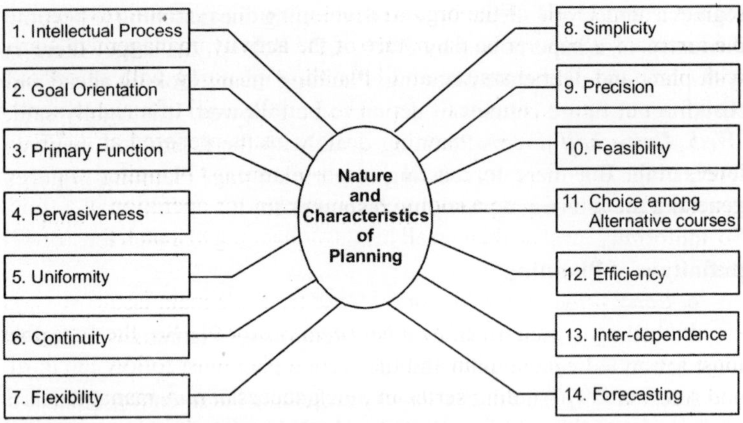

Fig. 5.1: Nature and Characteristics of Planning.

intellectual process. A planner should mainly consider the following questions:

(i) What is to be done?
(ii) How is it to be done?
(iii) When is it to be done?
(iv) By whom is it to be done?

These questions are needed the well-thinking process for executing the action.

2. Goal-orientation: All planning is connected with certain goals and objectives. Planning has no meaning without being related to goals and objectives. It bridges the gap between where the person is and where he wants to go at the minimum cost. Koontz and Weihrich write, "Plans provide a rational approach to pre-selected objectives."

3. Primary Function: Planning is the most basic and primary function of management. It occupies first place and precedes all other functions of management which are designed to attain the goals set under planning. This is so because the manager decides upon the policies, procedures, programmes, project, etc. before proceeding with the work. The other functions of management—organizing, direction, coordination, and control—can be performed only after the manager has formulated the necessary planning.

4. Pervasiveness: Planning pervades all managerial activities. It is the job of all managers in all types of organizations. It is undertaken at all segments and levels of the organization—from the general manager to the foreman. Whatever be the nature of the activity, management starts with planning. The character and breadth of planning will, of course, vary from one job to another—depending on the level of management.

5. Uniformity: There may be separate plans prepared at different levels in the organization, but all the sub-plans must be united with the general plan to make up a comprehensive plan for operation at a time. So, uniformity must be there in all levels of planning to match the general plan.

6. Continuity: Break in work diverts from the main issue. So, it is essential that planning must be a continuous process. So, the first plan must follow the second plan and the second plan must follow the third, and so on in never-ending series in quick succession. A manager starts planning before the work is started and when one task is accomplished planning for the other begins and this process continues. Thus, planning is a continuous process.

7. Flexibility: Plans should be dynamic and flexible. In case a man finds any such thing happening, he immediately brings in changes in his planning according to the changed facts or situations. So that he can reach the goal as soon as possible. A flexible plan can meet the demands of an organization easily.

8. Simplicity: Simplicity must be there so that every employee, especially the lower-level employee can understand easily.

9. Precision: Precision gives exact, accurate meaning in its scope and content. It is the soul of any planning.

10. Feasibility: Planning is based on facts and various experiences rather than poetic or philosophical matters. So, it depends on existing resources.

11. Choice among alternative courses: If there are choices then planning will play a big role. The planner selects the best possible alternative for executing the work.

12. Efficiency: A good plan attains the optimum relationship between output and input as well as the greatest satisfaction. Greater efficiency involves a greater plan of action.

13. Interdependence: There may be different plans for different organizations. Good plans are interdependent and interrelated to each other so that maximum outcomes bring out easily.

14. Forecasting: Planning is nothing if forecasting is not achieved properly. It is the synthesis of various forecasts where short-term, long-term, special terms are involved. So, planning is done because of fulfilling particular targets. The future is anticipated and the proper decision taken. Earl Strong says, "Planning is anticipating" and Ackoff writes, "Planning is anticipatory decision making". So, forecasting is the essence of planning.

So, it can be stated that planning is an intellectual, dynamic, continuous process. Its primary function is management. It focuses on objectives. It secures efficiency, economy, and accuracy. Planning involves forecasting. Any planning is limited within the five Ms viz., men, money, machine, material, and management.

Importance of Planning

Why planning is important for any organization:

1. Increases efficiency: Planning makes optimum utilization of all available recourses. It helps to reduce the wastage of valuable resources and avoids duplication. It aims to give the highest returns at the lowest possible cost. It thus increases the overall efficiency.

2. Reduces business-related risks: There are many risks involved in any modern business. Planning helps to forecast business-related risks. It also helps to take the necessary precautions to avoid these risks and prepare for future uncertainties in advance. Thus, it reduces business risks.

3. Facilitates proper coordination: Often, the plans of all departments of an organization are well coordinated with each other. Similarly, the short-term, medium-term, and long-term plans of an organization are also coordinated with each other. Such proper coordination is possible only because of efficient planning.

4. Aids in organizing: Organizing means to bring together all available resources, i.e. 6 Ms. Organizing is not possible without planning. It is so, since, planning tells us the number of resources required and when are they needed. It means that planning aids in organizing efficiently.

5. Gives right direction: Direction means to give proper information, accurate instructions, and useful guidance to the subordinates. It is impossible without planning. It is because planning tells us what to do, how to do it, and when to do it. Therefore, planning helps to give the right direction.

6. Keeps good control: With control, the actual performance of an employee is compared with the plans, and deviations (if any) are found out and corrected. It is impossible to achieve such control without the right planning. So, planning becomes necessary to keep good control.

7. Helps to achieve objectives: Every organization has certain objectives or targets. It takes working hard to fulfil these goals. Planning helps an organization to achieve these aims, but with some ease promptness. Planning also helps an organization to avoid doing some random activities.

***8. Motivates personnel*:** A good plan provides various financial and non-financial incentives to both managers and employees. These incentives motivate them to work hard and achieve the objectives of the organization. Thus, planning through various incentives helps to motivate the personnel of an organization.

***9. Encourages creativity and innovation*:** Planning helps managers to express their creativity and innovation. It brings satisfaction to the managers and eventually a success to the organization.

***10. Helps in decision-making*:** A manager makes many different plans. Then the manager selects or chooses the best of all available strategies. Making a selection or choosing something means to make a decision. So, decision-making is facilitated by planning.

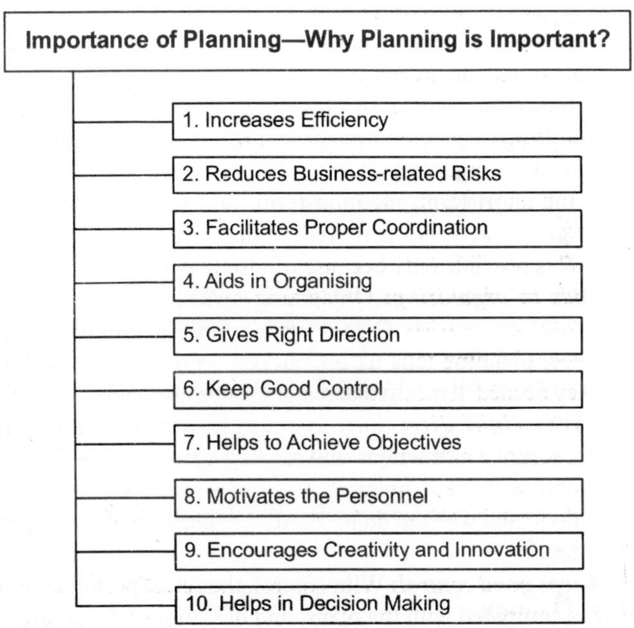

Therefore, planning is necessary for the efficient functioning of every organization irrespective of its size, type, and objectives.

Types of Planning

There are four types of planning as follows:

***1. Operational Planning*:** An operational plan (OP) is a highly detailed plan. It provides a clear picture of how a section or organization will contribute to the achievement of its goals. OP is a day-to-day task-oriented method. The plan covers—what, who, when, and how much.

***2. Strategic Planning*:** It is a long-term strategy. It includes the highest level overview of the entire phenomenon. It needs long-term decisions; it may take two years to the next 10 years. This strategic plan is vision, mission, and values. It is related to "why".

***3. Tactical Planning*:** Tactical planning is about what is going to happen. It supports strategic planning. It is different from operational planning in the sense that it asks specific questions about what needs to happen to accomplish a strategic goal, but operational plan asks how the organization will generally do something to accomplish the organization's mission.

***4. Contingency Planning*:** Contingency Planning or CP is a plan that made when something unexpected happens or when something needs to be changed. CP is helpful in circumstances that call for a change.

Steps of Planning

The steps of the planning process are:

1. Develop objectives.
2. Develop tasks to meet those objectives.
3. Determine the resources needed to implement tasks.
4. Create a timeline.
5. Determine the tracking and assessment methods.
6. Finalize plan.
7. Distribute to all involved in the process.

Another team of planner considers the steps of the planning process as shown in Fig. 5.2.

Models of Planning

The basic strategic planning process model is as follows:

1. Identify the purpose.

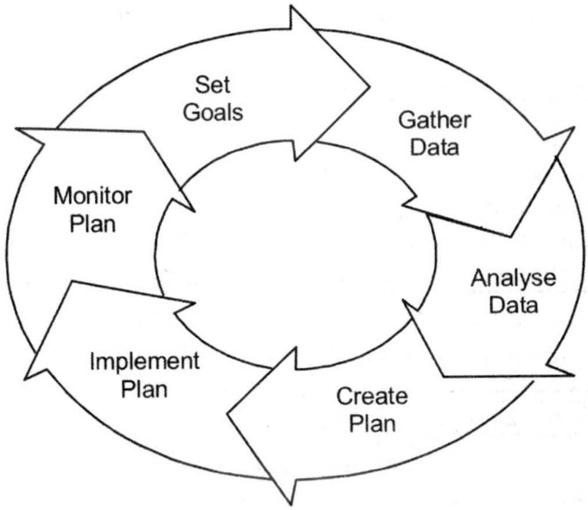

Fig. 5.2: Steps of Planning.

2. Identify specific approaches and strategies.
3. Identify action plans to achieve the strategy.
4. Monitor and update the plan.

This strategic planning model is best suited for new organizations that never did the project before, small or busy organizations.

Educational Planning

Meaning of Educational Planning

Planning is essential in the field of education entitled "Educational Planning" which is a major requirement in contemporary society. The complexities of the present scientifically developed and technologically advanced society have given a special position to the need for planning in education.

So educational planning is a systematic design of action. It helps to frame the aims and objectives of education. It is helpful for social groups and any individual through maximum utilization of available resources. From a practical perspective, educational planning is defined as a process utilized by an administrator while performing the role of a leader, decision-maker, and change-agent, and so on.

Now-a-days, educational planning is very necessary. Today's modern societies have increased the need for and significance of educational planning. Educational planning is required due to limited natural resources, due to overpopulation, due to ecological matter, due to unscientific applications in the society. To handle these problems, it is necessary to take good educational planning. In educational planning, there must be functional efficiency and good organizational health.

In today's life, educational planning is very much required. A society needs its requirements. Society comes from darkness to light with the help of educational planning. Not only society but also its every aspect needs educational planning. It can be cleared by giving some examples, day by day increasing population needs its help, decreasing natural resources needs its help, and ecology needs its help. It becomes a necessity to deal with these problems and it becomes mandatory for competence planning. Educational organizations are the active agent which bring a desirable change in the society. For increasing functional efficiency and effectiveness an educational organization plays a pivotal role and educational planning becomes a necessity for smooth functioning.

Definition of Educational Planning

It can be defined as "the process of setting out in advance, strategies, policies, procedures, programmes, and standards through which an educational objective or set of objectives can be achieved". It is a detailed and systematic process that does not happen by chance. It is always goal-oriented.

According to Coombs (1970), "Educational planning is the application of rational, systematic analysis to the process of educational development to make education more effective and efficient in responding to the needs and goals of its students and society."

Educational planning is a process utilized by an administrator while performing the role of a decision-maker, a leader, and change-agent, and so on. Higher-level effectiveness comes through educational planning. It is future-oriented.

Characteristics of Educational Planning

1. Logical,
2. Systematic,
3. Scientific process,
4. Progressive,
5. Mission-oriented,

6. Future-oriented,
7. Curriculum-oriented, and
8. Remedial.

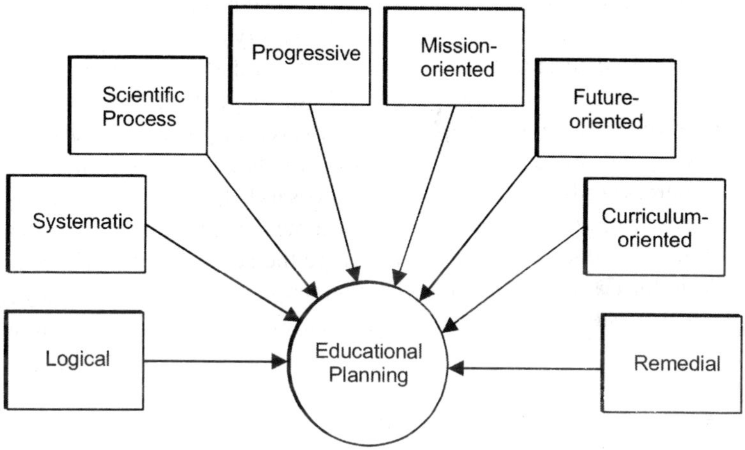

Fig. 5.3: Characteristics of Educational Planning.

Nature of Educational Planning

1. *Forecasting:* By forecasting, any event or condition or situation is known. By knowing its matter a good plan is taken. Forecasting has educational value. It tells what type of personality you are or types of students or number of students.

2. *Interpretation*: Educational planning gives interpretation to any data for its betterment. Translation and operational activities are to be done through educational planning.

3. *Goals and Objectives*: Educational planning fixes the aims and objectives of any organization or institution and fulfils the goals accordingly.

4. *Decision-Making*: Proper decision-making comes through proper educational planning. Educational planning gives good decisions or optimal decisions. It gives the best choices to people.

5. *Operations Optimization*: It is helpful for operative action. It enhances the existing situation and gifts a good future by guiding one.

6. *Problems Prevention*: Educational planning prevents problems related to education, institution, or any organization. Big problems are easily sorted out by good educational planning.

7. *Management Change*: A managerial tool like MBO, PERT, and various forecasting techniques work for achieving specific objectives of an organization.

8. *Complexity Resolution*: Educational Planning is complexity resolution. It is a process for coordination and control and works as coordination. It is helpful for any project for doing good work.

Need and Significance of Educational Planning

The need and significance of educational planning:

1. *Final success*: To make every programme of an educational institution or organization grand success.
2. *Saving agent*: Proper educational planning saves time, effort, and money as planning in every field is a time-saving, effort-saving, and a money-saving activity. To fulfil the target in time, educational planning is essential.
3. *Sound method*: It is a sound method of solving educational problems by avoiding the trial and error method of doing things.
4. *Smoothening administrative process*: It checks wastage and failure and contributes to the smoothness, ease, and efficiency of the administrative process in the field of education.
5. *Multiple facilitators*: Through proper planning in education, education can be the best means by which society will preserve and develop its value system, way of life of an individual, knowledge, skills, application, and culture of the nation.
6. *Work as a blueprint*: Educational planning is the most essential means for preparing a blueprint for any organization or any institution.
7. *Purposeful oriented*: Becoming any educational journey goal-oriented and purposeful educational planning becomes necessary.
8. *Intellectual benefits*: Educational planning is essential to sustain, maintain, and enhance the thinking process of any person or any organization.
9. *Universal aims and objectives*: It is necessary for the sense that every nation needs its planning to highlight the universal aims and objectives.
10. *Utilization of resources*: There must be good educational planning in the educational sector. If a school has Rs. 10 lakh for buying its books and extending the building. So the school administration

should work according to its budget otherwise school authority may face problems. By planning the authorities do smooth work. They are aware of their strength and weaknesses. They can minimize their work according to their strategies. They can adopt new tactics in fulfilling their objectives.

11. *External demands*: Educational planning is needed to meet the demands of the world. Good educational planning explores the knowledge and opens the door of science, advancement, and technology.
12. *Best possible means*: Educational planning provides and explores the best possible means of making the wide use of available resources leading to the maximum realization of the educational goals.
13. *To facilitate personnel*: It facilitates the gathering of educational experts, supervisors, teachers and administrators for deciding about the realization of purposes of the educational programme.
14. *Equal importance*: Educational planning has great importance in the sense that it gives equal importance to the purposes of different classes of experts such as economists, politicians, sociologists, scientists, educationists etc.
15. *To achieve maximum effectiveness and efficiency:* An adequate plan helps to direct and coordinate the actions of workers to achieve efficiency, effectiveness. The adequate plan gives good productivity to the man.
16. *Help in administrative decisions*: In the administrative field, need various types of decisions for smooth working or progress. Whether they can take direct action or indirect action according to their administrative policy.
17. *Decision-making*: In school, generally, three areas of decision-making are seen. These are budget, personnel, and curriculum. Where a budget is a plan of how to spend an amount of money over a particular period. It gives acknowledge how much money to be spent on something. In a personnel decision, the process and growth of a school are dependable. Good personnel decision gives smooth progress to a school. It is the power of a school to determine how best to staff the school. The school's personnel work systematically for fulfilling its target.
18. *Clear choices*: Good educational planning gives the best choices. Planning enables a nation to make its choices clear in terms of the aim and objectives.

19. *Optimum utilization of resources*: Through proper planning, an institution can maximze utilization of its resources within a specific time. Educational plans are designed to avoid imbalances and enormous wastes and replenish the steadily aggravated shortage of teachers. It is essential for the best utilization of available resources.

Types of Educational Planning

1. *Administrative Planning:* It is planning for an administrative perspective. Here responsibilities are vested to different levels like primary, secondary, higher secondary, higher general, technical, or professional. This educational planning prepares planning on the duration of an educational programme, organization, and coordination of various programmes. It not only prepares the above-mentioned things but also does financial allocation or budget for the programme, engagement of education officials in the programme. For smooth management, administrative planning is doing a great job. At least it is said that it deals with the distribution of responsibilities and powers for different education.

2. *Academic Planning:* It deals with smooth academic transactions of the syllabus for any course at any level of education. So, it is also called curricular planning. It maintains the needs and demands of an individual or society. Here diagnostic evaluation, formative evaluation, and summative evaluation are needed for the smooth progress of an institution. And remedial instruction is given for fulfilling the target.

3. *Co-curricular planning:* Co-curricular planning is beneficial for both, for a student as well as for educational organization too. This planning includes student welfare services, social and cultural activities, planning for games, and sports too. Without co-curricular planning, no institution gets its all-round development.

4. *Instructional planning:* Instructional planning deals with classroom activities. It deals with the emotional as well as the organizational climate of the classroom. It includes for specification or instructional objectives, organization of learning activities, selection of appropriate means for presentation of learning experiences. Monitoring the instructional progress and selection of suitable evaluation techniques.

5. *Institutional planning:* Institutional planning deals with the needs and requirements of every organization or institution to be achieved through the creation and maintenance of a planning atmosphere in the institution. Institutional planning includes all types of planning including

academic, co-curricular, administrative planning, planning for discipline, planning for utilization of resources.

Education can be categorized in another six types as follows:

1. Micro planning, 2. Macro planning, 3. Long-term planning, 4. Short-term planning, 5. Management planning, 6. Grassroots planning.

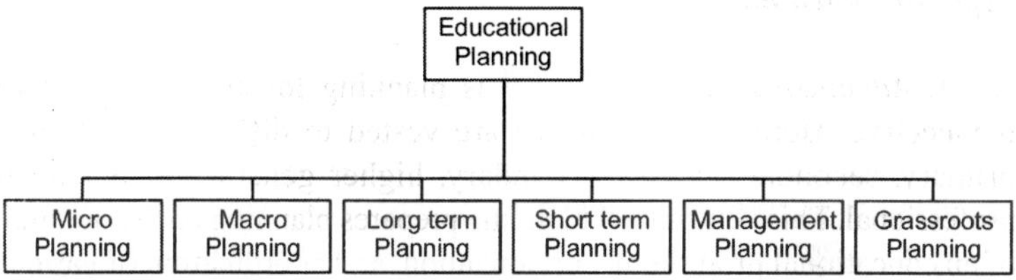

Fig. 5.4: Types of Educational Planning.

Steps of Educational Planning: There are seven main stages of educational planning:

1. Defining educational problems,
2. Analyzing the problems,
3. Conceptualizing and designing plans,
4. Evaluating plans,
5. Specifying the plans,
6. Implementing the plan, and
7. Feedback of the plan.

Models of Educational Planning

Based on peoples' description and understanding, there are various types of educational models. A model is a conceptual representation to explain facts, an object, or an event, or any real system. It serves as a guide. It explains the educational process and works as a framework for handling and solving the educational planning problem.

Adam came up with the interactive-rational model of planning in 2006. It has tremendous educational implication.

This model focuses on the analysis of the means to get the plan goals or objectives. The propositions of the model include:

(a) The knowledge needed for planning is objective, cumulative, and capable of being expressed in codified, abstract language.
(b) Planning provides an algorithm for responsive efficient change.
(c) Planning models and methods have universal applicability or at least require little situational adaptation. This rational model is a systematic, less participatory, and less adaptive. This model is objective-oriented. Its cost-benefit analysis is imperative.

The universal applicability of the planning model suggests that planning should be adaptive to reflect the social environment.

The interactive model of planning emphasizes the need for the value of interchange of ideas, opinions, and knowledge in the planning process. The interactive model is more adaptive and less structured than a rational model of planning. It recognizes the importance of information exchange in planning, the dynamism of participation, and the interaction of individuals and systems with the environment. Other than an interactive-rational model of education, there are other three models as follows:

1. Technicist Model
2. Consensual Model
3. Political Model

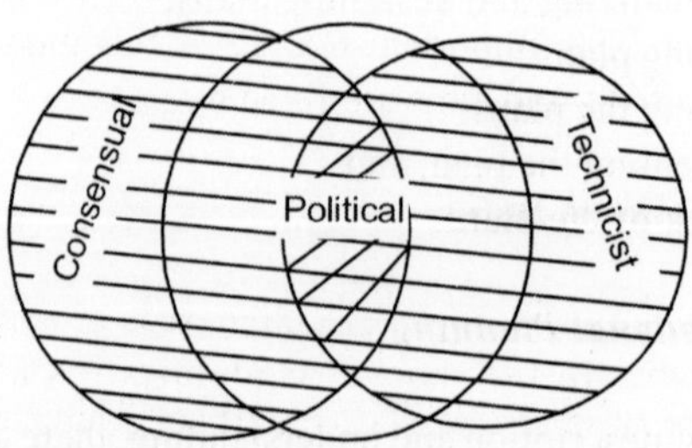

Fig. 5.5: Model of Educational Planning.

1. ***Technicist Model***: It is a popular model among all models. It is an expert-driven and linear process of decision-making. This model describes plan implementation as the execution of plan goals and objectives. Here, success is measured in terms of achievement of plan objectives and implementation is a linear process of change. It gives a good evaluation that's why it provides feedback to modify implementation activities. It provides information for future planning also. This technicist model can be applied in planning for teacher supply and demand. It deals with other aspects like space allocation, cost analysis in education, plant construction, and prediction of enrolment of students in school. The success of this model depends on the function of prior planning, information availability, and administrative capacity.

***2. Consensual Model*:** This conceptual model emerges from the interactive model of Adam (2006). It views educational planning as an open human system, located in a social environment. The main feature of this model is that meaningful interactions and actions presuppose understanding and that every legitimate action comes as a result of the consensual agreement. The consensual model evolves from social interaction or effective communication and is grounded in practice, Friedman cited in Adams (2006). Here in this model, plan goals are not permanent. But there is a suitable place for modification by discussion and replaced over time. This model can be used enhancing participation, agreement on particular issues, effective communication, and decision making in the educational process. This model requires the meaningful involvement of education stakeholders in planning educational change.

***3. Political Model*:** The last model of educational planning is a political model. It views educational planning as a process of bargaining, the exercise of power, and negotiation. Educational planning is influenced by political ideology and its power. Most of the educational planning or plan is decided by polity, there is no doubt. Polity decides and gives the direction of a plan. The important feature of this model is bargaining. Educational objectives and aims are fixed by polities.

Education Planning in India

Education Planning is one of the essential areas of concern in all Five-year Plans in India. In the time of modernization and globalization education planning is very necessary. In all levels which are elementary, secondary, vocational, higher, technical education planning is important and the Indian government has been emphasizing the need to develop it since the 1990s.

What are the Hindrances for Education Planning in India?

The major problems of Education Planning in India are as follows:

1. High drop-out rates.
2. Wastage of resources.

3. Low levels of learning achievement.
4. Low participation of girl students.
5. The problem of brain drain.
6. Inadequate school infrastructure.
7. Mass illiteracy.
8. Teacher absenteeism rate high.
9. Large-scale teacher vacancies.
10. Inadequate teaching or learning material.
11. Inadequate government funding.
12. Lack of public involvement in provisioning of educational services.
13. Variation in the literacy rates for the special groups of citizens.
14. Variation in inter-state literacy rates.

Steps taken by the Government in Accelerating Education Planning in India

The growth of education at all levels has been emphasizing at Central as well as State level. The Zilla Saksharta Samiti or District Literacy Society plays also an important role in pursuance of adult education. The first step taken by the Indian Government is to initiate measures for universal elementary education among all. The other significant steps on the Education Planning in India are—

1. To increase the number of institutions, teachers, and students at the elementary level.
2. To provide for incentives like free textbooks, free uniforms, and scholarships.
3. To offer a centrally sponsored programme of Nutritional Support to Primary Education or Mid Day Meal Scheme.
4. To launch the Sarva Siksha Abhiyan (SSA) Scheme.
5. To launch the National Literacy Mission for providing functional literacy to the non-literates between the age groups of 15 and 35.
6. To provide free and compulsory education for children.
7. To improve the Industrial Training Institutes, Boards of Technical Education and Engineering Colleges, and Polytechnics and Apprenticeship Schools.
8. To upgrade the Indian Institutes of Technology and Indian Institutes of Management.

9. To progress in new technology-based areas like biotechnology, bioinformatics, and nanotechnology.

Conclusion

Planning or educational planning is an action of plan or blueprint in the hands of the planner to accomplish aims and objectives of an organization or institution within a specific time in the best manner. It is a detailed programme or method, the scheme worked out beforehand to achieve a set objective. It is rightly remarked that the *Well plan is half done.* Like planning in any field, educational planning has to explore the best possible means of making the greatest use of available resources leading to the maximum realization of the educational aims and objectives, both individual and social. Educational Planning is a process where an administrator works as a decision-maker, leader, as well as change-agent, and so on. An administrator uses Educational Planning for good decision-making. Educational Planning is a basic management task. High effectiveness is achieved by well educational planning. Its uniqueness lies in its future-orientation or anticipation mode. In Educational Planning there are five types of planning, *viz.* administrative planning, academic planning, co-curricular planning, instructional planning, and institutional planning. Technicist model, conceptual model, political model are there in educational planning. The planners frame the aims and objectives of education and by these models, they achieve their goals or accomplish their target. There are some barriers to education planning in India. To overcome these hindrances Indian Government takes some strategies like increasing institutions, teachers; launching mid-day meal scheme, launching SSA scheme, adult education programme, enforcing RTE Act, 2009 etc.

REFERENCES

Dewey, J. (1916). *Democracy and Education: An introduction to the Philosophy of Education.* New York: Macmillan.

Dewey, J. (1935). "Toward Administrative Statesmanship." *The Social Frontier,* 1(6), 9-10.

Hanushek, E.A., and Woessmann, L. (2012). "Do better schools lead to more growth cognitive skills, economic outcomes, and causation". *Journal of Economic Growth, 17*(4), 267–321.CrossRefGoogle Scholar.

Meredith, J.R., and Mantel, S.J., Jr. (2012). *Project Management: A Managerial Approach*. Danvers, MA: Wiley. Google Scholar.

Pinto, J.K. (2013). *Project Management—Achieving Competitive Advantage.* New York: Pearson International Edition. Google Scholar.

PMI. (2017). PMBOK® Guide—Sixth Edition. Google Scholar.

Rand, G.K. (2000). "Critical chain: The Theory of Constraints Applied to Project Management. *International Journal of Project Management, 18*(3), 173–177.CrossRefGoogle Scholar.

Somech, A., and Oplatka, I. (2014). *Organizational Citizenship Behaviour in Schools: Research and Practice for Improving Educational Systems Worldwide.* London: Routledge. Google Scholar.

Yemini, M., Addi-Raccah, A., and Katarivas, K. (2015). "I have a dream: School principals as entrepreneurs." *Educational Management Administration and Leadership, 43*(4), 526-540. CrossRefGoogle Scholar.

https://education.stateuniversity.com/pages/2386/School-Based-Decision making.html 18.03.2020.

https://www.businessmanagementideas.com/management/planning-management/characteristics-of-planning/19378 09.04.2020.

https://kalyan-city.blogspot.com/2012/02/importance-of-planning-why-planning-is.html 09.04.2020.

https://kalyan-city.blogspot.com/search/label/Education 09.04.2020.

https://online.alvernia.edu/articles/types-of-planning/10.04.2020.

https://www.heflo.com/blog/business-management/strategic-planning-process-model/10.04.2020.

http://www.yourarticlelibrary.com/india-2/educational-planning/educational-planning-in-india-meaning-and-definitions-and-everything-else/63739 10.04.2020.

http://www.yourarticlelibrary.com/organization/planning-organization/planning-importance-elements-and-principles-function-of-management/70029 10.04.2020.

https://www.academia.edu/37925596/Types_of_Educational_Planning_Reasons_for_Planning_Education.

Unit 2

Education and Development

Unit 2

Education and Development

6
Education and Development

Smt. Naipali

Introduction

Education is the fundamental right and the process of facilitating learning. Education gives skills, moral values, habits etc. Educational methods include teaching, training, discussion, research etc. By education we can take place under the guidance of educators and can take place in formal or informal settings and any experience that has a formative effect on the way same thinks, feels, may accept educational and practice of teaching is related between applied linguistics and language pedagogy.

Education has these stages in common way as pre-school or kindergarten, primary school, secondary school and then college, university etc.

Our Constitution has fundamental rights. Education right is fundamental right so every person has right to get education and no caste, no region, no religion boundations every person is free to get the education according to our Constitution.

History

Education is not a new topic but this is a very ancient beginning in old times that time *Rishis* have given education by many methods as a *Dhanush-Ban*, *Talwar, Bhala,* and many other weapons etc. Education began in prehistory, as adults trained the young in the knowledge and skills deemed necessary in their society. In preliterate societies, this was achieved orally and through imitation. Story-telling passed knowledge, moral values, and skills from one generation to the next generation. As cultures began to extend their knowledge beyond skills that could be readily learned through imitation, formal education developed and schools came into existence.

Plato founded the Academy in Athens, the first institution of higher learning in Europe. In China, Confucius (551–479 BCE), of the State of Lu, was the country's most influential ancient philosopher, whose educational outlook continues to influence the societies of China and neighbours like Korea and Japan. Confucius gathered disciples and searched in vain for a ruler who would adopt his ideals for good governance, but his Analects were written down by followers and have continued to influence education in East Asia into the modern era. After the Fall of Rome, the Catholic Church became the sole preserver of literate scholarship in Western Europe. The Church established cathedral schools in the Early Middle ages as centres of advanced education. Some of these establishments ultimately evolved into medieval universities and forebears of many of Europe's modern universities.

Formal Education

Formal Education occurs in a structured environment whose explicit purpose is teaching students. Usually, formal education takes place in a school environment with classrooms of multiple students learning together with a trained, certified teacher of the subject. Mostly schooling systems are designed around a set of values. The International Standard Classification of Education was created by UNESCO as a statistical base to compare education systems. In 1997, it defined 7 levels of education and 25 fields, though the fields were later separated out to form a different project. The current version ISCED 2011 has 9 rather than 7 levels, created by dividing the tertiary pre-doctorate level into three levels.

Primary and Secondary Education

Primary Education is related to International Standard Classification of Education Level—Primary education consists of the first five to seven years of formal, structured education. In general, primary education consists of six to eight years of schooling starting at the age of five or six, because about 89 per cent of children aged six to twelve are enrolled in primary education. Some education systems have separate middle schools, with the transition to the final stage of secondary education taking place at around the age of fourteen. Because mostly referred to as primary schools or elementary schools. Primary schools are often sub-divided into infant schools and junior schools and in our country school education based on a national curriculum framework designed by the National Council of Educational Research and Training, and for example compulsory education spans over twelve years with 8 years of elementary education, five years of primary schooling and three years of upper primary schooling. Secondary education has a longer history in Europe where grammar school or academies date from as early as the 6th century.

Depending on the system, schools for this period, or a part of it, may be called secondary or high schools, gymnasiums, lyceums, middle schools, colleges. The exact boundary between primary and secondary` education also varies from country to country. but is generally we can say about the matter now we come at the topic of the lower secondary education. This is related at ISCED level-2. Upper Secondary education is related to ISCED level-3. They lead to skills relevant to employment and the skill necessary to engage in tertiary courses etc.

Higher Education

Tertiary is related to higher education. We can say higher education also called tertiary, third stage. Tertiary education is normally taken to include undergraduate and post-graduate education. Colleges and universities and institutions provide tertiary education.

Tertiary education the ISCED distinguishes 4 levels. ISCED 6 is equivalent to a first degree, ISCED 7 is equivalent to a masters or an advanced professional qualification and ISCED 8 is an advanced research qualification.

Higher education typically involves work towards a degree-level or foundation degree qualification. A high proportion of the population (up to 55%) now enter higher education at some time in their lives. Higher education is, therefore, very important to national economies, political, social and by getting higher education any people can get many other economic sources.

Education Sector

The education system is a group of institutions as a B.Ed. Course, M.Ed. Course, BTC, JBT, and other teacher's training etc. Primary purpose is to provide education to children and young people in educational settings. It is related to principals, teachers, school nurses, students etc. The rest of the education system through various elements such as education policies and guidelines to which school policies can refer curricula and learning materials, as well as pre- and in-service teacher training programmes. The school environment—both physical (infrastructures) and psychological (school climate) is also guided by school policies that should ensure the well-being of students when they are in school. The education sector is fully integrated into society, through interactions with numerous stakeholders and other sectors. These include NGOs, stakeholders involved in health, child protection, justice and law enforcement.

Purpose of Education

Education's main aim is different at different places, and times, and have used educational systems for different purposes. The Prussian education system in the 19th century, for example, wanted to turn boys and girls into adults who would serve the state's political goals. Some writers say about the purpose of the education that it is the base of life and education gives moral values, civilization and better employment etc. For example, in the 21st century, many countries treat education as a positional good. In this competitive approach, people want their own students to get a better education than other students. This approach can lead to unfair treatment of some students, especially those from disadvantaged groups.

Administration of Education

The education at the State level is primarily the responsibility of the State Governments; the Union Government is concerned only with the coordination and determination of academic standards in respect of higher education, research and scientific and technical education. The problem of standards and coordination in the sphere of higher education is now the responsibility of the University Grants Commission. Coordination in regard to primary and secondary education is secured through All-India Councils. The Union Government is also managing Central Universities of Delhi, Aligarh, Banaras and Shantiniketan and other such institutions of national importance as may be decided by the Parliament of the country. The Director of Education controls the Elementary and Secondary Education in States with the help of inspectorate, which is directly responsible for the supervision of schools. The Universities in India are purely autonomous bodies, whereas secondary institutions are partly under the State Government, partly under local bodies and largely under private control, but recognized and aided by the State Departments of Education.

Education System in India

After gaining Independence in 1947, making education available to all had become a priority for the government. As discrimination on the basis of caste and gender has been a major impediment in the healthy development of the Indian society, they have been made unlawful by the Indian Constitution. The 86th constitutional amendment has also made elementary education a fundamental right for the children between the age group 6 to 14. According to the 2001 Census, the total literacy rate in India is 65.38 per cent. The female literacy rate is only 54.16 per cent. The gap between rural and urban literacy rate is also very significant in India. This is evident from the fact that only 59.4 per cent of rural population is literate as against 80.3 per cent urban population according to the 2001 Census.

The present education system in India mainly comprises primary education, secondary education, senior secondary education and higher education. Elementary education consists of eight years of education. Each of secondary and senior secondary education consists of two years of education. There are quite a good number of educational institutes in India that can compete with the best educational institutes of the world. The Indian Institutes of Technology (IITs), Indian Institutes of Management (IIMs), Indian Institutes of Science, National Law Schools, Jawaharlal Nehru University are some such institutes. The growing acceptance of distance learning courses and expansion of the Open University system is also contributing a lot in the democratization of higher education in India.

Education Commission

After the achievement of Independence, our leaders introduced Five Year Plans with a view to effect the development of the country in various fields. In these plans education, too, found an important place. So plans have been made for the development of various stages and kinds of education. However, the execution of these plans made aware of certain inherent weaknesses due to which the expected success was not being achieved. Education appeared to be one of the areas, which indicated many problems and needed efforts for immediate solutions. Thus, the

Government appointed the University Education Commission in 1948 and Secondary Education Commission in 1952 for suggesting reforms in education. The recommendations of these Commissions could not be implemented in their entirety. Consequently, the defects in the area of education persisted. For removal of these defects the Government of India appointed an Education Commission in 1964 under the Chairmanship of Dr. D.S. Kothari. The Commission is thus popularly known as 'Kothari Commission'. The Kothari Commission said, *"While the fundamental values to which the universities owe their allegiance are largely unrelated to time and circumstances, their functions change from time to time. Their tasks are no longer confined to the two traditional functions of teaching and advancement of knowledge. They are assuming new functions and the older ones are increasing in range, depth and complexity."*

The Commission emphasized that the Universities must learn to encourage individuality, variety and dissent within a climate of tolerance. The Indian universities should strive to assist the schools in their attempts at qualitative self-improvement. Universities should conduct experimental schools, run advanced courses for teachers in various school subjects, assume greater responsibility for the training of teachers at all levels, develop new curricula, textbooks and teaching materials. Most important responsibility is to lower the dominant place given to examinations, to improve the standard in every aspect and by a symbiotic development of teaching and research, to create at least a few centres comparable to those of their type in any other part of the world.

National Policies on Education in India

The National Policy of Education cannot be overemphasized, as it is related to the essential development of a country. It was in 1968, for the first time that a National Policy on Education was formulated for preparing suitable hands for shouldering responsibilities in the various fields of our national reconstructions. Number of programmes were included in this policy, *viz.* free and compulsory education, development and protection of all the Indian languages, equality of educational opportunities, identification of gifted children, provision of work experience and national service scheme, science education and research, education in Agriculture and Industries, reform in examination system, part-time education and correspondence curriculum etc.

On April 20, 1986, a New Educational Policy was placed before the Indian Parliament for consideration and approval. It was a result of the renewed priority assigned to Education by the Government of Late Shri Rajiv Gandhi.

The basic recommendations of the policy were related to national form of education, more emphasis on learning, delinking degree for any service, vocationalization of education, importance on moral values, emphasis on reforms in the examination system, education of the weaker section of the society, starting of an All India Educational Service, starting of Open Universities, establishing many Navodaya Vidyalayas, women education. For raising the standard of women, special attention has been paid on their education in the new educational policy in order to minimize the prevailing distinction between men and women.

The National Policy on Education, 1986 and its Programme of Action, which was the result of deliberations, consultations and consensus was reviewed and updated in 1992. The introductory part of the POA envisages that given the rich diversity of our nation it would be in the fitness of things if each State and Union Territory formulates a State POA in accordance with their situational imperatives as well as with the POA, 1992.

Experiments in Indian Education

The revolution was crushed but the sparks continued to emanate and the fire of revolution remained burning in the hearts of Indians. One of the sparks that emanated from this fire was that of educational revolution. Men in position made efforts to open such educational centres that followed the education pattern of Vedic and Buddha era and was also in keeping with the pattern followed by the other progressive nations of the world.

It was decided to impart education of nationalism, cooperation and social unity, besides various other subjects. It also aimed at creating in the student love for the country, for society, for independence and for human beings and boycott foreign language, dress, communalism and untouchability. Consequently, some such institutions were founded that did not have any interest in the Government financial help and its educational policy. The important ones among these were the Viswa-Bharti, Vanasthali Vidyapeeth, Gurukul Kangri, Jamia Millia etc., these institutions received encouragement. These institutions continued their struggle for life during the British in the hope of a better future atmosphere and started developing after the country achieved freedom.

Progress of Technical and Vocational Education

After Independence the attention of the country has been focused on this deficiency and efforts have been made in the sphere of technical and vocational education. The Secondary Education Commission (1952-53) and the Kothari Commission (1964-66) have emphasized the importance of vocationalized education and they have recommended that education at least up to secondary stage must be vocationalized. The Kothari Commission also emphasized the need of production-oriented education and the necessity of work experience for all students at all the stages of education. The Basic Education Scheme as advocated by Mahatma Gandhi was a definite step towards vocationalization of education but the Government has not been able to promote this scheme well. As far as Commercial education is concerned during the period between 1857-1902, it did not show any marked progress like agricultural education. Except the Punjab University, no other university had recognized it.

Vocational and technical education in India has developed mainly in relation to assessed future demand for manpower and has largely been responsible for the growth of our industrial structure. According to the Planning Commission, *"The technical education system represents a national resource of science and technology with specialized laboratories, sophisticated instrumentation facilities and more importantly, teams of highly qualified scientific and engineering personnel on their faculty. These internal resources should be utilized not merely towards technological self-reliance but also to bring about progressive improvement in the quality of technical education."*

Scenario of Educational Development in India

According to the Constitutional Amendment of 1976 some of the subjects of education have been placed under the joint responsibility of the Centre and the State. The Centre is responsible for determining the standard of higher research, science education, technical education and higher education. Aligarh University, Banaras Hindu University, Hyderabad University, Jawaharlal Nehru University, Delhi, Visva Bharti University, Shantiniketan and North Eastern Hill University, Shillong and some other centres of higher learning have come under the direct control of the Central Government. All Educational Institutes, Scientific and Technological Institutes of national importance are run on the finances obtained from the Centre. Hence, these are under the control of the Central Ministry of Education.

The Universities in India in the present times can be classified in various categories like Central Universities, State Universities, Deemed Universities, Private Universities, Agricultural Universities, Institutes of National Importance and Open Universities. These universities play an important role not only in the sustenance of a just and vibrant society but also in the continuation of its rich democratic tradition. After Independence, the number of institutions has increased significantly. The expansion of the system normally refers to one, or a combination of an increase in the number of institutions; a growth in student enrolment; an increase in the number of teaching and non-teaching staff, the diversified structure in terms of courses. Improving the quality of and access to higher education and research in India has become all the more important keeping in view the growing need of qualified human resources in various sectors of the economy.

The Central Advisory Board of Education has been constituted to assist in the functioning of the two Governments and ensure that parity is maintained in the field of higher education. Open Universities provide the facility of distance education to people who are unable to pursue regular courses. Distance education is provided on academic, technical and professional subjects. These universities offer undergraduate, post-graduate and doctoral programmes. They also offer diploma and certificate level courses. As agriculture plays an important role in the Indian Economy, setting up of adequate number of Agricultural Universities were considered very important in India.

Technical Education in India

The technical education system in the country covers engineering, technology, management, architecture, pharmacy etc. The Ministry of Human Resource Development supports the programmes at undergraduate, graduate, post-graduate and research levels. The technical education system at the Central level comprises Indian Institutes of Technology, Indian Institute of Management, Indian Institute of Sciences, National Institutes of Technology etc. and All India Council for Technical Education:

Professional Education in India

Higher education also deals with the professional education. For this, a network of public and private polytechnics and vocational institutions, controlled and supervised by the councils specializing in each discipline, exist. Professional councils, like All India Council for Technical Education (AICTE), Distance Education Council (DEC), National Council for Teacher Education (NCTE), Medical Council of India (MCI) and others are responsible for recognition of courses, promotion of professional institutions and providing grants to undergraduate programmes and various awards.

Adult Education

In the education of adults, the emphasis has not been only on making them literate, but an attempt is also made for education of the personality in order that they may fulfil the responsibilities of citizens of a democracy intelligently. In 1973, a Programme of Adult Education was launched. Its objective has been to educate 30 crores adults within the age range of 15-35 years by the end of the 20th century. The main purpose of this Adult Education Programme is to increase the working efficiency of the adults.

Women Education in India

The Government has paid special attention on women education since 1957-58. In the programmes made for the same special provisions have been made for arrangement of stipends, appointment of lady teachers, residential accommodation for women teachers and training of women teachers. By 1995, i.e. within 48 years the progress of women education had reached such a point that there remained little difference between the percentage of educated boys and girls. Under Adult Education Programme for women the objectives have been to make women over 15 years of age literate and to make them economically self-dependent by educating them and developing other skills in them. Another aim has been to give them training in rearing up children, family planning and information about health principles etc.

Educational Research and Training

The National Council of Educational Research and Training (NCERT) was established by the Central Government in 1961 for implementing the educational policies and plans of the Central Ministry of Education. The Council contributes in the educational progress by cooperating with various universities in the country and Boards of Education in various States. The Council runs four Regional Colleges of Education situated in Ajmer, Bhopal, Bhubaneshwar etc.

Development of Languages in India

Development of Hindi—national language, development of Indian languages and development of English. The Central Government has established a Kendriya Hindi Sansthan at Agra, which makes researches in new Hindi teaching methods, constructs Hindi teaching materials, publishes Hindi books, awards degrees to trainees. For the development of other Indian languages, a Central Institute of Indian Languages has been established. The Central Government has opened at Hyderabad the Central Institute of English and Foreign Languages.

The University Grants Commission

The University Grants Commission of India is a Union Government body that provides funds for government-recognized universities and colleges. It is the body that provides recognition for universities in India. Its central office is in New Delhi, and it also has a southern regional office in Hyderabad. UGC conducts NET examinations for the appointment of teachers in colleges and universities, nevertheless, some years back the NET had been exempted those having M. Phil. degree to teach at graduation level. However, Ph.D. holders can teach at Post Graduation level since June 2006. The National Knowledge Commission was constituted on 13th June, 2005 as a high level Advisory Body to the Prime Minister of India. The vision for NKC was articulated in the address of Dr. Manmohan Singh, Prime Minister of India, *"the time has come to create a second wave of institution building and of excellence in the fields of education, research and capacity building."* The report is a compilation of the recommendations submitted by NKC till November 2007 on reforms relating to education. These include, *viz.* Right to Education, English language, Vocational Education and Training, Higher Education, Medical Education, Legal Education, Management Education, Open and Distance Education and Open Educational Resources etc.

Role of The Yashpal Committee, 2009

The Yashpal Committee, 2009 emphasized that at the undergraduate level students should be exposed to various disciplines, like humanities, social sciences, aesthetics etc., in an integrated manner. This should be irrespective of the discipline they would like to specialize in, whether general or professional higher education like medicine, engineering etc.

Targets and Achievements in Eleventh Plan Development in Education

Prime Minister Manmohan Singh has termed the Eleventh Five-Year Plan as *"India's Educational Plan"*. The Eleventh Plan, approved at the meeting of the National Development Council in December 2007, places the highest priority on education as a instrument for achieving rapid and inclusive growth. At INR 2.70 lakh crore, it constitutes 20 per cent of the Plan, representing a credible progress towards the target of 6 per cent of GDP. The Eleventh Five Year Plan presents a comprehensive strategy for strengthening the education sector covering all segments of the education pyramid. It is through universal literacy, access to education and knowledge-based industrial development that India will believably march ahead to join the front ranks of the great nations of the world overcoming the challenges of ensuring that everyone has an access to education and skill building in their activity.

Conclusion

Many countries are now at large scale changing the way they educate their citizens. The world is changing at an ever rapid rate, which means that a lot of knowledge becomes outdated and inaccurate more quickly. The emphasis is, therefore, shifting to teaching the skills of learning: to picking up new knowledge quickly and in an agile progress a way as possible. Some country's schools have even begun to move away from the regular subject-focused curricula, introducing instead developments like learning where students study concepts like climate change, natural sciences, computer science, social sciences etc. Education is also becoming reserved for all children and adults. Some governmental bodies have even proposed compulsory lifelong education. Because without education any person cannot get success and better civilization and moral values and better employment. Despite all the efforts to develop the education system in India, access, equity and quality of education in India continue to haunt the policy makers till this date. This has mainly been due to the widespread poverty and various prejudices. The inability to check the drop-out rates among the marginalized sections of the population is another cause of worry. Many aspects of the current educational set-up demand review and change. Until concrete steps are taken to reformulate our methodology of imparting education, we shall continue to underutilize, even waste our youth, and this could have serious consequences in the future.

REFERENCES

Assmann, Jan (2002). *The Mind of Egypt: History and Meaning in the Time of the Pharaohs*. p. 127.

"Plato". *Encycloaedia Britannica*. 2002.

Why is Confucius Still Relevant Today His Sound Bites Hold Up.

Nuria Sanz, Sjur Bergan: *The Heritage of European Universities,* 2nd edition, *Higher Education Series No. 7*, Council of Europe, 2006, p. 136 Sources References.

ISCED 2011 classification.

Revision of the International Standard Classification of Education (ISCED), retrieved 05-04-2012.

Government of India, *Report of the Yashpal Committee on Higher Education: The Report on 'Renovation and Rejuvenation of Higher Education,* 2008, New Delhi: Ministry of Education.

Basu, Aparna, *The Growth of Education and Political Development in India, 1898-1920*, 1974, New Delhi: Oxford University Press.

UGC Annual Report 2005-06, New Delhi: University Grants Commission and *Selected Educational Statistics*, New Delhi: Ministry of Human Resource Development.

UGC Annual Report 1996-97 and 2005-06 (New Delhi: University Grants Commission); and *Selected Educational Statistics* (New Delhi: Ministry of Human Resources Development).

UGC, *Model Act Committee Report*, New Delhi, 1964. p. 8.

Thakur, R.S. and Arun C. Mehta (1999), *Education for All: The Year 2000 Assessment*, Core EFA Indicators, New Delhi.

7

The Role of Education in Development of Economies

Tamara Nije Tawfiq Dawoud

The link between education and the economy is closely related. Education contributes to development directly through the education of human manpower and scientific knowledge, which is the fruit of scientific research that is linked to education, and the instilled attitudes towards work, organization and society, all of which favour development in one way or another. The economy provides different resources for education. Education is seen in many studies as multiple benefits at the individual and national level: it raises productivity, investment and savings, improves quality of life, helps technological change, improves income distribution and equal opportunity, contributes to influence (cognitive skills, personal ambition, competition and creativity, health etc). Noting that not every education is necessarily conducive to development, education may (devour resources from the first to be spent in other more feasible aspects, misallocation of resources within or use them efficiently low, contribute to graduate unemployment and brain drain etc.), so pay attention. The quality of education provided in to serve as the first....

What is Development

1. The Concept of Development

Development includes the ability of individuals to build, organize, direct, innovate and invest, as well as their ability to increase and expand the size of education to include each individual, which helps to grow, and thus investing the energies of individuals and involving them in development efforts and development is thus the goal and means of human being:

- Development is a voluntary intervention process for society and the ability of society to utilize human and material resources to improve the quality of life.
- Development is a dynamic process that results from the voluntary intervention of the community.
- Development is not a purely economic phenomenon, but a radical change that extends beyond the physical and financial aspects of people's lives. It is a multidimensional process that involves the reorganization and reorientation of economic and social systems and structures in a country.
- Development in the traditional sense means the extent of the ability of the national economy, which has been stagnant for a period to achieve an annual increase in the national rate of 5-7% or more).
- United Nations studies for the years (1950-1956) deviated from the state of development by the definition that "development processes can guide the efforts of citizens and the government to improve socio-economic conditions in communities and help them to contribute to the progress of society to the fullest extent possible."
- Modern development: This is a multidimensional process that involves radical changes in social, behavioural and cultural structures, political and administrative systems along with increasing rates of economic growth, equity in the distribution of national income and the eradication of absolute poverty in a society.
- Development is the process by which efforts can be directed to both parents and the government to improve the socio-economic conditions in the communities to help them integrate into the life of the nation and contribute to its progress as much as possible.

General Objectives of Development

- Raise the economic, social and cultural level of citizens and improve their living conditions.
- Satisfy the basic needs of community members.

- Achieve homogeneity between the layers of society by dissolving class differences and creating equal opportunities for all according to their abilities.
- Emphasizing the popular participation in development efforts from the beginning to the end because the role of man as a citizen in his society is realized and is becoming more and more prominent by his direct contribution according to his capacity at every stage of the developmental building that is intended to achieve in his country.
- Changing individual lifestyle and modifying their lifestyles, production and behaviour for the better.
- Changes in social, behavioural, cultural and political structures.
- Increasing the capacity of society to utilize its human and non-human resources.

The Most Important Pillars of Development

- *Structural change:* A change that requires the emergence of new social roles and organizations that are qualitatively different from the existing roles and organizations in society, and this is a major shift in phenomena, systems and relationships prevailing in society.
- *Strong impulse:* Society needs a strong impulse or a set of impulses to effect change and governments are largely responsible for the impulse.
- *Appropriate strategy:* Means the outline or outlines of development policy in the transition from underdevelopment to self-growth.

Development Characteristics

- Development is an ongoing process.
- Development is an inclusive and multidimensional process that encompasses the whole of society.
- Development is an investment process that uses available resources to improve the means and conditions of life.
- Planned process development.
- Development aimed at welfare.
- Development is an administrative responsibility.
- Development must be attractive and highly attractive to shareholders and beneficiaries.

The basic principles that must be met for the project to be considered a development project:

- Development projects should be part of State policy.
- Development is a process of continuous and inclusive change, i.e., it is a social process, not an economic process.
- The necessity of joining citizens and the state in implementing the development project.

Islam and Development

- Islam has a distinct vision of the concept of development, as portrayed by the Pakistani economist Dr. Khurshid Ahmed through the Islamic concept of development has the characteristics of inclusiveness and balance, so as to include the physical and spiritual aspects together, and meets the need of the individual and the community in perfect harmony and harmony.
- The development effort is concerned with the human being. This means that development is directed to the human being and to the promotion of his physical, social, cultural and environment.
- The process of development in the Islamic concept is a multi-dimensional activity and is not limited to one side without the other, and Islam seeks to strike a balance in life between different factors and forces.
- Islam tries to re-balance the quantitative and qualitative variables, and this is what economic development seeks in its application framework.

Optimal use of resources and the equal and equitable distribution of human relations on the basis of justice and truth.

- Education in most Arab countries, despite the large numbers and the multiplication of institutions and high spending on them and despite the full picture of bright reports, still between them and education that leads to human development and thus to comprehensive development is a huge bonus, may become a conflict and sometimes, when education truly becomes in the service of comprehensive and effective development, it plays its role because it is this development that achieves the strong economic, political, administrative, technological, cultural and social entity. Be it difficult.

Types of Development (Economic-Social)

Economic Development is defined as:

- Deliberate actions that would increase national income over a period of time more than population growth.
- The continuous increase in per capita income over a long period of time must be accompanied by an increase in the standard of living and welfare of the individual and increase the capacity of the individual to produce and reform the balance of payments.
- The process by which there is a real increase in the national output of a given economy over a long period of time.
- Economic development depends vitally on the creation of a workforce with the technical skills necessary for modern industrial production and creates a philosophy that calls for accommodating and inciting economic and technological change.

Social Development is defined as:

- Continuous improvement of the standard of living and well-being of the population, working in tandem with economic development.
- A scientific and realistic approach to study and guide the growth of society from different aspects, taking care of the human side in order to create interdependence between components of society.
- Processes of social change inflicted on social construction and its functions in order to satisfy the social needs of the human being and therefore include two basic elements are the change of old conditions and the establishment of a new social construction from which new relationships and new values and ideas emerge.

Education and Economic Growth

The importance of human capital in economic competition and economic growth is evident. The interest of countries in establishing universities and linking them to the production system and the needs of society attest to this recognition.

The literature and development experience suggest that sustained growth is driven by increased productive capacity and investments in tangible assets (such as innovation, education and training), which are the centre for achieving long-term productivity and employment goals. Most of the literature underscores the role of education and training as key determinants of productivity and its importance in raising competitiveness, leading to long-term employment levels.

By examining the determinants of economic growth in a large number of countries between 1960 and 1995, Barrow & Lee (2000) found that an important determinant of growth was the initial stock of human capital in countries and the characteristics of their populations. He showed that growth is positively correlated with the primary level of the average years of schooling at the secondary and higher levels of adult males. He explained that higher education workers are complementary to new technologies and play an important role in the diffusion of technologies, which is a key element in the development process. Primary education does not play a significant role in growth, but it is a prerequisite for crossing the educational ladder to higher stages of developmental return. What is striking is that its results have shown an insignificant correlation between years of secondary and tertiary education in females and growth, which is difficult to accept by advocates of women's education and empowerment in development and society (some economic researchers have criticized Barrow's findings and explained some of her dilemmas).

They have returned this results to some explanations, including that the employment of an educated mirror has not yet reached the degree to which the impact of education on development is evident. Perhaps such a conclusion applies to the education of women in the Arab world, taking into account the modest contribution rates of women to economic activity at least as measured by statistics. The study pointed out that the education of women at the primary level stimulates economic growth indirectly through its impact on reducing fertility rates in the population, which is considered by many economists and demographers is an important element in both economic growth and social development.

Education was not a clear determinant of growth in the study of Jerusalem, Fattah and Imam (2003). The researchers studied the relative contribution of both capital and labour.

The growth of aggregate factor productivity over economic growth was the result of the dominant contribution of capital to the contribution of both labour and aggregate factor productivity growth during the period 1960-1977. The study showed that the growth of total factor productivity has a positive impact on East Asian countries. In the Middle East and North Africa, the results were mixed in terms of the impact of education on the growth of total factor productivity. While the effects were positive in Egypt, Morocco, Tunisia and Turkey, the impact was negative in other countries in the sample, including (5) oil countries.

Difference between Economic Growth and Development

- The words "economic growth" are synonymous with the words "increase in national income"; economic growth tells us the real values of GDP during certain years.
- Economic growth "is a long-term (continuous) increase in the capacity of the national economy and its ability to supply the population with diverse commodities. This increased energy depends on renewable technology and the structural, behavioural and ideological adjustments required by the growth process."
- Development includes a broader concept, and development does not have its requirements unless this increase in national output is accompanied by drastic changes in economic, social and political structures. Development is a rapid and cumulative increase over a period of time.
- Development is a comprehensive and integrated process resulting from continuous voluntary intervention to create interaction between:

  The societal energy of any society, i.e. the total human abilities and skills and the size of the quality of natural elements, and

  The developmental capacity of the community, i.e. the will of the society and its ability to utilize its social energy and to improve the quality of life of its children.

Reasons or Sources of Economic Growth

In the analysis of development or growth, it is generally observed that the causes or sources of economic growth are concentrated in factors such as:

- *Increased labour input:* Resulting from population growth and increased rates of contribution to economic activity.

- *Improved quality of labour input:* People are becoming more educated and healthier than they were in the past, and as a result, society's stock of human capital has increased, contributing to greater productivity.
- *Increase in natural capital:* In order to increase the nation's stock of natural capital to be spared. That is, to give up some of its current consumption in order to produce capital goods that allow for greater future consumption. Additions to the physical capital stock enable individuals to produce more per hour or in other words increase productivity.
- *Economy size:* The larger the size of the enterprise and the market grows economy. The experience of nations suggests that output exceeds input increases.
- *Technology improvement:* When new information (knowledge) is applied to production processes, it is able to reduce the amount of resources needed to produce, they also offer new products and materials that were not of economic value. One recent study estimates that "advances in knowledge" contributed about 28 per cent of the total increase in output in the United States between 1929 and 1982.

Education and Labour Market: Conceptualization

The relationship between education and the labour market is intended to guide the educational system at all stages, levels and types to prepare for the needs of the economic system of manpower in various economic sectors. A situation like this entails creating an educational system in a very different way, whether the attitude is to guide the educational system to prepare the civilized, social and cultural rights of a society with a particular specificity and identity, especially if the position is to build a civilized project, and this does not, of course, mean the negation of the function of preparing the strong working for the economy and its development. To this end, considerable and complex differences have arisen between advocates for linking education to the labour market directly and automatically, and among advocates of a civilized, social and cultural function of the educational system, including preparation for the labour market. The following are some theoretical trends in this context:

Economic Theory

Economic studies and researches have been concerned with measuring the potential relationship between the variable of education and the variable of economic growth, depending on the GDP of each country. However, there have been several objections to the artificial accumulation of indicators and their integration in a strange and tendentious manner. "These methods outline signs of the inability of economic science to build a satisfactory theory of the relationship between education and development, and to understand the actual state of the educational system's interaction with the economic system."

However, three types of economic analysis of the relationship between education and economic growth can be identified:

The First Type of Economic Analysis

This type of analysis uses the method of international comparison between the level of education and the level of economic growth, and proceeds from the following hypothesis, that the high level of education leads to a higher level of income of educated individuals, as a result can be said that investment in education helps to rapid economic growth, and studies conducted. Based on this hypothesis, it become clear that this theory is difficult to prove in practice. Arab oil countries, for example, despite the expansion of education and availability, but the increase or decrease—that is income—for individuals or society is linked to other variables outside the relationship between education and the economy and the labour market and the experience and skills required. The whole equation was important as a result of the huge oil resources and the desire of the state to invest these funds and distribute them to the people of society, which led to the expansion of the size of the labour market, and the use of foreign labour, regardless of the output of education and its ability to satisfy. The need for labour, and that rising or changing per capita income is not as much a result of education as it is mainly due to huge oil revenues.

The Second Type of Economic Analysis

This type of analysis derives its origin from the theory of human capital, and focuses primarily on the study of the relationship between economic growth and human capital. Although the example of the United States is used as proof of this relationship, this example reveals that the growth of the American economy and the expansion of its labour market since the nineteenth century was a result of several integrated factors determined by five factors:

1. Increase the workload by 34 per cent.
2. Capital investment by 15 per cent.
3. The economies of small size resulting from the growth of the internal market by 9 per cent.
4. Education by 23 per cent.
5. Progress of knowledge by 20 per cent.

One criticism of this theory, which was put in the question: Why some countries are delayed economically, despite the abundance of holders of scientific degrees in them and the spread of education is widespread?

The Third Type of Economic Analysis

This type of economic analysis is based on the integration of educational planning with economic and social planning in a particular country, and this model of analysis is limited to secondary education and university education because they are more related to productivity than primary education. This model relies on the influx of secondary and university degree holders as a reserve for a qualified workforce, which remains a burden on the national economy if it is not employed, or its qualifications are not commensurate with the needs of the labour market.

One of the observations taken on this model of analysis is that the economy requires a qualified workforce, and not necessarily holders of secondary and university degrees qualified and able to enter the labour market directly, and can compete for jobs and occupations. The labour market always has other accounts, and even if it does not have it, qualifications required from secondary or university education graduates fill the shortage of foreign labour from abroad, in order to balance the supply and demand of the desired qualifications in the labour market. This is almost what is happening today in many advanced industrial countries that employ qualified and unqualified foreign labour force for two types of labour market areas, jobs that are not acceptable to those countries and advanced technical and scientific work in which these countries require expertise and high-level minds, Education and specialization, both from their children and from foreigners. In other words, this is happening almost in the Gulf countries and Libya, where the labour market depends on foreign workers, while there is a surplus of graduates of secondary and university education, it is always more than the direct relationship between education and employment. Other variables in the analysis are such as the quality of work and social values associated with work, the need to work by others, the quality of investment and the companies that implement it.

Thus, the relationship between education and the labour market varies depending on countries and their rates of economic growth, their relevance to the global economy, international conditions and the politics of a country's economy. South Korea's economy and labour market are very different from Cuba's and its labour market, and without a direct mechanical relationship between education and the labour market, quality education can provide trained labour anywhere in the world, especially in the light of developments in the global economy today.

Importance of Education (Socio-Economic)

Advantages of Education: Education is seen in many studies as:

- Increases productivity/raises investment and savings/helps to change technological development.
- Contributes to influence cognitive skills/contributes to influence personal ambition, competition and creativity.
- Encourages women's contribution to economic activity (paid work).
- Parent education raises the quality, health and subsequent status of the child.
- Helps to improve and distribute income and equal opportunities.

There are many studies of such linkages but without always confirming the causality or even the direction of the relationship and the extent of the slowdown, but not every education is necessarily conducive to development.

Education may—

- Devour resources from the first to be spent in other more feasible aspects.
- Misallocates resources or uses them in low efficiency.

- Harms the abilities of individuals by finding learners who are not needed for careers or creating unjustified aspirations and hence the cause of learners' unemployment.
- Contributes to brain drain.

Social Importance of Education

1. Preparation and production of leadership elements.
2. The composition of civilized human.
3. Increase the enjoyment of human life.
4. Narrowing the gap of civilization.
5. Facilitate communication and interaction between different individuals and peoples.
6. Increase the ambition of individuals and push them to rise in the social ladder.
7. Stimulates minds and souls and increases their willingness to accept change and bring it about.
8. Provides a cultural climate for individuals and society.

Economic Importance of Education

1. Provide better opportunities for scientific progress and technological development.
2. Providing the members of the society with the technical and technological skills required for development.
3. Demand for goods and services increases.
4. Creating means of objective thinking and discovering the capabilities of individuals.
5. Assisting individuals to accept and bring about change.
6. Education is a national human investment.
7. Capital development of labour force.

The Role of Education in Achieving Development Goals

Significant progress in education can contribute significantly to paving the way for the world to achieve the broader Millennium Development Goals, particularly in the following three areas:

First: Addressing poverty through economic growth: Achieving equitable economic growth is the way to reduce poverty. There is strong evidence linking education to higher levels of economic growth and productivity. A study of 50 countries between 1960 and 2000 revealed that spending one additional year in education increases the average annual growth in GDP by 37 per cent. Another study found that spending an additional year in school education increases per capita income by 10 per cent. Inequalities in education are also an expression of income inequalities. Wage inequality in Indonesia, the Philippines, Vietnam and India is closely linked to the widening gap between those with higher education and lower levels of education attainment. The poor also leads to large-scale economic growth and provides significant benefits in poverty reduction.

Second: Improving children's health and reducing mortality: The links between education and public health are certain. Maternal education, both at the secondary and primary levels, can lead to lower child mortality, and children with educated parents are often better nourished. Indonesia and Bangladesh, for example, data from household surveys reveal that high levels of parental attainment severely reduce the likelihood of delayed child development.

Third: Encouraging Democracy and Citizenship: Education that equips people with literacy and other skills enables them to participate in community life and to hold government bodies accountable. And what it's like.

Evidence in sub-Saharan Africa shows that education plays an important role in building support for multi-party democracy and anti-autocracy, and in a recent assessment under the OECD PISA International Student Assessment Programme that science education shows that students are critical to environmental issues and entrench a sense of responsibility for sustainable development. These are in turn tools that people can use to hold governments accountable and demand change.

REFERENCES

Abdul Ghani Al-Nouri (1988). *New Trends in the Economics of Education,* Dar Al Thaqafa, Doha, Qatar.

Abdullah Al-Rashdan (2001). *In the Economics of Education,* Dar Wael for Publishing and Distribution, Amman, Jordan.

Al-Mahdi, Magdi Salah (2013). *Economics of Educational Quality,* New University House, Alexandria, Egypt.

Arab Centre for Educational Research for the Gulf States (2012). *Education Economics,* Kuwait.

Ashour Kattoush, Foreign Hajj Fowder: *The Malaysian Experience in Human Development and its Success Components.*

Faleh Hassan Khalaf (2007). *Education, Economics and Planning,* Modern Book World, Amman, Jordan.

Farouk Abdo Feleh (2004). *Economics of Education: Solid Principles and Modern Trends,* Al-Masirah Publishing and Distribution House, Amman, Jordan.

Gul, Muhammad Zahid (2013). *The Turkish Renaissance Experience,* Nama Centre for Research and Studies, Beirut, Lebanon.

Ismail Mohamed Diab *et al.*: *Yearbook of Education and Psychology,* Volume XVI Studies in Education, Economics and Planning.

Kaddouri, El Hadj (2005). *The educational waste of students of the Faculty of Science and Engineering Sciences,* University of Algiers-Ouargla model, Master Thesis, Faculty of Arts, University of Ouargla, Algeria, pp. 39-69.

Mahmoud Al-Jaafari, Darine Lafi (2006). *The degree of adaptation between graduates of Palestinian higher education and the requirements of the Palestinian labour market,* Institute for Palestinian Economic Policy Research (MAS), Ramallah, Palestine.

Ministry of Commerce and Industry, *Migration of Arab Minds,* Central Department for Small and Medium Enterprises Support Programmes, Egypt.

Ministry of Education and Higher Education, and UNESCO (2014) *National Assessment Report on Education for All (2000-2015),* Ramallah, Palestine.

Mohammed, Ahmad Al-Haj (2012). *School Economics,* Dar Al-Masira, Amman, Jordan.

Oraba, Rabeh and Awali Hanan: *What is Intellectual Capital and Investing in Human Capital,* Website.

Rifai, Aqbal (2011). *Quality Standards and Accreditation in Schools,* Al-Sahab for Publishing and Distribution, Cairo, Egypt, pp. 41-82.

Tamimi, Saad, *Malaysian Development Experience,* Adhwaa Centre for Research and Strategic Studies. www.adhwaa.org.

Tamimi, Saad, *The Experience of Malaysian Development,* Lights Centre for Research and Strategic Studies. www.adhwaa.org.

UNESCO (2010). Summary of the Way to Equity for the Disadvantaged, *EFA Global Monitoring Report.*

UNESCO (2014). Education and Learning Achieving Quality for All, *EFA Global Monitoring Report 2013/2014.*

UNESCO http://www.unicef.org/english/

United Nations Educational, Scientific and Cultural Organization (UNESCO) (1998): *Education for All Situations and Trends, Missed Opportunities: When Schools Fail to Perform Their Mission—Repetition and Drop-out in Primary Schools*. UNESCO, France.

Wadih, Adnan (2007). *Economics of Education, Development Bridge,* p. 68, Arab Planning Institute in Kuwait, Kuwait.

8

Education and Development

Rambat Nur Sasongko

Education is basic human right. Undeniably, education provides many services to the lives of humanity. Therefore, the government, wherever the country is located, makes education a "compulsory education programme". The government also makes "education as a tool for development". Through education can prepare young people who are educated, knowledgeable, capable, character, and skilled in development. Development is not only in the scope of advancing the economic order, but also building a prosperous family life, building a harmonious social order, and building a prosperous, and harmonious nation and state order.

Introduction

Now, education is a basic human right. As a primary need, the position of education ranks first that must be given to humans. In some countries, both developed and backward countries, education is used as "compulsory education" (McGraths, 2018). Education is not a second or third requirement, but it is compulsory for the state, society, or parents to provide education for children or future generations. The word "mandatory" has implications for those who provide education will be free from the bondage of the law. Conversely, parents or education providers who do not provide education to their children will be given a penalty.

How important is education for the younger generation, placing educational status as a strategic thing, compulsory, as primary needs, and cannot be avoided. In essence, education is a conscious human effort to prepare students for the success of life's role in the future (Sasongko and

Sahono, 2016 and Mense, 2018). Nelson Mandela, a president of South Africa, explained that education is the most powerful weapon that you can use to change the world. Soekarno, the first Indonesian president, explained that education was a reflection of the life of the nation and determined development progress. An expert in Western education M.J. Langeveld defines education as an effort to guide underage humans towards maturity, so that they can be independent and morally responsible. Carter V. Good provides a definition of education as a process of influencing someone to attain attitudes and behaviour in life in society. John Dewey gives a description that education is an instrument for preparing democratic citizens (Rich, 1986). Some of the terminology about education, in essence aims to prepare young people to become citizens who are able to play a role in the nation's development in the future (Sasongko and Sahono, 2016).

Education is closely related to national development (Rich, 1986; Lynch, Mogdil and Mogdil, 2010; Al-Kremeen and Al-Amarat (2019); and Al-Zoubi and Abu-Orabi, 2019). That is because the development of a nation is largely determined by the presence of education. Education determines the success of national and state development. A nation of high quality, because the quality of education is also high. In fact, there are three variables that determine each other. Education can produce human resources. Human resources can determine the success of development. Likewise, development can determine the quality of education delivery and the quality of human resources. The relationship can be described as follows:

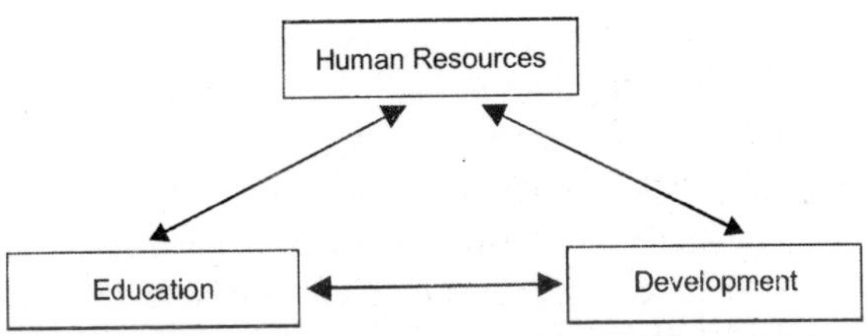

Fig. 8.1: The Relationship between Education, Human Resources, and Development.

Development is a process of changing the order of life that includes social, political, economic, infrastructure, defence, technology, education, institutional, and cultural changes (Lynch, 2017 and Bartz, 2019). According to Rogers and Shoemaker, development is a social change in which new ideas are introduced in a social system that aims to generate income per capita and a better level of life by using more sophisticated production methods and more efficient socio-economic organizations (Lynch, 2007 and Mense, 2018). Development aims for the good and welfare of society. Development aims to realize social justice, equitable prosperity, equal treatment in the eyes of the law, material, mental and spiritual well-being, happiness for all, peace, and security. To achieve this development goal, the community must be educated, so that they are aware of their roles, contributions and responsibilities in filling out the development.

Highly educated people certainly contribute better to development, than less educated people (Lemoine, Jenkins, and Richardson, 2017). The tendency of highly educated people is more aware of the role and contribution to the country's development, because he has been educated to be a leader in development. A highly educated person has been prepared how he should determine the work that will be used as the source of his livelihood, so that he is more successful in his life. In contrast to someone who is poorly educated, has little knowledge and limited skills, then he will get a menial job that may be insufficient to meet his daily needs.

The Role of Education in Development

In the order of national and state development, education occupies a strategic position for the progress of a nation and the country itself. Education is not only used as a "political instrument" to advance the country's development status, but it is also used as an indicator of "adapting human culture". Education is the only "humane" indicator for the civilization of state development (Sasongko and Sahono, 2016).

Many roles of education for nation and state development include:

1. Education as a human culture: Human beings who are cultured are organizing education (Sasongko and Sahono, 2016; and Cunha and Magano, 2019). In real life, education is divided into three areas, namely: (a) Informal education held in the family environment. Family education is first and foremost education. It is the family that educates children to smile, laugh, talk, stand, walk, be ethical, practice religions/religious rituals, manners, domestic duties, and so on. (b) Non-formal education organized by the community. Through education in the community, children are educated to respect the rules of society, maintain good values in the community, uphold the cultural traditions of the community, maintain customs, and so on. (c) formal education held in schools/

madrasas/universities. Education in this sphere is most important. Educated children can write, read, count, draw, dance, speak foreign languages, master science and technology, conduct research, conduct innovation, and so on. The whole is human culture, as a necessity and human rights.

2. Education as an agent of change and innovation: Education is an instrument for introducing change, renewal, and modernization in science and technology (Lynch, 2007; Atkinson, Mathur, and Zucker, 2019; and Al-Zoubi, 2019). Education can change children think in new ways, carry out activities with new technologies, develop new lifestyles, habits based on the modernization of life, develop discipline, ethical ethics, social responsibility. Good changes in the order of ideas, knowledge, attitudes, behaviour, lifestyle, real practices, life skills, and life patterns, can be done through educational efforts. Likewise through education someone can be introduced by a student or a student doing research that produces an innovation. For example research in the field of computers that find innovations about digital technology, research in the field of medicine find innovations of new medicinal ingredients, research in education find innovations in learning technology, research in the field of languages find innovations in effective communication, and so on. Educational services prepare innovative people as agents of change in development.

3. Education as a political instrument for the country: The state has an interest in the organization of education. Education is directed to support the vision and mission of the country, so that all human resources produced by education can contribute to the achievement of the country's goals (Ciferri, 2018). The development of the country can run effectively, when graduates from schools or colleges produce superior quality human resources, so that they can contribute to the interests of the country. Education is the only political tool of the state that prepares the state apparatus and people who are in the state bureaucracy, become cadres of leaders and members of political parties, leaders and government staff, leaders and members of people's representatives. Even education graduates who work outside the government, are also prepared to become citizens who have the role of supplying and filling development in accordance with their line of business.

4. Education as an instrument for ideological and political development: The ideological and political development in a country aims to ensure that citizens become loyal to the country, the wheels of development can run safely, and the people's welfare can be realized.

This ideological and political development can only be done through education services. In a country such as the USA and Indonesia, the government requires all schools to provide civic education subjects. The purpose of these subjects is to produce students become good citizens, love the motherland, be loyal to ideology and the Constitution, and be accountable to the country. Indeed there are differences between countries that have certain dogmatic ideologies, such as China producing humans who have communist ideological ideologies, compared to the USA which produces humans who have democratic and humanist ideologies. Education is the most effective political tool to support the interests of the state, both as a tool for political socialization, as a tool for political mobilization, and as a tool for political integration (Sutisna, 1982).

5. Education as an instrument for economic development (Sutisna, 1982 and Chabbott, 2003): Initially economists were reluctant to accept that the progress of economic development is a good service from education. Education is a human investment in preparing for manpower development. The wheels of development can run productively with quality human resources. Educational services have prepared humans to have knowledge and skills that are useful for development. These services are social capital and also at the same time as high-value economic capital. Quality people have a positive impact on the creation of new jobs, entrepreneurship, and/or become a part that contributes to economic progress. Conversely, humans who lack quality education, can cause unemployment, disease, and even hamper economic development. Educated people have been given the provision to live successfully through the development of livelihoods in agriculture, fisheries, plantations, trade, transportation, tourism, industry, oil, and so on.

6. Education as an instrument for social and cultural development: It has been mentioned above that education is also a social and cultural capital (Chabbott, 2003; and Sasongko, 2019). Highly educated people have intelligent qualifications and broad insight in the socio-cultural field. They are more aware about social-cultural literacy, such as easy to get along with all people in this world, easy to adapt to the social and cultural settings of certain communities, have a high tolerance for various differences in life, appreciate various types of art and culture, have more ethics and good manners in the community, selecting cultural values, maintaining customs and cultural heritage of the community, and so on. These globalizing literacy skills and socio-cultural adaptation are good services from education. Therefore, education is used as an instrument of social and cultural development.

7. Education as an instrument for the development of scientific and technological progress (Sasongko and Sahono, 2016): It has been recognized by the public that the advancement of science and technology is the result of thinking from clever scholars and inventors in certain fields. To become someone who has the nickname of clever scholar and inventor, one must take certain education and innovation. They continue to study, persevere, be creative, conduct research, and innovate to find truth and innovation to answer certain problems. In the field of scientific discovery, for example John Locke discovered the theory of empiricism education (1702), John Dewey discovered the theory of education "learning by doing" (1884), Albert Einstein discovered the theory of relativity (1907), Sergio Ferrara, Daniel Z. Freedman, and Peter van Niewenhuizen discovered the theory of supergravity (won the Physics Breakthrough Prize, 2019), James Peebles discovered the Big Bang theory (cosmic microwave) (got the Nobel Prize, 2019), and so on. In the field of technological inventions such as Zacharias Janssen invented the microscope (1590), James Watt invented the steam engine (1765), Robert Fulton the inventor of the ship (1807), Thomas Alva Edison the inventor of the light bulb and the film projector (1893), Rudolf Diesel invented the combustion engine with diesel (1897), J.L. Baird and C.F. Jenkins invented television (1920), and so on. Some of these examples, show that through education a person can be educated to become a scientist or practitioner in the development of science and technology. Development in the field of science and technology is the basis for development in a society, country and even the world.

8. Education as an instrument to defense and security development: Educational services have also been recognized by the world that defence and security in a country can be created through the education process (McBride, 2019). Various countries have established a university or defence and security education institution, so that the graduates have the competence to be a safe and peaceful state manager. Education provides a variety of knowledge, experience, attitudes, behaviours, and various defence and security management skills. Some knowledge starts from planting and awareness of patriotism, responsibility towards the state, defending the country, the importance of security for development, strategies for maintaining security, maintaining national unity and integrity, and so on. On the other hand, a country that lacks investment in education to maintain and secure the country, the country's defense becomes fragile, lacks sustainability, the state is insecure, development does not work well, the economy is in ruins, it is easily intervened by other countries, and even the country becomes destroyed.

9. Education as an instrument for building religion and belief: (Sasongko and Sahono, 2016): Religion and belief are subjective dimensions in a person or society. Some countries have declared the religion to be a religious state. For example Iran and Saudi Arabia, making Islam as a religious state. Some countries with a pluralistic population do not make a particular religion a religious state. As in some Asean countries (Indonesia, Malaysia, Singapore, Thailand, Cambodia, Brunei and Darussalam), the USA, the United Kingdom, South Africa, and so on do not make the majority of the religion used as a religious state. Even development in the fields of religion and belief is the main scale of national development. Even religious education is the subject of curriculum in a particular educational institution. The development of religion is a strategic thing, because the religion professed by a person and the community can be a social capital for development. The government, which has an effective national development strategy, places the proportion of religious development as the main programme. The construction of places of worship built by the government has gained sympathy from religious communities to support the government. The government can utilize religious leaders and their people for the sake of creating national security. Countries that do not care about religious development, quickly become destroyed because of lack of religious tolerance.

10. Education as an instrument to reduce development barriers: Development in a country, whether in the fields of economy, trade, agriculture, industry, transportation, ideology, politics, social and culture, or religion, often experiences obstacles and even becomes inoperative. Such conditions are factors that hamper development (Lynch, 2007 and Chabbott, 2003). The most important factor inhibiting development besides limited natural resources, is the low quality of human resources. Low quality human resources, such as low quality education can cause poverty, unemployment, social disease (crime, sex workers, beggars etc.), and low quality of life. To overcome this, the government adopted a policy that education must be directed to overcome national development barriers. Through education the graduates have been prepared to have positive awareness, attitudes, and behaviours that make a significant contribution to the country and even the world. Education is directed so that graduates can create jobs and/or can work in accordance with their fields. If graduates of this education can get a decent job and income, in turn will get welfare. Thus it can contribute to the creation of social justice, increased economic growth, and high per capita income.

Theory of Education and Development

Education and development have functional relationships. The relationship is analogous to variable X and Y. Variable X has the task of influencing variable Y. Variable Y is the variable that is affected. The constellation of this relationship had an impact on the birth of a new theory which gave a stressful description that education was an instrument that could not be bargained by development. Harbison and Myers's statement in 1964 which said that education was the "key to modernization" and according to Schults in 1968 that education was an "investment in humans", was now proven to be true and recognized by various experts in the fields of economics, politics, and social culture (Sasongko and Sahono, 2016).

Earlier scientists, such as Thomas Hobbes, had placed the educational position as "Leviathan" and determined for the development of a country in the future (Rich, 1986). The statement has now become a reality and cannot be denied by any country and anywhere. Education is the main capital for the survival of the nation and state. Likewise, John Locke who has empiricism, gives the question that education is a miniature of "civil government" for state development (Rich, 1986). Education in the school environment is a basic capital for students to gain valuable experience for life in the future.

Geovanni Gentile who clearly provides the statement that education is a tool for the formation of a sense of nationalism (Rich, 1986). In various countries, education is used as the backbone for fostering a sense of nationalism. These methods are effective ways of fostering good citizens. I.L. Kandel and John Dewey have agreed to place education as an effective instrument for "social change" (Rich, 1986). Social changes that occur in a country because of the awareness of the need for democracy to obtain prosperity and happiness. Human collective ideals can be realized, when someone has an adequate level of education. In line with Kandel and Dewey, Harold Rugg also gave a statement that education is a tool of "social reconstruction" for the development progress of a nation. Through education can be reconstructed the order of people's lives which in turn to achieve development goals.

The views of the experts as mentioned above, even though they have been put forward in the past, now reap proof that his statement is true. Education which is considered by Thomas Hobbes as "Leviathan", at the present time the majority of countries in the world have made the education programme must be funded by the state budget with the largest portion.

Likewise, a statement from John Locke, Geovanni Gentile, I.L. Kandel, John Dewey and Harold Rugg, have now become reality and truth. Conditions like this make the hypothesis a thesis that is true, so it tends to be a theory that is recognized by experts in development.

R. Solow, an economist, provides clarification with a residual approach (Sutisna, 1982; and Shiza and Kariw, 2011). Solow said that about 10 per cent of economic growth can be influenced by population growth and physical resources, while the remaining 90 per cent is caused by "residual" factors, where education plays a very large role. Education contributes to the provision of managers with technical knowledge and quality as leaders, employees and workers with the will, ability, skills, and loyalty.

The residual approach calculates the contribution of capital, inputs in the form of labour and physical resources to the growth of production, and whatever is left as residual (residual from the human quality factor). Another approach is the correlation approach which uses an analysis of the relationship between educational activities with a number of indicators of economic progress. Harbison and Myers have conducted research into the relationship between the proportion of formal education and national per capita income in 75 countries (Sutisna, 1982). The results show that there is a high correlation at all levels of high education compared to low levels of education, to contributions to national per capita quantities.

The rate of return approach is a method of calculation that assumes that the income of educated people comes from investments in education (Sutisna, 1982). This approach is quite concrete which places education as a cause of the quality of one's income. This approach uses a cost-benefit analysis, expressed as a percentage of investment returns in education and its output in the form of productivity and profits from education expenditure (McGraths, 2018).

Theory of W.W. Rostow on "The Stage of Economic Growth" which says that economic growth can take place in several temporal stages. The most vital stage is "take off", where economic growth can be achieved on the strength of its own support, the condition of society has undergone a basic structural change in its social and political (Sutisna, 1982; and Chabbott, 2003).

Some of the theories referred above provide strong indications that economic growth and the progress of national development can go well, if you get a positive contribution from education. Education can provide awareness to the community to create conducive social and political conditions.

Education Quality as an Indicator of Development Success

Development is a change that includes mental attitude (Septarina and Sasongko, 2019). People must develop their own qualities, before they can change their physical environment. The process of developing self-quality requires a relatively adequate investment of cost and time. Unlike planting rice, three to four months can be harvested, with costs and time that can be predicted accurately. Likewise, the construction of factories, bridges, buildings, road facilities, oil palm plantations, and so on, can be done with relatively fast time.

Changes in human mental attitude requires a long learning process. Development in primitive societies can be introduced into modern times through the education of their children. It is impossible to change his parents who are old with the target of a lot of mental attitude changes. Changing behaviour to be dressed ethically is also difficult, let alone changing your lifestyle and mindset. Changes in life patterns and other mindsets can be done gradually, and even then through the younger generation and the sincerity of their parents (Lynch, Mogdil and Mogdil, 2010).

The implementation of education carried out in three regions, both in the domestic area with informal education, community areas with non-formal education, and public areas with formal education, should really be the target and orientation of integrated education (Sasongko, 2019). The target and orientation of the administration of education in the three regions are mutually sustainable and determine human quality. Talking about human quality is the target of implementing quality education. Quality education is a combination of the quality of education in the three regions. The three domains of providing education, if done with quality, can produce superior quality human resources and are ready to succeed the development programme. This condition has an implication that the quality of education is an indication of the success of development.

Development in the domestic area in the form of education organized by the family is a strategic programme that needs to be the focus of national development (Sasongko, 2019). Sometimes, the government in a country is less concerned about the implementation of education at home. Family education seems to be a matter for parents only. What about parents who have many children and then divorced? Who are the children at home who will educate them? It is possible if you have a house, what about people who do not have a house? These conditions can cause children at home to not receive proper education, lack of parental attention, lack of nutrition, malnutrition, and may lead to criminal behaviour in the family and community. This is where the presence of parents becomes very vital in building a prosperous family. Family education is an urgent education to be implemented. Complete parents can educate children to have competence to be able to see properly, hold, smile, laugh, talk, crawl, stand, walk, be ethical, have good behaviour, carry out religious/belief rituals well, polite, respectful towards parents, help carry out tasks in the household, family responsibilities, and so on. In short, through education in the family can produce children who are mature, independent, and have character. If this family education can be held with quality, then a happy and prosperous family can be realized.

Educational development in community areas (non-formal) is complementary (Sasongko, 2019). Even so, this out-of-school education has a very important role in the development of quality human resources. Non-formal education organized by the community has the service of preparing students in accordance with the needs of the surrounding community and creating a lifelong learning community. Children can be educated to respect the rules of the community, maintain good values in the community, uphold the cultural traditions of the community, maintain customs, maintain community order, be able to play an active role in building their home villages, prepare workers who are ready to work in the community, and so on.

The implementation of formal education that is usually held by the government in the form of schools, madrasas, universities, or certain education units (Sasongko, 2019; and McBride, 2019). This formal education is tasked with organizing government programmes in terms of compulsory education. Through education in this sphere children educate can write, read, count, draw, dance, speak foreign languages, master science and technology, conduct research, conduct innovations, and so on. The government in providing education, assisted by community foundations, or religious foundations, organizes private education. Both public and private education units must refer to national education standards, so that the implementation of education can be guaranteed quality. These formal education services can, among other things, educate the life of the nation and state, produce graduates who are ready to work in the labour market, guarantee development programmes can run efficiently and productively, and eliminate barriers to development.

Furthermore, a description of the education organizers, indicators of quality education, and contributions to development can be visualized as shown in Table 8.1.

Table 8.1: Contribution of Education Organizers to Development

S. No.	*Education Organizers*	*Quality Education Indicators*	*Contribution to Development*
1	Informal Education	• Complete parents • Parents care about the physical, mental and social growth of the child • Parents educate their children responsibly • The implementation of good character education	• Helps the government organize education according to the expectations of a prosperous family • Produce children who are physically, mentally, morally, and socially mature and independent • Produce children of character • Generate a harmonious family
2	Non Formal Education	• The surrounding community cares and works together to organize education • The community organizes non-formal education according to the needs of the environment/ labourmarket	• Helps the government organize education according to the needs of the community • Produce a learning community • Produce graduates who can be absorbed in the world of work
3	Formal Education	• The government organizes education according to national education standards (content standards, processes, graduates, educators, education personnel, facilities and infrastructure, costs, management, and evaluation) • Organize compulsory education programmes	• Educating the life of the nation and state • Produce graduates who are ready to work in the job market • Development programmes can run efficiently and productively • Remove barriers to development

Conclusion

Education has a very strategic role, mandatory, as primary needs, and basic human rights that cannot be avoided. Many educational services for the lives of humanity, making education as a tool for development. Education aims to prepare young people who can build social justice, equitable prosperity, equal treatment in the eyes of the law, material, mental and spiritual well-being, happiness for all, peace and security. Through education can be realized "manpower" that realizes the role, contributions, and responsibilities in the success of development.

Education and development are an inseparable unit. Education prepares "manpower" that is ready to build, and development prepares and succeeds the delivery of quality education. Various theories of education and development provide strong indications that economic growth and the progress of national development can go well, if you get a positive contribution from education. Education can provide awareness to the community to create conducive social and political conditions.

The positive correlation between education and development can be given the meaning that education has a lot to contribute to development. Development can begin by creating quality education in the areas of informal education, non-formal education, and formal education. If these three areas for the development of education can be carried out with quality, it can be ensured that quality human resources can be available and can realize the development of a quality nation and state as well.

REFERENCES

Al-Kremeen, H.A. and Al-Amarat, M.S. (2019). "Organizational Slack and Its Relation to Leadership Styles of School Principals at Secondary School in Tafilah Directorate of Education." *Journal of Education and Human Development*, 8 (1), pp. 133-145.

Al-Zoubi, A. and Abu-Orabi, S.T. (2019). "Impact of Internationalization on Arab Higher Education: The Role of Association of Arab Universities." *Journal of Education and Human Development*, 8(1), pp. 69-85.

Al-Zoubi, A. *et al.* (2019). "A Model for Jordanian National Qualifications Framework." *Journal of Education and Human Development*, 8(3), pp. 101-112.

Atkinson, L.; Mathur, S.R.; and Zucker, S.H. (2019). "Sustainability of an Urban Teacher Education Programme." July Press: *Journal of Education and Development*, 3(3), pp. 21-31.

Bartz, D.E. (2019). "Organization Members Directing their Career Development", *Journal of Education and Human Development*, 8(1), pp. 43-47.

Chabbott, C. (2003). *Constructing Education for Development: International Organization and Education for All*. New York: Routledge Palmer.

Ciferri, A. (2018). "Socio-economic Inequalities in the Americas—A Mitigating Educational Approach." July Press: *Journal of Education and Development*, 2(3), pp. 8-12.

Cunha, M.N. and Magano, J. (2019). "Principal's Management Strategy." *Journal of Education and Human Development*, 8(3), pp. 126-132.

Lemoine, P.A.; Jenkins, W.M.; and Richardson, M.D. (2017). "Global Higher Education: Development and Implications." July Press: *Journal of Education and Development*, 1(1), pp. 58-69.

Lynch, J. (2007). *Education and Development: A Human Right Analysis*. London: Cassell.

Lynch, J.; Mogdil, J.; and Mogdil, S. (2010). *Education and Development: Tradition and Innovation (Innovations in Delivering Primary Education)*. London: Cassell.

McBride, A.E. (2019). "Cultural Immersion for Teacher Educators: Stimulus for Growth." *Journal of Education and Human Development*, 8(3), pp. 10-15.

McGraths, S. (2018). *Education and Development*. New York: Routledge Perspectives on Development.

Mense, E.G. *et al.* (2018). "The Development of Global Higher Education in a World of Transformation." July Press: *Journal of Education and Development*, 2(3), pp. 47-53.

Rich, J.M. (Ed.). (1986). *Reading in The Philosophy of Education*. Belmont, California: Wadsworth Publishing Company, Inc.

Sasongko, R.N. (2019). *Determining Factors of Success of Character Education Management and its Implementation Facing of the Era of Industrial Revolution 4.0: An analysis at elementary school, Province of Bengkulu*. Advances in Social Science, Education and Humanities Research, 295 [Proceeding on 1st International Conference on Educational Sciences and Teacher Profession (ICETeP 2018)], pp. 74-79.

Sasongko, R.N. and Sahono, B. (2016). *Design of Education Management Innovation*. Jakarta, Indonesia: Shany Publisher.

Septarina, L. and Sasongko, R.N. (2019). "Quality Management: Impact of Leadership Mobilization on Institutional Quality." *International Journal* of *Research Science and Management*, 6(5), pp. 1-8.

Shizha, E. and Kariw, M.T. (2011). *Education and Development in Zimbabwe: A Social, Political and Economic Analysis*. Rotterdam, The Netherlands: Sense Publishers.

Sutisna, O. (1982). *Education and Development: The Challenges to Innovation in Education*. Bandung, Indonesia: IKIP, Bandung.

9
Education and Economic Development

Reena Trivedi

Education is a means to acquire knowledge, skills, beliefs, values and good habits. Education does not mean bookish or theoretical knowledge but to apply the attained knowledge practically. Through education we learn how to meet challenges and overcome obstacles in the dynamic social and economic circumstances. Education makes people productive for the economy, improve skills, provide better earning opportunities, eradicates unemployment problem, reduces poverty, improves standard of living, promotes entrepreneurship, technological advancement etc. Learned and knowledgeable individuals help society to work smoothly and economy to develop faster.

Mahatma Gandhi viewed education not just literacy but an all-round development of an individual. He wrote, "Literacy in itself is no education. Literacy is not the end of education or even the beginning. By education I mean all-round drawing out of the best in the child and man—body, mind and spirit." He insisted that education must be compatible with the changing circumstances. "True education must correspond to the surrounding circumstances or it is not a healthy growth." *Gandhiji*.

Even several years back education was considered as the most potent weapon to transform social and economical goals in a desired way. Sustainable economic development can be achieved by improving quality of human capital. Education is a measure to enhance the quality of human capital of a country. Economist Adam Smith realized that the acquired ability of human being contributes to increase production in an economy. Modern economists also identify that investment in education or human capital is crucial for economic development. Education raises productive power, income level, standard of living and national income of an economy. Investment in human capital and physical capital is needed equally. Educated workers increase the marginal productivity of physical capital. It raises labour productivity, national output and national income. Economic development through investment in human capital not only raise real output but also consumption level and well-being of the society. Therefore, every government gives importance to education in its economic policy. Education is positively related to per capita income and real Gross Domestic Product of an economy. Education produces skilled labour and raises their earning capacity.

The study of "Entrepreneurship Selection and Performance: A Meta-analysis of the Impact of Education in Less Developed Countries" conducted in 2004 by Van Der Slvis, Mirjam Van Praag and Wim Vijverber analysed the effect of schooling on the selection of entrepreneurship and its impact on less developed countries. It provides the conclusion that marginal year of schooling raises the enterprise income by 5.5 per cent. This result differs in urban and rural areas in male and female etc. It was found in the study that more educated labour force prefer to indulge in non-farm business rather than doing farming. Educated women mostly prefer wage employment rather than self-employment. Uneducated women mostly found doing low-income activities or agriculture. This provides conclusion that education provides better earning opportunities.

Investment in education provides more productive workers which contributes to increased productivity, output level leading to economic growth. Skill development includes education and training of people. More skilled population in a country increases its competitiveness at global level and also promotes sustainable development. Skilled labour produces a positive impact on Gross Domestic Product. But this requires an increased level of investment in education. Education brings technological innovations which makes labour force and production process more efficient as well as productive.

Economic development means the increase in average productivity of economy in a given period of time which is measured by its Gross Domestic Product. Gary S. Becker in his book, *Human Capital: A Theoretical and Empirical Analysis with Special Reference to Education,* analysed the investment in education and its cost-benefit expectations. He asserted that people like to bear the cost of education if they expect better earnings in the future that compensate the educational costs later. He did not relate education to only technological innovation but also adaptation to 'changing technology'. He tries to explain the cause of economic growth of developed countries by applying diminishing marginal returns theory. This theory means that if one factor of production is variable while all other factors are fixed, after a point addition of variable to fixed factors yield diminishing level of output. The same concept applies to investment in education as variable factor, keeping all other factors unchanged would bring diminishing returns over some time. In developed countries, additional investment in education produces negative effect on productivity through overeducated labour-force and oversupplied work places. In developing countries, an additional increase in investment in education produces positive effect on production and increases productive efficiency. He established a 'cause-effect' relationship between education and economic growth without mentioning any intermediate variable. Market economy works with demand and supply conditions. If there is an excess supply of educated workforce without any demand for them to adjust them in high earning jobs then education would not create economic growth in that case. He wrote, "the expansion in education as countries get richer no more implies that education causes growth that does a larger number of dishwashers in richer countries implies that dishwashers are an engine to growth." This contradictory statement was given for developed countries and this relationship does not exist in developing countries like India.

Economist Keynes analysed that the demand creates the supply. 'Principle of Acceleration' describes that an investment to increase the supply of output of a product should be made if there is an increase in demand for that product. This concept also applies to education. If there is no demand of highly educated workforce in a country, further increased investment in education will provide excess supply of skilled human capital leading them to migrate towards technological advanced countries.

Human capital and economic development are correlated. Indian Government realized the importance of human capital in the Seventh Five Year Plan. This Plan dictates, "Human resources development has necessarily to be assigned a key role in any development strategy, particularly in a country with a large population." Human capital promotes economic development of a country in the following ways:

- Education promotes skilled and specialized manpower who can handle complex technology and machines efficiently. In this way, human capital promotes the productivity of physical capital. Increased production leads to economic development.
- Educated and trained human capital increases innovations in production process. This further increases production, Gross

Domestic Product and economic development.

- High education provides better employment opportunities to the people which increases their income level, standard of living, productive capacity, reduces income inequality and leads to economic development.
- Investment in human capital increases the worker participation rate, the production level and economic development.
- More educated workers learn more easily and adapt themselves more quickly to complicated tasks.
- Education facilitates skilled manpower which encourages their working capacity to increase productivity.
- Education promotes entrepreneur's ability and technological advancement needed for social and economic development.
- Investment in education generates higher returns per worker.
- Education is a powerful instrument for reducing poverty and inequality.

Today; society must be an 'educated society' to progress and to survive in a better way. Changes are continuously taking place in the modern world e.g. new techniques, new innovations and new abilities. Education is the only means to keep a person out of ignorance and superstition. The development of a nation depends on development of its people. A nation needs to develop human potentialities to develop materially, economically, socially, politically or culturally. Educated man-power of an economy determines its performance in terms of international trade and also globally. A trained and efficient workforce can hold a comparative advantage over the workforce of other countries. Difference in human resources among different countries determines development level to a great extent, apart from other factors. Higher literacy promotes critical thinking. It also uplifts a person economically. Employers pay higher wages for a job require higher level of education.

Cobweb Model

The Cobweb Model explains the effect of workers learning new skill, wage fluctuation and supply of workers overtime. The model describes that when a worker learn new skill, wage increases in the short-run. But, when more workers get trained overtime and enter the workforce in search of higher wages, labour supply increases. The excess supply of trained workers results in lower wage rate. When wages decrease, less workers are interested in a particular job which leads to reduced labour supply. The cycle again starts with training more workers and increasing their wages in the short-run. This model considers the positive relationship between trained manpower and their earning by considering the supply of labour at that time.

Economic development involves not only reduction in poverty, inequality and unemployment but also includes improvement in quality of life, environment protection, good education, better health and nutrition etc. The *World Development Report 1991* published by World Bank asserts, "The challenge of development is to improve the quality of life, especially in the world's poor countries, a better quality of life generally calls for higher incomes but it involves much more. It encompasses as ends in themselves better education, higher standards of health and nutrition, less poverty, a cleaner environment, more equality of opportunity." The concept of economic development includes higher growth of Gross Domestic Product and improvement in quality of life. According to Prof. Amartya Sen, "Economic development consists in enlargement of opportunities for people and freedom of human choice." The new concept of economic development includes freedom from ignorance and illiteracy. A Human Development Index is prepared by United Nations Development Programme (UNDP) on the basis of certain indicators in different countries. These indicators are literacy, life expectancy and per capita income of a country. Human Development Index is a better indicator of economic development.

Education and Higher Rate of Gross Domestic Product (GDP)

Education promotes a higher rate of Gross Domestic Product which raises productive capacity of the economy and an improvement in living standard of people. However, it is also true that faster economic growth may not always lead to higher living standard of the people if the growth process is not inclusive. If the growth process is inclusive then the growth of GDP leads to higher production, higher income, more consumption of goods and services thus raise their standard of living. Higher GDP growth increases pubic revenue required for financing anti-poverty programmes started by the government.

Education and Reduction of Poverty and Unemployment

Education and poverty are inversely related. Education provides better avenues of employment which reduces poverty level. Poverty is reflected in the form of deprivation of basic amenities of life, hunger, undernourishment, widespread illness, lack of education etc. Economic development eradicates poverty only if the income distribution in the society is equitable. Unemployment is one of the reasons of poverty. Education is a means to shift population from agriculture to industrial and service sector. Gainful employment provides better livelihood to people.

Education and Industries

Education mobiles surplus labour towards industries. Import substitution based industries improves balance of payments of a country and promotes economic development. The demand for agricultural products is inelastic in foreign countries. To promote exports of primary products by developing countries would deteriorate terms of trade. These countries should concentrate on import substituting industries to promote economic growth, reduce poverty and unemployment in the country. Prof. Ragner Nurkse advocated 'a balanced growth strategy' to break 'vicious circle of poverty' in developing countries. Investment should be made simultaneously in different industries so that workers employed in different industries could generate demand for each other product and promote balanced economic growth. Moreover, industries require highly educated and trained manpower tend to pay higher wages.

Education and Quality of Life

Education improves quality of life and well-being of a person. It is an indicator of human development of a country. The accumulated knowledge and skills lead towards a happy and satisfied life. Happier people are healthier people with high life expectancy. Education improves the mental, physical, emotional health and a more meaningful life. Human quality of a country significantly affects its economic development.

Education, Social Benefits and Development

Education benefits the society as a whole. Education promotes feeling of unity, togetherness and compatibility within a society. The more educated a country's citizens are, the more the country will develop. Education not only leads to financial stability but also provides mental stability to the people. It improves social skills, awareness of citizenship, knowledge, tolerance, adaptability and understanding level of a person. Society works with more educated and informed electorate, lower rates of violence and crime, lower rate of poverty, improved health and nutrition and helps society run smoothly. Education promotes social and individual well-being and this has a positive impact on economic development also.

Education and Sustainable Development

Education provides knowledge and skill to understand complex environmental issues. It helps a person to understand his duty, decision and actions towards environment. Economic development must be environment healthy and sustainable for the future. Education promotes knowledge, skills, values, understanding and practices needed for sustainable development. It makes a society aware towards environmental protection and conservation necessary for development. Sustainable development promotes a better economy with meagre waste and pollution, more employment, equitable wealth distribution, environmental protection, conservation of natural resources for stable economic growth.

Education and Workers Productivity

Education provides knowledge and skills to workers. Industries require higher education and training are ready to pay higher wages to workers. Skilled workers can perform tasks more efficiently which raises economy's productivity. Educated labour-force better understand scientific advancements and also adapt advanced technology in the economy. Education contributes to the increase in labour productivity, increase in wages and standard of living. Educated labour force is more mobile, adaptable and have creative thinking power. Education promotes employment, wages, social-equity and economic development. More educated workers enable a firm to take advantage of new economic opportunities result in improved performance and its profit level. Skilled labour raises production and lead towards sustainable economic development.

Education and Physical Capital

Physical capital include buildings, equipment and machinery needed for raising quantity and quality of production. Efficient use of these resources is necessary to raise productivity. Human capital is crucial to innovate, utilize and upgrade physical capital needed for economic development. Investment in education facilitates high quality human capital to increase production level. Modern and scientific ideas lead to technical progress. Human capital promotes physical capital by utilizing advanced technology in production process.

Education and Human Capital

Education provides knowledge, talent, skill, ability, intelligence, experience, training, wisdom and judgement to an individual. Education is necessary for human capital. In India, the rate of human capital formation is continuously increasing after independence because of qualitative improvement in each generation. The present workforce of India is qualitatively more superior human resource as compared to past generation. The service sector is constantly developing and the India's balance of payments position is improving. The growth rate of economy is increasing in response to improvement in service sector due to cumulative growth of human capital in India. The Government of India has recently launched some schemes to provide job-oriented education to increase the supply of skilled labour. The scheme 'Kaushal Bharat, Kushal Bharat' has set the target of training 400 million citizens by the year 2022. Some other programmes, like Pradhan Mantri Kaushal Vikas Yojana (PMKVY), National Policy for Skill Development and Entrepreneurship 2015, Skill Loan Scheme, Digital India, National Skill Development Mission etc. are started to provide skilled human resources to the economy needed for its development.

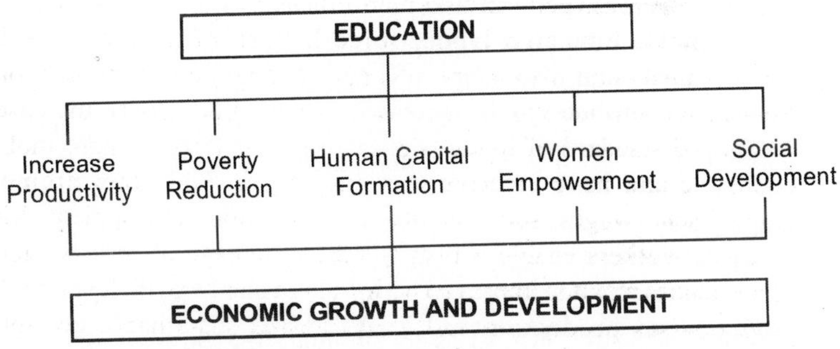

The above figure shows the various roles of education. It leads to increase productivity, reduce poverty, human capital formation, women empowerment, social development etc. through which economic development is stimulated. In spite of being a developing country India has shown very good performance in many fields so as to be noticeable among top advanced countries of the world. In terms of nuclear weapon, in case of marine equipments India has got third place of the world. This level of development become possible due to education. Technical and vocational education and training is the key to increase economic efficiency.

Education and Women Empowerment

Education is very potent tool to remove inequalities between men and women. It empowers women in the society by providing gainful employment opportunities, making them aware about their rights and privileges. Many social evils reduced with the rise in female literacy rate in India. These evils were child marriage, *purda pratha*, female infanticide, *sati* system, dowry system etc. Education is the means through which social and economic status of women in the society has been increased. Education reduces social injustice to the underprivileged section and provide the opportunity for their upliftment and inclusion.

Education affects the growth rate of an economy either directly or indirectly. It is very difficult to develop a nation with illiterate population. In today's world the demand of technology and digitization is increasing day by day. We can meet these challenges with education. There is a need to change the education policy of India which could adopt the raising needs of skill and technology to generate better job opportunities to our students.

The New Education Policy of India will be implemented after few months. The Draft National Education Policy 2019 was already submitted to Ministry of Human Resource and Development. Many suggestions and feedback have been received in this respect. This policy must focus on economic development of India which can be achieved through effective skill training to increase employment and effective implementation of technology to improve teaching-learning process. Government of India would like to revise the education policy to fulfil the changing requirements of our country's education, skills, knowledge, innovation, research etc. so as to eliminate the shortage of skilled manpower and to promote science, technology, industry, agriculture and academics in our country. Human capital with required knowledge and skills is needed for development of a country. It increases individual's productivity, employer's profitability and economic growth. Vocational skills increase labour mobility and improve earning capacity. Education lead to reduction in population growth, removing social evils from the society, reducing poverty, achieving gender equality, sustainable development and inclusive growth.

Quality education is among one of the seventeen global goals that has to be achieved by the year 2030 "*Agenda for Sustainable Development*." Under this main focus is given to ensure completion of primary and secondary education, equal access of education, quality technical and vocational education to all. It will be helpful in improving the quality of human capital. There is a need to equip our students with skills, critical thinking, problem solving, digital literacy, training and creativity to provide better employment opportunities. India aims to achieve the goal of becoming a USD 5 trillion economy by the year 2025 for which real GDP growth rate of 8 per cent is required. This goal can be achieved by increasing savings and investment rate, export promotion and other economic variables. But, most important variable is a good quality demography of our country. Human quality can be improved through providing better employment opportunities to our population which could directly and indirectly assist in the economic development of India.

Human Development Index (HDI) *and* ***Physical Quality of Life Index (PQLI)*** are used for measuring human quality of different countries of the world. Human Development Index is a statistical method to measure human development of a country on the basis of Life Expectancy, Education and Per Capita Income. HDI assess the effect of human capabilities on the economic development of a country. It indicates that social and economic factors both affect human quality. The countries with high human development are developing at a faster rate than countries with low human development. In 2018 HDI report, India ranked 130 among 189 countries of the world which improved to rank 129 in 2019. The UNDP India resident representative, Shoko Noda said in an official release, "For countries like India, which have shown great success in reducing absolute poverty, we hope that the 2019 Human Development Report sheds light on inequalities and deprivations that go beyond income. How we tackle old and new inequalities, ranging from access to basic services such as housing to things like access to quality university education, will be critical to whether we achieve the Sustainable Development Goals."

Human Development Index for Indian States in 2017 shows that Kerala ranked first with high human development status and Bihar ranked last having low human development status. Kerela with high human development index also ranks first in terms of education and life expectancy while Bihar with low human development having lowest literacy rate among all Indian states. This indicates that education has direct impact on human development which further promotes economic development of a state or a country.

Physical Quality of Life Index (PQLI) is an another concept used for measuring human quality of a country. National income and per capita income as an indicator used in HDI does not depict the real condition of economic development of a country. There are many limitations related to it. Due to unequal distribution of wealth in the society, increasing income of a country may not be the real indicator of well-being. PQLI is the average of three indicators—Education, Life Expectancy and Infant Mortality Rate. The high level of physical quality of life is considered as a high level of economic development of a country. This indicator is related to the living standard of people, and their basic requirements. It is the real indicator to measure well-being of the country. A healthier and educated demography determines the quality of human resource of a country which is a crucial factor needed for its economic development.

Education promotes national output through educated workers. Highly educated workforce raises marginal productivity of physical capital, total output and national income. The positive effect of human capital is needed to offset the diminishing returns of investment in physical capital. Education is needed for satisfied life for a person and at the same time to promote self-sustained growth of a nation. Human capital is a crucial input to production function. The social rates of return on education are higher than the private rates of return on education. Educated people are aware about the socio-economic situation of the nation. Investment in human capital promotes productivity and work efficiency. It influence values, beliefs and behaviours of a person making him more development oriented. Prof. Schultz argued that education is a productive investment. Education provides skilled labour-force required for industrial development. Economists who favour 'Human Capital Theory' assume that most effective way to national development is through improvement of human capital *via* education. They advocated that the preconditions for economic development are investment in education and improvement in technology. There is a strong correlation between the levels of educational attainment and lifetime earnings in future. Prof. Kless and Wells advocated, "provide a basic justification for large public expenditure on the expansion of formal school systems in developing countries. Its appeal was based on the presumed economic returns to investment in education both at the macro and micro levels. Thus government's intensified efforts to invest in Human Capital so as to achieve rapid economic growth and development." Increased enrolment rates and reduced drop-out rates are necessary to attain maximum benefits from school education. But, there are differences in high enrolment rates and low attendance rates in schools. Public expenditure on education as a proportion to Gross Domestic Product is constantly increasing. Education facilitates the process of economic development through following ways:

- Enhancing human skills and talents.
- Increasing per head productivity.
- Promoting entrepreneur ability.
- Development of Human Resources.
- Promoting innovations and research.
- Increasing employment opportunities.
- Enhancing per capita income and national income.
- Reducing poverty and inequality.
- Developing individual personality—physical, mental, social, emotional, moral etc.
- Developing self-confidence, self-sufficiency, social-efficiency and judgement power.
- Fostering democratic values.

In these ways, education plays a pivotal role to promote economic development of a country. The real development of an economy can be achieved through inclusive development of the society. The role of education cannot be ignored. Investment in education today is for betterment of people tomorrow. The National Policy on Education (1986) advocated education as a "unique investment in the present for the future."

REFERENCES

Bartel, P.A. and Lichtenberg, F.R. (1987). "The Comparative Advantage of Educated Workers in Implementing New Technology." *Review of Economics and Statistics.*

Dreze, J. and Sen, A. (1995). *India: Economic Development and Social Opportunities*, New Delhi, India: Oxford University Press.

Godbole, M. (2001). "Elementary Education as a Fundamental Right: The Issues", *Economic and Political Weekly*, 36.

Goel, S.C. (1974). "Education and Economic Growth in India", *Comparative Education*, Vol. 10, No. 2.

Gounden, A. (1967). "Investment in Education in India", *The Journal of Human Resources*.

Government of India. (2011). *Educational Statistics at Glance*, New Delhi, India.

Govinda, R. (2005). "Elementary Education: Progress and Challenges", *Yojana*, 49.

Gray S. Becker (1994). *Human Capital: A Theoretical and Empirical Analysis with Special Reference to Education*, The University of Chicago Press, Chapter 2, pp. 15-28.

Human Development Report, 2019, UNDP.

India Human Development Report 2018, IARM, Planning Commission, Government of India.

Ministry of Human Resource Development (2014). *Statistics of School Education 2011-12*. New Delhi—Bureau of Planning, Monitoring and Statistics, Government of India.

Ozturk, I. (2001). "The Role of Education in Economic Development: A Theoretical Perspective", *Journal of Rural Development and Administration*, Vol. XXXIII, No. 1.

Philip Stevens and Martin Weale (2003). *Education and Economic Growth*, National Institute of Economic and Social Research.

Selected Socio-Economic Statistics India, 2011, Ministry of Statistics and Programme Implementation, Government of India.

Tilak, J. (2004). "Free and Compulsory Education", *Economic and Political Weekly*, 39(7).

10

Education and Economic Growth in India

Zubair Ahmad Parray

Introduction

Education is a very important factor in overall development and progress of any country. Since the early days of independence India has always focused on improving the literacy rate in the country. Even today the government runs many programmes to promote Primary and Higher Education in India. Let us study more about them.

Human Capital and Economic Growth stay hand in hand together, keeping an eye on the development of the country. Long back the Indians recognized the importance of human capital. The Seventh Five Year Plan dictates, "Human resources development has necessarily to be assigned a key role in any development strategy, particularly in a country with a large population". Looking at the below-mentioned points, one can certainly say that both, human capital and economic growth are interdependent on each other. Human capital theory explains it as:

- Skilled and specialized workers can handle complex machines or techniques, which unskilled workers cannot. This human capital increases the productivity of physical capital. This increases productivity and hence increased production leads to economic growth.
- New methods of production can be introduced by innovative human capital and these facilitate an increase of production and economic growth in the form of an increase in GDP.
- A higher rate of participation of human capital and equality amongst them leads to higher employment rate. As the employment increases, there will be a rise in production. Also,

the standard of living increases by an increase in income and increase in employment opportunities helps in reducing inequalities of wealth. The increment in employment rate and reduction in income inequalities are indicators of economic development.

- A positive picture of the society can be depicted when the process of human capital formation goes in right direction. All the conventional and orthodox school of thoughts gets eradicated and hence the rate of participation in the workforce increases the production level.
- Education in India means the process of teaching, learning, and training of human capital in schools and colleges. This improves and increases knowledge and results in skill development hence enhancing the quality of the human capital. Our government has always valued the importance of education in India and this is reflected in our economic policies.

Growth in Government Expenditure on Education

There are two areas where government expresses the expenditure:

- As a percentage of total government expenditure.
- As a percentage of Gross Domestic Product (GDP).

The percentage of expenditure on education out of total government expenditure is the indicator of the importance of education in the scheme of expenses before the government. The commitment level towards the development of education in our country can be shown by the percentage of expenditure done on education out of total GDP.

During 1952-2010, the percentage of total education expenditure out of total government expenditure increased from 7.92 per cent to 11.10 per cent. At the same time, the percentage of GDP of the country increased from 0.64 per cent to 3.25 per cent. As the expenditure on education was not constant during that time, the growth of country was irregular in that era.

Expenditure on Elementary Education in India

In comparison to expenditure on elementary education and higher education, the major share was grabbed by the elementary education. On the contrary, expenditure per student on higher education was higher than that of elementary education. As the expansion of school education is going on, we need more trained teachers who have studied at educational institutes. Therefore, expenditure on all levels of education should increase. Himachal Pradesh spends Rs. 2005 as per capita education expenditure as compared to Bihar which spends Rs. 515. This results in differences of educational opportunities between states.

Free and Compulsory Education

The Education Commission (1964-66) recommended that at least 6 per cent of GDP should be spent on education to make a recognizable growth rate in education. In December 2002, the Government of India, through its 86th Amendment to the Constitution of India, declared for free and compulsory education as a fundamental right to all children in the age group of 6-14 years.

The Tapas Majumdar Committee was appointed by the Government of India in the year 1998. The Committee estimated an expenditure of Rs. 1.37 lakh crore (approx.) for 1998-99 to 2006-07, to cater all Indian children of 6-14 years age group, under the umbrella of school education. Currently, the expenditure is around 4 per cent, which has to be increased to 6 per cent to reach desired results in years to come. Government levies education cess at the rate of 2 per cent on all union taxes. The revenues from education cess will be earmarked for spending on elementary education.

Future Prospects

Indian Government considers education as a key area where the extreme growth and development is required. So various future forecasts have been considered and policies are drafted. The vision is to ensure that education in India is of the highest quality and available to the whole population without discrimination. Let us look at some projects the government wishes to implement successfully.

Education for All—A Dream

Though the education level has increased for both youth as well as adults, still the number of illiterates is as much as the population was at the time of independence. The Constituent Assembly passed the Constitution of

India in the year 1950. Free and compulsory education for the children till 14 years of age within 10 years from the commencement of Constitution was noted as Directive Principle of the Constitution. Following are the factors which make education for all a dream:

- Gender bias
- Low rural access
- Increasing number of illiterates
- Privatization
- Low expenditure on education by government.

Improving Gender Equity

The differences between male and female are reducing and the same can be seen in literacy rate, showcasing a development in gender equity. Still, hard work left to promote the education of women. There are various reasons, such as:

- The social status of women
- Healthcare of women and children
- Improving economic independence.

Therefore, we cannot feel satisfied with the upward movement in literacy rate as long miles to go for gender equity. Kerala, Mizoram, Goa and New Delhi are having high literacy rate, whereas, Bihar, Uttar Pradesh, Arunachal Pradesh and Rajasthan are educationally backward states. Social and economic poverty are main reasons for educational backwardness.

Higher Education

People in India face great difficulty to reach the higher levels in the current education system. As per National Sample Survey Organization data, in the FY 2007-08, the unemployment rate was 18.10 per cent for youth with education up to secondary level. Whereas unemployment rate for youth with education up to primary level was only 11.60 per cent. The government should take emphasis on allocation of higher education and improve the students.

Education and Economic Development

Several empirical studies made in developed countries, especially in the U.S.A. regarding different sources of economic growth or contributions made by the factors such as physical capital, wage workers, education etc. have shown that education and the development of human capital is a significant source of economic growth of a nation.

Rate of Return Approach

The economic growth and the contribution of education has also been measured through the rate of return approach. In this approach rate of return is calculated from expenditure made by individuals on education and the measurement of the flow of an individual's future earnings expected to result from education. The present value of these is then calculated by using appropriate discount rate. This method has been used by Gary S. Backer who measured income differential arising from the cost or expenditure incurred on acquiring a college education in the United States. His estimates show that the rates of return on education in the U.S.A. for urban white population were 12.5 per cent in 1940 and 10 per cent in 1950. It is worth noting that estimates of rate of return on investment in education are based upon private rates of returns to individuals receiving education. However, by assuming that differences in earnings in a market economy reflect differences in productivity, the rate of return on investment in education is taken to be the effect of education on the output of the country.

Expenditure on Education and Income

Another approach to measure the economic growth and the contribution of education is based upon the analysis of the relationship between expenditure on education and income. Using this approach Schultz studied the relationship between expenditure on education and consumer's income and also the relationship between expenditure on education and physical capital formation for the United States during the period 1900 to 1956. He found that when measured in constant dollars, resources that are allocated to education rose about three and a half times:

(a) relative to consumer income in dollars, and
(b) relative to the gross formation of physical capital in dollars.

This implies that the 'income elasticity' of the demand for education was about 3.5 over the period or, in other words, education considered as an investment could be regarded as 3.5 times more attractive than investment in physical capital. It may, however, be noted that these estimates of Schultz only indirectly reflect the contribution of education to economic growth.

Consumption Benefits of Education

We have explained above the investment benefits of education and therefore, its effects on productivity and national output. But investment benefits are not the only benefits flowing from education. Education also yields consumption benefits for the individual as he may "enjoy" more education derive increased satisfaction from his present and future personal life. If the welfare of society depends on the welfare of its individual members, then the society as a whole also gains in welfare as a result of the increased consumption benefits of individuals from more education. Economic theory also helps us in quantifying the consumption benefits derived from education.

External Benefits of Education

We have explained above the investment benefits and consumption benefits flowing from more education both for the individual and for society. The analysis of benefits has been based on the assumption that private interests of individuals are consistent with the social good. However, private and social benefits do not always coincide for instance social benefits may exceed private benefits. This is the case with the education of an individual which not only benefits individual privately but also others. First, education makes people better neighbours and citizens and makes social and political life more healthy and meaningful. Secondly, the most important external benefit of more education is its effect on technological change in the economy. More education, especially higher education stimulates research and thereby raises productivity which undoubtedly benefits the society. The individual inventor may not receive earnings equal to his contribution to the research. Denison's study of contribution of education to growth whose main findings have been mentioned above clearly shows the external benefits of education. After estimating the contribution of labour (including educated labour) and physical capital to economic growth he obtained an average residual of

0.59 percentage point. Denison attributed this to the increase in knowledge which is the direct result of research and indirectly of higher education. "If the entire residual indeed stemmed ultimately from education, as some human capital enthusiasts have implied, this would mean that education, directly or indirectly, contributed over 40 per cent of total output growth and 80 per cent of increased productivity from 1929 to 1957." If Denison's residual is regarded as mainly due to research stimulated by additional education then this is indeed a major external benefit of education.

Education, Inequality and Poverty

An evaluation of the role of education in economic development must not be confined to judging its impact on growth in output but should also include its impact on structure and pattern of economic development as well as on the distribution of income and removal of poverty. In the 1950s and 1960s, the most important objective of development was the maximization of rate of economic growth, i.e. growth of material output and in conformity with this the economics of education also focused on estimating the contribution of education to the growth of national output. But now-a-days policy of economic development has been increasingly concerned with the distribution of income, i.e. how gains of economic growth are distributed and whether poverty is being reduced. But recent studies have revealed that education, given the present education system, has tended to increase the inequalities in income distribution rather than reducing them. The adverse effect of formal education on income distribution has been explained through establishing a positive correlation between level of education received by an individual and the level of his life-term earnings.

Education and Rural Development

If the objective of raising the standards of living of the people in general and removal of mass poverty is to be attained in less developed countries like India, then rural development must get the highest priority. In the 1950s and 1960s in most of developing countries, the modernization and development of the urban sector was given the highest priority in the development plans and more resources were allocated to this sector. But in recent years, the thinking among economists all-over the world has undergone a significant change, since the development of the large scale industries and the urban sector has failed to solve the twin problems of poverty and unemployment. It has now been increasingly realised that it is through the emphasis on agricultural and rural development in the strategy of development that the problems of poverty and unemployment can be solved. Since 80 per cent of the population of less developed countries directly or indirectly depends upon agriculture, rural area needs to be given the highest priority.

Now, education can play an important role in agricultural and rural development provided it is suitably modified and given a rural bias. The present system of education has a strong urban bias so that it is ill-suited to the requirements of agricultural and rural development. Moreover, the emphasis in the present education system is on general education rather than on vocational education. A relevant and meaningful education can raise the productivity of the rural labour in agricultural work. It can create new employment opportunities if during the schooling students are educated and trained in some useful vocations. Moreover, education to the poor people will induce in them desire to have fewer children with the result that not only their private level of living will rise, but it will also help the general economic development by checking the growth of population. Above all, education will bring about improvement in their health and nutrition. Phillip H. Coomb, an eminent educationist and economist, has classified different types of education that should be provided to the rural people so as to promote rapid rural and agricultural development. They are:

(i) General or Basic Education

This should cover teaching the students about reading, writing, elementary mathematics and about understanding of basic science and one's environment. This type of education is being currently provided.

(ii) Family Improvement Education

Under this students should be provided knowledge, skills, attitudes which are useful in improving the quality of human life. Accordingly, this should cover subjects such as health and nutrition, family planning, child care, home repairs and environment improvements etc.

(iii) Community Development Education

This type of education should be so designed as to improve the working of rural institutions and processes so that rural community should be developed. This should cover subjects such as local self-government, cooperative enterprise, running rural development projects etc.

(iv) Occupational Education

Under this students should be educated and trained for performing various agricultural activities properly and efficiently and for imparting education regarding particular agricultural skills and occupations. This would enable the students to make their living through self-employed occupations in agriculture, agro-industries and other non-agricultural works after completing their education.

Role of Education in Economic Development of Nations

Education in every field is one of the fundamental source for economic development. No any country can attain its sustainable development without substantial investment in human capital. Education enshrines people's understanding among themselves and the world. It improves the quality and standards of their lives and leads to extensive social benefits to individuals and society. Education raises people's productivity and creativity, it promotes entrepreneurship and the technical advances. "Education is the most powerful weapon you can use to change the world" said Nelson Mandela. In addition it plays a very critical role in securing economic and social progress and in improving the income distribution. However, economic development is a complex process and economists have had a difficult time identifying the fundamental factors. At its core, this process is one in which financial and human capital are combined in ever more sophisticated and productive ways, and that is why certain countries advance in this process much more rapidly than others. According to Adam Smith, *"the acquired abilities of all the inhabitants are a kind of capital," what is now called "human capital,"* as one of the four types of fixed capital that contribute to production in the national economy. Some economists began to wonder if poor countries might be poor because they lacked human capital. They deduced that rich countries devastated in World War-II were able to quickly employ massive amounts of new physical capital, while the poorest countries seemed unable to successfully utilize even small amounts. They conceived that a nation's capability to productively use physical capital is a function of its level of human capital and that if human capital does not increase along with physical capital, then economic development cannot proceed. In addition, it is notified that human capital is more likely to be the constraint to development because foreign investors are eager to invest in physical capital, but not in human capital. Economists now accept that investment in education, or human capital, is an important element in the economic development process. Econometric studies provide very strong and consistent evidence that more educated workers are more productive and that they earn higher salaries. There is also no doubt that average levels of education and national income rise simultaneously. So, this idea not only support Adam Smith's view that acquired abilities are a form of capital but also proves that education plays a large and critical role in the economic development process and that it most likely is the limiting factor in this process.

The relationships between the two capitals (human capital and physical capital) are complementary. There is some variation in the relative amounts of the two types of capital, but no country has high level of only one type. For example, the U.S. has more human than physical capital, while Japan has more physical than human capital, but both countries have high levels of both. Similarly, studies show that economic development does not occur automatically. If it did, there would not be such large differences in the magnitude of the capital stocks between countries. However, there are some other characteristic which are not present in the less developed countries, facilitated historic investment in both types of capital. It is also evident that whatever these characteristics are, they vary widely across countries because levels of capital/adult vary widely. If human capital and physical capital are complementary, then historically either type of capital or both could have been the factor limiting investment in the other type of capital. Human capital is created initially by providing children with primary and secondary schooling. Private financing of this type of investment is not feasible for poor children. Countries that are highly developed today have a long history of providing free or highly-subsidized education to the poor. A review of their history suggests that the initial impetus for this schooling had a religious basis, but that as the public's level of education and income rose, their demand for schooling rose, and the financial support from private donors was replaced or greatly augmented with public funds. If poor countries wish to achieve high levels of national income, they need to provide public funding for the universal education of the poor, at least at the primary and secondary levels of schooling. The evidence on returns to education indicates that investment in schooling is subject to diminishing returns, but that the macro marginal return on all education is still considerable in highly-educated countries. In less-educated countries, the marginal macro returns are much larger, in excess of 50 per cent, but since most of this return is indirect, the magnitude of the marginal returns to education is not generally appreciated. These very high macro marginal returns to education make it possible for poor countries to grow very rapidly if they make a major commitment to raising their average level of schooling. The evidence also indicates that educated workers raise the marginal productivity of physical capital and of other workers. In highly educated countries, the spillover effect on other workers is very small, but in less-educated countries this effect appears to be much larger. Finally, in all countries the positive effect of rising human capital on the productivity of physical capital is required to offset the diminishing returns to investment and make rising investment in physical capital financially viable in the development process. Finally, the human capital and physical capital are complementary; the education has both direct and indirect effects on national income. So the human capital and physical capital are both required for economic development and that each has a positive external effect on the productivity of the other. To end with Education is the key to solve every problem, no nation could achieve sustainable economic development without substantial investment in human capital.

How Education Benefits a Nation

Globalization and international trade require countries and their economies to compete with each other. Economically successful countries will hold competitive and comparative advantages over other economies, though a single country rarely specializes in a particular industry. A typical developed economy will include various industries with different competitive advantages and disadvantages in the global marketplace. The education and training of a country's workforce is a major factor in determining how well the country's economy will perform.

A successful economy has a workforce capable of operating industries at a level where it holds a competitive advantage over the economies of other countries. Nations may try incentivizing training through tax breaks, providing facilities to train workers, or a variety of other means designed to create a more skilled workforce. While it's unlikely an economy will hold a competitive advantage in all industries, it can focus on a number of industries in which skilled professionals are more readily trained.

Differences in training levels is a significant factor that

separates developed and developing countries. Although other factors are certainly in play, such as geography and available resources, having better-trained workers creates spillovers throughout the economy and positive externalities. An externality can be a positive effect on an economy due to a well-trained workforce. In other words, all companies benefit from the external factor of having a skilled labour pool from which to hire employees. In some cases, the highly-skilled labour force might be concentrated in a specific geographic region. As a result, similar businesses may cluster in the same geographic region because of those skilled workers (e.g., Silicon Valley, CA).

(i) For Employers

Ideally, employers want workers who are productive and require less management. Employers must consider many factors when deciding whether or not to pay for employee training:

- Will the training programme increase the productivity of the workers?
- Will the increase in productivity warrant the cost of paying for all or part of the training?
- If the employer pays for training, will the employee leave the company for a competitor after the training programme is complete?
- Will the newly trained worker be able to command a higher wage?
- Will the worker gain an increase in bargaining power or leverage for a higher wage?
- If increases in pay are warranted as a result of the training, will the increases in productivity and profits be enough to cover any pay raises as well as the overall cost of the training programme?

While employers should be wary about newly trained workers leaving, many employers require workers to remain with the firm for a certain amount of time in exchange for the paid training.

Businesses may also face employees who are unwilling to accept training. This can happen in industries dominated by unions since increased job security could make it more difficult to hire trained professionals or fire less-trained employees. However, unions may also negotiate with employers to ensure its members are better trained and thus more productive, which reduces the likelihood of jobs being shifted overseas.

(ii) For Workers

Workers increase their earning potential by developing and refining their capabilities. The more they know about a particular job's function, the more they understand a particular industry, the more valuable they become to an employer. Employees want to learn advanced techniques or new skills to vie for a higher wage. Usually, workers can expect their wages to increase at a smaller percentage than the productivity gains by employers. The worker must consider a number of factors when deciding whether to enter a training programme:

- How much extra productivity would he or she expect to gain?
- Is there a cost to the worker for the training programme?
- Will the worker see a wage increase that would warrant the cost of the programme?
- What are the labour market conditions for better-trained professionals in that field?
- Is the labour market significantly saturated with trained labour already for that speciality?

Some employers pay for all or a portion of the training expenses, but this is not always the case. Also, the worker may lose income if the programme is unpaid and prevents the employee from working as many hours as was done previously.

(iii) For the Economy

Many countries have placed greater emphasis on developing an education system that can produce workers able to function in new industries, such as science and technology. This is partly because older industries in developed economies were becoming less competitive, and thus were less likely to continue dominating the industrial landscape. Also, a movement to improve the basic education of the population emerged, with a growing belief that all people had the right to an education.

When economists speak of "education", the focus is not strictly on workers obtaining college degrees. Education is often broken into specific levels:

- Primary—elementary school in the U.S.

- Secondary—middle school, high school, and preparatory school.
- Post-secondary—university, community college, vocational schools.

A country's economy becomes more productive as the proportion of educated workers increases since educated workers can more efficiently carry out tasks that require literacy and critical thinking. However, obtaining a higher level of education also carries a cost. A country does not have to provide an extensive network of colleges or universities to benefit from education; it can provide basic literacy programmes and still see economic improvements.

Countries with a greater portion of their population attending and graduating from schools see faster economic growth than countries with less-educated workers. As a result, many countries provide funding for primary and secondary education to improve economic performance. In this sense, education is an investment in human capital, similar to an investment in better equipment.

According to UNESCO and the United Nations Human Development Programme, the ratio of the number of children of official secondary school age enrolled in school to the number of children of official secondary school age in the population (referred to as the enrolment ratio), is higher in developed nations than it is in developing ones.

The enrolment ratio differs as a metric from calculating education spending as a percentage of GDP, which does not always correlate strongly with the level of education in a country's population. GDP is the Gross Domestic Product, which represents the output of goods and services for a nation. Therefore, a country spending a high proportion of its GDP on education does not necessarily ensure that the country's population is more educated.

For businesses, an employee's intellectual ability can be treated as an asset. This asset can be used to create products and services that can be sold. The more well-trained workers employed by a firm, the more that firm can theoretically produce. An economy in which employers treat education as an asset is often referred to as a knowledge-based economy.

Like any decision, investing in education involves an opportunity cost for the worker. Hours spent in the classroom means less time working and earning income. Employers, however, pay more wages when the tasks required to complete a job require a higher level of education. As a result, although an employee's income might be lower in the short-term to become educated, wages will likely be higher in the future, once the training is complete.

(iv) Cobweb Model

The Cobweb Model helps to explain the effects of workers learning new skills. The model shows how wages fluctuate as workers learn a new skill, but also how the supply of workers is impacted over time.

The model shows that as workers learn a new skill, higher wages occur in the short-run. However, as more workers get trained over time and enter the workforce, to chase the higher wages, the supply of workers increases. The result is lower wages due to the excess supply of workers. As wages fall, fewer workers are interested in the job leading to a reduction in the supply of workers. The cycle begins again with training more workers and increasing their wages in the short run.

Since training and education take time to complete, shifts in the demand for particular types of employees have different effects in the long and short term. Economists demonstrate this shift using a Cobweb model of labour supply and labour demand. In this model, the supply of labour is analysed over the long term, but the shifts in demand and wages are viewed in the short-term as they move toward a long-term equilibrium.

(v) The Bottom Line

The knowledge and skills of workers available in the labour supply is a key factor in determining both business and economic growth. Economies with a significant supply of skilled labour, brought on through formal education, as well as vocational training, are often able to capitalize on this through the development of more value-added industries, such as high-tech manufacturing.

4. Economic Development in India

The economic development in traditional views, no discrimination was pitched in economic growth and development in the beginning of the evolution in its developments. Since the seventies, it has been thought necessary to distinguish between the economic growth and economic development. There are two views to interpret in its terms of planned changes in the structure of national products and the occupational patterns of labour force and also the institutional and technological changes that bring about such changes in the accompany. It may be noted that Kuznets in the study of 'Modern Economic Growth' interpreted the process of modern economy which involves the structural changes. In this view during the process of economic growth share the agriculture in both national products and employment of labour forces declines and in the industries and services increases. Various strategies of development which were suggested until 'seventies' generally focused on rapid industrialization so that structural transformation and the changes could be achieved. For this purpose appropriate institutional and technological changes were recommended to bring about such structural changes. Thus, economic growth means more output and economic growth implies both more output and changes in the technical and institutional arrangements by which it is produced—C.P. Kindleberg. Hence, by the traditional views, economic growth and development implies structural change. Structural change refers to changes in technological and institutional factors which causes shift of labour from agriculture to modern manufacturing and services sectors and also generate self-sustaining growth of output.

The Concept of Economic Development in Modern Era: The experience of the developing countries during the sixties and seventies showed that whereas target rates of economic growth were in fact achieved by creation of more employment opportunities, rise in wages and improvement in income distribution did not operate. The problems of poverty, unemployment and income inequality further worsened instead of getting reduced during the process of growth in the nineteen fifties and sixties in the developing countries. For instance, in India, Dandekar and Rath found that 40 per cent of rural population in India lived below the poverty line in 1968-69. Using somewhat different approach, B.S. Minhas estimated that 37 per cent of rural population in India lived below the poverty line in 1967-68. Similarly, the magnitude of poverty and unemployment and the extent of income inequalities also increased in many other developing countries. Hence, we can say, due to the failure of traditional strategies of development in solving the problems of poverty, unemployment and inequality, it was realised in the seventies that the concept of development should be broadened so that it should signify that well-being of the people has increased. This led to the view that economic development should not be judged on the basis of growth in GNP alone. Therefore, when we regard the well-being of the masses as the ultimate objective of development, we have to see whether poverty and unemployment are decreasing and how the increases in gross national product or national income are being distributed among the population. Recently, the concept of economic development has been further widened so that it now involves not only reduction in poverty, inequality and unemployment but also requires improvement in quality of life which includes cleaner environment, better education, good health and nutrition. Thus World Development Report 1991, published by the World Bank, asserts—"The challenge of development is to improve the quality of life, especially in the world's poor countries, a better quality of life generally calls for higher incomes but it involves much more. It encompasses as ends in themselves better education, higher standards of health and nutrition, less poverty, a cleaner environment, more equality of opportunity." Thus the concept of economic development has been greatly broadened. Today economic development is interpreted as not only in more growth in Gross Domestic Product (GDP) but also in terms of good quality of life which, according to Prof. Amartya Sen, "consists in enlargement of opportunities for people and freedom of human choices."

The economic development is lying under certain goals which are as following three objectives:

1. To Achieve a Higher Rate of GDP Growth.
2. To Eradicate Poverty and Unemployment.
3. To Expand the Freedoms Enjoyed by the People.

Evolution of Economic Development: The study of development economics as a separate discipline is relatively new as about 70 years ago in 1950s, the problem of economic development of poor developing countries did not constitute an important distinct branch of economics. The classical economists such as Adam Smith, Ricardo, Malthus, and Marx are extensively dealt with the problems and the issues of development of the economies. However, with the appearance of neoclassical economics propounded among others by Alfred Marshall and A.C. Pigou, were mainly concerned with explaining efficient provision of resources in a free market economy, development economics dealing with the developing economies found no place in their works. The renewed interest and public concern with the development of poor countries began only after the Second World War when the poverty of the underdeveloped countries of Asia, Africa and Latin America posed a great challenge to the peace and progress of the world as a whole and also many underdeveloped countries got freedom from the colonial rule.

Economists laid stress on capital accumulation, mobilization of surplus labour for growth and industrialization based on import-substitution through economic planning and with active role of the government. It was thought that due to market failures, development through free market, as emphasized by neoclassical economics, would neither achieve efficient allocation of scarce resources nor brings about desired GDP growth rate to remove poverty and employment. Since rate of domestic saving in these underdeveloped countries was inadequate to bring about a desired rate of growth, the need for foreign aid to supplement domestic saving was emphasized in early approaches to development based on application of Harrod-Domar growth model.

REFERENCES

http://outlookafghanistan.net/topics.php?post_id=16303#ixzz65Quksept

http://www.economicsdiscussion.net/essays/economic-development-essays/essay-on-economic-development-in-india/29939

https://www.investopedia.com/articles/economics/09/education-training-advantages.asp

https://acta.mendelu.cz/media/pdf/actaun_2018066010253.pdf

https://ideas.repec.org/p/dun/dpaper/210.html

https://www.jstor.org/stable/40703680?seq=1

Unit 3

Economic Approaches of Education

11

Economic Development in India through Education

The Policies, Discrepancies and the Possible Solutions

Afshan

> "India is not a country we live in but a country that lives within us."
> –*M.K. Gandhi*
>
> "India is a large, complex, very important country."
> – *Hillary Clinton*

The above-mentioned quotes do not come close to describing how India came to be one of the most talked about countries in many aspects; historically, politically, socially, and religiously. Ever since the ancient times of the Achaemenid, India has been the epicentre of the world, making history as she goes along. From the ancient empire that arose on her lands to the 6th of December 1971 victory and the peace treaty with Pakistan to the 22nd of July, 2019 launched lunar mission Chandrayaan-2, Indians never failed to impress and garner the awe of the world. Historical events are witnesses on how grand and mysterious she is. India went through a lot of changes and conflicts that have changed the shape of the society altogether. Most of these changes and conflicts have risen because of the unfortunate overall descent of the country and the multi-faceted failures of the state to deal with the people's demands and the country's many problems.

After the UPA Government lost election on 11th of May, 2014 and India entered its transitional path into strong nationalism and a hopeful achievement of a better life for her people, a lot of questions and problems have come into the light, most importantly its dying economy and the hard fact that Indians do not seem to be getting the education they need in order to thrive and better themselves. In 2011, 26 per cent of population was completely illiterate and most recently, India has been placed last in terms of quality of primary education; India officially has the worst primary education system in the world. Even with impressive improvements in the country's infrastructure especially in utilities and telecommunications (an increasing access to internet and better telecom services), with an average GDP growth rate of circa 6 per cent throughout the new millennium, the overall development of the country is deteriorating. For example, India saw its ranking settle among the lower 49 per cent of all developing countries in the UN's 2005-16 Human Poverty Index. Hence, the reason for the study that I conducted presents itself; does the answer to India's ailing economy lie within its educational sector? And if so, how much impact on economic growth could education reforms produce?

The previous literature discusses the relationship between economic growth and education including the role of government involvement. Alkire and Santos (2010) mention that a resource-based policy of the government has little effect on the educational sector. They argue that the educational attainment of students is almost unaffected by government policy. Using UN data, they clarify that an active involvement of government in the education sector is deemed as a failure. While Alkire and Santos might strike some important points regarding that matter, I argue that the question should not be just about resource management in the education sector, but also about the quality of the outcomes arising from those resources.

Krishnankutty and Chakraborty (2012) ask whether a resource based public education policy can be counter-productive. They also explore the proactive role of the government as a factor determining public education spending behaviour (across countries), and the relationship between public education spending and schooling returns. Self and Grabowski (2003) link public expenditure on education to growth as well as Ansari and Singh (1997) and Pradhan (2009). Dutta (2006) shows that a strategic environment, when a government spends more on the education sector, students may underinvest in their efforts, which may dampen any spillover effect on economic growth.

In this Chapter, I focus on the quality of the educational system and human capital in India. Specially, the following questions are explored: Has the path to growth and development been hindered by an inefficient educational system? What needs to be done in terms of improving the quality of education in order for India to have more qualified workers? How can "labour and education" work together in order for India to move from a developing to a developed country? From the study conducted, I find that despite the important illiteracy rate that seems to persist in India, Indians spend half of their lives in educating themselves and building their human capital. However, that time spent on education yields little in terms of building the stock of human capital for Indians. Therefore, any potential the educational system has of contributing positively to economic growth is not currently being used effectively.

To answer these questions, I use an endogenous growth model similar to that used in Krishnankutty and Chakraborty (2012). The model focuses on the relationship between government involvement in the educational sector, in terms of spending on education, and the impact it has on the productivity of schooling and the average growth rate of the economy. In their model, the authors aimed for cross-country results on how government involvement in education can negatively affect the average growth rate of the economy. In my analysis, I apply their growth model on India and try to establish a positive relationship between the quality of education and the average growth rate of the country. The results that I reach support my hypothesis that increasing the quality of education will in fact contribute in increasing the average growth rate of India's economy by significant strides.

The study proceeds as follows: Part I present a brief history of India's economy and where it appears to be going, while also shedding some light on potential policy prescriptions that could help resolve the issues mentioned *a priori*. In Part II, I present a simple endogenous growth model, the purpose of which is to measure how effective the educational system in India is. Part III concludes with possible solutions for improving the Indian educational system so that it can begin to contribute positively in the growth of the Indian economy.

Part I: Economic Policies in India

This part discusses a brief history of economic growth and reforms in India. Under the Congress Government, India has seen different economic approaches and policies to better the economic situation and turn the country into an economic stronghold. The goal is to understand the path of growth to date, as well as to reinforce that a poor education system has limited the access to economic growth among the country's poor, even with the different economic policies applied "for their benefit".

According to the Asian Development Bank's 2018 report, India is considered to be the third largest economy of Asia and the 5th globally. The Indian economy is known to be well-diversified and driven mainly by industry, tourism revenues, trade services and agriculture. As of 2019, India's population stands at 1.38 billion with a distinctive characteristic of being poor and having financial hardships. Over the past 50 years or so, the Indian economy has seen many reforms and policies implemented to restructure and redesign the market to better cope with the regional and global markets, as well as cope with the people's demand of a better and improved lifestyle.

1. A Populist Outlook

India was known to be one of the "must-watch" countries in terms of economic development during the late 50s to the end of the 60s. Following the 1947 August Independence that disposed of the British rule, the Indian economy went through a major change, most importantly on the economic side. During Nehru Government, the economy was mainly driven by a populist agenda hence, eliminating the massive concentration of resources and riches in the hands of the elite capitalists of the disposed British.

Prime Minister Nehru's most important policy was to revolutionize the public sector with more state-owned factories and companies being built. By the late 50s and early 60s, India's most sizeable businesses were nationalized which helped the late PM's economic vision at that time; to remodel the structure of wealth by transferring ownership from a narrow stratum of capitalists to the poorer and ordinary people. This direction brought on a more balanced socio-economic status to the society. The social curve eventually flattened, aided by a dramatic increase in university education, expansion in industry and services, as well as an emerging public sector. As a result, the previously poorer strata of Indians moved up to the middle class (http://www.oecd.org>emp). He was able to transform India's society from a poor and helpless society into a working and driven one.

The results were staggering; the country's economy grew at an average of 7.5 per cent per year for almost a decade. The manufacturing contribution to the GDP increased from 12 per cent to 17 per cent in the early 70s. The afore-mentioned sector became the largest employer of Indians making India a country with a very large share of labour force in the manufacturing sector. Unemployment decreased from 6 per cent in 1956 to 3.8 per cent in 1972 a record low (mospi.nic.in>default>files).

This was due to the rapid growth of the public sector after nationalizing most of the companies and factories and to the increasing number of graduate students because of the expansion of free education.

The newly empowered public sector was not accompanied by proper training and skill enhancement to the poor, low skilled farmers that came to acquire a large portion of the agriculture resources from the more educated and well-capitalized landowners (following the PM's Land Reform Act). That resulted in a poorer quality of agrarian produce and poor marketing for it (especially the cotton which is India's main agriculture produce) a poorer labour productivity and effectiveness.

2. Opening up the Economy

Following PM Nehru's government, the late PM Indra Gandhi ushered in a new economic agenda, one that depended on the alliance between policies and economics. The economic changes expected from the opening-up policy were to transfer power from the state, the government, the military establishments and the public sector to a newly emerging private sector. One of the major impacts of the economic policy was on the social aspect. The middle class saw its structure transform under the pressure of different forces of change such as the rise of the private sector and the increase of Foreign Domestic Investments (FDI). With those effects in play, the public sector saw its role decline in the 70s and 80s with substantial income gaps between workers of both sectors. The opening-up policy adopted at that time created a new wave of financial liberalization for the Indian economy. It upgraded the country's job market, created a momentum and triggered an increase in a number of industries. The private sector became the leading economic player in the country for the three following decades, pushing aside the decaying role of the public sector. With the new "opening-up" policy set in motion, the low growth rate during PM Indra Gandhi's government ranged around 0.9 per cent as opposed to an average growth rate of almost 1.6 per cent during Nehru's government (Goel, 1974:148).

However, because of the sizeable income gap between the decaying public sector and newly emerging private sector, the former's top talent and elite university graduates moved to much better paying jobs, leaving a vacancy that was hard to help better the public sector. Millions comprising India's middle class, found themselves stuck in that sector since the focus of the government was directed at the private sector. The public sector was left stuck with an increasing marginalization and stagnancy and low wages. Despite the previous, the public sector remained the backbone of the economy up until the early 2000s with the Indian economy opening up to the labour markets as well, more than 30 million Indians were lured to work in the Gulf States following the first oil boom between 1974 and 1985. The resulting social mobility in that period was not due to an overall socio-economic equality or higher education and professional standing like Nehru's policies. This mobility was supported by an increase in domestic purchasing power. The middle class in India was now defined as a function of the disposable income of families and no longer by education or professions.

With that being said, it is important to mention that having the middle-class status in the economy be determined as a function of the disposable income, rendered it vulnerable to the new economic forces in play. Economic crisis caused immense pressure on the middle class where the middle class saw its purchasing power eroded, with real-wages in the public sector being affected by high inflation. The newly adopted policy was not flexible enough to respond to the social dynamics of the time. With the sudden surge of new economic opportunities and an upgrade of the country's job market, the skills of the Indian middle class were mismatched with the period's skill demands and requirements.

3. False Hope for Development

P.V. Narsimha Rao was able to turn the economy into a different version of itself. The economic reform the new PM then wanted to adopt focused on strengthening and solidifying the country's economic foundations so as to have change come in a less disruptive manner. With the improvement of the people's economic conditions in mind, Rao launched a programme of economic upliftment with the help of the World Bank and the International Monetary Fund (IMF). He wanted to improve living conditions, expand high-employment sectors and decrease poverty through enhancing the source of foreign currency, most importantly the agriculture sector (with almost 1.5 million Indians working in the sector by 2007, representing 4.3 per cent of total GDP and accommodating 10 per cent of the workforce) (Sreenivasulu, 2013:33).

As a result, labour force participation increased following the flow of FDI in the country, especially in the agriculture and tourism sector and a combined effect from the industry and services sector (that includes the telecoms sector).

Table 11.1 : Correlation between Education spending as a share of GDP and GDP growth rate, India. We can observe a definite persistent negative trend between g per cent and t between 1990-2015.

Year	*1990*	*1995*	*2000*	*20005*	*2010*	*2015*
Education, cash (Budget, Cen. Govt.)	3.80	4.79	5.00	5.00	4.00	4.00
GDP annual growth rate	5.7%	4%	6.2%	7%	6.8%	7.5%

Source: Indian Government Finance Statistics and the World Development Indicators.

Despite the trend of employment in the industrial sector is lower than the one in the services sector, its contribution to the employment of the Indians is not negligible, reaching as high as 55.1 per cent of total employment in 2010-11. Following the restructuring of the economy's infrastructure and an important flow of FDI in the 2000s, the employment trend in the services sector grew tremendously, pushing it to become the highest employment sector between 2001 and 2005. Despite its minor decline during 2010-2011, the services sector still contributed to about 45 per cent of the employment in the country. Following the ambitious restructuring of the economy, unemployment and inflation reached all-time highs during Rao's government. At a rate of 18-21 per cent in the 25-54 age group, unemployment attacked the country's core labour force (and is still in the double digits following the demonetization and instability the country is witnessing). This came to affect a sizeable section of the middle class's living standards.

Now the Modi government has proposed a draft National Education Policy. In the meanwhile, the collapse of government schools has intensified. The system is almost totally corrupt from the top downwards—with teacher's posts and transfers being sold. Many government school teachers are inevitably incompetent as a result and a good number of them do not even attend schools, particularly in villages and remote areas. Education quality is pathetic: Himachal Pradesh and Tamil Nadu children undertook the PISA test in 2009 and came out at the bottom of the world.

The government has a heavily skewed and iniquitous school funding model. It massively subsidises a few chosen high-quality schools in big cities but funding is meagre for the majority of the schools—with most of it being siphoned off on the way. Government school infrastructure is, therefore, in shambles.

The poorest parents are most affected. As a result, they have switched enmasse to private for-profit schools where fees are often as low as Rs. 200

per month. The mushrooming of such low-cost private schools reflects the point that Gurcharan Das had made in 2012 in his book, "India Grows at Night"—that most sectors of India's economy have become privatized because of chronic government failure. It is important to note here, as well, that there is absolutely no government funding for such low-cost schools—the poor are entirely on their own, which defeats the entire point of having government involvement in education.

4. What Went Wrong?

In my opinion, the main problem plaguing the economy is the lack of consistency between the different policies applied. With every government that came to power in India since the Independence was overthrown, there has been no uniformity in terms of views and perceptions of the essential changes needed, or even an idea of what the alternative model should be in order to develop India's economy. The common mistake committed by the aforementioned policies was their ignoring of the fact that the Indian society and average workers were still unequipped with necessary skills and tools to compete in a global and more open market, and become more effective and productive as workers.

Interestingly enough, out of 22 million workers, 42 per cent are either illiterate or semi-literate. This has led to the Global Competitiveness Index to classify the Indian workers as "working poor", not only because of the stagnation of real wages in the public sector over three decades, but because Indians have the lowest level of productivity. India has been ranked 137 in terms of the labour market efficiency (http://gcr.weforum.org/). Indians were considered "unemployable" due to their lacking skills domestically and internationally. Following the new "opening-up" policy and the rapid implementation of the socialist policy, the Indians were in no way prepared to face a competitive and demanding global market with new technology and demanding skills. Enhancing the Indians' skills should have been the number one objective for both policies, to match up with their agenda of propelling the economy forward.

Following what has been mentioned above, the perfect remedy for the ailing economy lies within the educational system of the country. Over the past 70 years, the skills and tools acquired by the Indian workers have not been sufficient to increase their productivity and value in the market. Education refers to not only schools and universities, but also to training and enhancing the Indians' set of skills so that they are more able to compete and produce on the labour market. In the last Global

Competitiveness Index of 2019, India was placed last (58th place) in terms of quality of primary education. The Adequacy of Education Index has placed India at 37th place (http://www.quora.com). Even if Indian workers enhanced their skills, they would be given unnecessary skills and sometimes unrelated to the labour market demands rendering them unable to work with what they have. Educational policies thus far have only served in expanding or minimizing the educational system increasing or decreasing the number of years of schooling. They have not served the economic growth and failed to link what the youth acquire during their "student" life to what they will face in the labour market.

Part II: Method to Solve the Problem?

In this part, I attempt to quantify the major defect that has affected India's educational system: lack of quality. "Quality" is an ambiguous indicator and difficult to measure seeing as how the word itself expands over a wide spectrum of definitions. In my opinion, the education sector has a great potential in contributing to the growth rate of the Indian economy. It is my belief that if properly developed and reformed, the education sector could have a positive spillover effect, mainly on employment. I use the model to determine the level of productivity provided by the present educational system and try to establish a link between the quality of education and the growth rate of the economy. If a positive relationship exists, I can then examine how much the growth rate changes given a change in the productivity of education.

I acquired data on the percentage share of education in the Indian GDP from the Indian Government Finance Statistics (GFS) over the period of 1990 to 2019. I also acquired data on the annual growth rate of GDP from the World Development Indicators (WDI) over the same period. These two data sets help determine whether there exists a link between the quality of education, the share of education in GDP and the annual growth rate of the economy.

The Model

My analysis utilizes the model of Krishnankutty and Chakraborty (2012). This study discusses the relationship between government involvement in education and the growth rate of the economy. The economy has two major sectors: the goods producing sector and an education sector. There is a fixed time allocated between schooling and producing goods such that l_{Ht} is time allocated to schooling (time spent on education) at date *t*. Time allocated to schooling contributes to an individual's stock of human capital in the next period, denoted by h_{t+1}. Specially, the law of motion for human capital follows:

$$H_{t+1} = (1-S_h)h_t + A_H g^n{}_t (l_H h_t)^{1-n}$$

The previous equation represents the human capital production function, where $S_h E\ (0,1)$ is the depreciation rate of human capital and $n\ E\ (0,1)$ is a schooling technology parameter. Public spending on education is denoted by g_t, while $l_H h_t$ represents private spending on education; the time spent on education by the households given a level of pre-acquired human capital. It is also the opportunity cost of diverting time from goods production to human capital production.

It is important to mention that the productivity of the schooling input depends on these factors:

1. A_H is the education productivity parameter, or in the context of my study, the quality of the education in India. This particular parameter helps determine how much additional human capital the Indians get for an additional input of schooling time.
2. Public spending on education, g_t, represents the second factor affecting the productivity of the schooling input in terms of how much the government spends on the educational infrastructure.
3. Another important parameter for my analysis (as well as it was for Krishnankutty and Chakraborty) is *n*, which represents the infrastructural role of the government in the education sector. In other words, it represents a schooling technology parameter and determines how involved the government was in the past in the education sector. Krishnankutty and Chakraborty (2012) call it the *government bias in education*. This parameter represents the tying point in the relationship between public spending on education and the growth rate of the economy.

With the given parameters and information that I was able to gather on India's education spending share in GDP and growth rate over 1990-2019, I was able to identify a specific A_H and l_H as follows:

$$n = 0.0694 \quad A_H = 0.1575 \quad l_H = 0.4967$$

The results obtained coincide with the reality of the educational sector in India. The government bias to education is high enough to actually mirror the country's recent attention to "improving" education especially since the 2000s. The education productivity parameter A_H or the quality of the education stands at a low rate of almost 0.16. Think of human capital as a swimming pool being filled with a hydro pump. If the hydro pump is of a good quality and effective, the additional hour of working that pump is worth that hour spent filling up the pool. Applying this analogy to the Indian situation, we find that an additional hour of education adds relatively little to the Indians' overall stock of human capital.

However, when we look at the time Indians put into their education l_H, we can establish that approximately half of their "time" is dedicated to educating themselves. With an important weight given to education by the government, a relatively high level of effort going towards human capital investment and a low productivity of schooling, one cannot help but think that all the recent investments done in the educational sector are going to waste.

Relationship between Quality of Education and Growth Rate?

After describing the state of education in India, I proceeded with establishing a relationship between the quality of education and the average growth rate of the economy. The purpose of this study would be to test whether or not an increase in the quality of education will have an impact on the average growth rate of the Indian economy, given everything else constant. Moreover, the balanced growth path defined above determines two optimal responses to this structural change:

1. The optimal response of households is spent on education, and
2. The optimal response of the government in adjusting the welfare maximizing level of government spending on education.

The study fixes the government bias for education at the country-specific level of 0.0694. I then proceed with increasing the quality of education by 20 per cent, 40 per cent and 60 per cent. These increases should have an impact on the time spent on education, the education spending share as a per cent in GDP and of course, the average growth rate of the economy. The following results were found:

Table 11.2: Changes in parameters as a result of increases in the quality of Education

Year	*1990*	*2000*	*2010*	*2019*
Increase in A_H	*20%*	*40%*	*60%*	*80%*
l_H	0.5575	0.6014	0.6343	1.0013
t (%)	5.68	6.72	7.65	8.95
Y (%)	5.02	7.54	10.04	11.68

Source: http://en.m.wikipedia.org>wiki (Education in India).

As shown from the table above, an increase in the quality of education has a positive and significant effect on all related to education. By increasing the education from its initial level of almost 16 per cent to 60 per cent, the number of hours spent on education jumps from 0.4967 to 0.6343, an increase of almost 28 per cent. To accommodate that 60 per cent increase in quality of education, the government has to increase its spending on education (as a per cent share of GDP) from 4.5 per cent to almost 8 per cent. But the most important result of all is the positive effect the increase of education has on the average growth rate. By increasing the quality of education by 60 per cent, the average growth rate jumps from 2.49 per cent to 10.04 per cent an increase of almost 303 per cent, 4 times the average growth rate!

However, the quality of education has kept declining in recent years and the number of employable individuals did not meet the market demand for labour. Furthermore, 27 per cent of youth, many of whom come from poor backgrounds, do not compete basic education by age 19.

The academic performance of students from different backgrounds demonstrates inequality. For example, students from urban areas have better access to school and therefore tend to perform better than students from rural areas. The same goes for the performance of male students in relation to female students.

However, education in India has a different value to employers. For example, the secondary level test results are equal to those in Latin America, yet the latter has a much higher income per capita than India. Additionally, students' test scores in India are still below the average of the Organization for Economic Co-operation and Development (OECD). Those numbers are not improving quickly enough to combat labour shortages.

Part III: Conclusion and Recommendations

India has undergone a lot of economic policies that contributed in shaping the India we know today. From a socialist/populist outlook on the economy to an open free market, one can only say that the system Indians are dealing with is nothing short of a "Frankenstein", a hybrid of different policies that lack consistency, continuity and coherence. It is because of the latter reason that we find Indians struggling to improve their socio-economic status (Shelley, 1818:39). They are facing a high level of unemployment (with 18-21% unemployed among the under-25 and with university degrees), a high level of poverty (with 27.5% of the population below the absolute poverty line), complications with receiving high quality medical care to tend to their needs, and above all, a poor quality of education that leaves them unprepared for the requirements of the global and domestic job market (http://en.m.wikipedia.org>wiki).

One of the most important sectors that could actually help alleviate some of the pressure off of the average Indian is education. By education, I not only refer to the schooling system and universities but also include training and skill enhancement programmes to arm the workers with the required and necessary set of skills needed to compete in the domestic and global labour markets. It goes without saying that the quality of education in India is very low hence, Indians have a very low rate of return on education. By analyzing economic growth in India, I was able to establish a relationship between quality of education and average growth rate of the Indian economy.

It was shown that by increasing the quality of education, average growth rate will significantly increase; a 20 per cent increase in the quality of education will lead to an increase of almost 102 per cent in terms of average growth rate! (Ahmed & Narain, 2008:61). However important these results are in linking the quality of education to the growth rate of the economy, they appear very much unbelievable and stand on their own without taking into consideration other factors and sectors in the economy. The results shown above are meant to display how vital an educational reform in India is and how, if properly reformed and the quality of the education provided improved could contribute positively to the growth rate of the economy. The analysis in this chapter determines the impact of an exogenous increase in the "productivity" of the education sector. Given this change, the study determines the welfare maximizing response in government spending on education. This welfare maximizing level internalizes the opportunity cost of the increased taxes associated with more government spending. This is said: the exogenous increase in quality of education ignores what resources may be required to achieve this change. While difficult to quantify, this one time increase in resource use may not be negligible. Therefore, it is advisable that future research expand in order to include other sectors in the Indian economy that might help put the effect of the increase in educational production on the growth rate into a more focused perspective. For now, the question is; how should the government proceed with such a result?

Investments in the educational sector (whether private or public) should be well targeted and aimed at improving the quality of school facilities and not just increase their numbers. Chatterjee (2008:147-158) mentions that state-schools in India lack playgrounds, music programmes, art rooms and even laboratories; they are very rare and even if one crosses paths with such facilities, they are in a very poor shape. Instead of just increasing their numbers, resources should also be directed at increasing the facilities' quality in order to create a conducive educative environment. For example, more equipped laboratories with the necessary tools to help with certain subjects, mainly the sciences.

Another way to increase the quality of education would be to eliminate the concept of "overcrowding". The ratio of students to teachers stands at 40-50:1, which represents a great burden on the teacher who receives a salary of US 281/month (21,000 Indian rupees/month). We find that some teachers—if not all of them—take on a second and even a third job to cover their necessities and be able to live comfortably (especially with a high inflation rate in the economy). This tends to overwork the teachers and increases the likelihood of poor performance in class. Some economists and experts suggest that the main outlook of any educational policy should be on the schooling quality and recognizing the importance of cognitive skills (Alkire & Santos, 2010:25). It does not just lie in expanding the educational system because if the quality remains the same, then any expansion is nothing but a waste of investments and efforts. Possible solutions are various. First, to help reform education and in turn, advance with the labour markets, a qualitative transformation of the institutional framework behind the educational system in India should take place. By quality, I refer to the quality of the curriculum presented to the students, the method of teaching and the cadre of professors and teachers available, and how the students in both schools and universities are able to acquire the skills needed to face the labour market, link education to labour.

One other possible solution could be to revise India's Labour Law of 2003 and set-up an autonomous institution responsible for capacity building throughout India. More investments should be directed to improving technical and vocational education and training. If properly reformed and maintained, on a short and long run basis, employability will improve dramatically and have workers better skilled and trained. However, I cannot stress enough of how important it is to reform the schooling process and the way students in India are being taught. The system is one that depends on the ability of the students to cram for examinations and neglects their ability to analyse, think strategically and logically and create. The students' purpose is to get high enough grades to go to one of the ivy leagues in India because "it is the social decorum". Technical schools are ignored completely although they have the potential of generating high levels of employment and talents.

What we lack in India in terms of education is the vision of developing the youth's abilities and skills, to make them think and analyse, to relate what they are studying for the real life. Education is all about developing a decent and worthy character in the youth rather than developing their ability to cram subjects that will eventually leave them unprepared.

In short, reforming the education correctly will create a ripple effect that will affect the labour market which in turn will have an impact on poverty and inequality. Eventually, growth will be induced and sustained as long as correct education is implemented.

In order to compensate their poor wages, some of the teachers take on private tutoring and according to CAPMAS (India's Central Statistics and Mobilization Agency), over 60 per cent of private investments in education (the households' resources) go to private tutoring (http://www.ft.com>content). The latter has a very negative effect on those students who do not have the capacity to pay for these private lessons in that the teachers themselves tend to go over the material very lightly and superficially so that students would be encouraged to attend these private lessons.

One way to eliminate that loss of resources and better the educative process is to (i) reduce the strain on the teachers with a class capacity of max 20-25 per teacher, (ii) provide incentive to teachers in order to better focus on their work inside the classroom by increasing the salary based on performance evaluation. Government and third-party personal monitor the professors a few times each semester and write a report detailing their in-class work, and (iii) the government should provide high quality training for the teacher in order to eliminate the "unqualified teachers" dilemma.

Some accuse the government of having a tight centralized control over the curriculum across the country. By "centralized control", I mean that the Ministry of Education provides state schools with specific lesson plans and controls the curriculum: what should be included in the material and what should not, what the students should be exposed to and what they should not know. This is done by having government officials visit the classrooms and observe the teachers' in class time. This gives the teachers a very tight space in which they can teach; they cannot go beyond what the material states.

One way to overcome that obstacle would be to have the Ministry of Education loosen the grip on how and what should be taught and focus more on how it should be handled by the teachers. The Ministry should allow the teachers to cover the material in the best way they see fit in order to develop the students' skills, knowledge and way of thinking. Curriculums should be provided by the schools and not by the Ministry as a way to avoid politicizing the content (like when it occurred during Rao's government and post-2014 where examinations had a compulsory examination question where students had to thank the government on its efforts).

Learning in India has become all about examinations and focus entirely on how high up a student can get in terms of grade points. That being said, pedagogical methods and approaches have come to be shaped around helping the students memorize and cram as much information as they can in order to exactly reproduce that information during examinations. Critical thinking, logic analysis, understanding and creativity become a needless luxury in the eyes of the students. Following this track, we can notice that high degrees of concentration and effort are pooled into getting "overrated" grades in the National Examinations (surpassing the 100% at times) in order to get admitted into India's faculties who require at sometimes, a minimum of 98 per cent to be admitted (without further requirement such as language skills). Such faculties include the Faculty of Engineering, Medicine and Pharmacy who have become the main target for any student. The rest of the branches are shunned out especially the technical colleges and vocational training.

Those who fail in being admitted in those high-tier schools face the poor funded, low quality technical colleges where the students face a future of low status. Possible solutions to solve the above-mentioned dilemma would be to:

1. Shift the focus from solely getting high grades to actually understanding the material at hand and developing one's skills

that will serve in the labour market later on. Examinations have become the key determinant of students' future tracks. Instead, each faculty and university should have an admission test that does not depend on the students' performance during the National Examinations. These admission tests would test the students' skills on critical and logical thinking, language, ability to analyze and produce ideas instead of reproducing them.

2. Technical colleges and vocational training are just as important as any other faculty or university in India. Resources should be focused on improving the quality of education in those colleges, and increasing their funding instead of just focusing on the prestigious universities (where only a small per cent of the students end up actually working in their respective fields because of high supply and low demand in engineering and medicine in the country).
3. The third key step to improve these numbers is to provide jobs for graduates in fields that often suffer from unemployment, mainly social science and law graduates. Information regarding careers and majors should be made clear and available to students.
4. Improving education in India will also require reallocation of finances, job description access and encouraged competition between universities. Policies should aim towards including poor students and addressing inequalities and hierarchy issues in the education system.
5. Improving the quality of education in India can also help to develop and diversify the economy. The government aims to bring well-educated and proactive youth into an open, globally-driven market in order to stimulate the economy, though no plans have been announced yet.
6. The techniques suggested by the Indian Human Development Report include improving accreditation status of its universities and integrating different programmes and evaluation methods. In addition to these techniques, universities can be encouraged to use innovative skills and adopt a demand-driven economy. Such changes will encourage graduates to pursue diverse careers, decreasing dependency on foreign labour.

Ever since Prime Minister Nehru's socialist policy, education has been accessible to all Indians, from schools up to higher education. While that may have been an important move in his economical/political agenda, a free access to education has caused a huge burden on the National Accounts of the country. Instead of having a free access to education in all its stages, free access to education should be admissible up till 6th grade (the end of the primary cycle). Afterwards, up to the 12th grade (the end of the secondary cycle); the government covers only a part of the expenses (half-subsidies). However, university access should not be permitted to all. At this point, equal attention should be given to prestigious schools and technical ones. Students with special skills, who excelled in their national examinations and were able to secure a spot in any school (whether it be a scientific or technical one) is eligible for a government backed grant or scholarship. Private scholarships are also encouraged to alleviate the pressure from the government. In the spirit of relating the educative process to the labour markets, faculties and schools of different genres should be encouraged to apply a "Co-Up" programme as a way for students to cover a part of their educational expenses and gain experience working in the field of their study.

Having discussed the possible ways of reforms and the benefits that could come out of it, it is only right to mention the costs mirroring those benefits:

- Training the teachers to become more effective and productive will most certainly demand a reallocation of the government's resources and a review of its national budget to incorporate such trainings effectively. Increasing taxes is one way the government could respond to such a reform. To determine the welfare maximizing tax rate that could incorporate these training costs, an extension of the model used in this chapter could be possible since the tax rate is already incorporated. It is also possible to relate the tax rate the Indian Government wishes to apply to an effective level of education spending in GDP, the government should reallocate its resources in a manner to support a certain level of education spending that should match the tax rate as well as the level of quality needed to be reached. This could also be a very useful extension to this chapter.
- Decreasing the subsidies on education could also be met by an increase in school tuition fees and with higher taxes perceived in the future of this reform, if not handled effectively and in a welfare maximizing way, the reform could backfire with poorer families taking their children out of school given the high costs they will incur.

- Decreasing the student-teacher ratio will require a more deepened and heavier infrastructure to support that decrease. Seeing as how the numbers of students in India are huge, more schools and classes could be needed to support that cut and even, several school shifts which is already a norm in government schools. Aside the fact that this will be a burden on the government's budget, the productivity level of one teacher will decrease as the shifts pass by and if there are several other teachers teaching the same subject and covering the different shifts in the school day, this will mean more wages and therefore, an increase in costs.

REFERENCES

Ahmed, A. & Narnia, A. (2008). Towards Understanding Development in Lagging Region of India. Paper presented at the conference on growth and Development in Lagging Regions of India. Administrative Staff College of India. Hyderabad. India.

Alkire, S. and Santos, M.E. (July, 2010). Oxford Poverty and Human Development Initiative. UK.1-8. www.ophi.org.uk

Ansari, M.I. and Singh, S.K. (1997). "Public Spending on Education and Economic Growth in India: Evidence from VAR Modelling". *Indian Journal of Applied Economics,* 6(2). 43-64.

Chatterjee, M. (2008). Education and Economic Development in India. University of Dundee, Department of Economic Studies. http://ideas.repec.org> dun>dpaper.

Dutta, P.V. (2006). Returns to Education: New Evidence for India. *Education Economics,* 14 (4), 431-451.

Employment Trends in India. 32.1 Post Independence. Mospi.nic.in>default> files.

Goel, S.C. (June, 1974). *Education and Economic Growth in India.* Vol: 10, No. 2. 147-158. Taylor and Francis Ltd, JSTOR. http://www.jstor.org/stable/ 3098057.

India revises growth data as concern over official statistics mounts. (3 January, 2019) *Financial Times.* http://www.ft.com>content.

Krishnankutty, Ravish and Chakraborty, K.S. (December 2012). *Education and Economic Growth in India.* Indra Gandhi National Open University, Kolkata Regional Centre,/CFA/University Tripura. India.http://mpra,ub.uni-muenchen.de/485&4/

Kunda, A. and Mohan, P.C. (2008). *Employment and Inequality Outcomes in India.* JNU. Delhi. India. http://www.oecd.org>emp.

Pradhan, R.P. (2009). "Education and Economic growth in India: Using Error Correction Modeling", *International Research Journal of Finance and Economics.* 25, 139-147.

Self, S. and Grabowski, R. (2003). "Does Education at all levels cause growth? India, a case study". *Economic of Education Review,* 23(1), 47-55.

Shelley, M. (January 1, 1818). *Frankenstein and The Modern Prometheus.* Vol. 3. Lacking ton, Hughes Harding, Mavor & Jones, UK.

Sreenivasulu, E. (Jan-Feb, 2013). "Role and Importance of Education for Effective Growth of Indian Economy: An Overview." *Journal of Humanities and Social Science.* Vol 7, Issue 5. 32-35. www.iosrjournals.org.

Svickauskas, L. (1975). "The Productivity of Cities." *Quarterly Journal of Economics.* 89. 393-413.

The Global Competitiveness Report-2019, World Economic Forum. Geneva, Switzerland. www.weforum.org>docs.

What is India's rank in the world education system rankings? http://www.qura.com (July 23, 2018).

Education in India. http://en.m.wikipedia.org>wiki.

12
Education as an Investment

Rajni Bala

Introduction

An Investment in Knowledge Pays the Best Interest.

—*Benjamin Franklin*

Education is the most powerful weapon which we can use to change the world. Education in every sense is one of the fundamental of development. No country can achieve sustainable economic development without substantial investment in human capital. Education enrich the understanding level of people about themselves and world. It improves the quality of their lives and leads them to broad social benefits to individuals and society. There is a strong bond between education and economic development. Without education, economic development is impossible. It has been rightly said, "With majority of the population remaining uneducated, it is a futile attempt to commence economic development programme." It is utmost necessary to have educated and skilled workers for the purpose of economic development. The role of education in economic growth has both quantity and quality dimensions. Educational innovations and research are necessary and should be encouraged. Education has the power to improve the efficiency of the persons, which leads our nation to the prosperity and growth of national income. In the present chapter we shall study education as an investment but before this the meaning of education and economics must be clear to us. Here are some of the definitions of education and economics, through which we will be able to understand both the concept clearly.

Definitions of Education

Zakir Hussain: "Education is the work of whole life. It begins from the time of birth and continues till the last moment of death."

John Dewey: "Education is the development of all those capacities in the individual which enables him to control his environment and fulfil his possibilities."

T.P. Nunn: "Education is the complete development of individuality so that man can make an original contribution of human life to his best capacity."

Above given definitions explain us that the main work of education is complete development. Man should be careful about all the aspects of education, i.e. physical, mental, aesthetic, social, spiritual and as well as economic. Education is a fundamental driver of personal, national and global development.

Definitions of Economics

Dr. Alfred Marshall: "Economics is a study of man`s action in the ordinary business of life, it enquires how he gets his income and how he use it."

Beveridge: "Economics is the study of the general method, by which men cooperate to meet their material needs."

Pigou: "Economics deals with that part of social welfare that can be brought directly or indirectly into relation with the measuring rod of money."

Along with above given definitions, Adam Smith, father of Economics described Economics as "An enquiry into the nature and causes of wealth of nations." A number of distinguished economists gave the definitions of economics in their own words but it is clear that economics is a systematic body of knowledge. Knowledge means education, which are non-material economic goods. It is service rendered to satisfy a human want. It is limited and capable of being allocated to individuals.

Economic Aspects of Educaion

Education raises people's productivity and creativity and promotes entrepreneurship and technological advances. It plays a very crucial role in securing economic and social progress. Following points explain the economic aspects of education:

1. *Education as Economic Good:* A 'good' can be included under the scope of economic good only when its availability is limited and it is capable of allocation. Education is a non-material good. It is also a producer's and consumer's good. Education in the form of producer's good is acquired for the purpose of becoming a teacher, lawyer, engineer of mechanic or for any other profession. At the same time, it is consumer by those who receive it in the satisfaction of some for their wants. Again, education becomes a consumer's good when the purpose of acquiring knowledge is to enrich a person's life by increasing his or her capacity to use, enjoy or appreciate any material or non-material good that satisfies human want.

2. *Education as Industry*: A country's government spends its gross national income on different sectors of the economy, such as agriculture, industry and education every year expecting more returns than the previous year. The share of education is increasing every year in both developed and developing countries. Thus, education is indeed a "growth industry" which provides employment and services needed by the total economy as any other industry contributes to the gross national product to the country. It contributes substantially to the total economy of the country, and without it the economy would be all too poor.

3. Education as Human Capital: Capital is anything that involves costs but yields a stream of income over time. It is the sky to the production of income and consequently to economic growth. Education is considered as human capital and human capital can be described as the knowledge, abilities and skills of a individual, acquired through education, training and experience, which help the later to be more productive and thus improve his potential income earning. Ismael (1998), Becker (1964) and Mincer (1974) have emphasized on the fact, that by investing in human beings, we will gain some forms of benefits in the future. Thus, education as human capital is one of the most important components of sustainable economic development of a country. It plays a significant role in the economic development of any nation. It provides individuals with the required abilities for various kinds of works. The ability and capacity of an educated individual gets boosted so much so that whatever has been spent on his education, he has the capacity to produce more money than that. Education is a vital item of capital formation on which future productivity of a nation depends. On the whole, it can be said that human capital is a capital in the form of intellectual power which plays the most significant role in the increased production and increased income. Every country's development depend upon two factors, the first is natural resources and the latter is human capital.

Interlinkage between Education and Socio-Economic Variables

The education has several economic dimensions which are recognized by thinkers in India since long. For example, the eminent Sanskrit poet Bharthari termed education as indestructible and concealed wealth having significant use, value and exchange value. Economics of education as a discipline was born after 1930s when the Russian economist Strumlin estimated economic returns to education or more specifically after 1960s when on 28 December, 1960, T.W. Shultz presented his Presidential Address to the American Economic Association highlighting the economic contributions of education. Series of studies on estimating the economic value of education strengthened the foundations of this new discipline. The reciprocal linkage between economic variables and education also widened the scope of discipline.

It is well established that improvements in education are associated with long-term improvements in economic performance. There are three broad theories about how education influences economic performance:

- The basic human capital approach is that education improves the overall skills and abilities of the workforce, leading to greater productivity and improved ability to use existing technology and thus contributing to economic growth.
- The innovation approach links education to improving the capacity of the economy to develop new ideas and technologies.
- An extension of this is the knowledge transfer approach, which sees education as a means of spreading the knowledge needed to apply new ideas and make use of new technologies.

However, there is an important question as whether there is a casual link between education and economics and if so, in which direction. In general education and economics are likely to be interlinked. Having a more educated workforce enables firms to take advantage of new economic opportunities, leading to improved performance. Also, economic growth can lead to greater national and personal wealth, which increases the resources available and opportunities for education.

Economic Value of Education

Education contributes to worker's productivity and hence to aggregate productivity of the economy. Education can, therefore, be legitimately treated as a produced means of production or capital. A person with education can said to be endowed with educational capital. But, is educational capital is more analogy? Can this capital be clearly defined and measured?

Like any other capital input, educational capital can be defined and measured from two points of view: (a) in terms of cost of creating that capital, and (b) in terms of economic value created by the capital. The two measures do not necessarily lead to the same value. And large cost approach has been adopted for estimating the educational capital.

Education as An Investment

Education is the best investment. There is no better investment of your/our time and resources than education. Better jobs, more rewarding work, higher income, intellectual stimulation and understanding are the benefits of education rise after the course has been completed. The fact is that showing investment after individuals monetary rates of returns that are comparable to those received from other forms on investment. In fact, education is an essential investment where return are in the form of useful, dynamic and efficient citizen. Education also has investment value, those who acquire additional schooling earn more over lifetime achieve higher level of employment or more satisfying carriers. Investment in education makes an individual more informed and socially active citizen. On the whole, investment in education contributes more to national growth. Following points will help us to make clear how education is the best investment?

- ***Investment in education is a key for any prosperous society:*** Education is the best investment, one can make because it is the key for prosperity. An individual as well as a society or nation can be prosperous by getting or providing the right education to build the future of its country people.
- ***It is the investment with greatest returns:*** An investment in education always pays the greatest or highest returns. It also pays the best dividends that last for generation. An investment in knowledge pays the best interests also. In the words of Brad

Henry, an American politician, "No other investment yields as great a return as the investment in education. An educated workforce is the foundation of every community and the failure of every economy. Education is the key to a better economy and a controlled population."

- ***It improves the performance of people:*** Education is the better solution for the good lifestyle. It improves the performance of people. It improves the quality of their lives and leads to broad social and economic benefits to individuals and society. Investment in education plays a very crucial role in securing economic and social progress and improving income distribution.
- ***It increases the productivity:*** It is a fact well known that the more degrees you have better would be your economic performance. There is a deep connection between education and productivity and in this age where there is competition at every turn; education is what will help an industry and subsequently a nation to flourish.
- ***Investing in education means investing in yourself:*** In the words of Warren Buffet, "Investing in yourself is the best thing you can do. Anything that improves your own talents; nobody can tax it or take it away from you. They can run up huge deficits and the dollar can become worth far less. You can have all kinds of things happen. But if you've got talent yourself and you have maximized your talent, you have got a tremendous asset that can return ten-fold." It means if there is something essential for you to lead a happy, fulfilled life, something you don't quite know much about it, and your ultimate goal should be to upgrade your knowledge. Investing in education is investing in yourself and it is always the best start. Education opens the doors to jobs that they pay more, people with more education enjoy lower unemployment rates, it's important to pick the right major and invest wisely.
- ***It helps to build more powerful societies:*** Education has the power to put people on the path towards good health, empowerment and employment. Education can make a lasting difference in children's lives. It can be used for the upliftment of society since it helps elevate the social and economic conditions in the marginalized sections of society.
- ***Investment in education turns weakness into strength:*** Education helps to turn weakness into strength. Education gives

us the confidence to stand for ourselves. It improves our decision making capabilities, makes us mobile and gives us access to social networks. Many researchers have proven that in countries where women are subjected to gender bias, education helped them to stand up against marital violence, improved their capabilities and helped them to take charge of their own lives.

- ***Investment in education provides higher earning throughout life:*** The United States Department of Labour reports that job requiring a higher level of education and skills pay more attractive wages. When job requires a certain level of skill and expertise, employers will pay handsomely to make sure they attract people who can do the job. It is a real fact which can be seen in India as well as other developing countries also. Individuals having higher degrees are earning higher amounts and respectable positions with attractive vocation policies and other perks.

Alan B. Krueger is a highly respected economics professor at Princeton. He presents evidence showing that additional education will rise individual earning by ten per cent. This expert's opinion is verified by United States Census data showing that people with master's degree earn 15 per cent more than their peers. Modern employers are looking at skills and education level, and they are willing to pay more to have those skills at their disposal.

- ***Investment in education increases the self-confidence:*** An education is intangible and invaluable. Even if you lose your house, your car, your gold or any other material objects, no one can take the education away from you. You will still have your skills and those skills can carry you through your life. A higher degree gives you confidence. That simple piece of paper is more than a decoration for the wall of your professional office. It is your personal confirmation that you are smart, capable and worthy. The investment in education always gives positive returns in the form of self-satisfaction and self-confidence that carries us through life.
- ***Investment in education produces well-rounded citizens:*** Higher educational degree produces citizens who are intelligent, well spoken and well-rounded. Studies show that individuals having higher educational degrees are more likely to see the big

picture, so they are more inclined to save money and invest in their future. They enjoy more hobbies and are perceptive consumers who make more educated decisions. Educational institutions prepare people for life as they learn how to juggle schedules, manage their money and interact with people with whom they may not always agree. The experience helps students learn how to strive for more, reach for more and accomplish amazing things.

Yoka Brandt, Deputy Executive, Director of UNICEF says that education can make a lasting difference in children's lives but education is not just good for children. It is good for nations. Investing in education is not just the right thing to do, it is smart economics. Education can put people on a path towards good health; empowerment and employment. It can help to build more powerful societies and the benefits of girl's education extends to their own children who are often healthier and more educated because their mothers went to school. Brandt added that we have known for a long time that education can break the cycle of persistent poverty and disadvantages for children, families and countries. But to do this, government and the private sector need to not only invest more, but also invest more wisely in education. This is true in the context of Indian children and our families.

Benefits of Investing in Education

People, who learn to read, write and count will provide a better future for their families as well as their country. With improved education so many other areas are positively affected. In short, education has the power to make the world a better place. Following are the benefits of investing in education which are extracted from the article "*The Benefits of Education*" (http: www.globalpartnership.org)

- *It reduces poverty:* 420 million people would be lifted out of poverty with a secondary education, thus producing the number of poor worldwide by more than half.
- *It increases income:* One extra year of schooling increases an individual's earning up to 10 per cent.
- *It makes people healthier:* Children of educated mothers are more likely to be vaccinated and less likely to be stunted because of malnourishment.

- *It boosts economic growth:* Each individual year of schooling raises average annual gross domestic product (GDP) growth by 0.37 per cent.
- *It saves children's lives:* A child whose mother can read is 50 per cent more likely to live past the age of five.
- *It fosters peace:* If the enrolment rate for secondary schooling is 10 per cent points higher than the average, the risk is reduced about 3 per cent points. Education is the foundation of peace and prosperity.
- *It reduces fertility rates:* One additional year of school reduces the probability of becoming a mother by 7.3 per cent for women who have completed at least her primary education.
- *It prevents disaster related deaths:* Universalizing upper secondary education by 2030 would prevent 2,00,000 disaster related deaths in the 20 years that follow.
- *It reduces child marriage:* Each year of secondary education reduces the likelihood of marrying as a child by five per cent points or more.
- *It reduces maternal deaths:* If all mothers completed primary education, maternal deaths would be reduced by two-thirds saving 1,89,000 lives.
- *It promotes gender equality:* One additional school year can increase a woman's earning by 10 to 20 per cent.
- *It combats HIV and AIDS:* Women with post-primary education are five times more likely than illiterate women to be educated on the topic of HIV and AIDS.

Education is a way of forming an attitude of openness and adaptability because the whole life is learning, therefore, education should not end. A wide dissemination in a globle knowledge economy is due to the fact that higher education is a major contribution to economic competitiveness, which made the quality tertiary education to become an ever more important objective in both developing countries as well as in the industrialized ones. Attaining a degree in any field is often considered a rite old passage, and is a sign of commitment, a vested interest in self-improvement and the willingness to take your education and abilities to new heights. By making the investment in education, especially students not only learn the skills but also have the opportunity to better expand their skill-set and learning potential. By investing in education students open not just one door but the entire pathway to new opportunities and professional ventures. There is no doubt that investing in education produces a private benefit. Individuals who are more educated are healthier, more likely to get good jobs and pay higher taxes, less likely to participate in risky behaviours and more civically and socially engaged. But investment in education produces public benefits as well. Education is truly one of the most powerful instruments for reducing poverty and inequality and it sets the foundation for sustained economic growth.

Returns to Education in India

Whether to continue education beyond a certain level or to enter the labour market is an important investment decision. According to Human Capital Investment theory, an individual would prefer to attend the school only if the present value of the expected benefits from schooling exceeds that of they expected costs (Becker, 1993). Thus an important determinant of the demand for schooling or training is its expected benefits. Since the benefits depend upon the quality and quantity of an individual's labour input, which in turn depends upon the human capital acquired during schooling, the education-wage relationship can be used to measure the returns to schooling.

Investment in education can be evaluated in terms of their rates of return. In general, returns to education are higher for lower levels of education for example primary and decline with the level of education. This is due to the low cost of primary education relation to other level of education and considerable productivity differentiates between primary graduates and illiterate persons. Primary education also prides the basis for further education.

Investment in education is an investment in the future education opportunities yield enormous return for both students and societies. Investing in education may also be one of the keys to ending warfare and global conflict. Having a more educated population is good for economy. Especially investment in early childhood and lower secondary education is of utmost importance in influencing equality and equity. Investment in education benefits the economy because it enables a greater proportion of the population to gain skills that benefit the industry, allowing more people to become employed. A more educated society overall has lower crime rates, more equal economy and increased civic engagement. Education can also help people become more responsible adults. Education also benefits the economy through many saved on policing, mass incarceration and public safety. The Universal Declaration of Human

Rights declares Education as a basic human need. It enables people to advocate for themselves and encourages them to hold their communities. Education is also shown to be an empowering force, in general, increasing tolerance for other races and religions generating a sense of civic duty and responsibility and increasing concern for the environment and climate change. Above all, returns on investment in education are a useful indicator of the productivity of education and they serve as a incentive for individuals to invest in their own human capital.

Conclusion

Education is an investment worth making since it directly impacts lifelong earnings. However, occupation, race and gender play significant roles in one's potential earnings. Economics look at education as an investment that generates higher future earnings because more educated people are more productive and earn higher wages. Adam Smith opens the wealth of nations (1770) by stating that, "the greatest improvement in the production powers of labour and the greater part of the skill, dexterity and judgement with which it is anywhere directly applied, seem to have been the effects of the division of labour." We discussed earlier that education is a type of "human capital" when individuals spend resources on themselves or their children and these expenditures improve their future economic opportunities, we say that they are investing in human capital. So many examples of different types of human capital may be given such as health, formal schooling, technical training, professional training and informed learning. We must invest more effectively and equitably so that the children who are in need have access to quality learning. Education is an investment and one of the most critical investments we can make. This is true not only for India but for countries around the world. Venezuela and Philippines introduced Education 360 degree programmer to put an end to poverty through the holistic and systematic education plan. This type of programmer must be launched by our government because education is one of the major pillars of governance. It is holistic and systematic approach to uplifting the quality of local basic education. This type of programmers will provide platforms for participants (acting governance to flourish). Residents or citizens will be recognized as equal partners in policy formulation, planning and implementation. Education is indeed a most powerful investment for future. There is no time to lose. Educated children are at the heart of healthy, productive and prosperous societies. If that is the future, we want tomorrow we must invest today.

REFERENCES

Becker, G.S. (1976). *The Economics Approach to Human Behaviour*. University of Chicago Press Chicago IL.

Bellfield, Clive R. (Ed.); (2006). *Modern Classics in the Economics of Education*, Elger.

Blang, Mark, (1985), "Where are we now in the Economics of Education?" *Economics of Education Review* 4(1).

Chakraborty, A.K. (2007). *Principal and Practice of Education*; R. Lal Book Depot.

Education is considered as an Investment Economics—Essay. Retrieved from https//www.ukessays.com.

Janet, C. (1999). "Investing in Our Children: What we know and don't know about the costs and benefits of easy childhood Interventions", *Journal of Health Politics, Policy and Law*. 24 (6).

Paul, Schutz (1988). "Education Investments and Return", In *Handbook of Development Economics*. Hollis Chancery and T.N. Srinivasan (eds.) Amsterdam: North-Holland.

Schnittker, J., (2004), "Education and the changing shape of the Income Gradient in health". *Journal of Health and Social Behaviour* 45(3).

Schultz, T.W. (1960). "Capital Formalin by Education", *Journal of Political Economy*, December, p. 583.

Stephen A., Hoenack, (1996). "The Economics of Education in Developing Countries. An Assessment of the State of the Art", *Economics of Education Review* 12(4).

The benefits of education global partnership.org.

Tilak, Jandhyala B.G. (1987). *The Economics of Inequality in Education*. New Delhi: Sage Publication.

13
Concept and Types of Costs of Education

M.P. Tripathi

This chapter makes an attempt to highlight the concept of the costs of education and the various types of the costs of education. The chapter comprises: What is cost? How education is an investment? What is the concept of the costs of education? What are the different types of the costs of education? Countries worldwide are not only searching for alternative ways of financing education, but are also paying attention to reduce unit costs. Educational investment involves both social and private costs. The great interest by the World Bank and UNESCO to develop methodological guidelines for the estimation and analysis of costs has increased interest and the need to clarify methods of defining and measuring costs. The chapter ends with the description of importance of costs in educational planning, the complementary role between private and institutional costs and the nature of production process in the educational system, regional variations in the costs of education, the relationship between costs of education and economic development with some fruitful suggestions.

Economics of Education

The modern analysis of the Economics of Education had its birth with Adam Smith and Theodore Schultz's address to the American Economic Association in December 1960 on the notion that education can be regarded as an investment in human capital analogous to investments in physical capital. Individuals decide to invest in their own education, just as firms or businesses decide to invest in new machinery or products. The study of the Economics of Education has expanded considerably in scope over the last five decades emphasizing the role that education has to play in raising individuals' productivity providing estimates for the rate of return to education. Such estimates have been influencing in shaping the educational policies by international organizations such as the World Bank, UNESCO. The economics of education is a rapidly growing and evolving field that applies a diverse arrangement of economic theories, models and quantitative methodologies to understand and improve the performance of education systems.

Economics of Education is a study of human behaviour about schooling. The Economics of Education is the study of economic issues relating to education including the demand of the education, the financing of education and the comparative efficiency of various educational programmes and policies. Economics of Education is the application of the economic principles, concepts and laws to the process of education. Adam Smith's statement that "A man educated at the expense of much labour and time to any of those employments which require extraordinary dexterity and skills, may be compared to one of those expensive machines. The work which he learns to perform, it must be expected, over and above the usual wages of common labour, will replace to him the whole expense of his education."

Education as Investment

Human capital is one of the most important components of sustainable economic development of a country. Human capital can be described as the knowledge, abilities and skills of an individual, acquired through education and experiences. Education is considered as an investment in human capital. Education is the most powerful investment in the world. There were debates by researchers over whether education has a positive, negative or no relationship at all with the economic growth of a country. Barro (1991) finds that education has a positive and significant impact on economic growth. He observes that any rise in enrolment rate, raises GDP too. "Investing in education is critical to fostering growth and innovation for generations to come", said Susan Whiting, Vice Chairperson at Nielsen Global Survey of Educational Aspirations. The Draft New Education Policy 2019 puts an objective of increasing public spending on education, from the current 3.5 per cent of GDP to 6 per cent of GDP. The policy draft acknowledges the importance of investing in public institutions. The policy draft focuses on "Education, in Indian context, should be considered a public good and there is a need for greater public investment in the sector." For this, the government should use its fiscal powers to:

- Incentivize investments in education sector.
- Creation of specialized lending institutions not for education sector.
- Provide tax exemptions to minimize the costs of education.
- Creation of tax free bonds/securities for education that bring down the costs of education.
- Provide tax exemptions to increase savings for educational expenses.
- To empower citizens with requisite skills for Right to Occupation and Right to Livelihood.
- Allow tax exemptions for alumni donations to educational institutions.
- Sensitization about environmental protection and waste management.

Costs

In business and accounting, costs are the monetary value that has been spent by a company in order to produce something or creation of goods or services. The costs of any economic activity could be measured from numerous angles and perspectives. Costs are, also, amounts that have to be paid or spent to buy or obtain something or obtain services. Costs are expenditure required to produce or sell a product or get an asset ready for normal use. Every factor of production has an associated cost. Costs can have different relationships to output. Costs are used in different business applications, such as financial accounting, cost accounting, budgeting, capital budgeting and valuation. The cost of a product from the buyer's point of view is called the price. Expenditure can be expressed only in monetary terms, while costs can be expressed in monetary as well in real or physical terms. That part of expenses which has some relationship with the production process and the output only can be referred to as costs; and that part which has no such relationship with the production process and output is merely expenditure. To the economists, costs include the imputed value of goods and services, depreciation etc. For cost reduction in education sector, outsourcing to other companies for the tasks that are not directly linked to the schools target activities, such as cleaning, security, IT, food, etc., is to be made mandatory. Water and electricity must be used responsibly. Students are not always aware of this, so the school management needs to resort to modern equipments such as LED bulbs and electronic faucets to avoid wastage.

Categorization of Costs

There are different ways to categorize costs according to different criterion used. In order to understand the general concept of costs, it is important to know the following different types of costs:

A. Classification of the Costs based on the Nature of the Costs

1. Fixed costs

Fixed costs are those which do not vary with the changing of output. Fixed costs are also called overhead costs. The business incurs them regardless of the level of production. Examples of these include payment of rent, depreciation, taxes, interest on a loan, insurance, the cost of building, insurance and legal bills.

2. Variable Costs

These costs will fluctuate depending upon the output that the business generates. Less production will cost fewer expenses, and *vice versa.* Expenses on the purchase of raw material and payment of wages are examples of variable costs. For example, if you produce more cars, you have to use more raw materials. Labour and material costs are usually variable costs that change as the volume of production changes.

B. Classification of the Cost is based on the Nature of Expenses

1. Outlay Costs

The actual expenses incurred by the entrepreneur in employing inputs are called outlay costs. These include costs on payment of wages, rent, electricity or fuel charges, raw materials etc. We have to treat these as general expenses for the business.

2. Opportunity Costs

Opportunity costs are incomes from the next best alternative that is foregone when the entrepreneur makes certain choices for business. For example, the entrepreneur could have earned a salary as he worked for others instead of spending time on his own business and the money to invest in developing. Opportunity cost refers to the loss of earnings due to opportunities foregone due to scarcity of resources.

C. Classification of the Cost in Terms of Treatment

1. Accounting Costs

Accounting costs are those for which the entrepreneur pays direct cash for procuring resources for production. It is also referred as actual direct costs. These include costs of the price paid for raw materials and machines, wages paid to workers, electricity charges, the cost incurred in hiring or purchasing a building or plot etc. Accounting costs are treated as expenses. Accounting costs include variable and fixed costs.

2. Economic Costs

There are certain costs which are not included in Accounting Costs. These include money which the entrepreneur forgoes but would have earned had he invested his time, efforts and investments in other ventures. For example, the entrepreneur would have earned an income had he sold his services to others instead of working on his own business. Economic costs include both the actual direct costs (accounting costs) plus the opportunity costs.

D. Classification of the Cost in Terms of Traceability

1. Direct Costs

Direct Costs are related to a specific process or product. They are also called Traceable Costs as we can directly trace them to a particular activity, product or process. They can vary with changes in the activity or product. Examples of direct costs include manufacturing costs relating to production, customer acquisition costs pertaining to sales etc.

2. Indirect Costs

Indirect Costs, also, known as untraceable costs, are those which do not directly relate to a specific activity or component of the business, e.g. an increase in charges of electricity or taxes payable on income. Although we cannot trace indirect costs, they are important because they affect overall profitability.

E. Classification of the Cost in Terms of the Purpose

1. Incremental Costs

Incremental Costs are those costs which are incurred when the business makes a policy decision, e.g. change of product line, acquisition of new customers and upgradation of machinery to increase output.

2. Sunk Costs

Sunk Costs are those costs that have been incurred and cannot be recouped. Sunk costs are costs which the entrepreneur has already incurred and he cannot recover them again. These costs include money spent on advertising, conducting research and acquiring machinery. One can never claim these costs back.

F. Classification of the Cost in Terms of Payers

1. Private Costs

As the name suggests, Private Costs are the costs you pay. These costs are incurred by the business in furtherance of its own objectives. Entrepreneurs spend them for their own private and business interests, e.g. costs of advertising.

2. Social Costs

Social Costs, also referred to as True Costs, is the total cost to society. It is the society that bears social costs for private interests and expenses of the business. These include social resources for which the firm does not incur expenses, like atmosphere, water resources and environmental pollution. It includes the private costs and the external costs.

G. Other Classifications

1. *Marginal Costs:* Marginal Cost is the cost of producing an extra

unit. If the total cost of 5 units is 4000 and the total cost of 6 units is 4600. The marginal cost of the 6th unit is 600.

2. *Avoidable Costs:* Avoidable Costs, also known as escapable costs, which can be avoided.
3. *Explicit Costs:* These are costs that a firm directly pays for and can be seen on the accounting sheet. Explicit costs can be variable or fixed.
4. *Implicit Costs:* These are opportunity costs, which do not necessarily appear on balance sheet but affect the firm or business.
5. *External Costs:* This is the cost imposed on a third party.
6. *Individual Costs:* Individual Costs are those costs that are directly visible. Individual costs are of two types: Indirect and Direct costs.

Costs of Education

Human capital in the form of education shares many characteristics with physical capital. Both require an investment to create. Costs of Education are the measures of what a student, an institution of learning or the society has to spend for educating an individual or a group of individuals. Costs of Education may he incurred by producers (educational institutions) or consumers (students and their parents). The Costs of Education refer to the costs incurred by the governments or the private sectors for providing education to the citizens.

Categorization of Costs of Education

The way in which costs are classified varies considerably; likewise classification of Costs of Education varies. Though the World Bank and UNESCO have attempted to standardize definitions and ways of measuring costs, but not standardized methods of classifying Costs of Education. There is no standard terminology for the classification of Costs of Education. There is, however, some agreement on classification into distinct categories such as economic costs, direct costs and indirect costs, recurrent costs and capital costs, variable costs and fixed costs, unit costs and marginal costs, public costs and private costs, personnel costs and non-personnel costs, instructional costs and non-instructional costs. Some of the terminologies that are commonly encountered in educational costs analysis include:

(a) Opportunity Costs

Opportunity Costs component is very useful during the process of measuring the economic profitability of any service or business or investment. Attempting to rely solely on financial expenditures to estimate Costs of Education is inadequate. The term opportunity cost takes cognizance of the fact that each investment option involves a sacrifice of alternative opportunities to use resources. This sacrifice could be either for the present consumption or for some other form of investment. The opportunity cost of a commodity/service is the value of the next best alternative sacrifice made, in order to obtain that commodity/service. Therefore, there could be many alternatives to give up in order to get what is desired, the opportunity cost of a decision is the value of the most desirable alternative to be given up to get what is needed.

(b) Recurrent Costs

As the term implies, this is a cost that recurs regularly during the business and covers expenditures on goods and services that bring immediate and short-lived benefits. Thus, expenditure on consumable goods such as: infrastructures, resources and teachers' salaries fall under recurrent expenditure. The recurrent costs encompass what is incurred on personnel services and consumable supplies within one fiscal/financial year recurrently.

(c) Capital Costs

These costs relate to more durable items, e.g. Land, Buildings, and Equipment etc. These costs render useful services over a longer period of years if properly maintained.

(d) Social Costs or Public Costs

Social Costs or Public Costs are those costs that are financed by the governments, generally on the basis of taxes, loans, grants and other public revenue.

(e) Private Costs

These are those costs that are borne by individual students and their families. Examples of private costs include: school fees, purchase of uniforms, textbooks, upkeep and other costs.

(f) Fixed Costs

This cost is also referred to as an indirect cost. A fixed cost is that part of the cost which does not vary as the output changes. Examples include the rent of a building, wages of permanent employees and the cost of installing a broadcasting network among others.

(g) Variable Costs

A Variable Cost is a cost which varies with the change in the level of output. That is, if more output is produced, more variable costs are incurred and *vice versa*. This cost is also called a direct cost. When there are no operations, the variable cost is zero. Examples of variable costs include: wages of temporary workers, stationery expenses, publicity expenses and raw materials among others. However, it is important to note that in the long run, all costs are variable.

(h) Total Costs

This is the overall cost incurred for the production of a specific number of units of an education system. This cost can be expressed in terms of fixed costs and variable costs as shown below:

$$\text{Total Cost} = \text{Fixed Cost} + \text{Variable Cost}$$

(i) Average Costs

This is the cost incurred in producing a single unit of an education system. In an educational institution or setting, average costs indicate the amount of money or resources devoted to each student in the existing system. Average costs can further be distinguished into the following three categories, namely, Average total cost, Average variable cost and Average fixed cost.

(j) Marginal Costs

Marginal Costs refer to the extra expenditure incurred when one additional unit of a commodity is produced, i.e. one additional student is benefited. That is, it is an increase in the total cost due to the production of the last unit of the individual. In an educational setting, the marginal cost of enrolling an additional pupil/student is the extra expenditure incurred when the total enrolment is increased by one. In practice, it is often extremely difficult to identify marginal costs. However, the concept is important since marginal costs indicate the cost consequences of expanding the system/institution.

Private Cost of Education: The Issues

Unit costs of education means costs per unit learner, i.e. per student, per graduate, per credit, per total number of learners enrolled in a course in a particular financial year. Private costs, also referred to as Individual costs of education, are those costs of education incurred by a learner or by parents or guardians or by the family as a whole, i.e. the part of investments which are incurred either by the parents or students or both in a financial year for acquiring education. Private Costs of education may be classified into two broad categories: (i) Academic costs and (ii) Maintenance costs. Academic costs refers to the expenses on the items such as pre-admission cost, fee and funds given to the institution, private coaching fee, cost of books, stationery, project/thesis work, study tours and other instrumental to getting oneself formally educated. Maintenance costs, also known as the incidental costs, include expenses incurred on clothing, transport, boarding and lodging and other sundry expenses. Institutional costs refer to the expenses by an educational institution. There are number of issues related to the measurement of private costs of education. The students who belong to economically well-off and higher income groups spent larger amount than that of the lower income and low occupation groups of parents. It is not so easy to get the higher and professional education for the students belonging to the weaker sections of the society even in the present when the availability of higher and professional education is the public responsibility. Though, Governments contribute to the private costs borne by the students who belong to the weaker sections of society. The rising level of private costs of education has raised the equity issues in a very serious manner.

Difficulties in Cost Estimation in Education

Due to broader nature and span of the education, it is very difficult to estimate the costs of education. The main difficulties in estimation of costs in education are:

(i) Budgetary data are often inadequate for a detailed study of costs because they only cover expenditures rather than real resources or opportunity costs.
(ii) In most cases budgetary data only present the planned or provisional budget estimates rather than the actual expenditures.
(iii) There is apparent confusion in distinguishing between recurrent and capital expenditure.
(iv) Treatment of capital expenditure.
(v) Lack of uniformity in the methodologies used in analyzing costs.

Determinants of Educational Costs

Educational systems, throughout the world, have become so complex that they require detailed investigations into their various dimensions. Costs are one of such important dimensions. As education system has been viewed as an investment, it becomes more important to estimate the costs of education cautiously. It is necessary to attempt an analytical framework for the study of costs of education by presenting a brief discussion on the importance of analysis of costs of education in educational planning, organizing and development including some discussions on the different aspects of estimation of the costs of education. The estimation should describe the nature and quality of data available for educational planners and researchers, with particular reference to costs and financial aspects of education by highlighting the importance of analysis of costs of education in educational planning following a description on the taxonomy of costs of education. The costs incurred in imparting or acquiring education are mainly determined by the following factors:

(a) Educational demand,
(b) Educational technologies,
(c) Teacher salary structures and allowances,
(d) Drop-out and repeater rates,
(e) Utilization rates, and
(f) Market forces.

Conclusion

To ensure that educational costs are securely under control, educational planners should determine the amount of unused capacity in the existing institutions using the principle of Maximum use of Resources. For educational institutions to operate cost-effectively, it is important for them to operate within the economies of state. This can be achieved by adopting the strategies like: (i) Consolidating schools by reducing unit costs without disturbing the teacher-students ratio, (ii) In-Service courses for teachers who can teach more than one subject, (iii) Employing teachers who can teach more than one subject, (iv) Enhancing the utilization of the existing facilities/capacities, (v) Increasing the number of streams, (vi) Introduction of boarding schools to enable the students to use common educational facilities or equipments, (vii) Making school purchases in bulk, (viii) Incorporate multimedia in instruction and other process of education, (ix) Institutions should collaborate to jointly use expensive facilities, equipments and exchange of manpower. Hence, statistics on costs of education are of utmost importance for educational planning. Estimates of costs are essential for estimating resources required for educational sector and for various sub-sectors of education. They also help us in understanding whether resources allocated to education reflect optimal level or not and within education whether resources are optimally allocated between different layers. The decision to incur the costs on education from the individual point of view would be based on a relatively short term perspective. It may be necessary to note here that the costs of education, like any other money-based statistics, can be expressed either at current prices or at constant prices. When the costs of education are expressed at constant prices, they take care of price-inflation and thus represent the real costs of education. When we are computing costs of education for over a time period, it is necessary to compute the costs of education at constant prices. Costs of education expressed in current prices have increased in real costs of education.

REFERENCES

Balsara, M. (1996). *New Education Policy and Development Challenge*, New Delhi: Kanishka Publishers.

Burton A. Weisbrod (1962). "Education and Investment in Human Capital", *Journal of Political Economy*, Vol. 70, No. 5, The University of Chicago Press. https://www.jstor.org/stable

Dhar, T.N. (1978). *Educational statistics in India-organisational arrangements, problems and deficiencies*, NIEPA, New Delhi.

Education Commission (1966). *Education and National Development, Report of the Education Commission 1966,* NCERT, New Delhi.

Garg, V.P. (1985). *The Cost Analysis in Higher Education*, New Delhi: Metropolitan Book Co. Pvt Ltd.

Goel S.C. (1975). *Education and Economics Growth in India*, Macmillan, New Delhi.

Haldipur, R.N. (1974). *Local Government—Rural Development and Micro Level Planning*, Department of Personnel and Administrative Reforms, New Delhi.

Hallak, J. (1969). *The analysis of Educational Costs and Expenditures*, Paris.

Hallak J. (1990). *Investing in the Future*, UNESCO: Pergamon Press.

Heggade, O.D. (1992). *Economics of Education*, Bombay: Himalaya Publishing House.

Institute of Applied Manpower Research (1981). *Data Sources and Items of Information on Educational Statistics in India,* New Delhi.

Kothari, and P.R. Panchamukhi (1980). *Economics of Education: A Trend Report*, New Delhi.

Kumar, Krishna (1984). *Breaking Away Elementary Education, The Unfinished Task: A Future Supplement on Early Learning in India,* New Delhi.

Laxmidevi (1996), *Encyclopedia of Education Development and Planning Economics of Education*, Vol. V, New Delhi: Anmol Publications Pvt. Ltd.

Majumdar, Tapas (1983), *Investment in Education and Social Choice*, Cambridge: Cambridge University Press.

Marope, P.T.M.; Kaga, Y. (2015). *Investing against Evidence: The Global State of Early Childhood Care and Education*, Paris.

Mishra, S.N. (1972), *Project Evaluation with Special Reference to Education*, New, Delhi.

Muzammil, M. (1989), *Financing of Education*. New Delhi House.

Naik J.P. (1965), *Educational Planning in India*, Bombay, Allied Publishers.

Naik, Chitra (1982) "In and out of School", *Development Perspective on Children.*

Nair (1981), *Primary Education: Population Growth and Socio-economic Change*, New Delhi.

Natarajan, S. (1990), *Introduction to Economics of Education*, New Delhi: Sterling Publishers Pvt. Ltd.

Padmanabhan, C.B. (1971), *Economics of Educational Planning in India*, New Delhi: Arya Book Depot.

Panchamukhi, (1989), *Economics of Educational Finance*, Bombay: Himalaya Publishing House.

Patel, B.B. (1982), "Access to Higher Education in Equalisation of Educational Opportunities through Freeship: A Case Study", *Journal of Higher Education.*

Saxena, S. (1979), *Educational Planning in India*, New Delhi: Sterling Publishers Pvt. Ltd.

Shriprakash (1996), *Cost of Education*, New Delhi: Anamika Publishers and Distributors.

Singh, R.P. (1993), *Private Initiative and Public Policy in Education*, New Delhi.

Srivastava, A.B.L. and K.N. Hirinnaiah (1977). *Educational Statistics in India.*

Tilak, Jandhyala B.G. (1980), *Inequality by Sex in Human Capital Formation: Labour Market Discrimination and Returns to Education.*

Tilak, Jandhyala B.G. (1984), *'Centre-state relations in financing Education in India*, NIEPA, New Delhi.

Tilak, J.B.G. (1987), *The Economics of Inequality in Education*, New Delhi: Sage Publications.

Tilak J.B.G. (1994), *Education for Development in Asia*, New Delhi: Sage Publications.

Tilak J.B.G. (1992), *Educational Planning at Grassroots*, New Delhi: Ashish Publishing House.

Tsang, M.C. (1988). "Cost Analysis for Educational Policymaking: A Review of Cost Studies in Education in Developing Countries", *Review of Educational Research.*

UNESCO (1980), "Economics of New Educational Media. Vol. 2." *Cost and Effectiveness*, Paris.

Veena, D.R. (1987), *Education of Economic Growth*, New Delhi: Ashish Publishing House.

14
Cost-Benefit Analysis in Education

Kounsar Jabeen

Cost-Benefit Analysis refers a systematic comparison of the magnitude of the costs and benefits of some form of investment in order to assess economic profitability. All forms of investment involve a sacrifice of the present expenditure in order to secure future benefits in the form of higher levels of output. Cost-benefit analysis provides a means of appraising these future benefits in the light of the costs that must be incurred at present. The purpose of such analysis is to provide a measure of the expected yield of the investment, as a guide to the rational allocation of resources.

Cost-Benefit analysis (CBA) is a technique used to compare the total costs of a programme/project with its benefits, using a common metric (most commonly monetary units). This enables the calculation of the net benefit associated with the programme. As a technique, it is used most often at the start of project when different options or courses of action are being appraised and compared, as an option for choosing the best approach. It can also be used, however, to evaluate the overall impact of a project in quantifiable terms.

Cost-benefit analysis adds up the total costs of a programme and compares it against its total benefits. The technique assumes that a monetary value can be placed on all the costs and benefits of a programme, including tangible and intangible returns to other people and organization in addition to those directly impacted. As such, a major advantage of cost-benefit analysis lies in forcing people to explicitly and systematically consider the various factors which should influence strategic choice.

Decisions are made through cost-benefit analysis by comparing the net present value of the project's costs with the net present value of its benefits. Decisions are based on whether there is a net benefit or cost to the approach, i.e. total benefits less total costs. Costs and benefits that occur in the future have less weight attached to them in a cost-benefit analysis. The 'discount rate' will vary depending on the sector, but public sector activity generally uses a discount rate of 5-6 per cent. The sum of the discounted benefits of an option minus the sum of the discounted costs, all discounted to the same base date, is the 'net present value' of the option.

Cost	*Benefit*
Any negative effect on an organization resulting from the implementation of the project. Example: 1. Environment 2. Maintenance Costs 3. Labour Costs 4. Research and Development	A benefit is any positive effect on the organization resulting from the implementation of the project. Example 1. Increase in Productivity 2. Reduction in Costs 3. Saving Time

Cost-Benefit Analysis is an economic evaluation technique that compares the cost of the intervention with the benefit incurred, where the benefit is measured by monetary units. It focuses on the monetary outcomes. Here, both costs and consequences are measured in monetary unit. Cost Benefit Analysis is based on the monetary terms, it is quantitative project evaluation technique and it adopts broad societal perspective as it includes all costs and all benefits. After this analysis, an intervention should be chosen and undertaken if the benefit exceeds the costs. It is used to evaluate public expenditure programmes designed to produce different outcomes. The results are presented in terms of ratio of benefit to cost and return on investment. The outcome is usually expressed as the difference in cost net benefits. Net gains and losses are checked for the decision regarding any intervention. The outcomes of cost-benefit analysis are already known. Cost-benefit is reasonably more complex as every matter needs to quantify and it also considers opportunity cost and time factor. Cost-benefit analysis helps to identify the best ways to achieve given outcome. Designed to facilitate rational decision-making by systematically weighing the advantages and disadvantages of possible courses of action, cost-benefit analysis currently plays a key role in public policy-making and is broadly applied in a variety of domains such as law, health and safety, environmental protection and agriculture (Adler and Postner, 2006; Kornhauser, 2000).

Example

In 2005, the UK Government undertook a value for money analysis of Government investment in different types of childcare. The choice was between higher cost "integrated" childcare centres, providing a range of services to both children and parents, or lower cost "non-integrated" centres that provided basic childcare facilities. The analysis included both a 'hard exercise' and a 'soft exercise'. The hard exercise identified quantified and monetized direct costs and benefits. The soft exercise identified and described qualitatively non-negotiable impacts, leading to option ranking.

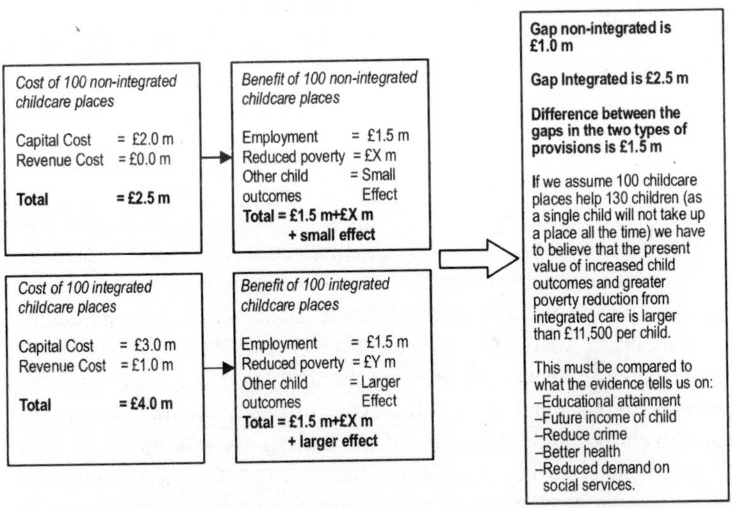

Source: Prime Minister's Strategy Unit. 2004.

Adesina (1981) noted that cost-benefit approach looks at each level of education as investment in the human beings with the purpose that the returns will help to improve the whole economy. It is the mode of analysis of current relationship between education and income. Education is perceived from two angles, namely:

The social rates of return: Social rate of return stresses the benefit to be consequent by the state of investing in a particular form of education. The cost of education is usually borne by the society as a whole and can be calculated by equating the total present value, earning of an average educated person before tax with benefits to be gained from alternative investments, in physical capital.

The private rates of return: This is the investment by private individual and the expected benefit for acquiring a particular type of education. This is calculated by equating the direct and out of pocket costs of student plus earning done by them while studying, to the present value of earning after tax e.g., direct cost + pocket money + foregone money.

Cost-Benefit Analysis consists of three steps—

1. Determining the benefits of an existing programme and placing a dollar value on those benefits.
2. Calculating the total costs of the programme.
3. Comparing the benefits and the costs.

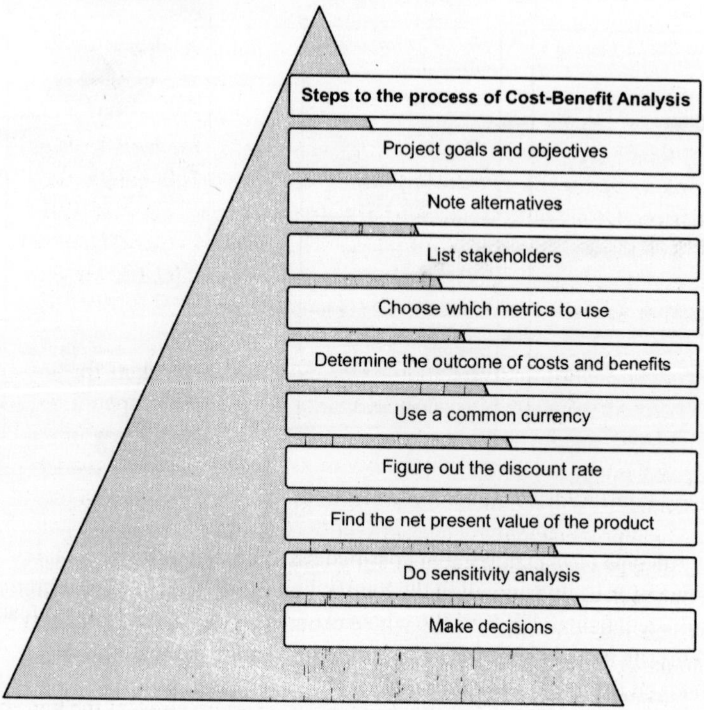

Cost-Benefit Approach in Education

The rate of return approach is also known as cost benefit or cost-effectiveness approach to educational planning. It emphasizes that the investment in education should be based on the benefits or return. The expenditure on education should be thought of as a form of national investment. Positive investment depends upon a closer relationship between education and manpower requirement of a country. Although so far the use of cost-benefit analysis in education has remained limited, a change is being felt (Levin, 2001). In the last two decades, the World Bank, UNESCO and the OECD have increasingly integrated cost-benefit analysis into educational policy-making (Vawda, Moock, Gittinger and Patrinos 2002).

According to UNESCO, education as an investment means two things:

1. Training imparted by institution, the learners must acquire productive capacity.
2. The level of earning of educated people must be higher. It happens then it is said that return on education is positive.

Many economists, academics and policy-makers now call to further expand the use of cost-benefit analysis in this area. For example, a recent report by the European Expert Network on Economics of Education, which is a think tank that is sponsored by and advises to the European Commission, Directorate General of Education and Culture, states that "Wider use of good quality CBAs/CEAs would surely be a step in the right direction to improve policy-making in the area of education within EU-Member States" (Muinch & Psacharopoulos, 2014:57).

- Cost-benefit analysis should normally be undertaken for any project which involves policy development, capital expenditure, use of assets or setting of standards. Depending on the nature of the issue, it will sometimes be very quick and easy. At other times, it will require complex economic analysis best conducted by a professional evaluator experienced in CBA techniques.
- The best cost-benefit analysis take a broad view of costs and benefits, including indirect and longer-term effects, reflecting the interests of all stakeholders who will be affected by the programme. It is thus important to ensure the analysis is as comprehensive as possible.
- Cost-benefit analysis (CBA) is traditionally based on conventional welfare economics, which provides a utilitarian account of value which relies on individual self-interest. In practice, people express preferences for a much wider set of

public goals. Techniques such as CBA rarely give proper recognition to these wider public preferences. Consideration should be given, therefore, to the prevailing understanding of the public good and how this is best served.

- In carrying out a CBA, it is critical to begin with an exhaustive list of all the different costs and benefits that could arise—even if some are later excluded. Otherwise, important aspects of the analysis could be overlooked.

Information on costs, benefits and risks is rarely known with certainty, especially when one looks to the future. This makes it essential that sensitivity analysis is carried out, testing the robustness of the CBA result to changes in some of the key numbers.

Model of Cost-Benefit Analysis

1. Define the framework for the analysis.
2. Identify and classify costs and benefits.
3. Drawing a timeline for expected costs and revenue.
4. Monetize costs and benefits.
5. Discount costs and benefits to obtain present values.
6. Calculate net present values.

Benefits—Cost of Education

The use of CBA in education, however, is also gradually expanding, and CBA has conducted and employed in a variety of ways. Most commonly, CBA has been used in its most basic form, which seeks to establish the monetary cost-benefit ratio of an existing policy or project. Most of the cases in which CBA is conducted on existing educational interventions or policies, the aim is not just to assess how well existing programmes or policies function, but to provide future recommendations regarding what ought to be done. In recent decades and especially since the mid-1990s, CBA has also been used to estimate the merits of future educational projects and policies. Although there are many similarities between CBA studies that examine existing educational interventions and those that examine future ones, there is a fundamental difference between them. While the former's primary aim is to assess policy, the latter are primarily designed as an aid to determining future policy.

Advantages of Cost-Benefit Analysis Approach

1. Possible to quantify the increase in productivity of an educated peon.
2. Suggest the directions in which education system in a society should expand.
3. Maximize the earning capacity of their product.
4. Minimizes waste in investment.
5. Economically oriented.
6. Emphasizes cost-benefit principle.
7. Relationship between the costs of gaining more education.
8. Increase in payment, which results from additional.
9. The analysis can show or suggest the directions in which education system in a society should expand, so as to maximize the earning capacity of their product.

Educational cost-benefit analysis is currently, and has been for some years, a widely accepted technique, used to assess the profitability of investment in education. Educational rate-of-return studies have been carried out in most developed countries and in many developing countries. In the great majority of cases, the results are in favour of additional investment in education, which the studies show to be profitable both from the point of view of the national economy and from that of the individual student.

Limitations of Cost-Benefit Analysis Approach

1. It is difficult to measure the benefits, which derive from investing in any type of education.
2. In developing countries, differential in earning of workers cannot be attributed to additional education acquired, but to other things such as habits, customers, family background, and primordial factor etc.
3. Primary education gives the highest return to society, according to some studies done on the calculation of the social rates of return for all levels of education which seems to be vague.
4. The salaries of civil servants are more influences by economic variables than by productivity consideration.
5. A financial return from education has been inflated in Africa due to particular type and level of education.

6. Civil servants salaries are much to economic context of the country, but little to productive consideration.

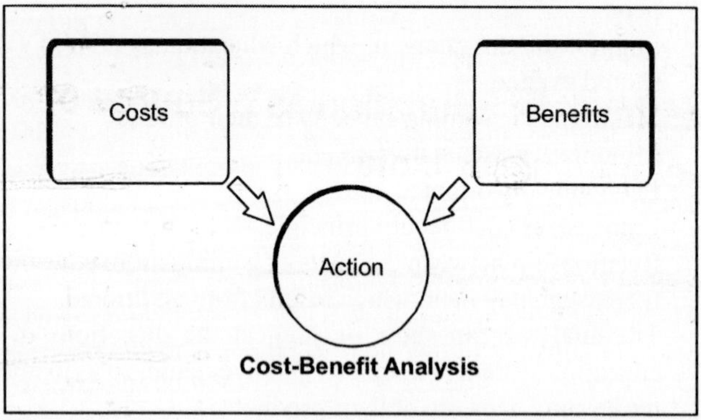

Source: https://www.bing.com/images/search?q=Cost+Accounting&FORM=IRIBEP

REFERENCES

Boardman, A., Greenberg, D., Vining, A., and Weimer, D. (2006). *Cost Benefit Analysis: Concepts and Practice.* (3rd. ed.). Upper Saddle River, NJ: Prentice Hall.

Levin, B. (2004). Making research matter more. *Education Policy Analysis Archives*, *12*, 56.

Prime Minister's Strategy Unit. (2004). *Strategy Survival Guide.* Retrieved from Cabinet Office website: http://www.odi.org.uk/resources/docs/7270.pdf

Society for Benefit-Cost Analysis. (2010). *The Society for Benefit-cost Analysis.* Retrieved from http://benefitcostanalysis.org/

15

Investment in Education as a Source of Development for India

Maliha Batool

Introduction

For the success of sustainable and democratic society, it is necessary that the majority of the citizens should have a minimum level of education. Education is the process of facilitating learning, or the acquisition of skills, knowledge, values, habits and beliefs. Education is most important in the life of every individual and for the society in general. Education does not only refer to the formal education that one attains from academic institutions but also that one gains informally through lessons of life and from our elders.

Education helps to reduce the level of ignorance and as one attains education one gets to learn about various things that take place in life and also learn better about how to handle various events of life. At an individual level it improves the chances of getting a job to an individual in comparison to those who do not have. It enables an individual to understand the real life situation and helps to develop the younger by developing confidence in the minds of younger and provide a solid foundation for rational and value-oriented and nation-building progress. Similarly, any type of vocational, technical or higher education enables a person not only attractive personality but also make them professionally fit in different spheres (Myers & Harbison, 1965; Mingat and Tan, 1986; Rena, 2004).

Via education one can improve his/her the living standards and it is the means of bringing improvement in the lives of the people as it increases the chances of getting job. It makes one fit in various social groups by making people able to communicate with other people and also makes society a healthy one by making people living in it healthy by developing social skills among its members. Education is a crucial tool in liberating the minds of people to an elevated state of potential.

For the Developing Countries

A good quality and basic education people of the knowledge and skills that they need to face daily life challenges, and take advantage of economic and lifelong learning opportunities. In every country it is also a key driver for fostering economic growth, achieving gender equality, reducing poverty and social development.

Education, particularly among the developing countries is helpful in rebuilding, bringing stability, structure and hope for the future, helping the future children and youth to overcome trauma caused by aggression, war, conflict or disaster.

India is the second in terms of population and 7th largest country in terms of area, depicting clearly the burden of population in India. Education is the means that can convert the huge population into human capital, i.e. developing the abilities and skills among the population of the country by turning them into a useful asset for the society. This process is termed as human capital formation.

"The process of acquiring and increasing the number of persons who have the skills, education and experience which are critical for the economic and the political development of the country. Human capital formation is thus associated with investment in man and his development as a creative and productive resource."...Harbison.

Turning of population into Human Capital backbone of any nation and is known as human resource. These human resources consist of students who with time turn into accountants, doctors, engineers, managers etc. The human capital formation is crucial in the economic development as it will change the traditional society into modern one, will increase the productivity of the physical capital educated persons can handle the tools and machines in a better and proper way and will facilitate the use of new technology and machinery and will foster growth by giving boost to innovation.

Investments made in education can accelerate economic growth. Proper utility of manpower depends on system of education, training and industrial experience of the people. Education is one of the most important factors of development for the country and it enriches the understanding among people themselves and enhances the understanding of the world. It improves the quality of their lives and leads to broad social benefits to individuals and society. Playing a crucial role in achievement of social economic progress and helps in improving the pattern of income distribution in a country. Education helps in raising people's creativity, productivity and helps in the promotion of entrepreneurship and technological advancement (Oztruck, 2008).

The most important and effective way of enhancing and enlarging the productive workforce of a country is the expenditure made on the education system as it is considered as a process of creating human capital. The main objective behind any nation and individuals behind investment in education is to enhance income, generating technical skill, creating manpower which can result in rapid economic growth and many other social benefits.

Education, Human Capital and Economic Growth

Becker (1993) comes with the viewpoint that education is prime factor resulting in the formation of human capital. Human capital is the key factor for growth, competitiveness, and development, in recent times, within the modern context of development, human capital forms the base of economic growth. Investment in education and health are the key drivers which are affecting economic growth of India.

Any kind of investment especially on education is the principal component in achieving economic growth and development of country (Brempong & Wilson, 2004).

There is bi-directional causality between the two, growth of human capital helps in economic growth and in the same way economic growth providing a platform for the growth of human capital (Sharma and Sahani, 2015; Chandra, 2010).

This link works through multiple pathways at the individual, firm and national level. Learning and skill building provide people with livelihoods, an opportunity to contribute to their societies. They also contribute vitally to the formation of one's meaning and identity in life.

Similarly, Khatak and Khan (2012), Barro and Sala-i-Martin (1995; 2004) found that there is effect of primary, secondary, and tertiary school attainment in any country on growth and development of a country. These come with the viewpoint that increase in enrolment enhance the growth and development of the country.

Expenditure on Education in India

After Independence much importance has been given to the expenditure on education as it is the means through which we can develop the country as a whole. Investment on education is the only way through which, with expenditure in few per cent, the future of entire country will be secure.

There are many reasons why government is focusing on investment in education, the most important is that it has a positive and significant impact on economic growth with the rise in enrolment rate there raises GDP too (Barro, 1991).

Expenditure on primary, secondary and tertiary education during recent years is shown below:

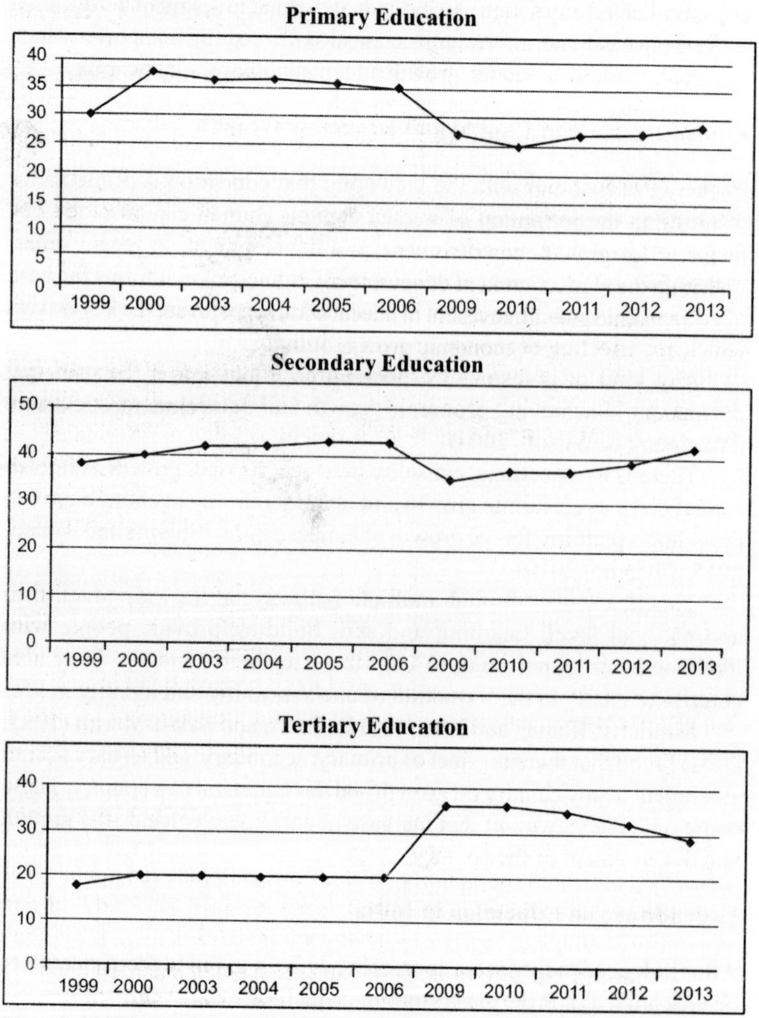

Fig. 15.1: Expenditure on primary, secondary and tertiary education (% of government expendiure on education)

Source: Authors own demonstration, WDI 2019.

Recent Developments for the Promotion of Education in India

Government has taken various effective Sarva Siksha Abhiyan Scheme, Mid Day meal scheme National Programme for Education of Girls at Elementary Education (NPEGEE), Rashtriya Aavishkar Abhiyan (RAA), Padhe Bharat Badhe Bharat, Beti Bachao Beti Padhao, Kasturba Gandhi Balika Vidyalaya etc. As the students are getting the free food in schools, the parents are more willing to send their children in schools as their families are too poor to afford two meals a day. Providing free school uniforms, free textbooks, and some other necessary items etc. Scholarships are being provided to poor so that these could get financial help for their studies. The Right to Education (RTE) Act was passed and enacted in 2009 which has made education a fundamental right.

National Policy for Skill Development and Entrepreneurship 2015 has been launched with a view to create aptitude and advance business enterprise at the same time. The National Skill Development Mission has been started in 2015 with a view of expanding the skilling eco-framework of about 7.6 million youth and about 1,500 Multi Skill Training Institutes have been started all-over the nation.

Prime Minister Mr. Narendra Modi recently has propelled the Skill India activity via 'Kaushal Bharat, Kushal Bharat'. Under this initiative, the government has set an objective for itself of preparing 400 million natives by 2022 which would empower them to discover the occupation of their interest. This initiative has been propelled with projects like: Pradhan Mantri Kaushal Vikas Yojana (PMKVY), National Policy for Skill Development and Entrepreneurship 2015, Skill Loan Scheme, and the National Skill Development Mission.

Conclusion

From the above discussion, we can say that education is the only means which can turn the huge population in India into human capital which is necessary for the country for an all-round development. At present education is not only needed for the development of intellectual skills and knowledge among the population but also necessary for effective growth and development of Indian economy. It is the education system which is bearing the responsibility of making its students as researchers, learners, innovators, scholars, and trainers.

REFERENCES

Annabi, N., Harvey, S., and Lan, Y., (2011). "Public expenditures on education, human capital and growth in Canada: An OLG model analysis." *Journal of Policy Modelling*, 33, 852–865.

Barro, R., and Sala-i-Martin, X. (2004). *Economic Growth* (2nd ed.). Cambridge, Mass.: MIT Press.

Barro, R.J., and Sala-i-Martin, X. (1995). *Economic Growth*, New York, McGraw-Hill.

Khattak, Naeem ur Rehman, and Jangraiz, K. (2012). "The contribution of education to economic growth: Evidence from Pakistan." *International Journal of Business and Social Sciences*, 3(4), Special Issue, 145-151.

Donou-Adonsou, F. (2018). Technology, education, and economic growth in Sub-Saharan *Africa. Telecommunications Policy.*

Preeti Sharma and Priyanka Sahni, "Human Capital and Economic Growth in India: A Co-integration and Causality Analysis", *USHUS—Journal of Business Management*, 14 (2), 1-18.

Mingat, A., and J.P. Tan (1986). "Financing Public Higher Education in Developing Countries: The Potential role of loan schemes", *Higher Education* 15, 283-297.

Myers, C. and Harbison, F. (1965). *Education, Manpower and Economic Growth: Strategies of Human Resource Development.* New York: McGraw-Hill.

Ozturk, I. (2008). The role of education in economic development: A theoretical perspective. *Available at SSRN 1137541.*

16

Economic Approaches to Education

D. Anita

Approaches to Education

Operational planning, also known as divisional planning is concerned with the implementation of the larger goals and strategies that have been determined by strategic planning; it is also concerned with improving current operations and with the allocation of resources through the operating budget. Approaches to Education is concerned with the problems of how to make the best use of limited resources allocated to education in view of priorities given to different stages of education or different sectors of education and the need of the economy and the educational planning strategies are based on certain approaches attempting to establish the relationship between education, economic development and economic growth. We are aware that a strategy provides a dual approach to problem solving. In a way, it is exploration of the most effective means to overcome difficulties and face competition in the developing society and deployment of limited resources (education and human resource) among the critical activities with the intention of achieving maximum returns. Approaches are underlined by numerous subjective value judgements as to the desired nature of an educational system.

The nature of the approach to educational planning depends on the aims of planning a policy and on the levels of decision-making. An integrated social and economic planning policy could have the dual aims of maximization of present welfare within the limits of available resources and maximization of future growth. In the sense, education is often considered as *investment*, then present corruption may have to be sacrificed for future growth (investment), and the two policies may be contradictory. Yet in another sense education has been considered as *consumption*, and thus the dual policies are not contradictory. Decision making takes place at micro and macro level. At micro level, the internal structure of educational decision are concerned, while the size of total spending on education in relation to aggregate national resources is dealt at macro level.

Social Demand Approach

The 'social demand' approach rests heavily on forecasts of private demand for education. It requires the education authorities to provide schools and find facilities for all students who demand admission and who are qualified to enter. Social Demand Approach was used in Rubbings Committee report on Higher Education in Britain. In India we popularly use while opening new schools and colleges. Social Demand Approach is similar to the *Education Flow Model.* It assumes that access to all branches of education should be available to those who are willing, qualified and have the ability to attain it. We need to examine the educational system as a complex mechanized production system where the inputs are the children, teachers, materials and building. Whereas the outputs are students educated in different areas and trained teachers, trained engineers etc.

Components of Social Demand Approach

- Get a reliable set of demographic forecasts year-wise.
- Age and population of school going children periodically.
- Forecasting enrolment of students and teachers.
- Differences in educational experiences.
- Specialization in various fields of education.
- Difference in inherent abilities, attitudes and aptitudes.

Steps Followed in Social Demand Approach Method

(a) To estimate the proportion of students completing school education and are likely to enter into higher education.
(b) To estimate how many of these successful school leaving students would actually apply for admission to colleges.
(c) To determine how many of the applicants should be given admission to higher education.
(d) To determine the length and duration of the study.

The major issue concerned in this approach is to forecast the future demands for seats keeping in mind social and educational trends as well as demographic changes. The underlying assumption in this approach is that expansion of education is beneficial to the economy. Additional expenditure on education is not a burden but it satisfies the future needs of the economy.

Achievements or Success of Social Demand Approach

- The society supports traditional cultural values.
- This approach is suitable political tool to meet the need to satisfy the demand of the general public. When the decisions are taken in a democratic way, i.e. through public opinion.
- In societies that are pessimistic in nature.
- To provide social security and safety to the employees against accidents.
- To improve human relations.
- The demand of education would be fully met and every person who plan to pursue a course provided he or she has eligibility would get an opportunity. It means that greatest good to the greatest number, different kinds and quantities of education.

Effects of Social Demand Approach in Educational Planning

- Social demand approach in educational planning is very much as the demand and supply in business. To attain profit and work accurately, the supply should meet the demand.
- If there is too much supply and demand is less, the company makes loss if there is too much demand and not enough supply then the company should make the supply larger to gain a higher and more substantial place in the market.
- When there is a variance between demand and supply, unemployment and underemployment of products professional institutions take place.

Social Demand for Education

Educational establishment try to meet the demand of the individuals in a society. Too many schools may lead to the closure of educational institutions where the demand is not high. Social demand for education can be low when the cost of schooling is high. But this does not mean that there is no demand for education. At elementary stage, education is free and compulsory for all and it becomes a part of social justice approach. But at the secondary and higher education levels, no such provisions has been included in our Constitution, therefore, here the education is provided on the basis of social demand approach. At higher educational level, students enrol on the basis of demand for education as conceived by the students and their parents and as per the educational facilities and capacity of a particular institution.

Precautions Taken Over to Fulfil Social Demand for Education

- Providing free and compulsory schooling by law.
- Enforcing universal education properly.
- Checking attendance rates or enforcing attendance law for raising the attendance of pupils attending the schools. This can be done by providing MDM, free uniform, free books and quality education

The approach is based on currently expressed preferences and does not take into account public expenditure on education *vis-à-vis* the benefits as the demand for education may far exceed the resources available in a vast country like India. The policy of the government to provide tuition free education at the secondary and higher education may accelerate the demand for education.

Criticism or Limitations of Social Demand Approach

One of the demerits of this approach is that although individuals purposely base it on the estimation of the demand for places, what the data actually show is a mixture of demand for places and supply of places or capacity available. In many cases, the number of places available determines the number of students who enter. For example enough number of graduates are not available for admission to the colleges of education as the number of new colleges has increased. Any kind of attempt is made to measure the demand for university places by collecting information on the part of students, who apply for these places, it is not at all clear that applications for entry into universities are not influenced by the students' own estimation in relation to the available number of places. This approach has no control over absorptive capacity of the economy for the trained personnel.

There are criticism that this method of social demand also will make resources spread with closure of establishment and therefore, when the attendance law is enforced, there will be a spread of resources for a growing number of pupils that will there not get the amount of assistance that they require. It means it would not be able to fulfil the demands of all. This approach may also result in a negative manner by a variance between the output of higher education and the demands of the economy. Social demand approach is deprived of stating whether the resources exhausted are economically allotted to the extent it has.

The availability of financial assistance and free education (Scholarships) can be used explicitly to influence individual demand by encouraging students either to remain in the educational system either to leave or enter a new institution and take specialized courses when given no financial incentive they might prefer other courses. Distance education and other non-formal educational systems are also having a direct influence on inflow of students to educational institutions, the types and pattern of courses available under these systems determine the response of students and effect increase or decrease of demand for seats in educational institutions in a country.

Manpower Approach is Need-based

'Needs' implies the three factors, i.e. capital, educated manpower and unskilled manpower are used in fixed proportions to produce a certain level of output. But, if these factors are to some extent interchangeable or in economic terms substitutable then the same level of output could be produced with different combinations of inputs, and in this case the optimum allocation of resources depends on the price of each factor. This means that manpower forecasting becomes even more difficult. It not only solves the problems of predicting technical change and new methods of production, but it also adds the demand for physical capital and manpower. Thus the view is that, education is an economic investment which produces the trained manpower needed by the economy. It suggests that manpower forecasting is necessary, but by no means solves the problems of how to allocate resources.

Manpower Forecasting or the Manpower Approach

An approach, which is concerned to seek the optimum allocation of resources and concerned with education as investment rather than consumption is the "manpower forecasting" approach. In this approach, the general demand and supply of human resources in diverse areas and levels of educational sector are estimated.

Manpower approach focuses mainly on three basic fundamentals:

- Specification of the composition of manpower need at some future date for example 2015-2020.
- Specification of manpower availability for example in 2000.
- Specification which reconciles the former specification with the later.

Methods of Forecasting Manpower

The methods for forecasting manpower necessities of an economy are diverge. It may use international comparisons of the ratio between manpower and output, or may be based on analysis and manpower utilization patterns in different industries, or on mathematical models of the economy based on constant or changing co-efficient between manpower and output. But the basic rationale of the approach is to forecast the manpower needs of the economy.

Nature, Importance and Working of Manpower Approach

It chiefly involves in forecasting demand for various levels in relation to a given structure of industry in near future.

This approach emphasizes that education produces the qualitative human resources with desirable knowledge, attitudes and skills as per the requirement.

If shortages or surpluses of certain types of manpower are predicted to develop over time, then the educational system is adapted such as to eliminate or remove them.

This may involve a large increase in educational expenditures and student inflows in the immediate period to meet these future technological requirements.

Appraisal and analysis of the existing employment conditions and the system of education is must.

For the development of the economy planning, the system of education *vis-à-vis* the manpower is essential. Development of skilled, trained and educated manpower in the long run reduces the risks and costs.

Usage of financial resources that are limited is the best possible way to fulfil the demands of employment sector without incurring wastage on account of unemployment.

In this method to make an appraisal of the number of students enrolled, the number of existing teachers and their qualifications, enrolment in teacher education institutions, as well as the existing number of school buildings, equipments, infrastructure and other facilities.

In manpower approach, the employer's requirement regarding occupational and professional qualifications for employees, their levels of training and abilities should also be assessed.

Manpower planning approach takes note of the fact that the teaching profession requires approximately 60 per cent of the highly qualified human resources of a country which competes with the demand for manpower in other economic sectors.

Manpower approach fulfils long term or long run goals. It is a thorough study of the occupational changes and technological progress as well as a particular level of educational standards.

The National Education Commission Report 1966 aims at manpower planning in other words to provide every educated person with a job and every available job with a trained and educated worker.

The Blaug Approach (1966) appears from the proposal that educational plans must be established on the basis of economic and social objectives. The method used is that proceedings in stages from the initial projections of a desirable GDP in a future year, as given by prior economic plan, to a supply of educated manpower of the requisite calibre and competencies required reaching in the target years.

Steps Followed to Achieve the Objectives of Manpower Approach of Planning

- Split down the target GDP under major sectors like primary, secondary and tertiary.
- The sectored GDPs are further divided into various industries.
- An average output or the productivity of labour is applied to the industrial GDP targets yielding the forecast of labour requirement by the sector or an industry.
- The working force or labour force is distributed as per the requirement among the occupational categories.
- Skilled manpower engaged in production and this improvement helps in achieving higher and higher targets of growth and production in industrial or production sector. At the same time,

they also help in increasing the agricultural production and services in an efficient way. It helps the entrepreneur in organizing the units of production and deciding what to produce, and on how and where to produce.

- The occupational structure of the labour force is converted into skilled manpower through education. It may be through formal education or skill training required to perform satisfactorily in the job achieved. For example ILO has made use of the training facilities available in institutions like Central Labour Institute (Bombay), Regional Labour Institutes (Kolkata, Kanpur and Chennai), IIMs and IITs. India also provides technical manpower for ILO.
- To meet the organizational requirement such as higher productivity, operational efficiency, quality of product and service manpower approach in educational planning is essential.
- At the same time to satisfy the needs of the individual employees like interests, challenges, achievement or accomplishment also manpower approach in education planning becomes important.
- Some benefits through Factories Act, 1948 for safe working environment, worker's compensation, health benefits. Under Employees State Insurance Act, 1948 some benefits like sickness, dependant's benefits, medical benefit, provident fund, pension, incentives, allowances for death are the benefits to improve and motivate employees as an addition to the stock of manpower.

Activities Conducted Related to Manpower

1. A survey of a sample of firms and industries may be carried out, where employed person may be asked to furnish facts and estimates related to present educational qualification for each job, hiring standards, adequacy of the present employee's job preparation for each job and expectation of future changes in these or other relevant factors.
2. NCTE had asked the state government to conduct future manpower requirement of teachers so that new teacher education institution may be established accordingly.
3. Government of India formulating manpower planning and programming model for educational planning.

Survey would require considerable investment in financial and physical terms. It requires periodic updating as well as considerable input of manpower from time to time.

Advantages or Merits of Manpower Approach to Planning

- It pays attention in knowing the educational imbalances and gaps in education.
- Manpower approach gives direction to estimate the educational requirement of the labour and training for the development of the country in near future.
- Manpower approach helps in getting rid of unemployment or underemployment by helping to the people to choose right education as per the requirement of one's need. This leads to challenge of education may create self-employment, that is development oriented creating more job opportunities.
- The contribution of manpower to job will be of optimum level.
- Education is cost-effective and manpower would be effective in productivity.
- Educational planning of manpower approach is an intellectual offshoot of an organized growth.

Disadvantages or Demerits of Manpower Approach to Planning

- Manpower approach does give clear or complete guidance as what is to be attained in various levels of education to the educational planner. Educational planning based entirely on manpower forecasting would be optimum in only one sense and would neglect the other aims of education such as social and political development. But concentrating for the moment only on the manpower aspects is it in fact impossible to forecast manpower needs because of economic, technological and other uncertainties that are involved.
- This approach neglects primary education as it is not work-oriented. Its attention is mainly on the education that contributes to manpower development through secondary education.
- It is not possible to forecast the level of economic development over a long-term period accurately. The economy does not grow just in terms of long-term projections; the estimates of manpower requirements are likely to go skewed. Manpower may go off

beam due to managing dismissals or compulsory retirement or due to high performance insight etc.

- Manpower needs are mostly needed in the urban employment. Education planner has not given any clauses about educational requirement to unskilled and semi-skilled workers in the urban areas and to the workers who live in rural areas.
- Manpower approach does not take into account the provision for education as a consumer good and it makes no provision for the social milieu. The occupational needs of the economy are not the whole of societies needs for education. The need for girls' education, which are not gainfully employment and education for cultural, political and social development should go hand in hand.
- Manpower needs are the consequent of the necessity related to economic development. But developing country is interested purely in the growth of the economy, i.e. increasing its national product in income. Its views are broader relating to social and political modernization. It wants an educational organization that is structured on value system giving knowledge, and skills that are the base for national development.

Criticism of the Alteration of Manpower Need into Educational Requirements

- A particular job may be employed by workers possessing varying levels of education. Highly educated may be underemployed or mal-employed.
- The conversion of manpower requirement into educational requirement through 27 years of schooling leaves a great deal to be fulfilled. We need vocational information and job training. But we see that 12 to 27 long years of formal or informal schooling becomes highly inadequate to work out in a realistic plan of manpower for employment in various sectors.
- Educational requirements may differ with the accessibility of educated manpower. It means, what an employer consider 'essential' may depend, to a large extent, on what type of manpower is available. Upgrading in terms of educational qualification is likely to occur when the supply of educated manpower has increased compared to the demand of the labour. Such scheme of progression is on the base of qualification in

the labour force is not vigorously followed in any of the educational plans that have been framed till present.

Assumptions of Manpower Approach

- It assumes that the labour market is at the point of disequilibrium or will be at the point of disequilibrium. The manpower approach is designed to reduce the probability of such disequilibrium. In a rapidly changing business environment, there is considerable scope for systematic, analytical and integrated approach through forecasting and planning. But, forecasting future events are uncertain and hazy.
- If we accept that economy is described by a production function in which substitutions among factors of production is not possible, any wrong assumption may result in a great loss or severe damage. Planning is a complex and complicated exercise which requires a high level of imagination, foresight, analytical ability, creativity and fortitude to identify alternatives and choose the most suitable strategy for direction and development resources. Planning requires not just preparation but all levels of everyday jobs.
- Manpower forecasts give a single prediction of expected manpower and educational needs. Forecasting ignores changes in supply. In India, the manpower approach is applicable in professional studies like engineering, medicine, agriculture, business environment etc. The performance of this approach depends upon the level to which the socio-economic variables are taken into account while making any educational model. While preparing an educational model planning they should not forget that the situations can never be static.

Rate of Return Approach

According to Blaug (1966), the rate of return approach takes into account a cross-tabulation of the labour force by age, education and earning before and after the payment of tax. From then, we construct age-earning profiles by years of schooling, that is, we use cross-section data to project life time earning associated with additional education. An allowance must be made for the difficulty that the earning associated with additional education cannot be entirely attributed to education along; individual earning are partly determined by local ability, family background, social class origin and character of a rental payment to a non-reproducible factor of production.

Educational planning influences the socio-economic development by enhancing the productive capacity of the people. It develops impartial distribution of wealth and makes possible social mobility of the people. The expenditure on education can be justified by its capacity to influence the process of national development.

Estimates of rates of return are now available for many different countries. There have been attempts to measure the returns to education in U.S.A., Britain, several Latin American countries, Israel, Kenya, Uganda and India. Having estimated the returns to education the next logical step is to compare the returns, or benefits of the investment with the costs, in order to measure the rate of return or yield of the investment.

In India, education has been constantly affected by insufficient resources. So it has become the responsibility of policy-makers to take policy decisions enabling Indian education to concentrate on courses at secondary and tertiary levels to maximize returns.

Rate of returns approach considers education as an investment in human capital and uses rate of return as a criterion in allocation of financial resources. That is, if the rate of return is low then the expenditure on education should be truncated or cut down. Theodore Schultz suggested that economic returns to education were simply the return to investment that had been made in human beings.

According to this approach, investment in education should be *done in order to get some returns*. The rate of return and investment must be equal like the other types of investment of capital, like investment in industry for the production of goods gives equal returns. This principle is called 'Equi-marginal returns' in economic theory and could be extended to educational sector.

Types of Rate of Return and Measurement of the Rate of Return

The search for investment criteria in the sphere of educational planning has been centred on the attempts to find the capital value of education invested in educated persons, and also find the private and social rates of return to various types of education. If these figures can be established, then a measure of the overall and marginal social contribution of education to economic and social development can be ascertained.

The rates of return look at education both as an investment for the whole community by means of social rate of return, and as investment for the individual by using the *private rate of return*.

Social rate of return: It measures the relationship between the before tax lifetime earning differentials associated with a particular type of education and the total social costs of that education is measured in terms of its opportunity cost. It furnishes the benefit to be consequent of the state of investing in a particular form of education. The cost of education is usually accepted by the society as a whole and calculated by equating the total present value earnings of an average educated person before tax with benefits to be gained from alternative investments in physical capital.

Private rate of return: It measures the relationship between after tax earning differentials and those costs that borne by the individual; provided a means of assessing education as a form of private investment. Since the information about age earning profiles is derived from a large sample, it shows what are the costs and benefits for an average worker. Of course, some individuals will earn more than this, and others will earn less, the average individual can expect for a university degree.

The information contained in such as an estimate of the private rate of return may help to explain the private demand for education. We can see the effect of the government's policy on subsidies and scholarships on the private rate of return. The higher the degree of subsidy, we find the higher the private rate of return towards education. But can the rate of return be used as any sort of a guide to allocation policy?

It is easy to see how to calculate the private rate of return, and to understand what it means for the individual. By choosing to go to school, or college, the individual incurs certain costs like fees, expenditure on books, and the earnings he foregoes while in school instead of working, on the other hand he can expect to be paid more throughout his life as a result of his education. If the extra earnings he receives less the tax he will have to pay as related to the costs he had to incur. This gives the *private rate of return* to schooling.

Therefore, in order to calculate the rate of return it is necessary to have information about the relative earnings of workers with different levels of education together with estimates of private expenditure on fees, books and so on, and the average earnings foregone by students the best way to obtain this information is to collect by means of a sample survey data on the age, educational qualifications, and earnings of a representative sample of workers.

Such surveys usually show that there is a *positive relationship between education and levels of earnings*. The data can then be used to construct age-education-earnings profiles, which will show the average earnings foregone by students in education. The age-education-earnings profiles together with estimates of tuition costs, therefore, provide everything that is needed to calculate the rate of return.

Utility of the Rate of Return

- The rate of return approach helps the policy-makers to evaluate the investment decisions in specific projects and programmes in a wider framework that is based on human capital theory.
- When social cost benefit rates are to be used for planning, the relation between earning differences at different educational levels and the rate of expansion of educated people is known.
- It helps in regulating the admission in various courses and policy decision regarding public investment and manpower requirement.
- The rate of return is positively helpful in saving the scarce resources.
- They also help the students who are going for courses that have a readily available employment market.
- It helps in saving the students from frustrating image of unemployment or underemployment in this country.
- Rate of return provides a useful guide to the allocation of resources between different types of investment. If the objective of planning is to maximize, the relation between economic benefits and costs.

According to Barrios and Davis (1980 : 86), the ex-post analysis after rate of return helps in:

- Identifying excess for higher education.
- Analysis of the distribution of burdens and benefits in education.
- The development of strategies for financing education.
- Identification of shortages and surpluses of educated persons.

Thus rate of return basically depends upon:

- Intelligence,
- Parental socio-economic status,

- Motivation and
- Aspiration.

In this approach, it is not easy to trait the rate of returns to education obtained. Hence, this approach is least frequently applied to education. This kind of approach in reality is not applicable to education due to problems associated with measuring rate of returns in education.

The 'Correlations' Approach

The first attempts to demonstrate that education was investment consisted in simply correlating some index of educational progress—for instance expenditure on education, per head, or enrolment rates, with an economic index—such as GNP per head. This was done both for different countries at one point of time—or for one country in different years.

In either case the correlation is positive: the more a country spends on education, the richer it is. This suggests that education adds to wealth of the country also. Unfortunately the relationship can just as easily states the other way: the richer a country is, the more it spends on education. So although simple correlation shows that there is a relationship between education and economic progress, it does not prove cause and effect. This is, of course, true of all correlation exercises. So although this approach is interesting and is being developed, with more sophisticated indices of education or economic levels and is being extended to inter-industry or inter-firm comparisons within countries, as well as international comparisons, it does not answer our basic question. The international comparisons are often used as a basis for deciding how much a country should spend on education.

The Residual Approach

Education and economic progress are positively correlated led economists to try to say how much of the increase in a country's national income could be explained by education. The first attempt, in America, to explain increase in national income by looking at the input of different factors had shown that output, or GNP, had grown much faster than the input of labour and physical capital. Comparing the rate of growth of input and output, construct a production function showing the relationship between input and output. The unexplained increase in output was termed 'the residual' such as technical knowledge and economies of scale. Denison in his famous book, *The Source of Economic Growth in the U.S. and the Alternative before us* tried to measure the contribution of these factors to the increase in American National Income, over 40 years, and came to the conclusion that increases in the formal education of the labour force—measured both in terms of increased years of schooling of the average worker, and increases in the number of school-days in the year-accounted for an important part of the residual. The significance of this research for education was examined by a study group of the OECD, in a book called *The Residual Factor and Economic Growth.* Denison's approach is criticized on technical grounds, as some of the assumptions he made about the form of the production function of the American economy—and also to see that how much does one factor contribute to the 'residual'. It also depends on how carefully one specifies the other factors. We can say that the attempt of how much increase in the national economy has taken place due to education without getting into the technical reasons was not successful. Denison concept of education as an investment for economic growth was a success. In other words, attempts to measure the contribution of capital and labour inputs to the growth of GNP per capita over time, using a simple linear homogeneous production function, and other restrictive assumptions, has resulted in a large "unexplained" residual factor that has also in some way contributed to the growth of output. Although much of the residual, has been attributed to technical progress embodied in capital and labour (due to improved quality of the labour force as a result of better education and improved health etc.), the exact contribution that expenditures on education has made to the overall increase is by no means clear, but it is assumed to have played a large part. If it could be ascertained then criteria could be established for the amount of expenditure on education in the future for a certain desired growth rate.

The Econometric Approach

The recent development of educational planning models, mainly of the input-output and linear programming variety, is designed to aid educational policy-makers in their decision making. These models are similar both conceptually and methodologically to the previous approaches mentioned, and the assumptions underlying them are basically the same. In this sense they may be regarded as an amalgam of these various approaches, and as such incorporate most of the advantages and disadvantages of them also.

Wage Differentials Approach

Wage differentials are well known as inter-industry, inter-firm, inter-area or geographical differentials. We see that wages are the price of labour that is influenced by its demand and supply that differ in countries, areas, industries and occupations.

Demand and supply: A difference in the skills and abilities of labour and in the demand for different type of workers in a labour market depends upon its own demand and supply conditions. Demand for labour depends upon the physical productivity of labour and the price of the product. Supply of labour is influenced by education and skill. The demand for skilled workers is high because the importance in the production process, relatively inelastic and they need training and qualification, their supply is low and inelastic. The supply of unskilled labour is high and elastic.

Due to area: For any type of job or occupation, wages are usually higher in one area than in others. Much of this difference is because of differences in the cost-of-living. However, most people are reluctant to move because they do not want to leave their friends, sell their house, be subjected to the cost and uncertainty of a new job in a new community, and the children may not want to change schools. People may also be unwilling to give up pension plans, health insurance, or seniority at their current job. Hence, wage differentials in different areas may persist, even if people know that higher wages can be earned elsewhere. Not only wages differ among occupations, but these also differ in case of workers working in the same occupation at different geographical regions. These differences are the result of working conditions prevalent in different regions of the country.

Movement of workers: Large scale movement of workers from low-paid to high-paid jobs would tend to equalize wages as the movements out of the lower paid jobs would reduce the supply of the type of labour and raise its price. Movements into highly paid jobs would increase the supply and tend to lower the price.

Trade unions: Some workers have their wages and salaries influenced by collective bargaining procedure. Trade unions force the employers to negotiate with representatives of the whole acting as a channel of communication between workers and employers. These differences arise because of the differences in the personal characteristics (age or sex) of workers working in the same unit and occupation. Though provision of 'equal pay for equal work' is certainly there, but it is still not the reality. Instances are there when woman worker is paid less than her male counterpart for doing the same job. Of course, there are other reasons also which cause wage differentials between male and female workers. Trade unions play their role in changing social attitudes showing significance to male employees.

Occupational licensing: The requirement for occupational licensing may also be an impediment to moving to a different area for higher wages. Many occupations require state licensing, such as law and medicine, so if a licensed worker wanted to move to a new state, she would have to obtain a new licence and may have to satisfy additional requirements. Many localities also have their own licensing requirements for certain occupations, such as for beauticians or barbers.

Wage Differentials due to Market Imperfections: In economics, there is an assumption that people migrate to higher paying jobs from lower paying jobs of the same type and with the same requirements. However, this can only happen if people know about the jobs. People tend to look for jobs in their own locality by searching the local newspaper or local Internet listings. Moreover, many people get jobs from their network of friends and acquaintances, who tend to live in the same area. Hence, the lack of information can lead to persistent differences in wage differentials for the same type of job.

Performance Pay

Many occupations pay a wage rate commensurate with performance, such as sales or managerial occupations. The purpose of performance pay is to attract the most highly qualified and productive workers, or as economists like to say, workers with highest marginal revenue productivity.

Performance pay is also used to motivate workers to work. Many employees paid a flat wage rate often linger or dawdle, which lowers their productivity and the employer's marginal revenue product. Dawdling employees can also lower morale, since harder working employees resent being paid the same as the dawdling employees. Performance pay helps to solve this principal-agent problem by aligning the interests of the employees with that of the owners of the firm—both want to make more money.

There are various types of performance pay. Piece rates are paid according to the amount of work accomplished. Many factories use piece rates to prevent dawdling.

Commissions are often paid as a percentage of sales, in such industries as real estate, insurance, securities, and retail sales. Royalties are paid to artists who actually create a product and, like commission, is usually a percentage of the sales price of the product. For instance, authors may receive 27 per cent of the price of a book for each book that they sell.

Bonuses and stock options are often paid to executives of the company so that they work harder to ensure that the company will succeed. Bonuses are lump sum payments paid at the end of the year after the employee's performance can be assessed. Stock options align the interests of executives of the company with those of the shareholders—if their shareholders profit, then they will too. Profit-sharing plans are often used to pay a percentage of the firm's profits to employees so that they work harder.

Efficiency Wages

Firms may also pay efficiency wages, which are higher than market wages, to attract more productive workers. Efficiency wages may lower the firm's cost of labour by hiring only productive individuals, with lower turnover, which can result in a more experienced workforce. Consequently, recruiting and training costs are also lower. Good employees also require less supervision and monitoring. Besides attracting the best workers, efficiency wages can make the threat of being fired more effective. If a worker is earning a regular wage at one company, then the threat of being fired is not much of a threat if he can easily find a job elsewhere paying the same wage. On the other hand, if he loses a job earning efficiency wages, then he will be less likely to find other employment paying a comparable wage.

Occupational Differences

Occupations in an organization widely differ from one another in terms of skill requirement and the extent of requirement and the extent of responsibility. Accordingly, wages vary from occupation to occupation. Such differences in occupations induce people/workers to undertake more challenging jobs, encourage workers to develop their skills by way of education and training. It is varying skill requirement for different occupations that shape the manpower planning in an organization—be it an industrial organization or educational institution.

Inter-firm Differentials

There are wage differentials of workers in different plants in the same area and occupation. Factors like differences in quality of labour employed by different firms, imperfections in the labour market and differences in the efficiency of equipments and supervision result in inter-firm wage differentials. Added to these are differences in technological advance, managerial efficiency, financial capability, firm's age and size, availability of raw material, power and transport facilities also account for differences in wages among firms.

Let us Sum up

These remarks suggest a few practical uses of social demand approach is providing useful projections of the demand for education, and forces the planner to think about some factors determining the demand. The manpower forecasting approach recognizes the role of education in providing trained manpower, although it is extremely difficult to forecast accurately.

These approaches attempt to provide the different types of guidance for the planner. While the social demand and manpower forecasting approach aim to provide actual targets for enrolment, the rate of return approach provides a 'direction-indicator'. The policy prescription from the rate of return calculation is "invest a little more or a little less" in a particular type of education, rather than build a certain number of new schools. Rates of return provide an estimate of the effects of the marginal change in investment allocation. Once change has been made, it becomes necessary to make a new calculation of rate of return, given the new supply and demand conditions.

If we once again ask the question "How can the economist help in the problem of allocating resources?" I think the answer is "by emphasizing the investment aspects of education, and by demanding that every benefit of education—whether economic, social, political or cultural, will be thought in terms of its cost. If educational planning is able to take account of the effects of changes in supply and demand on relative wage levels, and the need to talk in terms of 'alternative approaches'. What I think is important, is not whether a plan is based on manpower forecasts, international comparisons, rates of return, or any other technique but the resource allocation decisions should be made in a framework which includes consideration of both costs and benefits. A wage settlement in one market may cause wage demands in other markets. If one labour market is expanding and one contracting, a widening of the wage differential movement takes place in the market.

REFERENCES

Azad, J.L. Fundamentals of Educational Planning, Ibadan: Adejare Press.

Belman D. and J.S. Heywood (1989). *Applied Economics*, Taylor & Francis.

http://www.yourarticlelibrary.com/hrm/jobs/top-5-causes-of-wage-differentials-explained/35339

Madhurimalall and Sakinaqasinzaidi, (2017). *Human Resource Management—Approaches to Educational Planning.*

Maureen Wood Hall, The investment approach to educational planning, UNESCO: *International Institute for Educational Planning.*

Naik. J.P. (1965). *Educational Planning in India.* New Delhi: Allied Publishers.

Shii, S. *International Economic Review*, 2002–Wiley Online Library.

17

The Return from Education

Ahmad Mahmoud Ali Alghzawi

Introduction

Governments and individuals would not have increased their spending on education had it not been for material returns from education, irrespective of the non-material returns that outweigh the material value, as confirmed by research on education returns that educators, politicians and economists have justified spending on education given the returns from education. The contribution of learning to economic and social development has enabled officials of the education system to rationally deal with human and material education resources, and ways to optimize their use under economic processes and methods and the use of adequacy and productivity to correct existing imbalances and raise the effectiveness of performance, and to judge what has been done and achieved.

Yield Concept

Considering education as an investment process means employing the optimal education of its human and material resources in order to achieve specific material benefits over a given period of time, but the lesson in determining and measuring the returns to education. Economic return is the amount of monetary and non-monetary income generated by an investment over its useful life, in other words, the cost to be sacrificed for higher income in the future.

The return on education is defined as "the amount of increase in real national income that is associated with education and obtained by members of the labour force as a result of improved production and earning capacity."

Individual returns from education are: direct and indirect monetary income earned by graduates because of their educational levels resulting from investment in education, especially investment in post-secondary education.

Revenues of education: "are the economic and social gains of the individual and society that are associated with education." It is "the amount of increase in real national income that is associated with the additional education that the workforce receives."

Revenue in education is the sum of the outputs that are directly or indirectly attributable to education, which generate economic benefits by calculating the return or material gains that learners and society receive compared to the costs currently incurred. Yield is the interest rate that balances the current price of the expected return with the actual total value of the cost.

In the latest World Bank Report on Education in the Middle East and North Africa, which includes most Arab countries, it was noted that most Arab countries suffer from the trap of low productivity and low return on investment in education, where low productivity leads to low rates of return on education, which in turn leads to low investment in education, resulting in low productivity and so on. Recent literature in the theory of economic growth has formulated a variable of education in the form of human capital and introduced this variable in economic growth models where human capital is defined as the average number of years of schooling among the population aged 15 years and older (or 25 years and older).

On the basis of this definition, information shows that since 1960, Arab countries as a group have been able to invest in human capital in a remarkable way. The average years of schooling per person aged 15 years and over increased from 1.1 years in 1960 to an average of 4.8 years in 2000. This is a growth rate of human capital of about 4.2 per cent annually.

The rate of return on education is defined as "the relative increase in per capita income derived from employment in a competitive labour market, as a result of a one-year increase in school years."

Measuring the rate of return on education has become an important application area in studies of labour markets and education systems. In order to estimate the return on education, applied approaches have been developed to estimate this return at the individual level, where the private return on education is estimated through careful decision to invest in education by individuals.

The calculation of the rates of return for education is a prerequisite and a critical prerequisite for successful educational planning, both the individuals themselves and the authorities responsible for education, and knowledge of the returns from education is important to determine the demand for education.

Efficiency requires that rates of return for education and for all types of education be equal, and if not, then the transfer of investment resources from low-return education will in many countries there is a large discrepancy between the rates of return for basic, secondary and tertiary education, and in particular to the returns of basic education in the least developed (developing) countries which are very high and therefore, many economists like these countries. More resources allocated to education should be directed specifically to primary schools. The study of the returns to education has gone through two basic stages:

1. The first stage: The stage of the report where thinkers and specialists noted the fundamental differences between the educated and uneducated in the aspects of behaviour and production and other aspects, and these differences led them to determine the existence of positive effects and returns to education in the construction of man.

2. The second stage: The measurement phase, where researchers relied on the data of the previous stage and tried to measure some of the effects of education in the national income and individual and various aspects of personality after that, especially after the development of means of measurement and the availability of necessary data.

Divergent Views on Measuring the Economic Return from Education

Education men are divided into attempts to measure the economic return from education.

1. *The primary point of view:* Education is a high human phenomenon that is higher than calculation and above appreciation and that its value cannot be valued and cannot be calculated in any way.
2. *Second view:* Measuring the return of education helps to highlight its role in economic development at the individual and national levels, but they object to the use of the same methods and standards used by economists in the material fields.

Methodology for Estimating the Return on Education

Output is the sum of learners who have completed (did not complete or dropped out) their education in school—or institute or college—(how much and how much production) having achieved over a given time a level of achievement, growth or maturity represented by little or many knowledge, skills, values and attitudes. That is supposed to fit into the goals and objectives of education (this is how or the quality of production).

The outputs are appointed these learners after entering the battle of life and their integration into their institutions—really and emotionally—using what they have gained in school (or institute or college) and then the difference between (final output of education) and (outputs) as terms—is a difference in the time and place of the learner on production line and march of social and economic development and teams in the community.

The end result is a learner who moves from inside the school, institute or college outside with a qualification, certificate, or other degree as accomplished and expresses this which holds him to work and contribute to the development of himself and the society in which he integrates.

And the director: Is this learner after he exceeded the door of the school or institute or college and entered the arena of life and institutions already and became his work as an individual and as a member of the group "return" or feedback indicates the "sincerity" and "usefulness" of what he learned.

Minser (1958), Schultz (1988), Card (1995) and (1998) for the review articles in this field, it is important to recall that the incentive to develop the human capital approach has been an attempt to understand the role that individual decisions play on the basis of rational economic behaviour in explaining observed wage differentials *versus* income distribution theories that consider such behaviour beyond analysis. Human capital models are focused by individuals by excluding all non-competitive forces that result in income inequality. The basic assumptions of the model as developed by Minser are as follows:

- The length of training or education is the main source of inequality in workers' income, and training raises worker productivity, but training requires postponement of income for a future period.
- When making a training decision, individuals expect to receive higher incomes in the future that offset the cost of training.
- The cost of training is assumed to be limited to the alternative

cost, i.e. income that the individual would have received if he did not attend training institutions.

- It is assumed that individuals will not make a decision for future training after the end of the initial training period, and that the flow of future income after the end of the initial training period will remain constant during the practical period.
- Assumes that the interest rate used by individuals in discounting future flows is constant.

Education Return

In the United States of America and some countries around the world, many studies and researches have been conducted on this subject, which confirm the relative fact and general trend that there is a positive and significant relationship between education in its different stages and types.

And between development and economic and social progress and some studies try to classify the return (return) of education to:

1. Temporary consumer returns for example: give parents an opportunity to relieve the troubles of children by sending them to school, or some children enjoy school life and living among peers.
2. Long-term capital returns and an impact on the life of the individual and his future, such as: increase the capacity (and productivity) of the individual and acquire the skill or habit of reading insight and useful knowledge.
3. Individual or personal returns, such as: increase the income of the individual, or enjoy his free time.
4. Social returns, such as: increase national production, increase taxes on incomes, and increase the scientific and technological capacity of the state.
5. Financial returns, such as: increase the human capacity to save, or good spending.
6. Non-financial returns, such as: increasing the human capacity to understand him and to innovate.

The Importance of Studying the Revenues of Education

- Help to rationalize investment in education in the light of specific alternatives by comparing the returns on investment in education with the economic and social sectors, especially after the spread of education among the categories of society.

- Empowering educational planners and decision-makers in making the right decision to distribute expenditures among different types of education according to investment needs and returns.
- Contribute to knowing the suitability of education systems to meet the needs of development and the labour market of qualified and trained workforce, especially in the disciplines that increase demand, which limits the unemployment of learners.
- Help develop curricula in form and content of implementation and evaluation and develop modern teaching and learning systems that meet the needs of learners and the needs of development and the labour market.
- Push officials and educational planners to pay attention to scientific research to study the variables of education and its various phenomena and their relationship to economic and social transformations.

Applying the economic perspective and logic in measuring the returns of education, new terms and meanings have emerged in the field of education that seem strange, but they have become a reality that must be dealt with.

- *Capital goods:* It contributes to reducing the number of workers because the educated and trained worker is more productive than the uneducated worker, in addition to the development of education for its abilities and trends that increase the accumulation of physical capital, making education a store of intangible capital that gives importance to physical capital.
- *Some kind of human investment:* It is seen through the increasing productivity of the learner and society and thus increase their income.
- *Consumer durable goods:* It contributes to expand the knowledge and abilities of the educated person to upgrade his personality, and take care of his health, and raise the standard of living, and increases the pleasure of private and public life.
- *Social commodity:* It increases the effectiveness of the learner in dealing with the issues of society and reduce crime and

promotes taste and morality and increase the learner's acceptance of new lifestyles.

- *Political commodity:* It develops the characteristics of belonging and good citizenship and abide by the laws of society and gain the learner values of loyalty to society and support for the political system.

Measuring the Economic Return from Education

By calculating the cost and return through the cross-sectional sample and extracted the income of individuals at different levels of age according to the educational level of individuals and thus get the level of income per capita for different educational levels in successive ages. The method highlighted:

- The per capita income is highly correlated with the level of education.
- Income increases and reaches the highest level in the average age and then stabilizes and sometimes decreases until the retirement age.
- The incomes of individuals with higher education are very high for those who are less educated.
- Income is highest for those with higher education at a later age and sometimes continues to rise until retirement.

The Goal of Measuring the Return on Education

1. Statement of the contribution of education to economic development.
2. The educational plan provides useful background information on the links between education and the labour market.
3. Providing us with the cost of education in different stages, and the balance of supply and demand.
4. Helps to make different comparisons between the economic return from education and other investment projects.
5. Determines the stage of education, and educational programmes the most effective investment.
6. Directs the relationship between spending on higher education and the labour market, and wage policy in the country.
7. The scheme is useful in the distribution of investment in the

field of high return/suggest ways to increase the efficiency of education by increasing the return or reduce the cost/examination of the cost of education and compared with the increase in the incomes of the educated workforce.

Difficulties in Education

Despite the importance of measuring returns in education and mathematical calculation, there are systemic and practical difficulties of measuring the return in education as in other productive projects because education is an open system in which many factors and forces affecting it near and far, calculated and non-calculated, and interacts with each other. What surrounds it almost permanently, which makes the measurement process a very complex task because of the existence of methodological and practical difficulties. Perhaps the most prominent are:

1. *Difficulty in comparing costs with revenues:* Because of the difficulty of identifying educational objectives accurately in the form of criteria to measure performance, then the returns in education take different forms, including economic and non-economic, including returns at the level of the educated person, and others at the level of society, and if the returns can be calculated in the form of a net expected return on learning expenditure, it is difficult to measure and accurately define non-economic returns.
2. *Difficulty in identifying the types of expenditures invested in education and their sources:* Whether they are investment or consumer expenditures, and whether they are monetary or other material financial expenditures and their valuation.
3. *Difficulty in measuring the factors of production in education:* The productivity in education depends on many indicators difficult to quantify things intangible, as well as difficult to measure the effectiveness and productivity of the work of teachers, students and educational institutions (the real productivity of educational work).
4. *The difficulty of quantifying the unit of output in education:* As happens in the classification of goods and services as well as the difficulty of determining the monetary value of output because education does not work to sell its output at market prices.
5. *Difficulty in measuring the impact of education on labour*

productivity: The adequacy of labour and productivity may be due to factors other than education such as capacity. The impact of education alone is difficult to isolate and measure among the non-material elements affecting production.

6. The emergence of the economic return from spending on education is delayed because there is a long time between spending on education and obtaining a return on education, which may take between ten to fifteen years or more.
7. The apparent negligence of measuring social, political, and cultural returns from education because of the impossibility of measuring them in monetary and physical units.
8. Ignoring studies and research, measuring the role of science and scientific research in increasing the productivity of work since education is the basis of the growth of science and scientific research and through scientific research can develop tools and methods of production.

However, the aforementioned difficulties have not prevented the measurement of education revenues at least in the areas that can be calculated and come up with methods to avoid many difficulties. Other studies seek to measure other education revenues through qualitative indicators.

Problems Measuring the Return on Education

1. The exploitation of capital in education—building schools, for example—does not produce a product that can be marketed, and difficult to calculate the financial return as a social capital of the individual and when compared to other projects.
2. Restrict to present and past supply and demand situations, and use them to determine future needs.
3. The measurement of indirect economic benefits is neglected.
4. The problem of collecting facts and data required and accuracy in developing countries such as (individuals' income/expenses of each educational stage/school expenses/scholarships/labour market data/average income tax).

Ways and means of measuring the economic return of education.

Schultz argues that education returns can be measured in two ways—direct and indirect.

If the park is opened to people for a certain fee, the income of these fees represents the direct economic return. An indirect economic return is the available air, sun, tree and green landscape, and these economic benefits can be measured but difficult. This is the case for education. There are four ways to measure the contribution of education to the economy:

1. *Calculation of the return on the estimate of increase in per capita income:* There is physical capital, human capital/for every investment of capital there is what is called returnable measurable/there is difficulty to measure human capital but economists managed to do this and divided it to individual and collective return, and individual direct and indirect.

Direct return on the individual, based on the comparison between the profits of individuals and their level of education and the idea that education raises the level of qualification of the worker, which entails increasing productivity and this in turn leads to raise its level. Studies (Walsh) indicated that the financial value obtained by the individual as a result of education exceeds in all cases the expenses spent on it, and studies of Schultz, Lobel, Glick, Baker and Hothacker.

Objections:

1. Opposing the return of education from the individual and the society.
2. Individual return varies from one community to another.
3. The amount of income taken by the individual does not necessarily indicate the value of his work, because of the link to the social status and status of the family, and other social factors such as patronage.
4. Indirect return on the individual, such as respect for work and production, accept cultural change and advocacy, development of innovation and ambition of the individual, educational experiences, concepts and social skills and attitudes and tastes of individuals.

2. *Bonding Method:* It means to measure the interdependence between educational activity and the level of economic activity, and methods, comparing different countries at a fixed time, and discovering the previous link between the growth of education and the growth of national income. Research has been conducted on the correlation between

school enrolment rates and per capita national income and the existence of positive correlations between them despite the disparity between countries. There is a method of interdependence over time and means to measure the correlation between education and national income within a particular country over different periods of time, such as the Schultz study, during which he measured the correlation between education and national income in America during the period 1900 to 1956. As well as measuring the impact of education in the production of factories.

3. *The residue Method to know the Contribution of Education to Increase the General National Income:* Thus, the overall increase in the national production of a country is estimated over a period of time, indicating the role of determinable and measurable factors in that increase, concluding that what remains is due to some unspecified factors. A number of researchers pointed out:

- The percentage increase in the GNI that can be traced back to the capital and labour spent in a certain period of time and then considered the rest as a result of improvements in the quality of the workforce due to education.
- The remaining factor includes the elements of education, training and technological regulation.
- The remaining factor can be explained by economies of scale, improvement in the quality of human and non-human resources entering the production process.

4. *The Method of Calculating the Cost and Economic Return:* Cost-benefit calculation means comparing the cost of an investment project with the expected return with a view to determine its usefulness, and choosing to invest capital in a project that means sacrificing money at the present time in order to secure future benefits or return on that money.

Investor in the form of higher levels of income or production. So the concept of cost and benefit:

- Means comparing an investment project with the expected return with a view to determine its usefulness.
- The choice of capital investment in a project means sacrificing money at the present time in order to ensure future benefits or return on the money invested in the form of higher levels of production and income.
- Determining the relationship between spending on investment

projects and expected return is a very important process because it guides us to allocate financial resources on a sound basis.

How can investment in education be compared to other types of investments?

- Which types of investment contribute more to economic growth: investment in human capital or investment in physical capital?
- Are all types of education and stages equal in terms of the rate of return of them?
- What is the contribution of education to increase national income and per capita?
- What is the relationship of education to economic growth?

All of the above revolves around, the head axis is: "The relationship between investment in education and its return as education is an investment process that has a measurable return?"

Methods of Educational Cost Analysis

A. Method of Comprehensive Analysis: It deals with analyzing the status of education for the national economy and comparing education with the national income and the general budget of the country. This method is useful for comparative studies between different countries.

B. Method of detailed analysis of the total costs and unit cost by type of education (general education/special education) and stages, i.e. calculate the cost of pupils in education (primary/preparatory/secondary) and the purpose of spending on any study (direct costs of education/ indirect costs/social costs).

How to Calculate the Cost in Education?

- Cost in education means current expenditure on education.
- For the purposes of determining expenditure and return for an investment project, the actual total cost of the project includes financial expenses in educational investment—teachers' salaries, rent of buildings, the price of equipment, stationery, other materials and services.
- The rate of return on an investment project is the interest rate that balances the current expected rate of return with the actual

total value of the cost. That is, the rate of return is the interest rate at which the cost is equal to the value of the return.

- Interest rate of return is the trade-off between investment projects and the initial investment that achieves the greatest return.
- Data required to calculate the rate of return on education (income of individuals by age, level of education, gender, function and class/expenditure on education per stage/capital value estimates—buildings, equipment and laboratories—per stage/ value of school expenses per stage/average income tax/data of labour market, such as unemployment and employment rates. This is not available in many countries so resort to the cross-sectional sample to obtain the necessary data as estimated in India, Venezuela and the Philippines. If not available resort to data on the wage as happened in Uganda.
- The rate of return from a project that has no meaning unless compared to the rate of return from other investment projects, as well as the rate of return on investment at certain stages.

How to Benefit from Cost-Benefit Calculation?

1. The calculation of cost and return is directed to the planned direction of investment in any type of education, but in any educational stage is investment.
2. The cost-benefit calculation draws attention to the relationship between spending on high-level manpower education and the labour market, and the impact of changing salary and wage systems on the demand for education.
3. The cost-benefit calculation directs a better allocation of financial resources to higher-yielding types of education.
4. Cost-benefit calculation suggests ways to increase the efficiency of education by increasing yield or reducing cost.
5. The calculation of cost and return helps in examining the cost of education and comparing it to the increase in the income of the educated workforce.

REFERENCES

8th International Congress on Obesity. Paris, France, 29 August-3 September 1998.

Abbas, Abdin Muhammad (2003). *Education Planning Issues, Global and Local Economies,* The dar Egyptian Lebanese for publishing and distribution, Cairo.

Agima, Mohamed Abdelaziz, Mohamed Libyan (2001). *Economic Development: Concept, Theories and Policy,* dar University or for publishing and distribution, Egypt.

Ali, Ali Abdulkadir (2009). *Measuring the Return on Education,* the Arab planning Institute in Kuwait, Kuwait, p. 3.

Azeez, Salem Abdel (2002). "The economic importance of human capital and the role of education in it," a paper presented to the educational Seminar accompanying the Central Council of teacher Union.2\13-2\Arabs held in Algeria.

Bouhi, Shawqi (2011). Differences in Educational and Economic Planning.

El Din Zayed, Mohamed Assam (1997). Investing in Human Training at the project level, *Arab Labor Journal*, Issue 8, pp. 13-18.

Hamdan, Suhail (2002). *Economics of Education Cost of Education and its Revenues*. Aladdin Foundation, Damascus.

Hani Muhammad, Al-Saeed (2008). *Intellectual Capital: A Contemporary Administrative Breakthrough,* Dar Al-Sahab Publishing and Distribution Jordan.

http://www.kitabat.com dated May 24, 2015 from the writing of Alani Ihassan Atalla.

Ismail, Hajji Ahmed (2002). *Education Economics and Educational Planning,* Cairo, dar al-fikr al-arbi for publishing and distribution, Cairo.

Khalaf, Falah Hassan (2006). *Development and Economic Planning*, World of Modern Books, Jordan.

Khalaf, Falih Hussein (2006). *Development and Economic Planning,* Jadar for the World Book, Amman, Jordan.

Muhammad, Al-Moghrabi Kamel (2004). Organizational Behaviour, Concepts and Foundations of Individual and behaviour in 2004 Organization, 3rd floor, Amman, Dar thought for publishing and distribution.

OECD (1998), *Education at a Glance: OECD indicators 1998*, Paris.

18

Trend of Supply of Education

Kartar Singh and Nazia Hassan

Introduction

According to Professor Samuelson (1961), "Economics is the study of how men and society choose, with or without the use of money, to employ scarce productive resources to produce various commodities over time and distribute them for consumption, now and in the future, among various people and group in society".

According to *Dictionary of Webster's* "Education is the process of training and developing the knowledge, skill, mind, character etc., especially by formal schooling" (p. 461). Economics of education deals with:

- Production of education through which it is produced.
- Distributing education among groups and individuals which compete with each other.
- Expenditure on education, i.e. how much should be spent by the society on various activities in education and the type of activities selected in the field of education.

Economics of education is dealing with economic issues related to Education. Economic development of any country depends on its Natural resources (forest, agriculture, mineral fertile land etc.) and Human Capital (skilful educated people). To increase productivity within the country, Education is a prominent factor. Productivity can be increased when there is an investment in Human Capital, i.e.

- Education,
- Training (skill development), and
- Health Care.

Due to increase in productivity (through increased Human Capital) an individual gets higher pay and with this increased pay he can contribute in economics activity (paying taxes, increase in life expectancy with good medical care, increase in consumption etc.). It shows that educated workers are more productive, i.e. education refines all areas of resources.

Education also acts as a market where with—

- Producer's Goods—Human Capital.
- Consumer's Goods—Purchase of education and wants as a consumer.

So, Market is determined by demand and supply forces. Here let us understand **Supply** of education and **Demand** for education.

Supply of Education

Supply is concept of economics that describes the total amount of goods or services which is available to consumer. Supply is anything in demand that is sold in competitive market place.

Supply originates whenever there is demand for any product say Education. There is desire among people to acquire education and this desire is nothing but demand. For fulfilling the demand there is supply and same is applicable in education sector.

Supply of Education [Global Perspective]

Literacy rates at global level is rising during the course of the last two centuries, due to increase in enrolment rate at primary level. Education at secondary and tertiary level have also seen increased growth, through a drastic change in average years of schooling globally.

Production of education is financed by public resources as predicted by data on education production at global level.

Attendance and Enrolment at school are two measures of educational attainment. Focus is on attendance and enrolment rates basically at the primary level. Most of the developing countries have high Net Enrolment Rates as compared to attendance rates. This shows that most of the children who are enrolled officially, do not go to school regularly. Looking deeply at a report by UNESCO which mainly focuses on measurement of Exclusion from Primary Education (2005), depicts the relationship between these two modes of measurement. The source reports that "among the 59 countries with comparable data, in 24 countries participation rates drop by five percentage points for the primary school-age group when household surveys are used instead of administrative data." In 1998, the estimate is that out of the total population 381 million children were out of school. In 2014, this figure drops to 263 million, even when there is an increase in the global young population [OECD and UNESCO (2016)].

There is a continuous increment in average years of schooling at global level: Due to fall in share of the uneducated population over a period of time, focus at the lower level became less clear and undefined.

Australia is the fastest growing market for international students worldwide, with increasing records each year. Indian students with its high-quality institutions gets attracted with great variety of programmes in STEM and in fields of health basically taught in English, and in numerous opportunities for study and work even after completing their study.

Germany also has a similar surge, if on a smaller scale. The country is basically a good place for students from different countries including India, because of its specialization in engineering programmes with world class ranking and most important due to its free education.

New Zealand, the increasing inflow of students from different countries and majority from India in recent years was unusual for it was driven by enrolments at smaller private providers instead of universities.

Supply of Education [Indian Perspective]

In India, Ministry of Human Resource Development is a pioneer organization to look after the functioning of education in India.

India focuses upon achieving universalization of elementary education, increasing gross enrolment level and universal retention, thus it focuses on providing all essential facilities as been required. According to Article 21-A of the Constitution, RTE Act, 2009 came into operation by providing Free and Compulsory Education under the age of 6-14. Scheme of Sarva Siksha Abhiyaan (SSA) is working under RTE Act for construction and opening of schools, constructing toilets, providing drinking water and qualified teachers, academic support, free uniform and textbooks etc.

According to MHRD Annual Report (2016-17), the major focus of elementary education on all areas with the provision of all essential facilities. The main focus of SSA programme is for:

Table 18.1: A brief description of provision of Essential facilities by MHRD

Areas	*Year*	*Amount Sanctioned (in crores)*
I. Universal access		
• New school	2016-17	20744 (primary) 159175 (upper primary)
• Residential facilities	2016-17	826
• Special training for mainstreaming out of school children		642.4
II. Gender gap in elementary education		
• Girls education	2016-17	286
• Transport facilities		48.14
• Uniform	2016-17	2970
III. Inclusive Education	2016-17	
• Muslims		12117 (lakh)
• Scheduled Caste		983206 (lakh)
• Scheduled Tribe		998433.321 (lakh)
• Children with special need		57276 (lakh)
IV. Improving Quality	2016-17	787.64
V. Academic Support System	2016-17	
• BRC (6759 in numbers)		68.13
• CRC (76064 in numbers)		14.06

Source: Ministry of Human Resource Development Annual Report (2016-17).

I. Universal Access

SSA mainly works for universalization of elementary education (access and equity) so the main areas it has focused are—

New Schools

Under 2016-17, 20,474 primary schools have been sanctioned and 1,59,415 upper primary schools have been sanctioned under SSA Scheme of the Government of India.

Special Training for Mainstreaming out of School Children

There is provision of special training programme for marginalized community, i.e. SC, ST, OBC, Muslim community and children with special needs etc. Special training is provided for residential and non-residential courses. 642.04 crore have been sanctioned for special training of 11.29 lakh out of school children.

Residential Facilities

Provision of 826 residential institutes with capacity of 90,855 children has been made under SSA Scheme of Government of India.

II. Gender Gap in Elementary Education

Girls Education

SSA intervention is available to disadvantaged and weaker sections. It provides female students of primary and upper primary schools prescribed under RTE with uniform, textbooks.

Kasturba Gandhi Balika Vidyalaya (KGBV)

It is mainly for SC, ST, OBC, Muslim and BPL community and also for those from educationally backward background and for out of school girls. Till today 3609 KGBV have been sanctioned and 3,66,756 girls are enrolled under this scheme.

Transport and Escort Facilities

SSA provided Rs. 48.41 crore for transport facilities for 1.61 lakh children.

Uniform

2 sets of uniform to all girls from BPL families have been sanctioned under SSA scheme for 2016-17, i.e. Rs. 2970.83 crore have been sanctioned for free uniform for 75,96,410 children.

III. Inclusive Education

- Allocation of Rs. 1,27,1139 lakh from SSA approved for 88 Muslim dominant special focus districts, i.e. 19 per cent of total SSA allocation and allocation of Rs. 9,98,433.321 for 109 ST focus districts which is 13 per cent of total SSA allocation. Rs. 9,83,206.07 lakh for 61 SC focused district
- ***Children with Special Need (CWSN):*** Financial support up to 30,000 per child for integration of disabled children as per specific proposal. 26.21 lakh identified as CWSN and 23.11 lakh are enrolled. Total allocation for CWSN under SSA is Rs. 57,276 lakh.
- For improving quality various schemes launched such as NAS (National Achievement Survey) which is conducted every year like "Padhe Bharat Badhe Bharat" for class 1 and 2 focuses on functional learning in early grade. Rs. 787.64 crore were sanctioned for this programme. Rastriya Aavishkaar Abhiyaan (RAA) under SSA.

IV. Improving Quality

- NAS conducted every year.
- Padhe Baharat Badhe Bharat Programme. I and II class focusing foundational learning in early Grades.
- Rs. 787.64 crore approved for this programme.
- Rastriya Aavishkaar Abhiyaan (RAA) under SSA by APJ Abdul Kalam engage 6-18-year children in science, Mathematics and Technical innovations.
- Distance education programme for teachers.

V. Academic Support System

Academic Support Structure

6,759 BRC and 76,064 CRC to provide decentralized academic support, training, supervision to teacher and subject-wise teachers for each BRC/CRC for pedagogical and content support.

Factors Responsible for Rapid Increase in Supply of Education

There are factors which are responsible for increasing supply in education sectors, i.e. the factors due to which there is an upward mobility with respect to education sector. Such factors are demand for education, role of the government, urbanization and industrialization and access to education. Let us discuss these factors in detail:

I. *Demand for Education*

By demand for any commodity it means that wish or desire to get any particular good at a point of time. Demand for Education means the desire to be educated, there are various factors on which Demand for Education depends. These are given below:

Increase in Population

With increase in population more people are willing to pursue education this increases the demand for teachers, schools and other resources and accordingly there will be supply of all such educational resources and services.

Poverty Reduction

With economic development people have increased their income and standard of living which brought a wave of Revolution in Education sector. People want their upcoming generations to acquire knowledge for which there is need for more schools and educational resources. There is increase in demand for education for which provision has been made to meet the need of every individual.

Government Policies

Government has started various schemes and programmes such as Sarva Sikhsha Abhiyaan, Mid-day Meal, Padhe Bharat Badhe Bharat, RTE Act, 2009 etc. For increasing the level of education under these schemes, provision has been made by the government to increase Enrolment.

II. Government Role in Pushing Demand for Education

Government plays a vital role in increasing demand for education, the programmes and schemes initiated by government lead to increment in education, i.e. demand for education increases with government initiatives. There are some schemes which government have started to increase demand for education. These are as follows:

Free and Compulsory Education and Other Schemes

There is provision of free and compulsory education under RTE Act, 2009 for elementary education. It is mainly to increase enrolment level and also Universalization of Elementary Education.

Other schemes for Secondary Education, i.e. Rastriya Madhyamik Siksha Abhiyaan (RMSA) and for Higher Education Rastriya Uchchtar Siksha Abhiyaan (RUSA).

Provision of School

There is attention on improving education system in India since Independence and various measures have been taken by the government to uplift education. Schools are opened at mass scale under various Commissions of Education. National Education Policy (NPE) 1986 has brought a drastic change in education system and these changes can be seen from primary to higher level. Various schools such as Kendriya Vidyalaya, Navodaya Vidyalaya have been established. Since then much attention has been drawn towards education all across the globe.

Quality of Education (NAS conducted every year)

- Padhe Baharat Badhe Bharat programme. I and II class focus on foundational learning in early Grades.
- Rs. 787.64 crore approved for this programme.
- Rastriya Aavishkaar Abhiyaan (RAA) under SSA by APJ Abdul Kalam engage 6-18-year children in Science, Mathematics, and Technical Advancement.
- Distance education programme for teachers.

III. Quality of Improvement in Life (Urbanization, Industrialization)

With industrialization there is improvement in standard of living of the people. Urban migration has brought various changes in the life of the people and the biggest one is awareness about education among people. People have now realized the importance of being educated. People prefer to provide their children education in urban areas. There is an increase in Human Capital resources in urban areas.

Industrial revolution brought a drastic change in whole world. Due to industrial revolution, the world has started adopting new technology and innovations. These innovations were witnessed in every area, thus there were changes in education sector as well. People demand for education as they believe that it can upgrade their standard of living. With increasing demand for education there is an improvement in quality of living.

IV. Access

Provision made by the government to provide access to education so as to improve quality and strengthen the capacity for better education system. Universal education attainment can be achieved when there is access to education at primary, secondary and higher level. There are various factors which are important in universal access to education. These are as follows:

Impact of Access Increase on Gross Enrolment Ratio (GER)

In 1950, Government constitutionally committed itself to provide free and compulsory education to all children falling under the age of 14. Thus, a Constitutional Amendment was formed under which it became a fundamental right to provide free and compulsory education for children between the age group of 6-14. Even though, access to elementary education remains vague and poor quality of provision is unbalanced. Providing quality education in India is mostly a quantitative challenge. According to data generated by Ministry of Human Resource Development (MHRD) in 2004-05 there was enrolment of 182 million, out of which 1.04 million were of elementary schools (grades 1-8) across the country (GoI, 2007a). This accounted for approximately 82 per cent of children in the 5-14-year age group in that year (GoI, 2007b).

Demand for schooling in India has increased over the past two decades, but there is an inequality in access to education. The National

Policy on Education (1986) and its Programme of Action (1992) clearly states access to education at elementary level for every children irrespective of caste, location, creed or gender, should also be an increase in pupil-teacher's ratio (number of teachers per student) in reality, provision of school favours those who are better off, and groups that are backward or disadvantaged [including girls, poor children, children from Scheduled Caste (SC), Scheduled Tribe (ST), Other Backward Class (OBC)] group lack access to education and poorer quality of education is made available to them. Huge variations in access to education is seen in different states, people belonging to different social categories and geographical locations have access to varied forms of education. Policy-makers whilst making great strides to improve physical access to schools, have ongoing challenges to provide meaningful access to education for all children in India.

Educational Pattern for Access in India

There is an improvement in access to basic education in India, but there are certain areas that should be focused upon such as—

School supply: In 1986, primary schools were approximately 5,29,000 and have increased to 7,67,000 in 2005 and upper primary from 1,34,000 to 2,75,000. 87 per cent of residents have acquired primary school within a radius of 1 km in 2003 and in 2005 about 78 per cent of residents have acquired an upper primary school at 3 km (NCERT, 2005).

In addition, the number of schools, i.e. primary, pre-primary, upper primary and private schools increased considerably. Main provider of education remains government and local bodies handling around 91 per cent of primary and 73 per cent of upper primary schools. Many new schools particularly those opened under the Employment Guarantee Scheme are small in size. Most are located in rural areas. Around 28 per cent of children are educated in primary schools with an enrolment of students less than fifty in numbers (NUEPA-DISE 2005-06).

Questions of quality of provision persist with many schools having weak infrastructure and poor teaching and learning conditions.

Initial access to education: On the basis of data available for Gross Enrolment Ratio at the national level, India has almost reached an optimum level universal enrolment in primary education, i.e. India has achieved universal elementary education at national level in most areas. At the primary level, the average enrolment ratio across all India was 108.5 per cent and at the upper primary level 70.5 per cent in 2004-05. In various states, there is variation in GERs at primary level from below 80 per cent in Punjab, Chandigarh, to more than 120 per cent in Chhattisgarh, Arunachal Pradesh, and at upper primary from below 60 per cent in Jharkhand, Uttar Pradesh, Bihar to 100 per cent in Himachal Pradesh, Tamil Nadu.

Rural schools: Vast majority of students are from rural areas at national level, i.e. in 2005 total enrolment at primary level were 85 per cent. Poor quality of resources are available in these rural schools such as poor teacher-student ratio, poor school infrastructure, lack of teaching aid and teaching materials, no availability of land and drop-out rates are high. There are only three teachers in 80 per cent of primary schools.

Inter-state variations are quite vast. In the Census of India in 2001 reported that about 70 per cent of the total out-of-school children in India in the 6-10-year-old age group were concentrated in Uttar Pradesh, Bihar, Madhya Pradesh, West Bengal and Rajasthan. According to the 61st Round National Sample Survey (2006): 35 per cent of 5-9 years old have never been to school; and around 28.5 per cent of children dropped out of primary school in 2004-05.

Supply of Education at Higher Level (Indian Perspective)

On the eve of Independence there were twenty universities and five hundred colleges in India. As on March 2016, there have been increment in university to 799 and 3711 colleges. There is an increment in enrolment also, nearly 284.85 lakh students enrolled in universities and colleges in India. There are seven hundred ninety-nine universities and number of colleges is 39,071 whereas stand-alone institutions are 11,923.

Among these universities privately managed universities are 277, in rural areas there are 307 colleges and fourteen universities are reserved for women. Apart from this, there is single Central university in distance mode and number of State university is 1 and there are 118 deemed universities.

- General development grant of Rs. 1,52,234 crore has been provided to forty Central universities in 2015-16 and grant for maintenance of around Rs. 39.59 crore approximately that have been financed for Central Universities (24) and a medical college.
- In 2015-16, there has been sanction of amount of Rs. 1,458.11 crore to State Universities under general development purpose.
- Rs. 5347.70 lakh have been released to State Universities and

Rs. 5505.43 crore for Deemed Universities in 2015-16, under general development assistance.

- For achieving excellence in teaching and research there has been provision of assistance by UGC in the form of grant through which identified universities are labelled with the status of "Universities with Potential Excellence".
- Rs. 33.36 crore for launch of Skill Development based Higher Education.

Table 18.2: A Brief description of amount sanctioned at higher education by MHRD

Sl. No.	*Universities*	*Year*	*Amount sanctioned (crores)*
1.	Central universities	2015-16	1,52,234.00
2.	State universities	2015-16	1,458.11
3.	Deemed universities	2015-16	5,505.43
4.	Skill development at Higher education	2015-16	33.36

Supporting Factors in Supply of Education

Government Provision Towards Supply of Education

Govternment Burdens and Challenges

Challenges in Higher Education in India: Even in the 69th year of independence our education system is not fully developed. We do not rank among 100 top universities of the world, not even a single university lies among the top 200 universities of the world. There have been changes in government during these 6 decades. Various attempts have been made to boost the education system and there is implementation of education policies at all levels but they fail to set an example in the world. There are continuous efforts made by UGC for better working of education system and focus is on maintaining quality education in higher education sector. Despite all such efforts, India is facing lot of problems and challenges in education system. Some of major challenges in higher education system in India are discussed below:

- *Enrolment:* In higher education the Gross Enrolment Ratio (GER) in India is only 15 per cent that is very low if compared with developed and also, some of the developing countries. The supply of higher education institutes is insufficient with the increase of enrolments at school level, meeting with the growing demand in the country.

- *Equity:* In GER there is no equity among different sects of the society. GER in higher education in India varies among male and female to greater extent as suggested by previous studies. Apart from this there is regional variations too, in some states GER is high while some states are quite behind the national GER which shows a significant imbalance within the higher education system.
- *Quality:* In higher education, quality is a multidimensional, and a dynamic concept. Quality in higher education is amongst the foremost challenges being faced in India today. However, Government is continuously focusing on the quality education. Still large number of colleges and universities in India are unable to meet the minimum requirements laid down by the UGC and our universities are not in a position to mark its place among the top universities of the world.
- *Infrastructure:* Infrastructure deficiency is yet another major challenge to the education system in India especially those institutes which are governed by the public sector. These sectors face huge problem from insufficient physical facilities and infrastructure. Large number of colleges which are running on multiple (second and third) floor of the building basically have photocopy shops and readymade hosieries on ground.
- *Faculty:* Shortages of faculty and state educational system's inability to attract and provide well-qualified teachers is considered as big challenge to quality education for many years. Large numbers of scholars who have cleared National eligibility test/PhD remain unemployed despite lot of vacancies in higher education, these scholars and qualified candidates apply for post in other discipline and in other departments which is a largest drawback to the higher education.
- *Accreditation:* According to data provided by the NAAC (June 2010) "not even 25 per cent of the total higher education institutions in the country were accredited. And among those accredited, only 30 per cent of the universities and 45 per cent of the colleges were found to be of quality to be ranked at 'A' level" (Annual Report, 2016, Ministry of Human Resource Development of India, GoI).

- *Innovation and Research:* There are very few scholars in India whose work is cited by renouned Western authors. Inadequate focus on research is a major issue in higher education institutes in India. Inadequate resources and facilities, as well as, lack of quality teachers (faculty) to guide students. Majority of the research scholars do not receive a sound stipend and also not receiving their fellowships on time has adverse effect on their research as they are stressed and less motivated to proceed within their work. Moreover, Indian Higher Education Institutions are poorly connected to research centres. So, this is another area of challenge to the Higher Education in India.
- *Structure of higher education:* Management of the Indian education faces challenges of overcentralisation, bureaucratic structures and lack of accountability, transparency, and professionalism (Annual Report-2016, School of Education and Literacy and Higher Education, MHRD, GoI).

Due to increased number of affiliated colleges and students, the burden on functioning of administrative section of universities has increased significantly and the main focus on research and academics has vanished (Kumar, 2015).

Conclusion

There is detailed description about the concept of supply of education where supply is concept of economics that describes the total amount of goods or services which is available to consumer. Supply is anything in demand that is sold in competitive market place.

Supply originates whenever there is demand for any product say Education. There is desire among people to acquire education and this desire is nothing but Demand. For fulfilling the Demand there is Supply and same is applicable in education sector. There are various factors which are responsible for supply of education i.e. demand for education (increase in population, poverty reduction, government policies), role of government in pushing demand for education (free and compulsory education, provision of school and quality education), impact of industrialization and urbanization, access to education etc. These results in factors which helps in an increment in supply of educational resources required for quality education.

Various schemes of the government at primary, secondary and higher levels have increased universal education, has increased GER and pupil-teacher ratio in urban as well as rural areas. In recent scenario, the focus is made not only on quantitative approach towards providing educational resources rather focus should be shifted on providing qualitative educational access to all. Thus, supply of education is more focused towards qualitative aspects than quantitative.

REFERENCES

Annual Report (2015-16). Department of School Education and Literacy, Ministry of Human Resource Development, Government of India.

Brewer and McEwan (2010). *Economics of Education*, Academic Press, USA.

Bluag, M. (1972). *An Introduction to Economics of Education*, Hardcover, Penguin Books.

Coultas, Julie and Lewin Keith (2002). "Who Becomes a teacher? The characteristics of student teachers in four countries." *International Journal of Educational Development*, 22, 234-260.

Craig, H.J., Kraft, R.J., and du Plessis, J. (1998). *Teacher Development: Making an Impact*. Washington, DC.: U.S. Agency for International Development and The World Bank.

Education International (2003). *Education for All: Is Commitment Enough?* Brussels: Education International.

T.C. Charles, M. Rothschild (1994). "Studies of Supply and Demand in Higher Education." *Southern Economic Journal*. Vol. *79*(6).

Wayne. J. Andrew. (2000). "Teacher Supply and Demand: Surprise from Primary Research." *Educational Policy Analyses Archives*, Vol. 8, p. 47.

Unit 4

Education and Human Development

19

Developing Economics of Value-Based Education

Rethinking Problems, Challenges, and Nature of Education

Muqowim

Introduction

Smart Society 5.0 (SS-5.0) launched by Japanese Prime Minister Shinzo Abe in January 2019 at the Davos World Economic Forum seemed to be a *warning* to every citizen of the world regarding the effects of the Industrial Revolution 4.0 (IR-4.0). This can be a real '*warning*' since IR-4.0 has caused a number of negative influences on human values such as human degradation due to technological advances. Advances in information technology and communications (ICT) such as the emergence of artificial intelligence have also partially spoiled humans. Essentially, the advances of ICT should bring happiness, peacefulness and wisdom to human being. In fact, it has caused various anomalies for the development of universal human values. Therefore, the negative effects of the ICT advancement need to be immediately anticipated so as not to cause multidimensional losses such as physical, psychological, social and spiritual problems. SS-5.0 is a concrete movement in Japan to bring back humans to be able to control all types of technological devices. The objectives of SS-5.0 could be more easily achieved through the true sense of education process, not the education as formalism.

All educational practices with various educational components are essentially based on the nature of human beings since the ultimate mission of education is to achieve happiness in life. Thus, the underlying assumptions of all components in education such as human resources, approaches, evaluations, and learning resources in education should also be based on philosophies about humans and education itself. This chapter discusses the relationship between the concept and practice of education along with the challenges and developments in communication and information technology in the industrial revolution 4.0. The discussion begins with the elaboration about the fourth industrial revolution, then Smart Society and Spirit of Education is explored, followed with discussion on Education and Human Being, Happy Education, Re-meaning Education, Core Values-Based Management: State Islamic University Sunan Kalijaga's Experience, and closed by a concluding remark.

The Fourth Industrial Revolution and the Misleading of Education

IR-4.0 which is marked by great advances in information and communication technology is basically the achievement of the progress of modern human science as an answer to the problem of reality (Skilton and Hovesepian, 2018). Science and technology are created by humans to provide the best solution to the problems faced by humans, which always change from time to time. According to Thomas S. Kuhn, the author of *The Structure of Scientific Revolution,* the advancement of ICT in the IR-4.0 era is a form of revolutionary science. It is needed because the science developed earlier has been considered incapable in answering the challenges brought by the ever changing time. The challenges appeared as anomalies result in crisis which necessitate immediate revolutionary science (Kuhn, 2012). What needs to be emphasized here is that the advancement of science and technology is initially intended for the benefit of humans themselves, not to put humans under the control of science and technology. Therefore, it is questionable when the advance of science and technology lead to numerous negative effects in which humans are controlled by their own creation.

The advancement of science and technology in the industrial revolution 4.0 seems to cause humans to lose their lives because they are too spoiled by their creations. As a result, human beings are awfully dependent on science and technology. Among the negative symptoms are the fear of missing out, the emergence of narcissistic personality disorder (NPD), *Munchausen's* syndrome, voyeurism, internal Asperger syndrome (AIS), and social climber. Fear of missing out among others, is characterized by a feeling of simultaneous worry, anxiety or fear of being loss or outdated from the newly updated technology such as gadgets.

One of the symptoms of this psychological disorder is when people do not take along their Smart phone then they will feel 'like losing half of the soul'. They feel hopeless only because they do not carry the 'magic tool'. NPD, among others, is characterized by a penchant for showing themselves in cyberspace excessively while paying less attention to the reality around them. An attitude to always update social media status for the purpose of exaggerating situation has declined human beings' awareness of the purpose of life both personally and socially. By this reality, the popular dictum coined by Descartes (Clarke, 2003) '*Cogito Ergo Sum*' which means 'I think therefore I am' might then be replaced by a statement of 'I update my status therefore I am'. *Muncheon* syndrome is a mental illness in which people act like they are in big trouble then show it to other people through updating status in social media to obtain people's attention. Voyeurism, among others, is characterized by a desire to always 'peek' at other's status in social media and then feel sorry for the circumstances of others. This results in a willingness to always outperform other in terms of updating social media status. Symptoms of AIS are marked by psychiatric conditions in which people's act is contradict with their speech. There is a gap between what actually happens and what is conveyed through social media. Meanwhile, social climbing, among others, is characterized by symptoms of wanting to increase social status quickly through social media by presenting their life far from reality. These various negative symptoms caused by the advance of ICT alert the importance of restoring human spirit to be the controller of technology because humans are the creators of the technology.

Despite these various negative effects, the advance of ICT also bears a lot of positive outcomes. With the advancement of ICT, human beings are facilitated in overcoming many problems. Various technological advances used to be unimaginable and now it comes to the reality. Previously, it was difficult to imagine of being able to see various events or events that occurred in other parts of the world, now it is as if the world is in the grip. For instance, people can watch football matches of their favourite clubs any time. It used to be difficult to imagine an airplane that flies without a pilot, now that remote-controlled drones have emerged. Even some cars have been designed to move without a driver using autopilot system. In the field of transportation, if people wanted to take a taxi, they had to walk on to certain base or highway, now people just need to call the taxi through gadget, and then the taxi will come and be ready in front of them. In the culinary field, to have dinner or lunch people needed to find a place or food stall, but now they can tip their finger on their smart phone to order their favourite food and the dinner or lunch will come in front of the door.

In terms of profession, many jobs that used to be promising professions have presently been abandoned or are becoming less important. Some professions such as doctor or engineer which used to be the 'idol' and ideals among students since it promises a brighter future with higher income, recently it has been overshadowed by newer profession called *youtuber* or *influencer* developed by millennials which undoubtedly generate high amount of money. To start a business people do not need to build a shop because through online market this has been resolved. People can do transactions and earn extraordinary profits only by finger-tipping the gadgets in their comfortable sleeping rooms.

In the field of education, numerous applications are offered to facilitate people to be able to learn independently, such as Google or Khan Academy. These services force educational theorist as well as practitioners to change their mindset and offer educational innovation. If education is still oriented towards transfer of knowledge or just conveying knowledge, it will be left far behind or even overtaken with these various online services. If teachers only rely on traditional learning resources such as printed textbooks, then students may move on further by accessing online learning resources such as the unlimited number of e-books provided on cyberspace.

Nonetheless, among positive effects of the ICT advancement, one element that can never be replaced by any technology is associated with the core of education. The heart of education is to transform the soul from negative to positive state. This process can only be carried out by soulful people not a machine. Therefore, the advance of science and ICT in the industrial revolution 4.0 should be dedicated to fulfil humanity. ICT is essentially neutral. Which is not neutral is the way people look or perspective that they use understand the ICT. In the hands of a positive soulful human, ICT comprises valuable and meaningful devices for the good of humanity that is to facilitate more blissful and profound life. Conversely, in the hands of soulless human, ICT will bring them far from their humanity and even create misery of modern human (Nasr, 1990). Therefore, the advance of science and ICT should be in line with the ultimate goal of education, that *'the heart of education is education of the heart'*, the core of education is heart education. The advance of ICT in the IR-4.0 era should produce more positive soulful human beings. This, subsequently, depends on individual capability to control the devices as a coined adage 'man *behind the gun*'. The ICT as a neutral weapon will be greatly influenced by its users, human.

Smart Society and Spirit of Education

In www8.cao.go.jp, SS-5.0 is defined as *'a human-centred society that balances economic advancement with the resolution of social problems by a system that integrates highly cyberspace and physical space'*. According to this page, SS-5.0 is a human-centred society that is able to balance economic progress with the resolution of various social problems by using a system that combine cyberspace and the real world. From this understanding we can infer several points. First, no matter how great human progress has been made, the main focus remains on humanity. Whatever the model of community will be shaped, human should be placed as central point. Human is the subject of development as well as the subject of science and technology development. Human must not be degenerated only as the object of development. Secondly, the community must be able to balance economic progress by solving any arising problems. This is a sort of warning that a number of economic progresses, in fact, could raise many problems that are difficult to solve. This should not have happened because economic progress was supposed to bring about development on human being. Thirdly, the society that is formed should create a system capable of integrating cyber space which is reflected in the advance of ICT with the ever-changing real world. In reality, there is a broad gap between *'the problem of the earth'* and the *'problem of the sky'*, ideality versus reality. The advance of ICT is often not down to earth. It does not bring benefits to human survival, because humans are uprooted from their souls. Therefore, SS-5.0 craves ICT that serve human needs by generating more blissful, peaceful and loving human being. These several points remind us of the spirit of education.

Education is a process of humanization to create human being equipped with positive mental qualities. According to UNESCO, there are five pillars that should be developed in the field of education, i.e. learning to know, learning to do, learning to be, learning to live together, and learning to transform oneself and society (UNEP, 2012). The first pillar, learning how to know, is related to the cognitive domain, that education must develop this realm of knowledge. The second pillar, learning how to do, is related to the psychomotor domain, that education should familiarize everyone to carry out real action, not just knowing. The third pillar, learning how to be, is related to the affective domain, especially intra-personal skills, that the education process should develop a strong and tough and dignified personality. The fourth pillar, learning how to live together, relates to the social domain of education, that education should not only develop the intrapersonal realm of each student but should also develop interpersonal skills, because everyone lives in the context of space and time, especially with social and cultural settings so that each people should be accustomed to having social and cultural awareness. Meanwhile, the fifth pillar is related to the importance of the process of changing someone from an individual or social aspect.

Among these five pillars, the last pillar should be reflected when it deals with the educational process. This fifth pillar is intended to transform the other four pillars. In the first pillar, there are many levels, starting from the lowest level which is often called the *lower order thinking skill* (LOTS) to the *higher order thinking skill* (HOTS). Among examples of the lower level thinking skills are *memorizing* and *knowledge*, while higher level thinking skills might appear as *analyzing* and *applying*. Therefore, transformation in terms of cognitive context means making change from lower-level thinking to higher-order thinking. This also applies to other pillars of education. The *learning to do* transformation is a shift from accomplishment done due to external forces to increased level of accomplishment based on internal forces, self-awareness and creative thinking. The *learning to be* form of transformation may emerge as changes from doing without awareness to doing with full self-awareness based on values and in-depth meaning. Meanwhile, the transformation of the pillars of learning to live together with others can be seen from the change from passive communication to active, effective, synergetic communication. With this in mind, transformation is the core of education that is individual changes and environmental changes.

In the current era of disruption, self-transformation is inevitable because people are faced with two choices, whether they are going to disrupt or be disrupted (Kasali, 2018). The former means that people are the subject of change. People themselves determine the direction of change, become the trend setters and drivers, not followers and passengers (Kasali, 2014). While the latter means that people are the object of change, in a position to be driven by reality. Using Muhammad Iqbal's terms, *to disrupt* means people have *prophetic consciousness* while *to be disrupted* means people have *mystical consciousness.* The terms differ in that *prophetic consciousness* means 'the horizon dissolves in us', while *mystical consciousness* is 'when we dissolve in the horizon' (Iqbal, 1920). People who have prophetic awareness possess three main characteristics, i.e. he is able to carry out the process of humanization, able to carry out the process of liberation, and able to do the process of transcendence (Ahimsa-Putra, 2018). Humanization means the ability to explore and optimize all the human potentials that have been given by God. Each people are great and champion in their respective fields. Liberation means the ability to distance their selves or protect them from all things that can inhibit the growth and development of human potentials. Meanwhile, transcendence means the ability to place God as the only reliance on all matters, to believe that all occurrences in the universe are essentially a form of devotion and confidence in the existence of God. In Islam, this is relevant to the words of the Prophet about the importance of piety (character) wherever people are.

In education, self-transformation is the spirit of education itself (Osman and Hornsby, 2017). This process is an integral part of self-introduction to the Divine. In Islam, there is a popular saying among *Sufis*, *man' arafanafsahu, faqad 'arafarabbahu; man 'arafaqalbahufaqad' arafanafsahu'*. This expression denotes an understanding that to get to know God, one must begin with knowing his/herself, while knowing oneself must originate from knowing one's hearts. In the context of Islamic leadership, it is stated that each people is a leader, and every leader will be held accountable for what he/she leads. Self-transformation is a concrete form of becoming a self-leader, because the nature of leadership is to influence. Self-transformation is the process of influencing oneself positively. In inner-leadership, people have to influence all that exists within them including their thoughts, feelings, speech, writing and actions. If whatever they think, say, write and do are always under their own control, then they are able to become a self-leader. People have begun to learn to be self-determinant by providing a positive influence on everything they do.

Education and Human Being

Various problems in education should immediately be solved if educational practices and processes are returned to an awareness of the meaning and the nature of human and education. The meaning of education and human being cannot be separated because talking about education always means talking about human with their various potentials. At the same time, talking about human beings also means talking about the effort to optimize the potential of humanity through education. However, education should not be limited to formal education which, in practice, often turns out to imprison human soul. Changing the practice of education either in terms of institutional or educational alternatives, strategic learning, or curriculum is essentially a manifestation of the changing perspective of the meaning and philosophy of human as educational participant.

Education needs to be interpreted as an effort to help humans to achieve the self (*self-realization*) and to optimize all the potentials of humanity. By understanding this, all the processes leading to the realization of optimizing the potential of human is, regardless the place and time, is categorized as educational activity. Conversely, when there is a practice assumed as the process of education yet turns out to actually inhibit the development potential of humanity in various forms, then this cannot be called as the practice of education. It should be understood that if there are differences among educational practices done in different places and time then it is only a matter of technical implementation, not the essential meaning of education. In addition, as an attempt to carry out the transformation for the educational participant towards positive direction, education should also be able to transform society towards the formation of civil society that is open, democratic, and pluralistic. This is in fact the fifth pillar of education, i.e. learning *how to transform oneself and society*.

Human as learning creature also needs to be examined. A comprehensive understanding of the concept of human will result in the merits of the practice of education. Since, ontologically, knowledge is human, then the concept (science produced by human) of human being is also greatly influenced by human themselves. This is determined by the level of experience and knowledge as well as social setting surrounding them. In the context of the Islamic teachings, the meaning of human is also determined by Moslem understanding about the concept of human being contained in the *Quran* and *al-Sunnah*. Although the main references used by Moslem around the world is exactly the same, the understandings are various, as many as the number of the people. The point is that the spirit of Islamic teaching is always' *'shalihli-kullizamaninwa-makanin'* or virtuous and relevant to all places and time.

As a unique and multidimensional creature, no scholar is able to define exactly the nature of human being nor is able to formulate precisely the meaning of human. When philosophers approached the terms, they will end up in different formulations compared to the psychologists although they have the underlying assumption. Human being remains a mystery to life. It is not surprising that Alexis Carrel, Nobel Prize winner in medicine, wrote a book titled *Man the Unknown* (2017). Because of this, it takes a lot of perspective to understand the nature of human. A scholar of certain discipline will not be really confident to formulate the meaning of human fixedly, and then he/she must collaborate and cooperate with other scholars from various disciplines. To understand the meaning of human, at least, people need to utilize *philosophical* perspective which examines human being radically from the domain of ontology, epistemology and axiology, *psychology* which discusses human from the aspects of mental state, *biology* that studies human on the aspects of the structure of the physics as living being, *anthropology* which sees human as the unique cultural creatures, and particularly in Islam, *al-Qur'an* which defines the meaning of human being as divine creatures. With further scientific development, there will be increasing perspectives or multi-disciplinary that should be employed.

If the formulation of the meaning of education and the nature of human being taken from multiperspectives has been obtained, then the new practices and patterns of education can be formulated, though a comprehensive and final understanding on the two terms could not be agreed upon perfectly since the challenges are always changing from time to time. Understanding problems and challenges of the earlier era is certainly distinctive from that of the present time. Due to the awareness that the concept of education and human always changes, then the practices of education must also be changed. Accordingly, the effort to change the paradigm of education has to be carried out.

As a simple illustration, when the ideal human concept is that of physically strong figure, as perceived by the Greek Sparta, the *treatment* of all components of education is designed to realize the idea of that ideal human. The formulation of educational goals is more or less "*creating ideal human with strong physical characteristics*" (Batchelor, 2008). Social, mental and intellectual aspects may not be important and of priority in this context. The objective of this education is, of course, translated to a variety of indicators that lead to the characteristics of great human with strong physicality. To realize this, what kinds of curriculum are offered? The curriculum offered is subjects intended to realize the ideal human being [physically strong]. Subsequently, the relevant subjects offered in this educational model are sports, physical health, and nutrition. What about the methods, evaluation, facilities, and teachers? The approach and methods used are experiential and participatory learning and learning by doing such as running, swimming, push-ups, and lifting weights. These strategies are more important than the mastery and understanding theories and concepts. Learning evaluation is directed to check whether students are physically strong or not. To check the capability on running is by running and swimming by swimming. Learning facilities needed in this learning model is certainly that which provides complete range of facilities to produce physically strong human. What about the teacher? Only teachers who are able to train physically strong are suitable in this school. With this simple illustration, it can be understood that an understanding of human nature will influence further educational practices.

Joyful Education

Nel Noddings (2003) wrote an inspiring book titled *Happiness and Education.* Through this book, Noddings reminds us that happiness is the main purpose of life and education. He stated in the introductory of the book that "*happiness should be an aim of education, and a good education should contribute significantly to personal and collective happiness*" (Noddings, 2003: 2). He proposed the word 'should', because in reality almost all educational practices have not focused on this goal, although theoretically or conceptually many agree that the goal of the educational process is to achieve happiness both personally and collectively.

According to Noddings, the learning process will run well if all students are in a happy state. Learning competencies that have been planned are easily achieved when they take part in fun learning activities, even though the level of difficulty of the material presented is high. Conversely, learning competence is difficult to achieve if learning takes place in a rigid manner. Even though the material presented in class is in the easy category, the material is ultimately difficult for students to understand. This will affect the final quality of the students in particular and the quality of the education system in general, because the learning process involves many components such as curriculum, learning approaches and strategies, evaluation of learning, educators and education staffs, facilities and infrastructure, learning resources, finance, network management and development.

Even in the view of neuroscience research, human brain cells will develop and connect to each other quickly when they are happy. Endorphins and serotonin hormones will develop which causes them to study in a comfortable and calm state. This condition is often referred to as an alpha wave condition that allows individuals to be able to learn quickly because it is suggestible. People may have experienced reading a novel that is thick enough and finishing it quickly because they are in a suggestible state, they are happy to read it. On the contrary, it is difficult to understand the contents of the book if the reader dislikes the book. The learning atmosphere designed by educators in classroom or school should be comfortable and convenient for every student. This learning process is often called joyful learning.

People who are happy are rarely found to be rude, cruel or violent, either to other people or to other creatures such as animals and plants. According to Noddings, moral education should begin by creating a pleasant learning atmosphere where every student is happy. Students who are accustomed to experiencing happy values tend to behave positively, have stable emotions, be calm, and easily adapt to the surrounding. This has become social capital to build a harmonious society and a more peaceful and happy world, far from conflict and violence (Noddings, 2003: 2). Conversely, people who are educated in an environment full conflict and violence will result in many negative effects such as trauma, fear, anxiety, pessimism, and difficulty in adapting to the environment. This certainly has an impact on their future because they will surely face a new situation that has never been encountered before. If this is not immediately corrected, it will lead to a continuous chain of violence.

The importance of creating a happy learning atmosphere is also recognized by educators in Japan. A Japanese educator, Tsunesaburo Makiguchi, for example, created a happy atmosphere of learning at the elementary school level. Happiness is the main goal of elementary level education. Student who comes to school must be happy. The entire components in education must be created systemically and comprehensively, thus every student can learn happily. For many educational practices around the world, this idea might be a little strange because in many countries, fun learning only happens at the kindergarten level. As soon as the participants get into basic education, the classroom atmosphere has been designed rather rigid and even tends to be formal-administrative. According to Makiguchi such classroom atmosphere does not produce anything for students in the future. They will not experience positive values during class, less experience, and further feel and implement these values outside the classroom (Noddings, 2003: 3).

Happiness should be an indicator of the success of a learning process. Therefore, if the main goal of the educational process is to achieve student happiness, then there needs to be a way to evaluate the success of education whether it (happiness state) has been achieved or not. So far, an indicator of happiness in seeing the success of education has not been formulated. According to Noddings, "*Happiness is not the only aim of either education or life, but it is a central aim, and it can be used as an evaluative screen through which to judge everything we do.*" (p. 5). The educational domain that has been primarily used as the measure of success is cognitive domain, while the affective domain, especially the aspect of happiness, is rarely taken into consideration. In fact, all educational processes should be able to produce students' happiness in various situations, because everyone craves happiness. This is in line with an afterthought delivered by the Dalai Lama, "*Whether one believes in religion or not, we are all seeking something better in life—the very motion of our life is toward happiness.*" This is also in agreement with William James' statement, in his book *The Varieties of Religious Experience*, saying that happiness was the most important part of the main focus of human life. According to James, "*If we were to ask the question: 'What is human life's chief concern?' One of the answers we should receive would be: 'It is happiness'.*" (Noddings, 2003: 9).

The goal of happiness-oriented education seems to have received less attention, especially in the early 21st century, because almost all practitioners and thinkers of education emphasize more on the educational attainment standards along with economic indicators. The competencies generated in education are designed to familiarize with certain skills so that they are ready in the world of work. Measures of educational success are emphasized more on economic aspects than positive values, such as happiness and peace. This is proved by the various negative influences caused by IR-4.0, as explained at the beginning of this chapter. Of course, this is a real challenge of character education. Characters cannot be taught cognitively, but it must be familiarized and internalized effectively. According to Noddings, "*character education is experiencing a revival today, but its advocates make the mistake of supposing that character can be taught directly, virtue by virtue. In fact, the development of character may be very like the attainment of happiness itself; it may have to be aimed at indirectly.*" (p. 96). Education should provide more actual experiences on positive values, not talking about or teaching about these values. The value of happiness needs to be experienced and implemented, not talked about. Therefore, educators need to emphasize more on aspects of the experience of the value of happiness in school. Related to this, Noddings said that "*Happiness in the present is not incompatible with future happiness, and it may even be instrumental for future happiness. Educators should therefore give attention to the quality of students' present experience*". (p. 240)

Re-meaning the Education

Redefining education is urgent and critical because of several considerations. Firstly, education is not only seen from the conceptual aspect, but also in terms of practice. So far, there are often disparities between the realm of theory and real practices. Theoretically, the meaning of education has been formulated ideally, particularly in the field of Islamic teaching-based education, but the practice has not been fully ideal. As an illustration, education should produce human beings, but in reality, it is still "completely instant", human becomes incomplete character being. Education should produce individuals with happy soul, but in fact people often encounter educational products that tend to be upset and not ready to face the reality of life. Secondly, education tends to focus on physical-material aspects only, with less emphasis on mental-spiritual aspects. The former focuses on body awareness, while the latter is more on soul consciousness. The first educational model is more likely to regard education as a formal-administrative process that is routine-robotic, less touching to the heart of education, namely the soul itself. Meanwhile, the second type of education model emphasizes more on the soul, because the soul which is created as the device of the superstructure determines all educational practices. Thirdly, related to the second point, education should focus more on the aspects of *touching* rather than *teaching*. *Touching* means *transferring of values*, which is oriented more in touching the soul or superstructure. Meanwhile, *teaching* emphasizes more on *transferring of knowledge* which tends to stress on bodily aspect or infrastructure.

In line with the above thinking, there are a number of aspects that need to be reflected again as a form of re-understanding education, especially from the aspects of paradigms, policies, programmes, human resources, and practices (Rosado, 2006). From the context of the paradigm, the main goal of education is to bring to life the great and perfect qualities of each individual as a creature created by God the Most Perfect. This great quality is owned by every human being, which was attached when they are created by God. However, this quality is an abstract soul, not material. There are at least five soul qualities that every human being has when they were created by God, which is full of peace, love, happiness, power and purity. The main purpose of education is to enliven and implement these five qualities, not to discuss, explain nor discuss them. There is an adagium *the heart of education is education of the heart and from the heart*. If the process and practice of education is oriented towards reviving the five qualities, then every people can become a self that full of peace, love, happiness, power and sincerity (Lawrence, 2004). Whatever profession they have, if these five qualities embed in those people, then life will be beautiful and comfortable wherever they are. This aspect of the purpose of education is essentially related to the paradigm and philosophy of education.

Another important aspect related to the paradigm in education is the meaning of human beings. In the context of education, human beings need to be understood as multidimensional, unique and perfect creatures created by God. The multidimensional aspects of humans may appear in terms of physical, intellectual, mental, and social relation. Human beings are not only seen from the physical dimension that distinguishes one person from another. This can be seen from the weight, skin colour, height, gender, and face characteristics. If this aspect is seen predominantly, discriminatory actions will emerge among individuals, because of the massive proportions of the material dimension. Therefore, the element of mental, intellectual and social must also be emphasized. Every individual has different ideas and perception. Although the knowledge and experience are the same, the perception and the understanding of the phenomenon may be distinctive or even contradictory. In addition, each individual has a unique psychological development. What is experienced and felt by a person must be different, despite having the same literatures. In light of social aspect, everyone, according to Donna Haraway (1986), is conditioned in certain situations in which they have to accept. This is called as *situatedness*. When a person is born to parents with no formal education, living in a remote village of poor community, he/she cannot protest against God who is considered "as if" He was unjust to him/her. Instead of regretting and lamenting the existing conditions or inclining to be problem-based model, what needs to be done is behaving with more future-oriented attitudes. If the former tends to bring the past in the present context, the latter tends to bring the future to the present, *tomorrow is today*.

The second dimension that needs to be seen as the derivative of the first paradigm is policy. Educational policies established by leaders both in educational institutions and in government, should be based on certain educational paradigm. Educational policies include curriculum, learning approaches, educators, facilities, assessment, environment, financing, and management. All of these elements should be approached based on the educational paradigm, thus the educational policy will go in line with the paradigm. For example, in an educational institution in which the aim is to produce graduate profiles able to enliven positive values and become living positive model, then the designed curriculum should provide as much knowledge and experience as possible for the students. The cognitive, affective and psychomotor domains are also critical to be considered in designing the curriculum. Learning approaches as the derivation of the educational policies must also be carefully taken into consideration to produce better students with positive quality of life. This also applies to educational assessments. Education is considered successful if the graduates have and revive the quality of a positive soul, whatever profession they hold. To achieve this goal, education should be capable of being a positive model, not only performing the *teaching*, but also most importantly the *touching*.

Once the educational policy has been carefully formulated according to the appropriate educational paradigm, the educational programmes must also be able to describe the agreed paradigm. All activities offered to students must refer to the apprehended paradigm. In this case, the entire educational stakeholders must take care of and execute the paradigms and policies at the practical level including parents and community. Therefore, it should be understood that all the stakeholders are essentially teachers, who are able to present themselves as living positive models for students. Security guards, parking attendants, cleaning service employees, gardeners, drivers, cooks, and librarians must also be able to become positive models. Thus, synergy occurs and the shared spirit bonds the entire stakeholders. This undoubtedly indicates that human resources in education must also be a serious concern.

To date, educators or teachers are the only human resources considered to be critical in educational process. Meanwhile, other human resources are thought merely as complementary. Educational human resources development has been focused more on hard skills instead not soft skills. This should be reexamined since the success of educators is determined 80 per cent by their soft competence rather than hard competence. In teacher training, hard competence (HC) involves professional competence and pedagogical competence, while soft competence (SC) lies on personality and social competence. HC emphasizes more on technical knowledge and skills that distinguish the teaching profession from other professions. Meanwhile, SC is urgently needed in all types of professions. In other words, any profession requires the SC. This takes forms as responsibility, honesty, integrity, pro-activeness, initiative, commitment, co-working, communicative, tolerance, willingness to learn, willingness to change, and ability to adapt.

The last dimension of change in education is the practice of education. No matter how great the educational concepts and theories are; if they are not implemented, then it will only be a slogan. Thus, real action is required to initiate changes. The journey of a thousand miles will not happen without the first step. In terms of change, there are two phases that need to be accomplished, namely mental creation and physical creation. The first is related to paradigms, values, ideals, plans, dreams and goals, while the second is related to concrete actions. If it involves more than one person, the second step requires integration as well as shared ideas and perceptions to facilitate the realization of the dreams. Therefore, synergy, communication and team building are needed to realize the shared dreams.

Core Values-Based Management: The Case of State Islamic University Sunan Kalijaga

Since the transformation from the so-called State Islamic Institute (SII) into State Islamic University (SIU), this oldest Islamic based university situated in Yogyakarta Special Region, Indonesia, has changed not only legally, formally, and administratively, but also paradigmatically and philosophically. In terms of paradigm, this alteration can be seen from the new formulated core values offered by this university. The core values are integrative-interconnected, dedicated, innovative, inclusive and continuously improved. The emergence of these core values is, in fact, a form of the university's paradigm shift. This step is taken to present uniqueness and distinction that characterizes the university among its counterparts across Indonesia. In terms of marketing strategy, the university establishes particular *branding* and *positioning* to realize its vision, i.e. to achieve an excellent and leading Islamic university in the integration and development of Islamic and scientific studies for the development of civilization. The term 'scientific integration' (integrative-interconnected), first initiated by M. Amin Abdullah, the former chancellor, must be recognized as a new tradition in Islamic universities, especially related to the relationship between science and religion.

As the paradigm received its popularity, a number of SIU Sunan Kalijaga's counterparts across Indonesia embraced it as their respective paradigm. However, the model as well as the implementation strategy is diverse from one university to the others. As the pioneer, SIU Sunan Kalijaga Yogyakarta, spearheaded by M. Amin Abdullah (2006), offers a *spider web* model of the paradigm, in which the main source of science and technology is the *Qur'an* and the *Hadith*. These two main sources of Islamic teachings became the centre of inspiration for the emergence of various science and technology findings. Furthermore, accompanying this paradigm, the epistemology developed at this university is taken from

M. 'Abid al-Jabiry's thought, namely *bayani*, *burhani* and *irfani*. The *bayani* considers the sacred, texts, i.e. the *Qur'an* and the *Hadith* as the source of knowledge, whereas *burhani* reflects on reality (*al-waqi'*) as the source of knowledge, and *irfani* takes into account intuition (*dzawq*) as the source of knowledge.

These three epistemological models are designed comprehensively and in integrative manner and further applied in various levels at SIU Sunan Kalijaga such as in policy formulation, programme implementation, human resources management, as well as in real classroom practices. The epistemology is also applied in accomplishing the *Tri Dharma* (university's three primary services) involving educational services, research services and community services. The first services refer to the integrative paradigms. The second services are designed to study all the integrated issues. The third services are also shaped to implement the integrative paradigm in social environment. Thus, the entire aspects of educational policy, programmes, human resource management to educational practices in SIU Sunan Kalijaga covered in the three primary services should be based on the spirit of this integrated paradigm.

In daily basis, the integrative-interconnected paradigm is fundamentally equal to the *soft skills* that must be possessed by every academic community in SIU Sunan Kalijaga in overcoming the problems of life in their respective places. With this paradigm, the distinction between the profane and the sacred should no longer exist since the spirit of the integration is to abridge and integrate the both to create alumni as vicegerent of God (*khalifatullah fil-ardl*). Beside the integrative paradigm, the other core values offered this university is also implemented in the three services. The integrative-interconnected values accustom students to see various problems based on religious inspiration. In other words, religious values inspire and turn out to be the spirit in solving various problems. Because of that, the religious teachings taught in SIU Sunan Kalijaga are not delivered dogmatically and literally, instead they must be grounded in accordance with each study programmes. In light of nationalism viewpoint, the integrative values encourage academic community to become a role model of Indonesian characterized Islam, which actively provides solutions for the nation's challenges with values and spirituality of Islamic teachings.

The value of dedication is expected to produce devoted students and faculty members. By this value, it is also anticipated that the academia will embrace an attitude oriented to give, serve, love of work, promote the interests of the institution, as well as care for and loyal to the activities and professions they hold. As citizens, this value could habituate the academia to serve and give the best for the nation.

The innovative value encourages the academic community to alert and create willingness to changes, to learn, to look for alternative solutions of the existing problems, to think out of the comfortable zone, to be creative, to think the solution (solution-based thinking) rather than to think the problem (problem-based thinking), and to become a *positive trendsetter*. With this innovative value, it is expected that the graduates of SIU Sunan Kalijaga will be the trendsetter and the self-driver wherever they are. This value is also supposed to generate *trans-student* (above average student), not the *average student*. The former tends to think 50 per cent about present time and 50 per cent on the future, while the latter are likely to think 50 per cent about the past (problem) and 50 per cent about the present condition. Innovative values encourage students to ensure big investment for the future. Furthermore, this value is hoped to lead Indonesia to be increasingly taken into account in the world forum in regard to various science and technology findings generated by the graduates of SIU Sunan Kalijaga.

The inclusive value of SIU Sunan Kalijaga is believed to be able to produce tolerant, open-minded, appreciative on diversity and pluralism, peace lover academia and students who emphasize *soul consciousness* rather than *body one*. This inclusive value should be able to deliver students to be the agent of love and compassion for their surroundings. Recently, the emergence of a number of tensions, conflicts, violence, segregations, discrepancies and discriminations has been resulted mainly from the view of materialisms and attachment or 'layers' rather than values, soul and spirit. As a consequence, what appears is the attitude of selfishness, arrogance, anger, and greed because it is seen on the clothes and its attachments, not the aspects of the spirit of togetherness. In Islamic view, the best people to God are those with the best character and quality, not those with the best material. Multicultural countries such as Indonesia and India really need this inclusive value. Habituating this value at SIU Sunan Kalijaga will contribute positively to the development of Indonesia.

Finally, the value of continuous improvement is supposed to be able to familiarize all academics members, especially the students to improve the quality of life. It is so-called lifelong education in Islamic teaching, like the saying of the Prophet that Muslims are obliged to study starting from the cradle to the grave. It is also a manifestation of the implementation of the Islamic teaching stated in the *Qur'an* asserting about the importance of doing *muhasabah al-nafs* (self-reflection) on anything that have been through and to experience the benefit of improvement. "*O people of faith! Keep your duty to Allah and should each person pay attention to that which has been done for the day tomorrow (the Hereafter), and keep your duty to Allah. Indeed, Allah knoweth what are you doing*" (al-Hashr, 18).

Concluding Remark: Education 4.0

In early 2020, the World Economic Forum published a report on future education in accordance with technological advances, especially IR-4.0. This report is titled *Schools of the Future: Defining New Models of Education for the Fourth Industrial Revolution* (2020). At the top of the report, a title 'Platform for Shaping the Future of the New Economy and Society' is written, a platform to establish new economic and communities. If linked between the two, it seems that this book is an initiative formed by the WEF to provide an alternative picture of educational institutions which could be used as one of the future references in the context of a changing economy and society, especially now that it is within IR-4.0 and SS-5.0. WEF calls this report an illustration of 'Education 4.0'.

According to the WEF Report (2020), there are eight main characteristics of quality education in the IR-4.0 era, i.e., global citizenship skills, innovation and creativity skills, technology skills, interpersonal skills, personalized and self-paced learning, accessible and inclusive learning, problem-based and collaborative learning, and lifelong and student-driven learning. The character of global citizenship skills means that the education process should be able to equip and prepare students to become global citizens who are able to make a positive contribution in the global community to preserve the world. With these characteristics, every education process is expected to be more oriented towards making a positive contribution as citizens of the world, not thinking communally. The character of innovation and creativity skills means that educational practices equip each student with a variety of skills of innovation, problem solving, creativity, analytical thinking, and systemic analysis. The education process should focus on providing higher order thinking skills (HOTS).

In the third characteristic, technology skills, the quality of education among others appears on the learning content that gives greater emphasis on digital skills like programming, digital responsibility and clever use of technology. These characters have reminded us of the importance of digital literacy, not to just mastering the technology but also utilizing it as useful and meaningful tool for achieving human interests. However, sophisticated technology also has possibility to degrade the values of humanity if it does not lead to happiness and peace. Interpersonal skills are the main characteristic of quality education in the IR-4.0 era. The education process should be able to provide emotional and spiritual intelligence such as empathy, cooperation, negotiation, respect, leadership, tolerance and other social awareness. This confirms one of the characteristics of 21st century learning in which collaboration is a part of interpersonal skills.

The next characteristic of quality education is personalized and self-paced learning. Educational practice should not be measured by a single standard but rather looks at the uniqueness and individual needs of each student. The education process should meet every student's need. Therefore, the education process should be made more flexible to be able to respond to every challenge and change. Related to this feature, is the next character namely accessible and inclusive learning. With this character, the education process is expected to be able to accommodate every student's need, not only for certain interests. The education process should be designed to serve the needs of every student regardless of their background.

The next character of quality education is problem-based and collaborative learning. The educational process is designed to provide alternative solutions to daily real problems. Each student is familiarized with skills in identifying problems and providing alternative solutions. This is done collaboratively because each student is in the context of a multicultural society that has a variety of interests. Therefore, collaborative learning ability is very much needed in the IR-4.0 era. Finally, the last quality education requires lifelong and student-driven learning. This means that the education process should be able to accustom students as lifelong learners, wherever and whenever they are, they continue to learn. Learning is not carried out limitedly in the classroom covered in formal schooling. Real learning precisely occurs in real life. Because social context faced by each student is different from one another, the education process should equip them with the ability to learn independently. Education should also provide learning skills employed to solve the individual and social real problems in their respective places so that they can live positively and were able to make a positive contribution to their environment.

For education 4.0 to succeed, this report emphasizes the importance of applying five approaches in innovative pedagogies, i.e. playful, experiential, computational, embodied, and multiliteracies. Playful is an approach that emphasizes fun learning to better grasp the meaning of materials being learned. Therefore, learning must be designed meaningfully to enable student to think actively both personally and socially. Experiential is an approach that emphasizes aspects of experience rather than mastery of knowledge. The educational process must be designed to involve students in real world and solve the problems of surrounding reality, not mainly based on text-based books. This is very important in the process of internalizing positive values. Computational is an approach designed to equip students to be able to calculate quickly and accurately with existing technology such as computers. Data available in the internet of things era must be able to be processed accurately to meet the needs of students. Embodied is a learning approach that involves all dimensions of human beings, i.e. physical-kinesthetic, mental-psychological, social, and mental-spiritual. With this approach it is hoped that the educational process is not carried out mechanically-robotically without spirited, but it must be conducted in a purposive and meaningful way. Meanwhile, multiliteracies mean that the educational process should be designed involving many approaches because the contexts faced by learners are very diverse and connected with each other in a global society. People live as global citizens who are connected through sophisticated devices so they must have self and social awareness at the local, regional, national and international levels.

REFERENCES

Abdullah, M.A. (2006). *Islamic Studies di Perguruan Tinggi: Pendekatan Integratif-Interkonektif.* Yogyakarta: Pustaka Pelajar.

Budhananda, S. (2013). *Will-Power and Its Development*, Kolkata: Trio Process.

Campbell, J.R. and Rew, A. (eds.). (1999). *Identity and Affect: Experiences of Identity in a Globalizing World*, London: Pluto Press.

Clarke, D.M. (2005), *Descartes's Theory of Mind*, Oxford: Oxford University Press.

Feener, R.M. (ed.). (2004). *Islam in World Cultures: Comparative Perspectives*, Santa Barbara: ABC-CLIO.

Ferrer, J.N., Romero, M.T., and Albareda, R.V. (2005). "Integral Transformative Education: A Participatory Proposal" in *Journal of Transformative Education.*

Gandhi, M.K. (2010). *Ashram Observances in Action*, Ahmedabad: Navajivan Publishing House.

Gharajedaghi, J. (2016). *Thinking Systems: Managing Chaos and Complexity: A Platform for Designing Business Architecture*, Amsterdam: Morgan Kaufmann.

Iqbal, M. (2011). *The Reconstruction of Religious Thought in Islam*, Delhi: Shivalik Prakashan.

Iqbal, S.M. (1920). *The Secrets of the Self (Asrar-i Khudi): Philosophical Poem.* London: Macmillan.

Kalam, APJ.A. (2002). *Ignited Minds Unleashing the Power within India*, Haryana: Penguin Books.

Kallet, M. (2014). *Think Smarter: Critical Thinking to Improve Problem-Solving and Decision-Making Skills*, New Jersey: Wiley.

Kasali, R. (2014). *Self-Driving*. Bandung: Mizan.

Kasali, R. (2018). *Self-Disruption*. Bandung: Mizan.

Kuhn, T.S. (2012). *The Structure of Scientific Revolutions*. Chicago: The University of Chicago Press.

Lama, D., Tutu, D., and Abrams, D. (2016). *The Book of Joy: Lasting Happiness in a Changing World*, New York, Avery, 2016.

Levine, M. (2012). *Teach Your Children Well: Why Values and Coping Skills Matter More than Grades, Trophies, or "Fat Envelopes"*, New York: Harper Collins Publishers.

Maurer, R. (2013). *The Spirit of Kaizen: Creating Lasting Excellence One Small Step at a Time*, New York: McGraw-Hill.

Osman, J. and Hornsby, D.J. (2017). *Transforming Teaching and Learning in Higher Education: Towards a Socially Just Pedagogy in a Global Context.* Macmillan: Palgrave.

Pandiamani. (2013). *Values, Spirituality and Consciousness Development,* Rajashtan: Om Shanti Printing Press.

Popkova, E.G., Ragulina, Y.V., and Bogoviz, A.V. (eds.). (2019). *Industry 4.0: Industrial Revolution of the 21st Century*, Switzerland: Springer.

Rahman, F. (1982). *Islam and Modernity: Transformation of an Intellectual Tradition*, Chicago: Chicago University Press.

Salgues, B. (2018). *Society 5.0: Industry of the Future, Technologies, Methods and Tools,* Volume 1, London: Wiley.

Skilton, M. and Hevsepian, F. (2018). *The 4th Industrial Revolution: Responding to the Impact of Artificial Intelligence on Business*, Switzerland: Palgrave-Macmillan.

UNEP. (2012). *Learning to Transform Oneself and Society: Education for Sustainable Living, Policies and Practicies from Around the World*, UNESCO: Paris.

UNESCO. (2011). *UNESCO and Education: "Everyone has the Right to Education"*. Paris: UNESCO.

World Economic Forum. (2020). *Platform for Shaping the Future of the New Economy and Society. Schools of the Future: Defining New Models of Education for the Fourth Industrial Revolution*. Geneva: WEF.

20

Tracing the Changing Nature of Higher Education in India

Chetna Trivedi

Introduction

The institutions of higher education constitute a fundamental section of the social economic and political fibre of the state and society. Traditionally, they were seen only as centres relevant for learning and acquiring degrees. However, since the era of Modernity, they have become important centres for research, political confrontation, demands, experimentation and much more. They have been regarded as key institutions in the process of development and change. Therefore, they have an added responsibility of encouraging new cultural values, socializing members of the society apart from meeting the economic ends and producing graduates.

The higher education institutes act as shelters and safe homes for the socio-cultural refugees. They are definitely the centres of knowledge creation and they also act as catalysers of social mobility. The traditional professional culture of an open intellectual enquiry and debate is being gradually replaced with an institutional emphasis on performativity. Its evidence can be seen by the emerging importance laid on measured outputs: On strategic planning, performance indicators, quality assurance measures and academic audits (Olssen & Peters, 2007).

In India, with the advent of Neo-Liberal State since the late 1980s, there has been a shift in the public approach towards education consequently the public character is being shadowed and the profit-seeking private sector is coming to the fore. The post-liberalization period in the

Indian scenario could not keep the public nature of higher education immune from the Utilitarian approach eventually culminating in the commodification of higher education.

Higher education in India, which was labouriously *built for over a decade* in post-independent India, is being systematically dismantled (Haragopal, 2014). This transformation is taking place in a system which one could primarily term as the Neo-liberal regime and it has permeated almost all spheres of social, political and economic life.

This Neoliberal regime has greatly impacted the sphere of higher education. Since this neo-economic order is all pervasive, the higher education sector specifically is at its receiving end. Though in the beginning, the state did promote the establishment of higher education institutes for attaining nationwide development but under the pressure of new economic order, the relationship between the state and higher education has undergone a tremendous change. The domain of higher education which was predominantly state sponsored, changed its orientation, as the nature of state underwent a change from that of a Socialist to a Quasi-capitalist one. Where the state began to withdraw itself from essential domains of health education industrialisation etc.

The changing nature of the state also found its resonance in the changing mechanism of governance in the higher education. The new principles of governance are more in harmony with the doctrines of new pubic management, a system of management which goes in sync with the Neoliberal regime by focusing on extreme levels of performativity and measuring outputs. This system has consequences which are two-fold, i.e. it essentially transforms universities into factories for generating knowledge that could be put to immediate productive activity and it makes the state govern the higher education through market mediated principles. A major shift can be seen in the way higher education has been visualized in the subsequent Five Year Plans.

Higher Education in the Colonial Times

The Colonial policy of higher education was envisioned by the East India Company which was actually a trading corporation. The vision was based upon functional and instrumental conception of knowledge, promoted by the Utilitarian concept of 'useful education' (Prasad, 2012). It contained the policy advocated by Macaulay's infamous Minute of 1835. Therefore, the idea that the education system should provide equal opportunity to everyone and serve as a catalyst for social change, became an important part of the nationalist thought. University education was perceived as the engine for modernizing India and constituting it as an independent nation.

The two models had immense impact on the structures of higher education and universities in Europe. However, the British University System reflected heterogeneity. There were two British Universities along with one Scottish University and they were financially backed by the state.

On the other hand, there was Oxbridge which still reflected the model of medieval universities. They had relative autonomy from the state and had financial support from the land held by religious authorities and Anglican Church. However, during the second half of nineteenth century, they had to keep pace with the Parliamentary reforms and open their doors to Non-Anglican students and women. The universities in Britain were dependent upon grants from the University Grants Committee. However, the grant did not impose any supervision or restricted their autonomy through any provision.

The Indian University System has been majorly influenced by the British System and was established by the Colonizer East India Company which was primarily motivated to train and produce clerks and establish a system for higher education. However, the establishment of universities and the mode of imparting education was driven by a cross-current of various ideologies in Britain itself.

One cannot foresee the inherent debate in this policy until 1817 when the Evangelical pressure and the Utilitarian force came to dominate the educational policy in England as well as India. Initially, in the Company Act of 1813 and in the Educational Dispatch to Bengal in 1814, there was a presupposition that the natives of caste and reputation would not surrender themselves to the English way of learning. Therefore, the Indian predispositions were to be respected.

The logical keystone of the argument of the Orientalists was that the conquered people were to be ruled by their laws or in other words the British had to legitimize their rule in an Indian idiom. In contrast to the Orientalist view, the Anglicist view was held by Charles Grant in the British Parliament. Grant had also worked in India with Lord Cornwallis as a member of the Board of Trade in early 1780-1790s. Grant had lost his two children and suffered major financial setbacks while working in Bengal and his apprehensions regarding India had this personal vantage point. He was of the opinion that "the true cure of darkness is the introduction of light. The Hindoos err, because they are ignorant; and their errors have never fairly been laid before them. The communication of our light and knowledge to them, would prove the best remedy for their disorders; and this remedy is proposed, from a full conviction that if judiciously and patiently applied it would have great and happy effects upon them, effects honourable and advantageous for us." (H. Sharp, 1920).

The gulf between competing claims kept intensifying and came to an end only with Macaulay's well known Minutes along with William Bentinck's assertion and Auckland's Minute of 1839, both were influenced by the Utilitarian thinking of the eighteenth century Britain. The first three universities in India were established in 1857 in Calcutta, Madras and Bombay. These universities were supervised and controlled by the British exclusively and therefore, the universities were not autonomous in nature. These universities are also characterized as the first-generation universities. After the formation of Calcutta University Commission, some of its recommendations were taken into account by the British with regard to more transparency and governance of the universities in India. The idea of higher education in the Colonial times as argued by Aparna Basu, focused on producing a class of clerks who could provide a helping hand to the Colonial government for facilitating the process of Colonial rule (Basu, 1974).

Establishing the idea of higher educational institutions was appealing to the Liberals as well. They wanted to inculcate the English taste in a class of Indians and in this the missionaries sensed an opportunity to popularise the Christian way of life and conversion among Indians. (Vishwanathan, 1990). The model of higher education in India is predominantly derived from the Colonial government (Beteille, 2010). However, with the changing socio-political and economic context, the aims, objectives and approach of the State towards higher education continued to change. Initially, from the 1940s to 1980s, the idea of higher education was linked to promoting nation building. The idea of nation building here would refer to democratising the participation, increasing the number of people enrolling into higher education and producing individuals who can contribute to the task of nation building, but in the post-1980s, the whole idea of nation building itself was much influenced by the Neoliberal reforms taking place in India and the world at large.

The policy recommendations and approach of the state with respect to education have to be essentially seen in the light of this development. The idea then was to produce people who could be skilfully employed so there was a sudden rise in technological institutions and private and public universities. By the time National Knowledge Commission (2007) delivered its report, the sector of higher education became riddled with Commercialisation and Privatisation.

Hence, it is imperative to trace how higher education has been visualized in the Indian context since the beginning of the post-independent period. Before the 1970s, there appeared to be a fair consensus among the policy-makers and academicians that higher education was a channel for promoting chosen social values and national development. Higher education was supposed to constitute an academic community of the wider society, a section that was trained to reflect critically and respond to the society. 'Universities should be sensitive to enlightened public opinion and never let themselves be bullied or bribed into actions that they know are educationally unsound, motivated by nepotism or corruption (Report of Radhakrishanan Commission on Higher Education 1948, p. 37).

Their aim was to furnish intellectual leadership and moral tone of the society. While an autonomous university may not always achieve these goals but it was certain that a university which was not autonomous, could hardly ever achieve these great objectives. (Report of the Committee on Model Act for Universities, 1961-64, p. 5).

Higher Education in the Post-Independence Times

In Post-Independence India, higher education was necessarily seen as a machine of production of knowledge that has carry forward the task of nation-building and nationhood (Patnaik, 2009). Due to this reason, immediately after Independence, economic research and technological institutes were established and given importance (Beteille, 2010). However, this forced link between higher education and nation-building, in turn, distorted the role of universities as places of creating knowledge in a free and fair environment. Patnaik further argues that this imposition of the nation-building reduced universities to a place where higher education becomes a purely functional activity, detached from its quest for knowledge and truth, filled with artificiality, narrowness and outcome-based approach. Another problem is the fact that the task of nation-building through higher education, is seen as possible through only certain disciplines and segments (Patnaik, 2009). Now this further leads to a couple of problems, first is the exclusion of other disciplines, and secondly, research and training of certain types are appreciated leaving aside a large number of subjects.

The point which has been grossly missed by the policy-makers is that higher education institutes are not just centres of learning, but as a distinctive centre of learning, they play an essential role in knowledge creation and transmission. Along with this, they are also social institutions which play their role in making interaction between, young men and women and among generations (Beteille, 2010). The linking of higher education to nation-building and the role of the universities as machine to produce graduates, made it more important for the government to control the functioning of the universities, and not realise the fact that they are not just political institutions as was assumed by the British Raj at the times of their establishment. In independent India, they were much more than that. This is not to say that our universities have not grown, the massification of higher education led to the growth of universities but they are still far off from delivering what was being expected out of them, and the reason for this necessarily lies in the manner they are governed and this will be analysed further in the following section. Having said this, it must be noted that the period of 1970 to 1990 has been classified by N.V. Varghese as the stage of decline in the growth of enrolment in higher education. This has been exemplified by the fact that in 1970s, the gross enrolment ratio in higher education was 4.2 per cent and in 1990s it was 5.9 per cent when compared to the increase in the enrolment ratio from 1960 to 1970, i.e. 1.5 per cent in 1960 and 4.2 per cent in 1970 which shows a rise in enrolment ratio by 3.3 times (Varghese, 2015). The GER of higher education till 1990s has been categorised as the elite stage of enrolment of higher education in India. Varghese was of the opinion that the decline in the enrolment ratio of higher education in India is marked by the beginning of entry of private players in higher education as against decade of 1960 which was characterised as period of converting the private institutions into the public (Varghese, 2018). Pawan Agarwal stated that the colleges which were legally private but publicly financed dominated the higher education landscape till 1980s (Agarwal & Kamalakar, 2013). Hence, it was only with the adoption of cost recovery measures by the public institutions, which marked the beginning of privatization led to the massification of higher education in India. Moreover, one can argue that the public funding of the public institutions characterised the growth of higher education in its elite state while the process of massification was a market mediated process facilitated largely through private institutions and financed from the household. Having said this, till 2000, the GER in higher education remained below 10 per cent, i.e. 8.1 per cent and it reflected the elite nature of enrolment.

There were several reasons identified by R.K. Kale for the elite nature of enrolment, first being exclusion of many marginalised groups for the accessing higher education, only a certain class of people were able to secure a place for themselves in the universities. Despite the existence of reservation policies, the nature of higher education primarily remained exclusionary. Secondly, the GER was 4.7 per cent in 1980s to 10 per cent in 2000, there was a simultaneity in the process of massification and in the process of elitism in higher education. Thirdly, one could witness 'instead of giving autonomy and academic freedom, the government started regulating education, a tendency that only increased over a period'. (Kale, 2018). The massification of higher education occurred post the 1970s but could not realize the goal of inclusive and affordable education in its true sense.

The Planning Commission and Higher Education

Planning Commission which is a non-constitutional and a non-statutory body, has been conferred the task of preparing and devising India's five year plans for India's social and economic development. It was initially established in 1946 as an Advisory Board and from here the Planning Commission became an imperative organ of the Indian State for formulating its policies. When India became independent, a countrywide growth and development was much needed and much thrived for and educating the masses was an essential means to achieve it. To attain growth and development in the economic and technical domains, giving a thrust to the higher education was seen as fundamentally cardinal. The number of universities in India multiplied from 25 in 1947 to 348 in 2005. The significance of education in a planned economy was realised in the First Five-Year Plan itself. The need for a new structure of higher education was desperately felt for meeting the country's goals and objectives.

The Second Five Year Plan (1956-61) stated that there was acceleration in the number of students enrolled in the universities and colleges which affected the standards of education. Due to this acceleration, the Plan emphasised on developing the standards of colleges and university education. Education was declared the most crucial component for attaining the goal of economic development and technological advancement in the Third Five Year Plan (1961-66), thereby establishing a social order based on the values of freedom, social justice and equal opportunity.

In addition, it also stressed that 'programmes of education lie at the base of the effort to forge the bonds of common citizenship, to harness the energies of the people and to develop the natural and human resources of every part of the country' (1961; 573). 'The Seventh Plan (1985-90) had also emphasized on the importance of human resource development in the development strategy, particularly in a country with a large population. It was also marked by the National Policy on Education (NPE, 1986) and emphasized upon preparing the education system for 21st century challenges' (Aggarwal, 1992). It pointed out that 'trained and educated population in itself becomes an asset in accelerating economic growth and in insuring social change in desired directions'. Education facilitates the development of basic skills and abilities and cultivates such a value system which helps to achieve the national development goals, both long term and immediate.

It was stated in the Eighth Plan that since the objective of Plan efforts is human development, therefore, human resource development is quite imperative. Education acts as a catalyst and stimulates human resource development. As far as the domain of higher education is concerned, it has been noticed that the higher education system suffers from several lacunae like the institutions having sub-standard quality are mushrooming, the academic calendar is not adequately implemented, the curriculum is antediluvian, discrepancy in the quality of education provided and an acute dearth of support system for facilitating research.

In this backdrop, the following thrust areas were identified: "integrated approach to higher education; excellence in higher education; expansion of education in an equitable and cost-effective manner, in the process, making the higher education system financially self and supporting; making higher education relevant in the context of changing socio-economic scenario; promotion of value education; and strengthening of management system in the universities (para 1 1.7.1). It was also emphasised that there should be optimum utilization of resources along with their mobilization for creating a support system for the higher education sector, thereby, facilitating the country to successfully surpass all the tests in future especially in today's knowledge and information intensive era" (para 1 1.8.2).

The Ninth Plan revealed that degradation in the quality, lack of resources and pitfalls in governance were some of the grave issues that were crippling the development of higher education. The Plan laid emphasis on the fact that the country is suffering from major economic and technological changes so it becomes quite necessary that the higher education system prepares its products in such a way that they are competent enough to mark their presence in a fast moving social, economic and cultural environment. The universities are witnessing a sea change in their outlook and perspectives. Information Technology is leading to fundamental changes in the structure of modalities and modes of delivery. In the action plan, it was emphasised that teaching in Post-Graduate Programmes and Research would be oriented towards the applied field to establish relevance, need based specialisation and technological advancement driven by skill generation.

At the starting of the Tenth Five Year Plan (2002-2007), there was massive institutional infrastructure for the promotion of higher education and research in the country. The Tenth Plan marked its major goals, objectives, cardinal issues and focus as under: "The main objective in the Tenth Plan is to raise the enrolment in higher education of the 18-23 year age group from 6 per cent to 10 per cent by the end of the Plan period. The strategies would focus on increasing access, quality, adoption of State-specific strategies and the liberalization of the higher education system. Emphasis would also be laid on the relevance of the curriculum, vocationalisation, and networking on the use of Information Technology. The Plan would focus on distance education, convergence of formal, non-formal, distance and IT education institutions, increased private participation in the management of colleges and deemed to be universities; research in frontier areas of knowledge and meeting challenges in the area of internationalization of Indian education" (Approach to Tenth Fiver Year Plan 2002-2007).

The focal point of the Twelfth Five Year Plan was optimum utilisation of the existing infrastructure in higher education. The approach paper of Planning Commission for the Twelfth Five Year Plan was titled as "Faster, Sustainable and More inclusive Growth" and submitted in August 2011. It mentioned that the private higher education "accounts for about four-fifths of enrolment in professional higher education and one-third overall. This growth trend is likely to continue in the Twelfth Plan." (Twelfth Five Year Plan, Volume III, 2013).

For fostering the private investment, it called for "re-examination" of "not-for-profit" tag in the higher education sector. It recommended that the Higher Education Institutions (HEIs) should be advised to gather their own funds, have a reasonable tuition fees and give differential salaries to the staff etc. Provided the "widespread use of English language and low cost (of) living", it aimed to make India a "global hub for higher education." At the same time, the UGC gave its 12th Plan Document approximately on the same grounds. It also stressed on skill development and a planned expansion of skill based programme in higher education. Discarding the obsolete technology, moving towards the modernization of technical education, fogging of beneficial linkages with industries lacking developmental agencies were some of the aspects emphasised in the Twelfth Five Year Plan.

There was a special thrust on the enrolment in private institutions of higher education during the Eleventh Five Year Plan (UGC Report, 2011). The enrolment of students in private institutions increased to more than double as compared to the public institutions during this phase. The private institutions were outgrowing the number of students. The number accelerated in private institutions by 53.11 lakh, in State institutions by 23.72 lakh and Central institutions by 2.52 lakh. It corresponded to 58.9 per cent of total enrolment in the private institutions, while it was 38.5 per cent in the State institutions and 2.6 per cent in Central institutions.

The Planning Commission singled out the priorities, fixed the targets, indentified the resources gap and defined a time period for attaining these goals and objectives. The phase of 1960s witnessed substantial capacity build up in Heavy Capital Goods sector. The educational sector too caught up fast. The renowned and exclusive educational institutions like the IITs, IIMs, BARC, ISRO, IISC, CSIR, ICAR, DSE, ISI, TIFR stand as an evidence to justify the fact that funding made by this Central body was to equip the people to have their legitimate share in the global knowledge discourse. It would be significant to mention here that while 30 per cent of the total Central allocation got allocated for the Planning Commission (at that time), the higher education has commanded an approximately of 60 per cent of the budget for education from the Planning Commission.

A major deviation in the nature of higher education was noticed from being not-for-profit to 'for-profit' entity to subtlety and selectively allow the entry for profit institutions. Though, with reduction in the philanthropic investment, the higher education sector was already becoming a profit field. Since the major responsibility of massification was being shouldered by the private sector, it was only quite logical to allow them to enter legally. It could be said that 10th, 11th and 12th Five Year Plans played a major role in transforming the nature of higher education in India turning it into goods and services, which could be purchased by those who could bear its cost. Once the private sector was given a free hand it became almost impossible for the government to regulate the proliferation of these institutions and also ensure quality.

The 11th Five Year Plan also aimed at wiping off the non-performing colleges and limiting the system of affiliation. It observed that this system of affiliation is detrimental to the growth of higher education. However, the phasing out of the colleges was not an easy task to perform. How was the sub-committee to decide which standards to apply on colleges situated in varied socio-economic context and geographical disparities? And how can uniform standards be applied to judge and examine colleges and universities spread across various contexts?

The Changing Idea of Higher Education in India

The First Commission on higher education in post-independent India Ramakrishnan Commission, emphasized that higher education should take into account the changing socio-political scenario in the country and formulate aims of education. The major objectives were social efficiency, development of knowledge and wisdom, seeking higher moral values of life, cultural progress etc. It would not be a mistake here to mention the idea of higher education that John Henry Newman had articulated, in mid-nineteenth century. He insisted on the fact that knowledge should be seen as an end in itself and that alone is liberal knowledge. This idea was closer to the objectives laid down by the Ramakrishnan Commission.

The idea of liberal education was popular in the mid-nineteenth century and it was associated with the study of Theology, Mathematics and Philosophy. The aim was to enhance the moral character of the human beings. However, even at that time, the liberal education was applicable to the most common career followed by the Oxbridge graduates, namely the clergy of the church. The ambivalence of purpose became more sharp by the nineteenth century. Michael Sanderson's edited book, *The Universities in the Nineteenth Century* explains the nature, context and debate surrounding the universities in the nineteenth century (Sanderson, 2016). The period saw radical changes in the temperament and purpose of higher education. Since then, there have only been changes in the contextualization of purpose but the idea of having a material purpose always existed in the domain of higher education.

As the knowledge economy is acquiring the centre stage in twenty first century developmental world, higher education is assuming unprecedented significance *domestically* and internationally, since it has the responsibility of educating people for the new economy and its challenges (Altbach, 1998). Conventionally, higher education was seen as a public good, producing a huge set of externalities, benefiting not only the individual but also the society. However, this conception has marked a shift in the widespread introduction of Neoliberal Economics and Globalization in every country, contributing to massive privatization of education, as if it is a commodity to be traded. The 'public good' character is also being overshadowed and forgotten and the profit seeking agenda is thriving (Tilak, 2008).

From the last two decades it seems that the higher education systems around the globe have moved closer to textbook economic markets. (Marginson, 2012). To articulate the character of higher education as knowledge in itself, may seem problematic in today's context, especially as the knowledge economy is driven by outcome based measures and performativity. Still, it would be unfair and naïve to only characterise higher education in these terms, no matter how utilitarian the idea of higher education becomes, it would lose its character if it loses its idealism.

Higher education in the idealistic terms in today's context is not to negate the practicality and applicability of education but elevating it to a higher level of refinement (Pathak, 2009). The idea of higher education should be such that "useful branches of knowledge like computer science or biotechnology or financial economics by no means should be allowed to devalue a professor contemplating upon Tibetan Buddhism or African Culture" (Pathak, 2009). Else, we should be ready to find ourselves in a situation where "skill development policies are shaped and techniques are refined but wisdom as a form of deep reflection, collective exchange and a recognition and even a critique of inner values is out in jeopardy" (Barnett, 1994, p. 153).

In the Indian context, the idea was that higher education "must enable the country to attain, in a short time as possible, applicable and development of scientific and technological knowledge" (Bhatt and Aggarwal, 1969, p. 98). However, these would not be achievable if the foundational values are not inculcated and embraced, emphasised the Radhakrishnan Commission. It would be interesting to quote here that:

> In the name of practicality, we cannot forget the higher values of life, the danger is that we will have a number of scientists without conscience, technicians without taste who find a void within themselves, a moral vacuum and a desperate need to substitute something or anything for their lost endeavour and purpose. Indeed, it is refreshing to recall that we are building a civilization not a factory workshop and the quality of civilization depends not on the material development but on the character of man (Bhatt and Aggarwal, 1969, pp. 102-103).

However, as the National Knowledge Commission (2007) stated, the times are changing fast and education in terms of fulfilling needs is becoming more intense. We need to facilitate knowledge applicability in the sectors of health, industry and agriculture as the ability of a nation to use the knowledge capital determines its capacity to empower and enable its citizens by increasing the human capabilities. Also, the production of human knowledge ceases if it loses its fundamental queries.

The World Trade Organisation (WTO) and General Agreement on Trade in Services (GATS) made an entry into the arena of higher education in India in 2000. In the year 2005, a new strategy for reforms in the higher education sector was identified in India, i.e. the structure of regulation and cooperation between the investors and government in Private and Public Partnership (PPP) (Dahlman & Utz, 2005). The bureaucratic hurdles were relaxed for the Private players since a new cadre of knowledge labour was to be created (Prasad, 2014).

The principles of New Public Management (NPM), are being employed on the governance of higher education institutions. These principles are essentially based on the maximisation of output and performance based system increment. This makes the whole system of higher education, in a way, mechanic and robotic, the thrust is more upon quantity than quality it seems.

Conclusion

We have come too far from the objectives such as attaining higher moral value and cultural progress to output driven knowledge production which could be out to immediate use in the marker oriented knowledge economy. The trajectory of Indian higher education it seems, has suffered a downfall over the last two decades, even though, there has been significant emergence of numerous educational institutions and trends in higher education. The newly independent India built its thrust upon achieving excellence and building its human resources, technological and industrial capacity through higher education. Though, this process was not devoid of the foundational ideals of higher education.

However, as one can derive after reading various Commissions and Planning Commission's views on higher education that post the 1980s, specially higher education was turned into a skill development enterprise. This ideology which is dominating the world today is essentially material driven, what it does is it replaces the experience in life, with what corresponds to it, that is, the 'representational sensation', which is basically the objective consciousness of the word. Consequently, what we have in front of us is the reduction of the life world to the world of science, the reduction of the natural process to the abstract physio-mathematical parameters.

The contemporary global debate on education centres around the compulsions of preparing young people for the fourth Industrial Revolution, on one hand and seeking alternatives to State funding for the promotion of education, on other hand (Varghese, 2018). The golden period of the welfare State came to an end by the 1980s when the market and market forces became a unifying ideology, both in developmental debates and in political discourse. It can be claimed that the market became a dominant influence in public-policy and decision making. The process of Globalisation has not constrained the options available to the State with respect to policies but has also confined the walls of sovereignty. This process leads to the retrenchment of welfare policies in the developed countries and pushes the developing countries to introduce market friendly reforms in order to embrace themselves into the Neoliberal economies. The approach of these countries, regarding higher education, essentially underwent a change with these transformations.

Having introduced the structural adjustment policies in India, the success of these policies depended on the higher education sector. This has been best exemplified by Tilak, who was of the opinion that "as with the Globalisation and international competitions, the need for a more educated workforce is strongly felt. With an illiterate and ill-educated workforce, reforms programmes cannot even take off properly" (Tilak, 2003).

The above-mentioned proposition entails the opening of an economy by the government in which the private players will play a significant role and the reforms have to be introduced in respect of the regulatory measures. The academic regulators such as the API (Academic Performance Index) are framed in such a manner that more than an instrument of fostering intellectual stimulation they often lead to meaningless proliferation of academic endeavours. There is a grave danger that the whole discourse of higher education might turn into a process of providing services to the rather than transmitting knowledge and exchange ideas.

Higher education institutions is also a place where the young minds immerse in the process of learning and also unlearning what they have learnt all their lives without questioning (Ilich, 1971). Therefore, it is of grave importance that higher education is given its due, it should remain an area which is not overregulate and undergoverned rather aptly governed with mostly inputs from academicians.

REFERENCES

Aggarwal, J.C. (1992). *Educational Planning in India: Reports of Committees and Commissions, Five Year Plans, Statistical Tables* (Vol. 39). Concept Publishing Company.

Agarwal, P., and Kamalakar, G. (2013). "Indian higher education: Envisioning the future". *The Indian Economic Journal, 61*(1), 151-155.

Altbach, P.G. (1998). *Comparative higher education: Knowledge, the university, and development*. Greenwood Publishing Group.

Altbach, P.G. (2004). "Globalisation and the university: Myths and realities in an unequal world." *Tertiary Education and Management, 10*(1), 3-25.

Barnett, R. (1994). *Academic Community: Discourse or Discord? Higher Education Policy Series 20*. Jessica Kingsley Publishers Ltd., 1900 Frost Road, Suite 101, Bristol, PA 19007.

Basu, A. (1974). *The growth of education and political development in India, 1898-1920*. Oxford University Press.

Beteille, A. (2010). *Universities at the Crossroads*. Oxford University Press.

Bhatt, B.D. and Aggarwal, J.C. (Eds.).(1969). *Educational Documents in India*.

Chandra, P. (2017). *Building Universities that Matter: Where are Indian Institutions Going Wrong?*. Orient Black Swan, p. 9.

Dahlman, C., and Utz, A. (2005). *India and the knowledge economy: leveraging strengths and opportunities*, The World Bank.

Hasan, M. (Ed.). (1998). *Knowledge, Power and Politics: Educational Institutions in India*, Lotus Collection.

Illich, I (1971). *Deschooling Society*.

Kale, R.K. (2018) *Indian Higher Education: A perspective from the margin*, Aakar Books, New Delhi, 2018.

Marginson, S. (2013). "The impossibility of capitalist markets in higher education." *Journal of Education Policy, 28*(3), 353-370.

Olssen, M., and Peters, M.A. (2005). "Neoliberalism, higher education and the knowledge economy: From the free market to knowledge capitalism." *Journal of Education Policy, 20*(3), 313-345.

Pathak, A. (2009). *Recalling the Forgotten: Education and Moral Quest*, Aakar Books, New Delhi.

Patnaik, P. (2009). "Challenges before higher education in developing societies." *Social Scientist, 37*(7/8), 21-32.

Prasad, M. (2005). "Autonomy and the commercialization of higher education." *Social Scientist*, 43-48.

Sanderson, M. (Ed.). (2016). *The Universities in the Nineteenth Century*. Routledge.

Tilak, J.B. (2008). "Transition from higher education as a public good to higher education as a private good: The saga of Indian experience." *Journal of Asian Public Policy, 1*(2), 220-234.

Tilak, J.B.G. (2003). "Higher Education in India under Structural Adjustment", in Banerjee, Parthasarathi, and Frank-Jürgen Richter, (eds). *Economic Institutions in India: Sustainability under Liberalization and Globalization*. Palgrave Macmillan.

University Grants Commission. (2012*). Annual Report 2011-2012* (UGC).

Varghese, N.V. (2015). Challenges of massification of higher education in India. Research Papers, *National University of Educational Planning and Administration, New Delhi–India.*

Varghese, N.V. (2018). "Criticality, empathy and welfare in educational discourses." *Contemporary Education Dialogue, 15*(2), 122-142.

Viswanathan, G. (2014). *Masks of Conquest: Literary Study and British Rule in India*, Columbia University Press.

Planning Commission, Government of India. (2013) *Twelfth Five Year Plan, Volume III*, Retrieved from https://mhrd.gov.in/sites/upload_files/mhrd/files/document-reports/XIIFYP_SocialSector.pdf.

Ministry of Education, Government of India. *The Report of the University Education Commission (1948-49)*. (1962). Volume I, Government of India Press, Simla for The Manager of Publications Civil Lines, Delhi. Retrieved from https://www.educationforallinindia.com/1949%20Report%20of%20the%20University%20Education%20Commission.pdf

Planning Commission, Government of India, (2001). *Approach to paper to the Tenth Five Year Plan (2002-2007)*, Government of India, New Delhi. Retrieved from https://mhrd.gov.in/sites/upload_files/mhrd/files/document-reports/appdraft_1.pdf

http://mospi.nic.in/sites/default/files/Statistical_year_book_india_chapters/Five%20Year%20Plan%20writeup_0.pdf

21
Human Capital Formation Through Education

Kartar Singh and *Kiran Arora*

Overview

Skilled population contributes in the economic, social development of a country, if it is unskilled it is regarded as wastage. So, there is a need to accelerate the human capital formation for the development of a country.

In this chapter, at the first Introduction is mentioned that helps to understand the concept of human capital as well as human capital formation. After that its relationship with economic development supported with the data has been given. Description of Education and Health sector along with the data collected from different sources has been presented. At last recent initiates to boost human capital formation initiated by the Government of India has been discussed.

Introduction

India is still a developing country even after seventy-two years of Independence. The main reason behind this is the shortage of skilled manpower, inequality of income and wealth and lack of health facilities, which includes clean environment and safe drinking water. It is well said that the development of a nation depends to a great extent on human capital. So, Human Capital implies the development of different abilities, skills among humans through education, training and providing adequate health facilities. India's dream to become a developed nation can only be fulfilled through the formation of more human capital. As educated minds are the only way to open the door of economic development.

Development in Indian education cannot be envisaged, as many policies and programmes are initiated by the government for increasing literacy rates. According to the Census of India (2011), literacy rate in India is 74.04 per cent (Kerala is on the top with 93.91% and Bihar touched the bottom with only 63.82%) which is not satisfactory, if we compare with other developed countries like Poland, Russia, Italy etc. where more than 99 per cent population is literate. In the case of health facilities most of the population are suffering from poor sanitation facilities, safe drinking water which are the major factors contributing to the ill health of human beings. Different diseases like diabetes, asthma, high blood pressure, skin infection, eye infection, tuberculosis, cancer etc. are very commonly found in the Indian population. Even though many campaigns and drives are started by the Government of India but still we need more health facilities and care to eradicate these diseases.

Human Capital

Capital is something that is invested to get returns, in the same way, human capital is the investment in human beings to increase their productivity to get more gains from it. Broadly, human capital is defined as education imparted to the people, knowledge provided through training, skills development among people through different programmes so as to produce expertise human resources.

"Human capital is relatively young production factor. Because it is closely related to the production factors of labour and has features in common with the labour, analysis and research work are often not explicitly mentioned" (Tokarèíková, 2010). It implies that whatever expertise and knowledge a person got during his employment in an organization through experience and training helps in increasing the production of the organization, this is considered as human capital. M. Armstrong, defines the human capital as development of skills and enhancement of knowledge which an individual creates and use for increase in productivity of a nation.

Harbinson (1973) aptly summarized the importance of human capital to economic development by stating that "human resources constitute the ultimate basis for the wealth of nations. Capital and natural resources are passive factors of production; human beings are the active agents who accumulate capital, exploit natural resources, build social, economic, and political organizations, and carry forward national development. Clearly a country which is unable to develop the skills and knowledge of its people and to utilize them effectively in the national economy will be unable to develop anything else". The development of a nation depends totally on the manpower, as skilled and knowledgeable human resource contributes in the achievement of sustainable economic growth.

T.W. Schultz (1993) defined human capital as, an important element which help in enhancement of productivity and sustain competitive advantage through acquisition of knowledge with the help of education and training. He suggested following five ways for developing human resources:

(i) Enhancement in health facilities and services, broadly conceived to include all expenditure that affect the life expectancy, strength and stamina, and the vigour and vitality of the people;
(ii) Imparting on-the-job training, including aid type apprenticeships organised by firms;
(iii) Formal organisation of education at different levels, i.e. at the elementary, secondary and higher levels;
(iv) Study programmes for adults that are not organised by firms, including extension programmes notably in agriculture; and
(v) Facilitate the migration of individuals and families to adjust to changing job opportunities.

So human capital are those skills and abilities of a person which contribute towards increase in productivity. Hence, formation of human capital is pivot for economic growth and development.

Human Capital and Economic Development

Human Capital is one of the important components for economic development, as more you invest in the formation of human capital more output you will get in return. There exists a close relationship between human capital and economic development. An aware human with good health is the prime requirement of a healthy society. Human capital is a powerful source that can make a nation from developing to a developed one. A country with rich human capital can reach the heights of economic development, as it provides skilled and knowledgeable minds to the economy which further helps in increasing productivity of the nation.

Economic development of a country can be reflected through per capita income, higher literacy rate, decrease in mortality rate, employability of the youth, increase in growth rate, improved health facilities etc. It can also be assessed through Human Development Index, which includes three major areas, i.e. education, health and per capita income of a country. Ojo and Oshikoya (1995) in their study, "Determinants of Long-Term Growth: Some African Results" showed that the rate of literacy has strong impact on per capita income and concluded their study by stating that there exists a positive relation between human capital investment and economic growth. Skilled and knowledgeable labour force can positively enhance the country's wealth. If we want to transform from developing to developed nation, then formation of good human capital is the prerequisite. Even though the Government of India has launched so many policies and programmes for improving the condition of education and health and even increased the budget amount in last few decades, so now it is high time to utilize these expenditures effectively and efficiently for human capital formation.

Education and health are the two driving forces of economic development. In the last few years growth in these two sectors have accelerated, but it is not up to the mark. Expenditure on education as a percentage to GDP in 2018-19 is 3 per cent which has increased from 2.8 per cent in 2015-16. In the health sector, there is little change in expenditure as a percentage to GDP has only increased by 0.2 per cent from 1.3 per cent in 2015-16 to 1.5 per cent in 2018-19.

Different initiatives were started by the government to provide medical care to the citizens. Pradhan Mantri Bhartiya Jan Aushadhi Kendra (2015), Mohalla Clinic (2015) and many more are also started to provide proper medical facilities to all. Immunization of the children has also given emphasis to protect the child from different disease and some diseases like Polio, Tuberculosis are almost eradicated. The UN has set the target to eradicate Tuberculosis by 2030, but our Prime Minister moved five years ahead and pledged to end up Tuberculosis by 2025. No doubt these schemes and programmes have contributed a lot to India's progress but we need to push up more.

In India, the education sector is progressing as literacy rate is improving from last decades and in year 2016, Kerala became the first Indian State to achieve 100 per cent primary education through their literacy drive 'Athulyam'. Under the RTI Act (2009), children are receiving free and compulsory education from 6 to 14 years. Even in higher education the remarkable performance is being observed, that if we compare the higher education system from the time of Independence, it is found in the year 2017-18, there is 47.9 times increase in universities and 82.02 times in the case of colleges has been reported in All India Survey of Education initiated by Ministry of Human Resource Development. Rajasthan has secured the top position having 77 universities, then comes Uttar Pradesh with 75 universities and then Gujarat with 63 universities and so on. Although both the sectors are growing in their own inert way there is a need to accelerate the growth in these fields and investment in these two sectors should be the priority of the government.

Human Development Index is an indicator which is used to rank the countries based on the human development. The three indicators of human development suggested by Prof. Amartya Sen are Longevity, Education and Standard of Living.

Education

Education is considered as the backbone of a country, as it plays a major role in country's development. Earlier in India, the education was under the state list but in 1976, after 42nd Amendment Act was passed, it was moved from state list to concurrent list which confirms that education is the responsibility of both Central and State Governments. Here the pattern of School Education is 10+2 which consists of pre-primary, primary, elementary, secondary followed by senior secondary. But the National policy on education, 2019 (Draft) has revised the curriculam and pedagogical structure design for school education, i.e. 5+3+3+4, constituting of foundational stage (Grade 1-2), Preparatory stage (Grade 3-5), Middle stage (Grade 6-8) and High stage (Grade 9-12 in two phases, i.e. 9-10 and 11-12).

The gross enrolment ratio in our country is low, if compared with the developed nations. Although the number of enrolments have increased by 5 per cent annually from 2010-11 to 2018-19. It has been found there was a disparity in enrolment among different castes as well as states. In 2017-18, the gross enrolment among SC (Scheduled Caste) was 21.4 per cent and ST (Scheduled Tribe) was 15.9 per cent as compared to 25.4 per cent for all.

In the case of elementary education, India is progressing in the way of compulsory education to all students at the age of 6-14 years. Different programmes have been launched by the government in favour of RTE, 2009 (Right of Children to Free and Compulsory Education). In the Annual Report of MHRD, 2016-17, recent initiatives taken by the Department for improving the Quality of Elementary Education has been discussed below:

- Learning Goals are framed and will be displayed grade-wise from class 1-8, to ensure that all the children have achieved these goals.

- National Achievement Survey will be conducted yearly, for regular assessment of children learning levels and it also provides insight for any further changes required to improve their learning levels.
- Remedial Classes for grade-wise weak students are being organized.
- 'Enhancing the use of E-governance', for efficient decision making.
- Timely check on Teachers' Non-Teaching activities, to assess the time spent by them and its negative effect on education.
- 'Teacher Tenure Policy in rural areas' to fix their minimum teaching tenure.
- Extending the scheme, for vocationalisation at upper primary level.

Secondary education is a bridge between elementary education and higher education. It covers the age group of 14-18 years. One of the important scheme named RMSA (Rashtriya Madhyamik Shiksha Abhiyan) in 2009, had been initiated to provide access and improve quality of secondary education. It also aimed to ensure 100 per cent enrolment in secondary education by the year 2017 and universal retention by the year 2020. For improving the quality different initiatives like *Shaala Sidhi, Shaala Darpan, GIS Mapping, National Achievement Survey for Class X, Kala Utsav, Focus on Science and Mathematics, National Award for teachers using ICT for Innovation in Education, Database of Students and Teachers* are taken under RMSA. Vocationalisation of secondary education with the objective of enhancing youth employability has taken pace. Approximately, 4,86,000 students of 5,582 government schools are pursuing vocational courses across the nation (Annual Report, MHRD 2016-17).

Higher education is one of the essential components which contributes towards the welfare of the economy. In India, the higher education institutes are lagging behind in numbers. Although in the last few years, the number of universities has gone up to 851. So far, the number of universities are concerned, State Public Universities are leading with 383 in numbers followed by 295 State Private Universities, 123 Deemed to be Universities, 47 Central Universities and 3 institutes established under state legislature. These are tabulated in Table 21.1 along with pie chart (Figure 21.1).

Table 21.1: Number of Universities as on 31.3.2018

Types of Universities	*As on 31. 3.2018*
Central University	47
State Public University	383
State Private University	295
Deemed to be University	123
Institutions established under state legislature	3
Total Universities	**851**

Source: UGC, Annual Report 2017-18.

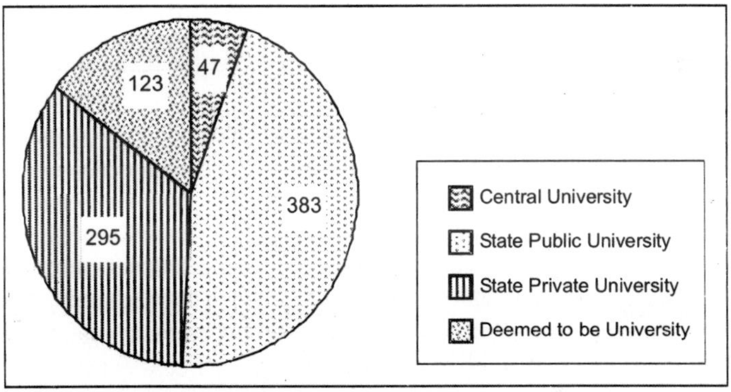

Fig. 21.1: Number of Universities in India.

The number of higher education colleges have also increased in the last few years and gone up-to 41,012. Constituting, 37,977 affiliated colleges, 1,550 constituent, 187 PG/Off campus centres and 1,298 recognized centres in India. These are tabulated below (Table 21.2):

Table 21.2: Number of Colleges in 2017-18

Types of Colleges	*2017-18*
Affiliated Colleges	37,977
Constituent	1,550
PG/Off Campus centres	187
Recognised centres	1,298
Total Number of Colleges	**41,012**

Source: UGC, Annual Report 2017-18.

According to the AISHE Report 2017-18, the number of colleges are less in Chandigarh and Delhi as compared to other states. Education comes under concurrent list which indicates the role of both Centre and State. Both Centre and State set a budget for the education sector. Even though the budget has increased in the last four years but still we need more amount to be invested in education for economic development. As education is the only sector in which investment gives maximum returns. Table 21.3 shows the expenditure on education.

Table 21.3: Expenditure by General Governments (Combined Centre and States) in Education

	2015-16	*2016-17*	*2017-18 (RE*)*	*2018-19 (BE**)*
Expenditure as % to GDP	2.8	2.8	2.9	3.0
Expenditure as % to Total Expenditure	10.4	10.2	10.1	10.6
Expenditure as % to Social Services	42.8	41.8	39.3	40.7

* RE—Revised Estimate.

** BE—Budget Estimate.

Note: Expenditure on 'Education' pertains to expenditure on 'Education, Sports, Arts and Culture'.
The ratios to GDP at current market prices are based on 2011-12 base

Source: Economic Survey 2018-19, Volume 2.

It has been observed from Table 21.3 that the Government of India is putting continuous effort on improving the education sector by investing more amount from the budget in this sector, i.e. expenditure as per cent to GDP in 2015-16 was 2.8 which was increased to 3 per cent in 2018-19, expenditure as per cent to total expenditure is also increased by 10.4 per cent to 10.6 from 2015-16 to 2018-19 (BE) but a decrease of 2.1 per cent has been reported in expenditure from 42.8 per cent in 2015-16 to 40.7 per cent in 2018-19 (BE). In the same way, other countries also set aside budgeted amount for education sector which is much higher than India. In 2017, Iceland was reported to be the country with highest percentage to GDP, i.e. 7.5 per cent, followed by Sweden with 6.8 per cent then Denmark with 6.5 per cent and so on.

Health

Health is one of the important components of human capital formation. There are many reasons or factors which affect one's quality of life, i.e.

food supply, water supply, sanitation and hygiene, global warming, etc.

World 7th happiness report published on 20th March, 2019 by UN depicts that 'Finland' is the happiest country in the world and 'India' has secured 140th rank among 156 countries. The three major sources of happiness included in it were a linkage between government policies and norms with happiness, power of pro-social behaviour and information technology. It shows that we need to push our economy.

Education and health are the two essentials for the development of an economy and share a close relationship. Health is the prerequisite, which contributes to the increment of productivity and education takes it to the extremes. More capital you spent on health; more will be the return on your investment in education.

From the last decade child care facilities have been improving in India, diseases like polio, tetanus have come to an end. Childhood mortality rate as shown (Table 21.4) has reduced as it is observed in NFHS-3 (2005-06) the mortality rate under five was 74 death per 1000 live birth but in NFHS-4 (2015-16) it has reduced to 50. The under-five mortality rate has been varying in different States of India, highest in Uttar Pradesh, i.e. 78 deaths per 1000 live birth and lowest in Kerala with 7 deaths per 1000 live birth. The infant mortality rate has also decreased from 57 to 50 from 2005-06 to 2015-16 along with decrement in neonatal mortality rate from 39 to 30 in the last decade.

Table 21.4: Mortality Rate Under Five Children (death per 000s' live birth)

NFHS-3 (2005-06)			*NFHS-4 (2015-16)*		
Under-five mortality	*Infant mortality*	*Neonatal mortality*	*Under-five mortality*	*Infant mortality*	*Neonatal mortality*
74	57	39	50	41	30

Source: National Family Health Survey-4 (2015-16).

The prevalence of malnutrition that results in stunting, wasting, underweight and overweight has decreased in the last decade (Table 21.5), but is very high when compared to other developing countries. According to Global Nutrition Report 2017, the three countries having wasted children are India with 2.5 million, Nigeria with 3.4 million and Indonesia with 3.3 million and it stands third with the 31 per cent of world's burden for stunting which is higher than any other developing country's average of 2.5 per cent.

Table 21.5: Health Status of Indian Children

(In percentage)

	2005-06	2015-16
Stunting	48	38
Wasting	20	21
Underweight	43	36
Overweight	–	2

Source: National Family Health Survey-4 (2015-16).

Status of nutritional health among adults is also alarming. Although huge improvement have been noticed in the health sector and different programmes and drives have been conducted by the Government of India, but still Indian population is impacted by malnutrition. It has been reported that 53 per cent of the women are anemic, which depicts that more than half of the women population have low hemoglobin resulting in the deficiency in upcoming births. More cases of thin and obesity are found in women, i.e. 23 per cent and 21 per cent as compared to men with 20 per cent and 19 per cent. The status has been shown (Table 21.6) along with the Graph (Fig. 21.2).

Table 21.6: Health Status of Indian Men and Women

(In percentage)

	15-49 years	
	Men	Women
Thin	20	23
Obese	19	21
Anaemia	23	53

Source: National Family Health Survey-4 (2015-16).

Women are the backbone of the society, who play a significant role in the development of a country. Although the health status of women population in India is not satisfactory as they are facing numerous health issues, the Government of India is putting continuous effort in improving and supporting their health conditions. Different drives like Janani Suraksha Yojana, Weekly Iron-Folic Acid Supplementation Programme, Scheme for Promotion of Menstrual Hygiene among adolescent girls have been initiated by the Government to provide good health and hygiene to the women.

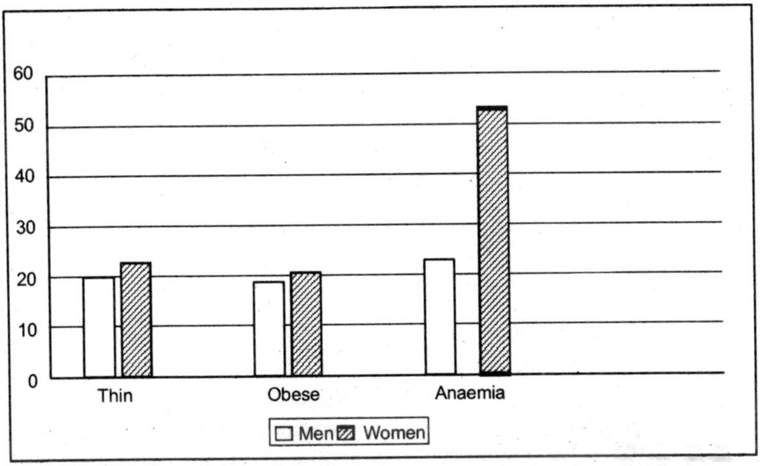

Fig. 21.2: Age Group 15-49 Years

The only way to improve the health status of a country is to increase the investment in health sector. More investment will bring new and modern opportunities to fight against these illnesses and contribute in the progress of a nation. Increase is witnessed in almost all the field of expenditure shown in Table 21.7, but only a slight improvement in the health budget from 1.3 per cent to 1.5 per cent in 2015-16 to 2018-19 has been noticed. The Government has targeted to raise it to 2.5 per cent by 2025 (National Health Policy, 2017).

Table 21.7: Expenditure by General Governments (Combined Centre and States) in Health

(In percentage)

	2015-16	*2016-17*	*2017-18 (RE*)*	*2018-19 (BE**)*
Expenditure as % to GDP	1.3	1.4	1.5	1.5
Expenditure as % to Total Expenditure	4.7	5.0	5.2	5.1
Expenditure as % to Social Services	19.1	20.5	20.3	19.8

Source: Economic Survey 2018-19, Volume 2.

* RE—Revised Estimate.

** BE—Budget Estimated.

Note: Expenditure on 'Health' includes expenditure on 'Medical and Public Health', 'Family Welfare' and 'Water Supply and Sanitation'.
The ratios to GDP at current market prices are based on 2011-12 base.

In this way improvement in expenditure on these two sectors are easily noticeable still there is a need to improve these figures for economic development of a nation.

Problems in Formation of Human Capital in India

India is facing the following problems listed below in formation of human capital:

Growing Population

India is one of the densely populated country, it stands second in the list of countries in terms of population after China. UNPD contends (world population) that an increase in mortality rate from 67 years in 2000-2005 to 70 years in 2010-2015 is one of the biggest reason for growth in population. The rapid increase in population results in reducing the per capita availability of present limited resources. It exerts pressure on the existing population and badly affects their employment opportunities.

Lack of Proper Health Facilities

Health facilities are one of the major social issue in our country. Thousands of people die daily due to lack of health facilities. Undernourishment among under-five children has been reported by NHFS-4, 38 per cent of the children are stunted, 21 per cent are wasted, 6 per cent are underweight, 2 per cent are overweight. Availability of clean drinking water, preventive medicines are not available to huge mass of population due to which productivity of human labour is deteriorating day by day.

Lack of Proper Training Facilities

Very few efforts have been done for skill development and enhancement in our country. Agriculture is one of the main sources of employment in India, still agriculture is the most ignored sector with low investment made by the government for the training of the farmers to increase their farm productivity.

Poverty

Poverty is one of the biggest challenges in India, where most of the people are unable to fulfil their basic needs. Even though many steps have been taken by the government to eradicate but it still persists. In India, poverty line is fixed on the basis of surveys conducted by the NSSO (2011-12), it has been found that more than 21.9 per cent population lives below the poverty line. Due to this, they are unable to afford the high-priced education and medical facilities.

Less Investment in Education

In India investment in education is very low as compared to other countries. Education is still a neglected sector in our economy. In the Annual Report of 2017-18 published by UGC, it has been found that Gross Enrolment Ratio for Higher Education in India is 25.8 per cent for the age group of 18-23 years. For the male population, it is 26.3 per cent and for female, it is 25.4 per cent. It shows that there are still some children who are not going to school.

Recent Programmes to Boost Human Capital Formation in India

Education and Health are the two priority sectors, which reflect wealth of an economy. Improvement in these two sectors contribute in reforming the country's economic condition. In India, these sectors are still lagging behind, if we compare it with other countries. So, the schemes are initiated by the Government of India shown in Table 21.8, to uplift the human capital formation in India.

Ayushman Bharat—National Health Protection Scheme

Ayushman Bharat—National Health Protection Scheme has been launched by the Government of India in 2018. It aims to provide pre- and post-hospitalization expenses to the 10 lakh families of India living below the poverty line. This scheme covers two health initiates i.e. health and wellness centres and National health protection schemes. It provides coverage of five lakh rupees per family per year for secondary and tertiary hospitalization.

Pradhan Mantri Kaushal Vikas Yojana

This scheme is proposed by the Government of India for skill development among Indian youth in the year 2015. The objective is to provide

Table 21.8: Recent programmes to Boost Human Capital Formation in India

S. No.	Schemes	Year	Objectives
1.	Ayushman Bharat—National Health Protection Scheme	2018	• To provide pre and post hospitalization expenses to the people living below poverty line
2.	Pradhan Mantri Kaushal Vikas Yojana	2015	• To develop employable skills among youth
3.	Pradhan Mantri Suraksha Bima Yojana	2015	• To provide accidental insurance coverage to the poor and unprivileged person
4.	Pradhan Mantri Jeevan Jyoti Bima Yojana	2015	• To provide life insurance to low income group people
5.	Pradhan Mantri Bhartiya Jan Aushadhi Kendra (PMBJAK)	2015	• To provide generic medicines to the masses at affordable prices
6.	Mohalla Clinic	2015	• To provide treatment for simple ailments at their doorstep
7.	Saksham or Rajiv Gandhi Scheme for Empowerment of Adolescent Boys 2014	2014	• All round development of adolescent boys • To make them self-reliant • To make them gender sensitized
8.	Sabla or Rajiv Gandhi Scheme for Empowerment of Adolescent Girls	2011	• All round development of adolescent girls • To make them self-reliant • Upgrading various home skills, vocational skills
9.	INSPIRE Programme	2010	• To motivate top science students for research

institutional training to the unskilled youth population by 2022. National Skill Development Council is the driving agency for the scheme. This skill training helps in increasing the productivity of the nation by making the human employable. Monetary rewards after completion of skill training through the authorised institute is also given to them with a bank account.

Pradhan Mantri Suraksha Bima Yojana

Pradhan Mantri Suraksha Bima Yojana launched by the Government of India in 2015. The objective of the scheme is to provide accidental insurance to poor and underprivileged people in India. The cheapest premium, i.e. Rs. 12 per year is taken from the insured person. Any person between the age of 18-70 with a bank account can get the benefits of this scheme.

Pradhan Mantri Jeevan Jyoti Bima Yojana

Pradhan Mantri Jeevan Jyoti Bima Yojana was initiated in 2015, by the Government of India. The objective of the scheme is to provide life insurance to poor low-income grade population. The person between the age group of 18-50 are eligible to get the benefits of the scheme. It provides life insurance coverage for 1 year with the cheapest premium of just Rs. 330 per year with the risk coverage of Rs. 2 lakh.

Pradhan Mantri Bhartiya Jan Aushadhi Kendra (PMBJAK)

Pradhan Mantri Bhartiya Jan Aushadhi Kendra has been set-up by the Government of India in 2014. The objective of this campaign is to provide generic medicines at affordable prices. These stores are opened in different districts of the country. In November 2016 this campaign is renamed as "Pradhan Mantri Bhartiya Janaushadhi Pariyojana" (PMBJP).

Mohalla Clinic

This is one of the initiative taken by the Government of NCT, Delhi in 2015. The aim of setting up of these Mohalla Clinics is to diagnose and treat the simple ailments of people at almost their doorstep. Setting up of these Clinics have created employment opportunities for people and also reduced the burden of government hospitals, in which the people use to go before these clinics.

Saksham or Rajiv Gandhi Scheme for Empowerment of Adolescent Boys

This scheme was initiated by the Ministry of Women and Child Development, Central Government in 2014. The aim of the scheme is to make adolescent boys more smart, aware, self-dependant; gender sensitised which contribute to the overall development of their personality. This covers the adolescent boys of age group 11-18 years. The different features of this scheme are awareness for their health needs, skill development trainings, mindset for respecting women, awareness of cleanliness, nutrition etc.

Sabla or Rajiv Gandhi Scheme for Empowerment of Adolescent Girls

Sabla or Rajiv Gandhi Scheme for Empowerment of Adolescent Girls was launched by the Ministry of Women and Child Development, Central Government in 2011. The aim of the scheme is to empower the adolescent women, make them self-reliant, provide awareness in health, nutrition and in different home and vocational skills. Adolescent girls between the age group of 11-18 are covered under the scheme.

INSPIRE Programme

INSPIRE (Innovation of Science Pursuit for Inspire Research) scheme is initiated by the Department of Science and Technology for talented students to study science in the year 2010. The objective of this scheme is to attract capable youth for research and innovation in science. It gives an opportunity to young achievers with an aptitude in science to avail scholarship, fellowship for carrying out research and also provide research grants to the researchers. Broadly this scheme has three programmes, i.e. Scheme for Early Attraction of Talents (SEAT), Scholarship for Higher Education (SHE) and Assured Opportunity for Research Careers (AORC).

Summarization

There is an urgent need on the part of the government to increase the investment or budgetary target for the priority sectors, i.e. education and health to achieve the targets set for economic development. Even though the increase was witnessed among all the social sectors, but this improvement is very low in the education sector as well as the health sector. Sound human capital formation policies should be made and implemented that would result in increasing human capital along with economic development.

REFERENCES

Armstrong, M. (2000). *A Handbook of Human Resource Management Practice*. London.

Harbison, F.H. (1973). *Human Resources as the Wealth of Nations*. New York: Oxford University Press.

MFHW: *National Family Health Survey (2015-16)*. International Institute for Population Sciences, Deonar, Mumbai.

MFHW: *National Health Policy (2017)*. Government of India, New Delhi.

MHRD: *Annual Report (2016-17)*. Government of India, New Delhi.

MHRD: *National Policy on Education (2019)*. Government of India, New Delhi.

Ministry of Finance, Department of Economic Affairs: *Economic Survey (2018-19)*, Volume 2. New Delhi.

Ojo, Oladeji and T. Oshikoya (1995), "Determinants of Long-Term Growth: Some African Results". *Journal of African Economies*, Vol. 4, No. 2.

Schultz, T.W (1961). "Investment in Human Capital." *The American Economic Review*, Vol. 51, No. 1, pp. 1-17.

Schultz, T.W. (1993), "The Economic Importance of Human Capital in Modernization", *Education Economics*, Vol. 1, No. 1, 13-19.

Tokarèíková, E.: Productivity of Human Capital. In: Proceedings of International Science Conference. Current Trends for Economic Development and Entrepreneurship. School of Business Administration in Karvina. Karviná. Silesian University in Opava, 2010, pp. 459-465.

UGC: *Annual Report (2017-18)*. Government of India, New Delhi.

WHO: *World Health Statistics (2018)*. World Health Organization.

22

Human Resource Management (HRM) and Human Resource Development (HRD)

With Reference to Education and Training

Umme Salma

Introduction

Human resource is one of the important resources along with natural as well as man-made resources. Natural resources are resources drawn from nature unaltered. Human beings with knowledge, skill and technology are able to harness these natural resources for development and advancement. Thus, human beings are considered as human resources, with their abilities, human resources are high in demand. The people who work for a company or organization and the department responsible for managing resources related to employees are considered as human resources. In the 1960s, the term human resources were first coined. During this period, the value of labour relations began to gather attention and motivation, organizational behaviour and selection assessments notion began to exist. The management and development of employees in an organization are the main task of human resource management. It is also termed as personnel or talent management. It involves overseeing all things related to managing an organization's human capital.

In the educational field, human resource management plays a prominent role and the principals, vice principals, head of the departments, teachers, parents, guardians constitute human resource management. Students, is their core responsibility, a prospective human resource, managing, nurturing, educating and preparing is the responsibility of

Human Resource Development (HRD). In fact, the prosperity of a society, nation and family is largely determined by the quality of these human resources. It is, however, only recently that Human Resource Management (HRM) has been acknowledged as key in raising schools' performance as well (e.g. Vekeman *et al.*, 2014). More specifically, by increasing teachers' competence and commitment, HRM holds the potential of increasing teacher performance and, consequently, of yielding higher student outcomes (see, for instance, DeArmond *et al.*, 2009). As the educational institutions are epicentres of human resources, the role of human resource management is significantly recognized. To increase the students' performances, the teachers and other human resources who deal with them have to be kept involved and motivated. And also help them to upgrade themselves and be efficient, the human resource management plays an important role.

1. Human Resource Management (HRM) and Education

In the present-day educational scenario, with the technological changes in education, a teacher has to promote meaningful and inclusive participation of all students in their schools. The socio-cultural practices and curriculum standards that are suitable and are constantly changing, making it challenging for teachers to keep up with trends and best practices in the field. To be a professionally developed teacher need to become appropriate educators enabling them to create significant and modified course directives for students in the present generation. Through professional development programmes, the teachers learn and get introduced to new teaching strategies, so that they are able to take class in a better way and make adaptation in their teaching style and curriculum to suit the needs of their students. The educators are introduced to new presentation methods, evaluation methods and record-keeping practices to make them more efficient. This makes them professionally efficient in their presentations and course evaluations. To be protective and supportive towards the physical and psychological needs of all the students in the classroom regardless of their strength and weakness, the teacher should be professional enough.

As teachers play a major role in student achievements (Rivkin *et al.*, 2005), the competency and efforts of their teachers determine the school's success in continuous success in students' achievements. HRM can be viewed as a means to motivate teachers to contribute to their schools' objectives. Further, there is a continuous stream of new psychological insights concerning pedagogy and learning that infuses schools (OECD, 2009, 2014). HRM provides opportunities to the teachers who want to upgrade themselves by incorporating these new insights into their daily practices, Human Resource Development (HRD) paves a way into the schools to offer these teachers constant professionalization. It is a fact that all-over the world schools have difficulty finding enough highly qualified teachers (OECD, 2014), and even if schools can find them, too many young teachers quit due to the fact that the work environment does not meet their expectations (OECD, 2009). Human Resource Management (HRM) systems can assist schools in attracting and retaining enough competent and motivated teachers (Loeb *et al.*, 2012). For a well organized and competent administration, a methodical human resource management system concentrates on recruitment and retaining the efficient principal and teaching and non-teaching staff (the people who are responsible for the administration of the school). Any conflicts among the teachers, problems of teachers and staff, shortcomings pertaining students etc. are efficiently dealt with by the human resource management. Recruiting and staffing and the maximum utilization of available resources to achieve organizational goals, in the efficient and effective deployment of organization's resources in a most efficient way possible is the responsibility of human resource management. To motivate and energize the teachers and school heads and other stakeholders in managing the functions of school smoothly, human resource management has a prominent role. It deals with the strategies to manage human resources, to equip teachers and school heads, and human resource management has a prominent role.

To improvise the effectiveness of an organization or institution, different developing and administering programmes are designed by human resource management. These programmes are designed including the entire spectrum of creating, managing and cultivating the employer-employee relationship. The functioning of school such as stating and opening is the responsibility of Human Resource Development. To enhance the human resources of school in the best way, human resource development is essential. The principal, vice-principals, head teacher, teachers, non-teaching staff, parents and community organizations all are part of human resources in educational institutions and Human Resource Development (HRD) focus on the enhancement and development of these human resources. The human resources department, being part of Human Resource Management (HRM), for most agencies and institutions, is responsible for:

- Managing job recruitment, selection, and promotion.
- Developing and overseeing employee benefits and wellness programmes.
- Promoting employee career development and job training.
- Providing orientation programmes for new hires.
- Providing guidance regarding disciplinary actions.
- Serving as a primary contact for work-site injuries or accidents.

1.1. Managing Job Recruitment, Selection and Promotion

In order to achieve the goals and targets set by the organization, committed and qualified workforce is needed. To ensure maximum utilization of resource assets, it is very important to use these human resources at appropriate times and appropriate places. Human resource development has to select the best efficient qualified candidates among the qualified resources who have high potentiality of performing successfully. In this process, the head of the institution and committee members to avoid resentment and frustration, should assess the knowledge, skills and attitude of the employees properly. It demands exceptional intellectual skills looking at the complexity of today's recruitment field. The skilled and efficient human resource manager looks at keeping the work force interested and motivated and sustains them in the workplace. The participation of candidates from all sections of society, people from weaker sections, physically challenged, socially and economically oppressed has to be ensured. Human Resource Development has to frame proper strategy for equality in employment and promotional appointments.

1.2. Developing and Overseeing Employee Benefits and Wellness Programmes

Any benefit that the employee receives in addition to direct remuneration is included in employees' benefits and services. The direct monetary value like pension, medical insurance etc. comes under the term benefits. The benefits and services in addition to regular income represent increased productivity of its employees. These benefits allow the employees to do their work without worry about their health and retirement. One of the greatest aspects for industrial growth is the welfare measures that facilitate motivation and retention of the workforce. It irradiates the social evils, ensures a happy and confident workforce. It in turn increases the image of the company and leads to increased productivity and continuity of recruitment. Good work atmosphere, provision of proper amenities, health benefits, employees' child welfare, recreation facilities, participation of labour in management in framing policies, getting feedback and follow up and provision of educational facilities are some of the welfare services in the workplace.

1.3. Promoting Employee Career Development and Job Training

Training and development are the efforts that are made within organizations to improve performance and self-fulfilment through a variety of educational methods and programmes. Today's workplace has a broad range of applications from instruction in highly specific job skills to long term professional development. Training and development is an integral element of strategy and recognized profession with distinct theories and methodologies. It means embracing continual learning and training and development leads promotion of employee growth and acquiring a highly skilled workforce. Human Resource Management (HRM) makes arrangements for professional job training for the teachers. Considering the importance of teacher's ability in thinking and solving classroom problems, HR arranges for on job training such as in-service training, onetime workshops or general pedagogical training to improve their classroom practices.

1.4. Providing Orientation Programmes for New Hires

To impart the essential knowledge and skills to new employees orientation programmes are organized. These orientation programmes expose the new recruits to the latest concepts, techniques and to develop skills to equip them to perform effectively in their new job. Human Resource Development (HRD) creates awareness among the people regarding the skills required for job performance and clarifies the job norms and standards; this helps people in understanding their roles better and reach the expectation of other members of the team. The Human Resource Management (HRM) team keeps the competent staff motivated, keeping their morale high. This leads to retaining happy working staff. They also see that unhappy employees are likely to leave.

1.5. Providing Guidance Regarding Disciplinary Actions

Human Resource (HR) has to look into the disciplinary actions related to the job-related behaviour that does not meet expected and communicated performance standards and end the employment of an individual who refused to improve. The primary purpose is to assist the employee to understand that a performance problem or opportunity for improvement exists and the main aim is improvement in performance. It is the department of human resource development to provide feedback to the employee and verbally reprimand for poor performance, provide written verbal warning to effort to improve their performance. If there is any misbehaviour, then provide an escalating number of days in which the employee is suspended from work and end the employment of an individual who refuses to improve. In a school environment, children are the most vulnerable and can be physically, emotionally affected by the adverse performance of the teachers; to look at the problems and for a safer environment, Human Resource (HR) has to provide guidance to the teachers regarding disciplinary actions for better performance.

1.6. Serving as a Primary Contact for Work-site Injuries or Accidents

The HR Department has to take appropriate care and provide proper training to prevent workplace accidents and prevent injuries. A safe workplace means stable employees. Care has to be taken to avoid injuries or risk or loss. The company or the HR department concentrates more on providing a safe environment at the workplace. The HR Department makes sure that the issues of the employees regarding health and safety are raised and heard. To prevent accidents, minor or major safety programmes have to be ensured to be followed. The HR Department has to identify the potential hazards scenarios; programmes have to be taken to avoid injuries and accidents resulting in harm and damage to personal and property. An efficient safety facilities and equipment should be provided and arrangement of prompt actions to be taken. An educational training programme has to be arranged to educate and guide the employees and employers regarding safety measures and in eliminating hazards. The HR also plans for emergencies in the workplace and also prepares to prevent any undue situations.

2. Human Resource Development (HRD) in Education and Training

To enable the workforce of any organization to exhibit their maximum skills and knowledge, to reach the goals and objectives of an institution Human Resource Development (HRD) is important. It provides a platform or the base where an organization can enhance and upgrade the skills of their employees through trainings and workshops and also keep the workforce motivated and inspired. HRD seeks to develop people's "knowledge, expertise, productivity and satisfaction, whether for personal or group/team gain, or for the benefit of an organization, community, nation, or ultimately, the whole of humanity" (McLean & McLean, 2001). Human Resource Development (HRD) is a part of Human Resource Management (HRM) to make their employees adapt to the fast pace of changes and advancement in the teaching and learning process. Due to these changes employees are compelled to become lifelong learners. Pellet (2007) states; globalization, growing competition for funding and staff as well as increasing institutional autonomy saw many changes in higher education institutions, this led to acquiring greater managerial and leadership competencies. People in the educational field encounter many challenges and different scenarios, Human Resource Development (HRD) helps in dealing with these challenges with appropriate skills. Therefore, Human Resource Development (HRD) always plays an important role in the teaching and learning process. Human Resource Development (HRD) works to create and maintain the relationship between employee and other staff members and thus enhances productivity. The core objectives of Human Resource Development (HRD) are to look at the availability of highly trained and skilled employees to meet the needs of the institutions. Human Resource Development (HRD) works on the four stages of framework—assessment, design, implementation and evaluation. With the help of these frameworks, it provides a set of planned and systematic activities to meet the present and future goals. Its training programmes ensure continuous growth and improvement of the individuals and getting maximum and desirable outcomes from the employees and enhance the company's productivity.

3. Characteristics of Human Resource Development (HRD)

- HRD is a structured approach where improvement is concerned with efficiency of employees.
- The learning outcome of the institutions at individual or organizational level is systematic and well planned.
- HRD deals with a constant uninterrupted improvement of managerial, technical, behavioural and conceptual skills of employees till retirement.
- HRD is versatile and deals with many subjects be it a

manufacturing organization or a service sector industry.

- HRD calls for action such as performance appraisal, management development, training, career planning, counselling, teacher's participation and quality circles.

4. Functions of Human Resource Development (HRD)

The functions of HRD depicted in the wheel can also be found in the most popular among the definitions of HRD, defining it as "the integrated use of training and development, organization development, and career development to improve individual, group and organizational effectiveness" (McLagan, 1989).

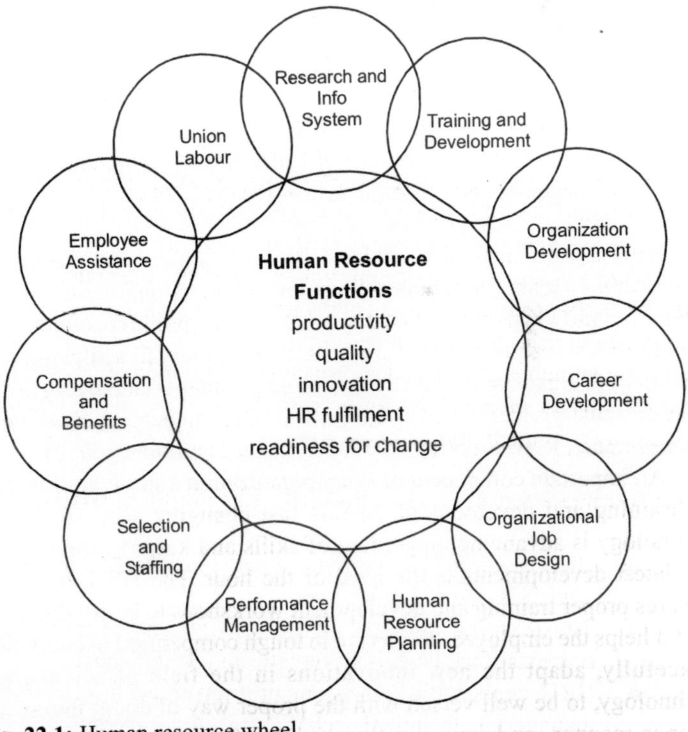

Fig. 22.1: Human resource wheel.
Source: McGuire & Jorgensen, 2011.

According to McLagan's human resource wheel, HRD comprises three distinct functions:

- Training and development,
- Organization development, and
- Career development.

4.1. Training and Development

Training refers to reactive and short-term activities that focus on changing or improving knowledge, skills or attitudes of individuals to perform a particular job or task. These activities mostly comprise skills, which are immediately needed and have an immediate benefit, whereas development activities concentrate on new skills and abilities aiming for future job opportunities. Usually Training and Development (T&D) measures comprise three major competence areas:

- Methodological competence (teaching, administration, IT-Systems, Finance, Legal know-how, Safety and Security etc.).
- Self-confidence and social competence (personality and soft skills, Time management, Work-Life Balance, languages etc.).
- Management competence (Leadership development, project management etc.) Natalie & Joo-Hyun (2014).

Various individual measures such as on-the-job training, mediation, mentoring, coaching and counselling for organizational units, project groups or individuals are included in T&D actions. While coaching refers to activities where employees are treated as partners in achieving both personal and organizational goals, counselling supports employees to deal with personal problems that could prevent them to achieve these goals (Bockelmann, Reif, Frohlich, 2010; Werner & DeSimone, 2012).

An important component of every organization's survival strategy is its training and development. In this fast changing scenario, where technology is advancing, upgrading of skills and keeping abreast with the latest developments is the need of the hour. The HR Department ensures proper training and development workshops to be conducted so that it helps the employees to survive in tough competition in every field gracefully, adapt the new innovations in the field of science and technology, to be well versed with the proper way of doing things in a proper manner, and improve their job performances and have job satisfaction. In India, school enrolment is nearly universal at primary level, study after study shows that children are failing to meet grade-level learning outcomes (ASER, 2015). At the same time, it is clear from research findings that, of the several school-based factors affecting learning outcomes, teachers can have the greatest impact (Hattie, 2012). As stated by the Organization for Economic Co-operation and Development (OECD) (2005, cited in OECD, 2009: 3) "raising teaching performance is perhaps the policy direction most likely to lead to substantial gains in student learning." It has also been recognized that quality among practicing teachers can be improved through more effective teacher evaluation (Borg, 2018). Thus, for the skill development process of teachers their skills have to be evaluated.

4.1.1. Human Resource Development and Teacher's Training

It is a known fact that good teachers are better at teaching students effectively. Students' achievement should be the core aim of the training and development of the teachers. Teachers have to spend whole careers developing new skills in response to meet the new challenges. Effective professional development training helps the teachers to have a lifelong career and learning. It boosts the students' outcomes and promotes growth. Training helps teachers to be active participants in their own learning. Indian Government recently has invested in the development of teachers and showed interest in introducing innovative strategies to meet the needs to educate the people in the educational field. Some of them are: a mandate for in-service teachers to receive 20 days of training per year under the Sarva Shiksha Abhiyan (SSA) programme; new online platforms hosting content for use in the classroom alongside professional development (for example, Diksha); the adoption of new models of in-service training (for example, mentoring, Teacher Activity Groups (TAGs) and online communities of practice in Maharashtra (Parnham *et al.*, forthcoming) and recent proposals to restructure the District Institutes of Education and Training (DIETs) to enable a greater emphasis on teachers' continuing professional development and support for school-level innovations and research projects (MHRD, 2017). Feedback and evaluation is the basic component in the assessment of a teacher. This helps them to assess themselves better and to further The Ministry of Human Resource Development's (MHRD) website, 1.1 million teachers are trained in pre-service teacher education institutes each year, while 3.5 million in-service teachers are trained through the Block and Cluster-level Resource Centres. In India, as elsewhere in the world, teachers are often encouraged to be change makers in their communities. Teacher evaluation is an integral part of any robust education system and for such a system to be in place in India it is clear that more work is needed in building awareness around teacher evaluation's function and its parameters (Bambawale, Hughes, & Lightfoot, 2018).

4.2. Organization Development

The second functional area of HRD refers explicitly to the development of the organization. Its purpose is to improve the relationships and processes between and among units, groups and individuals. Organizational development activities relate more to long-term strategies aiming for a holistic development of the organization in order to increase its overall efficiency (Werner & DeSimone, 2012). The close relationship between teacher development and school improvement or innovation has been emphasized by many authors (Fullan, 1992; Barth, 1990; Hargreaves, 1995). Barth offers a particularly arresting parallel between teacher and pupil development. Teacher growth is closely related to pupil growth. Probably nothing within a school has more impact on students in terms of skills development, self-confidence, or classroom behaviour than the personal and professional growth of their teachers (Barth, 1990). Human performance in the educational field reflects on the knowledge, skills, behaviours and values. Since, the abilities and skills will help the organization for better performance and productivity to enhance the problem solving capabilities and prepared to face the challenges in the educational field.

4.3. Career Development

Career development includes both career planning and career management. Career planning refers to skills assessment through counsellors, who assist employees in pursuing their career plans. Career management on the other hand is responsible for actually taking the necessary steps to achieve these plans. In the university context, the tenure track model is one example of designing adequate career paths for university teachers to eventually obtain a high level of professional stability (Werner & DeSimone, 2012). Ultimately, all HRD measures intend to cause greater efficiency and effectiveness through fully committed and skilled employees, who perform their work in alignment with the goals of their organization. In the 21st Century, teachers should know how to use technology effectively, ethically and appropriately connect to new study materials. For professional development facilitating skills learning opportunities among staff members is necessary. Education is a never-ending continuous process. It is the route or direction towards our development of life and process of leading life and building profession. The career oriented professionals can constantly upgrade their knowledge and skills through continuous education and become more proficient at their jobs.

5. A Framework for the HRD–Training and Development

In the opinion of Aimmaker, 2016, the 4 Stages of HRD Framework has been devised, this Human Resource Framework can be implemented as formal classroom training. This HRD Framework includes the processes and activities to develop and maintain the skills and competencies of the employees. The core objective is to ensure the availability of a highly trained and talented set of employees to meet future needs. HRD framework's main focus is to enhance the efficiency for better performance (Aimmaker, 2016).

Diagrammatic Representation of HRD Framework (Aimmaker, 2016)

HRD efforts should use the following four stages:

- Needs assessment
- Design
- Implementation
- Evaluation

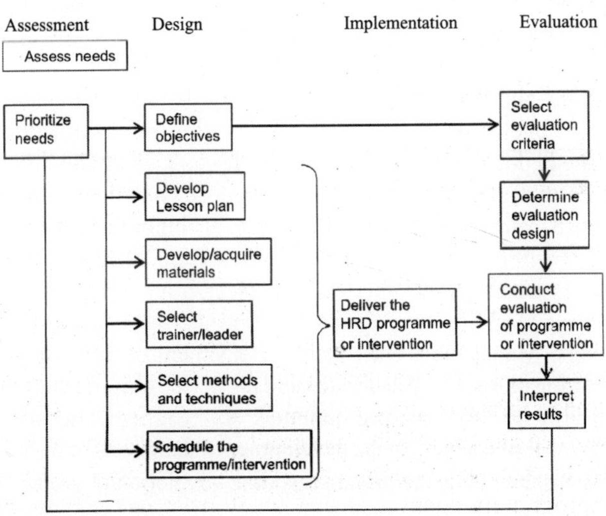

Source: Aimmaker, 2016.

5.1. Assessment

The Assessment in the HRD Framework involves prioritizing the need, understanding and examining the performance of the employees, job tasks and organizational environment. Above all, the need to acknowledge the gap between current competencies and skills needed for the production of a particular task is to ascertain. The organization goals and process of reaching those goals are determined through the *Need Assessment*. The *Gap Analysis* involves comparing the actual performance with the desired performance (Aimmaker, 2016). Human Resource Development needs to identify the training needs of each human resource of that institution and frame programmes that are best suited to their needs. Assess the target group requirement to plan the specific training programme to meet the current needs of the teaching and learning process. Who needs training and what do they need to learn? It should target to reduce the gap between the actual and expected performance of the human resource. Assessment needs a lot of hard work and inputs and research. It is the first process of human resource development.

Prioritize needs: Prioritize the needs of the employees or the need of human resources in the educational system cannot be overlooked. It will contribute directly to an improvement of the quality of education. Teachers are the catalyst in the educational institutions. Their credibility and trust towards their concern for the welfare of children and the community is linked to their ability to provide quality education. Thus, human resource development should look for the investment in teacher training, their professional upgradement, improvement in the working conditions and keep them motivated towards their profession. Human resource development department should prioritize in attracting able and motivated educational people to the profession. They should look at the remuneration paid, along with provision of incentives such as health insurance, retirement and pension plans, accommodation and transport provision. For effective classroom interaction, it has to prioritize in provision of the basic facilities in classroom, adequate classroom equipment, teaching-learning materials and also the maintenance of school buildings. Manageable class size, arrangement of alternative staff for substitution of teacher, pre-service and in-service training and workshops, organizing group learning schemes for teachers and supervisors, involvement of teachers in the development and reforms in the educational system are the needs the human resource development has to look at.

5.2. Design

It involves designing the HRD programme and intervention that includes training and development methods. It involves the training content and the delivery method (Aimmaker, 2016). The designing phase includes selecting the specific objectives of the programme, developing an appropriate and suitable plan for the implementation of the programme. The acquiring materials for the trainees to use and selecting the suitable method to conduct the programme and scheduling it at suitable timings. The designing plan also includes the selection and developing the content of the programme like choosing for professional training, classroom training, provision of learning materials etc.

Define the objectives: The objective to implement a training session should be mentioned beforehand. It is related to the goal of the firm and the skills required to achieve (Aimmaker, 2016). The main objective of human resource development in lieu of education is to understand and make known the importance of education and link education with economics, socio-economic and culture. It is the objective of HRD to acquire and improve skills of teaching-learning staff to achieve the goals of higher education and keep abreast with the latest developments in the educational field. HRD has to acknowledge the role of teachers and lecturers in the educational organization and provide opportunities for the development of personality, initiative and creativity.

Develop lesson plans: The development of the lesson plan involves a detailed description of the training course and instructions (Aimmaker, 2016). Human resource development after developing the objectives has to devise the lesson plans that are designed to communicate the objectives to the teaching learning resource and provide a guide and route map of organizing their materials and preparing themselves to achieve learning outcomes. The lesson plan designed should highlight the objectives to be achieved, explain the subject matter like areas to be dealt with to achieve efficiency, providing references and materials to deal with. The lesson plan devised by HRD should also explain the procedure followed to keep up the motivation of teaching staff, activities to do and to make aware of different lesson plans to be approachable. It finally has to look into final evaluation through different assignment techniques and providing proper and timely feedback.

Develop or acquire the materials: Acquiring or accumulating the training material is the next step of the HRD programme. These materials are related to classroom training or online training etc. (Aimmaker, 2016).

It is the responsibility of HRD to provide training materials necessary for any programme, it involves knowledge acquisition and retention and it should synchronize with the lesson plan developed. It should be directly related to the learning objectives, it must include hands-on practices or stimulation as possible so that people learn by doing, the materials thus designed should be in-control of the learner instead of the trainer. There should be provision of interaction with the trainer and with each other during training. The development materials should be broken into small chunks so that comprehension would be built up step by step. Computer instructions like word, excel powerpoint presentations and handouts, flip outs, posters, transparencies and graphic visual materials are some of the materials that help in learning developmental processes. Further, e-learning authoring tools such articulate studio and storyline or Adobe captivate for creating computer based e-learning modules. The material devised should keep in mind the learning and training objectives.

Select trainer or leader: The selection of the right trainer or leader is essential to enhance the skills of employees. It could be the immediate boss or a professional trainer (Aimmaker, 2016). The trainer should be professional enough, and keep the training motivated and inspired also explained about the importance of training. The trainer should manage the time productively and sustain the attention of the trainees throughout the training programme.

Select methods and techniques: The training could be delivered using any method or technique like a lecture, role play, conference or group discussion or online training technique (Aimmaker, 2016). The training covers a number of techniques to convey specific information—rules, procedures, methods, classroom lectures and conferences are well preferred. Utilization of audio-visuals or demonstrations makes a classroom presentation best media for the clarification of more difficult points. Reducing the structured lecture format and allowing trainees to provide feedback to the lecturer or creating discussion groups under the direction of a conference leader will remove the liabilities of lack of feedback and lack of involvement by the trainees. Films can also be used as a practical training technique. They can provide information and explicitly demonstrate skills that are not easily presented by other techniques. They may be produced by standard film distributors or produced internally by the organization. The conference, discussions to clarify and amplify those points, the film is used to emphasize the concepts. Simulation exercises and hands-on experiences is that part of training activity which unambiguously places the trainee in an artificial environment that closely presents actual working conditions. The simulation activities are case experiences, complex computer modelling, experiential exercises and vestibule training. Cases presentation provides a detail understanding of a specific problem a teacher may encounter in the classroom. These approaches help the employee to find and analyze the problem, evaluate alternative courses of action, and decide what course of action to be taken. To equip individuals to learn by doing, short, structured learning experiences such as experiential exercises are introduced.

Schedule the programme/intervention: The scheduling of the final training programme done after the accumulation of resources. It is based upon the organizational norms (Aimmaker, 2016). Human resource Department has to schedule the programme and be able to design the training programme based on the objectives to be fulfilled. A number of things have to be taken into consideration like what type of training is needed by the institution to reach its objectives. It has to consider the different learning styles for these training programmes and decide which learning style is suitable to achieve that objective. It also has to decide which mode of delivery to be used. The web-based training is more appropriate or mentoring to be used. A variety of delivery options have to be kept for the different training programmes. The HR Department has to decide whether the training be self-paced or instruction led. The kind of discussions and interactivity to be developed and how much the institution has to spend on this training. It also has to look into the budget to be spent on these training programmes. The HR Department has to divide to whom these trainings have to be developed; who is the audience; what are the job responsibilities of different individuals, it has to decide whether this training is suitable or whom and when to conduct. What needs to be taught, to decide the timeline of these sessions, to set a deadline to these training programmes to be concluded. HR Department has to communicate all the prospect employees about the training available and to get feedback for better evaluation.

5.3. Implementation

The implementation involves the successful delivery of the assessment and design phase as effective HRD programmes or interventions. The purpose of providing training leads to determine the methods of imparting effective HRD interventions. The content of the training programme is of prime importance. Following are the methods of the training programme: *On-the-job Training; Of-the-job Training; Apprenticeship Training; Distance/Internet-Based Training; Simulated Training; Computer-Based Training (CBT)* (Aimmaker, 2016). Deliver the actual design of the programme accordingly. One of them is on-the-job-training where an employee learns the job by actually doing the job. Off-the-job training involves the employees getting training away from the actual workplace. Case study method, management games, distance learning, sponsored higher education courses. Apprenticeship training is a combination of classroom training and on the job training. Some other training designs include internet based training; computer based training, stimulated training where the employee can actually feel the environment of the work. Implementing the HRD programme at the right time and in the right manner is an investment by human resource development for professional development and effective functioning of an organization. During the training implementation process, the trainee's queries and doubts should be answered, explanation of the logical sequence of the job, how to perform the job systematically and complete the job assigned to him. The mistakes should be corrected and resolved. Freedom and liberty should be provided to the trainer if the trainer shows comprehensiveness. The trainer should be allowed to learn by doing to gain new skills.

5.4. Evaluation

Evaluation of the programme is the final step of the HRD process and training sessions. The effectiveness of the HRD intervention measured during this phase. It is a significant and vital activity, so should be performed carefully. This is one of the most stages out of four stages of HRD framework (Aimmaker, 2016). For the effectiveness of training programmes, follow-up and feedback is mandatory. The trainees are given feedback on how well they performed. The HRD has to collect and describe and give judgemental views to make training effective. The evaluation made by HRD would assist in selection, adoption and modification of various instructional methods.

Select evaluation criteria: The evaluation criteria involves the reaction of the participants, noticeable changes in participants attitude, skills and knowledge, the difference in performance standard of the participant and at the same time the organizational performance overall (Aimmaker, 2016). While different institutions have different criteria for evaluation, there are some standard criteria for appraisal. These sets of appraisal factors are measurable and consistent. An organization can evaluate employees based on their knowledge of the organization, job they perform, regulations and their ability to perform work. A good measure of competence is certification in certain skill areas. Skills are the methods or tools an employee do his job. Another selection criteria is the reaching the objectives set by the institutions. Performance reviews are the best to review progress towards goals. Previous track record of the employee, attitude of employee, willingness to learn, cooperation, communication, loyalty etc. are also the criteria for evaluation.

Determine evaluation design: Designing the evaluation study is the second and vital step in making an accurate evaluation of the programme. The first method is the Time Series Design method that involves a series of measurements made before and after the HRD programme. In addition, the second method is called the Controlled Experimentation Method that is the most used and formal method of evaluation. Above all in this method, a controlled group is organized, and data is collected from training and controlled groups both before and after training, and then the review is done accordingly (Aimmaker, 2016). To determine the worth of a programme, evaluation is necessary; it decides how accurate any training conducted. Different designs are created based on the information that needs to be assessed. In an educational institution, a teacher asks the student to write a short note on the topic given and by the reflection given determines the students understanding and need to change in instruction if necessary; this formative evaluation is continuous evaluation. The summative evaluation is at the end of the programme; it reflects the effectiveness of the programme as a whole and makes suggestions to improve it. Process evaluation determines why a particular programme or training was successful or unsuccessful and provides suggestions as the further course of the programme. Impact evaluation are those that occur over a longer period of time, they provide a broader and complete view of the outcomes of any training or programmes. The evaluation that provides an idea of how well the programme has reached its targets is outcome evaluation; it is useful to assess the changing attitude and knowledge of the target audience. It is the human resource development department to decide which evaluation is suitable according to the training provided or the requirement of the institutions.

Conduct evaluation of programme or intervention: The evaluation of the HRD programme is through measuring three basic categories; reaction of the participants by understanding their liking or disliking about the session, learning of the participants related to skill development and knowledge after the meeting and behaviour change is also a noticeable factor (Aimmaker, 2016). The whole evaluation programme of the HRD depends on the feedback provided by the trainees. HRD has to get feedback from the trainees whether they like the programme and why, which part they don't like and what area they would like to improvise and implement. HRD has to evaluate whether there is any benefit of learning of skill or knowledge by the participants. Whether the whole training brought about any behaviour changes after participating in the training. HRD also has to evaluate if the mode of conducting training was satisfactory, in view of venue selection, technical hitches, development of the course conducted, the material provided, handouts and the power point presentation etc., are of useful. They have to look for the drawback if any and work for rectifying them.

Interpret results: The final result evaluated based on the objectives and goals set by the organization. The evaluator interprets whether the outcome matches with the desired effect or not. It would depend upon the behaviour of the participant after the training if a complaint came related to workability after training, Reaction of subordinates and manager and motivation towards the work (Aimmaker, 2016). Finally, the HRD interprets the evaluation results. The human resource development conducts any training, workshops, programmes to achieve the objectives and goals set by the institutions. After interpreting the whole training programme with the help of feedback given by the trainees and the employers, HRD now decides whether there have been any behavioural changes in the employee, whether they remained motivated towards their work. If the training has not reached the desired goals or accomplished any of the objectives, then further plan or design will be interpreted. Overall the evaluation of results shows the results on the scale of reaction, learning and behaviour of the participants.

Conclusion

Human resource is one of the important resources along with natural as well as man-made resources. As the educational institutions are epicentres of human resources, the role of human resource management is significantly recognized. To increase the students' performances, the teachers and other human resources who deal with them have to be kept involved and motivated. In the present-day educational scenario, with the technological changes in education, a teacher has to promote meaningful and inclusive participation of all students in their schools. To enable the workforce of any organization to exhibit their maximum skills and knowledge, to reach the goals and objectives of an institution. Human Resource Development (HRD) is important. It provides a platform or the base where an organization can enhance and upgrade the skills of their employees through trainings and workshops and also keep the workforce motivated and inspired. HRD works to create and maintain the relationship between employee and other staff members and thus enhances productivity. The core objectives of HRD are to look at the availability of highly trained and skilled employees to meet the needs of the institutions. People in the educational field encounter many challenges and different scenarios, Human Resource Development (HRD) helps in dealing with these challenges with appropriate skills. Therefore, HRD always plays an important role in the teaching and learning process. Human Resource Development (HRD) works on the four stages of framework—assessment, design, implementation and evaluation. With help of these frameworks, it provides a set of planned and systematic activities to meet the present and future goals. Its training programmes ensure continuous growth and improvement of the individuals and getting maximum and desirable outcomes from the employees and enhance the company's productivity.

REFERENCES

Aimmaker. (2016). *Four Stages of HRD Framework.* Retrieved on 18.4.2020 from http://www.aimmaker.com/four-stages-of-hrd-framework.html

ASER (2015). *Trends over time: 2006–2014—A supplement to ASER 2014.* New Delhi, India: ASER.

Bambawale, M., Hughes. J., and Lightfoot, A. (2018). *Exploring teacher evaluation process and practices in India: A case study.* (British Council) New Delhi, India. Retrieved from www.britishcouncil.in.

Barth, R. (1990) *Improving Schools from Within.* San Francisco: Jossey-Bass.

Bockelmann, C., Reif, L., and Frohlich, M. (2010). "Human Resources Management". In: *Higher Education Management and Development. Compendium for Managers.* Munster: Waxmann. S.159-173.

Borg, S. (2018) *Teacher evaluation: Global perspectives and their implications for English language teaching.* London, England: British Council.

DeArmond, M.M., Shaw, K.L., and Wright, P.M. (2009). "Zooming in and zooming out: Rethinking school district human resource management." In: Goldhaber, D. and Hannaway, J. (eds.) *Creating a New Teaching Profession.* Washington, DC: The Urban Institute, pp. 53-80.

Fullan, M. (1992). *Successful School Improvement.* Buckingham: Open University Press.

Hargreaves, A. (1995). "Kentucky fried schooling", *The Times Educational Supplement*, October.

Hattie, J. (2012). *Visible learning for teachers: Maximizing impact on learning.* London, England: Routledge.

Loeb, S., Kalogrides, D., and Be´teille, T. (2012). "Effective schools: Teacher hiring, assignment, development, and retention." *Education*, *7*(3): 269-304.

McGuire, D., and Jorgensen, K.M. (2011). *Human Resource Development: Theory and Practice.* London: Sage.

McLagan, P. (1989). *Models of Human Resource Development Practice*, Alexandria, VA: ASTD Press.

McLean, G.N. and McLean, L. (2001). "If we can't define HRD in one country, how can we define it in an international context?", *Human Resource Development International, 4*(3), 313-326.

Ministry of Human Resource Development (MHRD) (2017). *Guideline: strengthening,* District Institutes of Education and Training. New Delhi, India: NCTE.

Natalie, N., and Joo-Hyun, P. (2014). *Human resource development in higher education.* Retrieved on 16/4/2020 from http://donau.booktype.pro/human-resource-management-in-higher-education/human-resource-development-in-higher-education/

OECD (2009). *Creating Effective Teaching and Learning Environments: First Results from TALIS.* Paris: Organisation for Economic Cooperation and Development.

OECD (2014). *TALIS 2013 Results. An International Perspective on Teaching and Learning.* Paris: Organisation for Economic Cooperation and Development.

Pellert, A. (2007). "Human Resource Management at Universities." In: Pellert, A. and Pausits, A. (eds.): *Higher Education Management and Development in Central, Southern and Eastern Europe*, Waxmann.

Rivkin, S.G., Hanushek, E.A., and Kain, J.F. (2005). "Teachers, schools, and academic achievement." *Econometrica, 73*(2): 417-458.

Vekeman, E., Devos, G., and Tuytens, M. (2014). "The influence of teachers' expectations on principals' implementation of a new teacher evaluation policy in Flemish secondary education." *Educational Assessment, Evaluation and Accountability, 27*(2): 129-151.

Werner, J.M., and DeSimone, R.L. (2012). *Human Resource Development.* Mason, OH: South-Western Cengage.

23
Human Development Index

Y. Asha

Human Development Index

The Human Development Index is an index used to rank countries by level of "human development" which usually also implies whether a country is developed, developing or underdeveloped. A statistical tool used to measure a country's achievement based on the health of people, their level of education attainment and their standard of living. Long life in a country, Human Development Index (HDI) is higher, the education level is high and the Gross National Income per capita is higher, then the country scores high.

It is a social indicator measuring various aspects of human development like education, health care, poverty level, water and sanitation, livelihood issues, food and nutrition, security, gender equity etc. The human development index was first published in 1990 under the guidance of Mahbub ul Haq, former Finance Minister of Pakistan, economist with technical assistance from Nobel Laureate economist Amartya Sen and was further used to measure the country's development by the United Nations Development Programme (UNDP).

Pakistani economist Mahbub ul Haq devised and launched HDI that found its origin in the Annual Human Development Report produced by the Human Development Report of the United Nations Development Programme (UNDP) and with purpose "to shift the focus of development economics from national income accounting to people-centred policies."

Mahbub ul Haq formed a group of development economists including Paul Streeten, Frances Stewart, Gustav Ranis, Keith Griffin, Sudhir Anand and Meghnad Desai; to work on human development reports. Haq's work was utilized by Nobel laureate Amartya Sen in his own work on human capabilities. A simple composite measure of human development is needed to convince the public, academics and politicians to evaluate development not on economic advances but on improvement of human well-being, was strongly advocated by Haq.

1. Importance of Human Development Index (HDI)

The Human Development Index was framed to place emphasis on individuals, on their opportunity to realize satisfying work and lives. Evaluating a country's potential for individual human development provides a supplementary metric for evaluating a country's level of development besides considering standard economic growth statistics.

The main goal of this Index was to place people at the centre of development process in terms of the economic debate, policy and advocacy. The provision of choices and freedoms resulting in widespread outcomes is the characteristic of Development.

"People are the real wealth of a nation", Haq wrote in the opening lines of the first report in 1990. "The basic objective of development is to create an enabling environment for people to enjoy long, healthy and creative lives. This may appear to be a simple truth. But it is often forgotten in the immediate concern with the accumulation of commodities and financial wealth."

The United Nations General Assembly has formally recognized the report as "an important tool for raising awareness about human development around the world."

The main purpose of this Index is to examine the various policy choices of nations: if, for example, two countries have approximately the same gross national income (GNI) per capita, then it can help to evaluate why they produce widely disparate human development outcomes.

The 2010 Human Development Report introduced an Inequality-adjusted Human Development Index (IHDI). "The IHDI is the actual level of human development (accounting for inequality)" and "the HDI can be viewed as an index of potential human development (or the maximum IHDI they could be achieved if there were no inequality)."

The index is based on the human development approach, developed by Mahbub ul Haq, in terms of whether people are able to "be" and "do" desirable things in life—being well fed, sheltered, healthy, doing work education, voting, participating in community life.

Looking beyond 2010, this Report surveys critical aspects of human development, from political freedoms and empowerment to sustainability and human security and outlines a broader agenda for research and policies to respond to these challenges.

As Amartya Sen writes: "Twenty years after the appearance of the first Human Development Report, there is much to celebrate in what has been achieved. But we also have to be alive to ways of improving the assessment of old adversities and recognizing—and responding to—new threats that endanger human well-being and freedom."

2. Human Development Index (HDI) Indicators

The first Human Development Index (HDI) was published in the year 1990.

In 2010, published on 4 November (updated on 10 June), Human Development Report calculated Human Development Index using the following indicators:

A long and healthy life – Life expectancy at birth.
Education index – Mean years of schooling and expected years of schooling.
A decent standard of living – Means Gross National Income per capita.

These three indices are used:

1. Life expectancy index (LEI) $= \text{LD} - \dfrac{20}{85-20}$

   LEI is 1 when life expectancy at birth is 85 and 0 when life expectancy at birth is 20.

2. Education Index (EI) $= \dfrac{\text{MYSI} + \text{EYSI}}{2}$

   2.1. Mean years of schooling index (MYSI) $= \dfrac{\text{MYS}}{15}$

   Fifteen is the projected maximum index of this indicator for 2025.

   2.2. Expected years of schooling index (EYSI) $= \dfrac{\text{EYS}}{18}$

   Eighteen is equivalent to achieving a master's degree in most countries.

3. Income Index (II) $= \dfrac{\text{In (GNIpc)} - \text{In (100)}}{\text{In (75,000)} - \text{In (100)}}$

II is 1 when GNI per capita is $75,000 and 0 when GNI per capita is $ 100.

Finally, the HDI is the geometric mean of the previous three normalized indices.

$$\text{HDI} = 3\sqrt{\text{LEI} \cdot \text{EI} \cdot \text{II}}\,.$$

LE: Life expectancy at birth.

MYS: Mean years of schooling (i.e. years that a person aged 25 or older has spent in formal education).

EYS: Expected years of schooling (i.e. total expected years of schooling for children under 18 years of age).

GNIpc: Gross national income at purchasing power parity per capita.

3. Calculation of Human Development Index (HDI)

A single index measure is applied by the human development index to capture three key dimensions of human development: a long and healthy life, access to knowledge and a decent standard of living.

There are two steps to calculate the HDI:

3.1. Forming Indices for each of the Four Metrics

The indicator of the three dimensions recalibrated and combined to generate an HDI score between zero and one.

To construct the index, fixed minimum and maximum values have been established by UNDP for each of these indicators.

With the actual value for a given country, and the global maximum and minimum, the dimension (indices) values for each metric is calculated:

$$\text{Dimension index} = \frac{\text{Actual value} - \text{Minimum value}}{\text{Maximum value} - \text{Minimum value}}$$

Therefore, the dimension index is 1 in a country that achieves the maximum value and it is 0 for a country that is at the minimum value.

3.2. Aggregating the Four Metrics to Produce the HDI

These indices are aggregated, once each of the individual indices have been calculated, to get HDI.

The HDI is calculated as the geometric mean (equally-weighted) of life expectancy, education and GNI per capita as follows:

$$\text{HDI} = 3\sqrt{\text{Life, education, income}}$$

The education dimension is the arithmetic mean of the two education indices (mean years of schooling and expected years of schooling).

Countries are grouped into four human development categorized or qualifies—very high, high, medium and low.

Table 23.1: Human development indicators

Dimensions	*Indicators*	*Minimum*	*Maximum*
Health	Life expectancy (years)	20	85
Education	Expected years of schooling (years)	0	18
	Mean years of schooling (years)	0	15
Standard of Living	Gross national income per capita (2011pp$)	100	75,000

Source: UNDP (2014), Technical Note 1, p. 2.

The UNDP classifies each country into one of three development groups:

- Low human development for HDI scores between 0.0 and 0.5.
- Medium human development for HDI scores between 0.5 and 0.8.
- High human development for HDI scores between 0.8 and 1.0.

4. Limitations of the Human Development Index

The HDI notably fails to take account of qualitative factors such as cultural identity and political freedoms (human security, gender opportunities and human rights).

Many argue that the HDI should become more human-centred and expand to include more dimensions ranging from gender equity to environmental biodiversity.

The GNP per capita figure and consequently the HDI figure—takes no account of income distribution. If income is unevenly distributed, then GNP per capita will be an inaccurate measure of the monetary well-being of the people. Inequitable development is not human development.

There are likely to be significant variations in human development outcomes within as well as between countries. PPP values change very quickly and are likely to be inaccurate or misleading.

5. Human Development Reports

The Human Development Report Office (HDRO) works to publish the Human Development Report (HDR), an independent report commissioned by the United Nations Development Programme (UNDP).

Advance human development is the mission of Human Development Report Office. Contribution towards the expansion of opportunities, choice and freedom is its goal. It works towards promoting innovative new ideas, advocating practical policy changes, and constructively challenging policies and approaches that constrain human development.

The HRDO works on the Human Development Index (HDI), a summary measure of average achievement in key dimensions of human development: a long and healthy life, being knowledgeable and have a decent standard of living.

5.1 Human Development Report 2010

The Real Wealth of Nations: Pathways to Human Development

This report surveys critical aspects of human development from political freedoms and empowerment to sustainability and human security and outlines a broader agenda for research and policies to respond to these challenges.

"This time, we have taken three new indices—inequality adjustment HDI, gender inequality index and multidimensional poverty index—for our report", quotes UNDP Resident Representative in India.

The 2010 Human Development Report continues the HDI tradition of measurement innovation by introducing new indices that address crucial development factors not directly reflected in the HDI:

- *The Inequality-adjusted Human Development Index (IHDI)*: HDI data through the lens of inequality, adjusting HDI achievements to reflect disparities in income, health and education is examined.
- *The Gender Inequality Index (GII)*: A new measure of gender inequality, including material mortality rates and women's representation in parliaments.
- *The Multidimensional Poverty Index (MPI)*: A new multidimensional poverty measure at multiple factors at the household level, from basic living standards to access to schooling, clean water and health care.

India has garnered lowly 119th rank in the UNDP Index due to poor social infrastructure, mainly in areas of education and health care.

Norway has topped the HDI, with a score of 0.938, in a scale of zero to one, followed by Australia at the second place (0.937) and New Zealand with a score of 0.907.

The world's largest economy US is fourth with a score of 0.902.

In the South Asia region, Sri Lanka was at the top of 91st position with a value score of 0.658.

Even though India has made steady progress in the human development index over the past 20 years, the country continues to see rising inequality, Coeur-Bizot noted.

When inequality—especially in education and healthcare—is factored in India's HDI value would see a 30 per cent loss, according to the report.

In gender inequality index, India is at the poor 122nd position, among 138 countries. Bangladesh and Pakistan are ranked at 16th and 112th positions, respectively, indicating that these nations are better in gender equality than India.

During the last 40 years, life expectancy at birth in India has improved by 26 years, but less than 23 years in Bangladesh, the report said.

Average life expectancy at birth in India is currently 64 and when it comes to education, the average time a kid spends in school in India is 4.4 years.

Overall, China came 89th–0.663, Russia at 65th–0.719, Brazil at 73rd–0.699.

Bhutan was also part of the report but it was not ranked.

5.2 Human Development Report 2011: Sustainability and Equity: A Better Future for all

The 2011, Human Development Report argues that the urgent global challenges of sustainability and equity must be addressed together and identifies policies on the national and global level that could spur manually reinforcing progress towards these interlinked goals. The 2011 report projects how the world's most disadvantaged people suffer the most from environmental degradation, including in their immediate personal environment.

The report further emphasizes the human right to a healthy environment, the importance of integrating social equity into environmental policies and the critical importance of public participation and official accountability. The report concludes with a call for bold new approaches to global development financing and environmental controls.

A United Nations study has ranked India at 134 out of 187 countries in terms of HDI and observed that life expectancy at birth in the country has increased by 10.1 per cent a year over the last decades.

India's Human Development Index value for 2011 was 0.547 positioning the country in the 'medium human development category'.

The report said the 'mean' year of schooling for the country increased by 3.9 years between 1980 and 2011.

Rural Development Minister Jairam Ramesh, who was present at the report release, said India has made huge strides in the field of education and water supply system but admitted that the biggest block in the human development indices for India is in the field of sanitation where 58 per cent of open defecation in the world takes place in India.

He also said that the answer to the problem of sanitation is massive public investment in the sector on the lines of what the Central Government has done in education sector.

The HDI report highlights that reproductive right can further reduce environmental pressure by slowing global demographic growth. Some 120 national constitutions guarantee environmental protections.

5.3 Human Development Report 2013: The Rise of the South: Human Progress in a Diverse World

The 2013 report focuses on the "rise of the south" mapping the shift in global dynamics from the traditional power base in the west to newer emerging countries. This report identifies more than 40 developing countries that have done better than expected in human development in recent decades.

Besides the emerging economics of Brazil, China, India and South Africa, the report also acknowledges developing nations such as Turkey, Mexico, Thailand and Indonesia as playing a larger role on the global stage.

It estimated that by 2020, the combined economic output of the three leading developing countries—India, Brazil, and China—will surpass the aggregate production of Canada, France, Germany, Italy, The United Kingdom and The United States.

It underlines south-south cooperation as the key factor in boosting such development.

The report also underlines the need for global governance institutions to adopt a more equitable approach.

India's HDI value for 2013 is 0.586, positioning the country at 135 out of 187 countries. Among the BRICS countries, Russia secured the highest rank at 57, followed by Brazil at 79 and China at 91. South Africa and India secured 118 and 135 position respectively.

Presenting a review of India's progress in each of the HDI indicators, it said, "The life expectancy at birth increased by 11 years, early years of schooling increased by 2.5 years and expected years of schooling increased by 5.3 years."

On the parameters of multidimensional poverty index (MPI), which identifies multiple deprivations in the same households in education, health and living standards, India's 55.3 per cent of population were multi-dimensional poor, while an additional 18.2 per cent were near multi-dimensional poverty, the report said.

Introducing a new index, Gender Development Index (GDI), which is ratio of female to male HDI, in 2013 female HDI value for India stood at 0.519 in contrast with 0.627 for males. The GDI was calculated for 148 countries.

5.4 Human Development Report 2014: Sustaining Human Progress: Reducing Vulnerabilities and Building Resilience

Human Development report released by UNDP in Tokyo, Japan on 24 July, 2014, introduces a gender development index for the first time, which measures gender development gaps among 148 countries.

The overall gender gap is an 8 per cent deficit for women; the income gap is shockingly high—per capita income for men are more than double of that for women.

As per HDR 2014, improvement in human development measure has slowed in the past few years. The bleak picture of the vulnerabilities facing people across the world, exists in the form of financial crises, fluctuations in food prices, natural disasters and violent conflict significantly impede progress.

The report urges a threefold path: universal provision of social services, strong social protection and a return to full employment policies, all these would require a strong and active role of the state.

India is ranked at 135 with 0.586 score among the medium development countries. India is ranked 135 in inequality-adjusted HDI with a score of 0.418 with a coefficient of human inequality at 27.7.

In gender inequality index, India with a score of 0.563 is ranked 127 and in gender development index, India is ranked 132 with a score of 0.828 in multidimensional poverty index, India score 0.282.

Citing recent estimate of giving universal basic old age and disability pension, basic childcare benefits universal healthcare, social assistance and 100-day employment guarantee, the report says India would need to spend just about 4 per cent of its GDP to provide all this.

5.5 Human Development Report 2015: Work for Human Development

The Global Human Development Report 2015 asks a fundamental question—how can work enhance human development? The report deals with a board of work, going beyond jobs and considering activities as unpaid care work, voluntary work and creative work and put further the point that work can be a means to enhance human development by contributing to the public good, reducing inequality, securing livelihoods and empowering individuals. It suggest policies to harness human potential and achieve equitable and sustainable progress.

The link between work and human development are synergistic, work enhances human development. Globalizing of work and digital revolution brought about fast changes in the world of work. The benefits are not equally distributed and there are imbalances in paid and unpaid work particularly for women. Hence, creating work opportunities for both present and future generation would require moving towards sustainable work.

In 2015, India has been placed at 130th position with 0.609 score in the medium human development category, it has climbed five notches on account of rise in life expectancy and per capita income.

Life expectancy at birth increased to 68 years, on India's GDI, the female HDI value for India is 0.525 in contrast to 0.660 for males and India has GII value of 0.563.

The top three nations in the 2015 HDI are Norway, Australia and Switzerland.

India's neighbours: Sri Lanka (73), China (90), Bhutan (132), Bangladesh (142), Nepal (145), Pakistan (147) and Afghanistan (171).

5.6 Human Development Report 2016: Human Development for Everyone

Human development is must for everyone, caring for those left out, reaching them using universal policies, pursuing measures for groups with special needs and empowering those left out. Human development is about agency, self-determination and the freedom to make choices and shape outcomes.

According to the findings of the report is that although average human development improved significantly across all regions from 1990 to 2015, one in three persons worldwide continues to live in low levels of human development, as measured by the Human Development Index.

This is a concern in developed countries too, where poverty and exclusion are also a challenge, with over 300 million people—including more than one-third of all children—living in relative poverty.

The report also states that in almost every country, several groups face disadvantages that often overlap and reinforce each other, increasing vulnerability, widening the progress gap across generations, and making it harder to catch up as the world moves on.

This report highlights that:

- One in three persons worldwide continues to live in low levels of human development, as measured by the Human Development Index.
- More than 250 million people in the world face discrimination on the basis of their ethnicity.
- In 100 countries, women are legally excluded from some jobs because of their gender.

Speaking at the launch of the report in Stockholm, Sweden, on 21 March, 2017, UNDP Administrator Helen Clark called for "eliminating deep, persistent, discriminatory social norms and laws, and addressing the unequal access to political participation", saying such actions can contribute to poverty eradication and "peaceful, just and sustainable development….for all."

Sweden Prime Minister Stefan Lofven said, "leaving no one behind needs to become the way we operate as a global community." He stressed that "inclusiveness must guide policy choices" to overcome barriers that hinder progress on human development and the Sustainable Development Goals (SDGs).

Norway—0.949, Australia—0.939, and Switzerland—0.939 are the top three countries. SAARC countries—Sri Lanka (73), Maldives (105) were placed in "high human development" category, followed by India 131, Bhutan (132), Bangladesh (139), Nepal (144), Pakistan (147) and Afghanistan (169).

India ranks lowest among BRICS nations. Russia 49, Brazil 79, China 90, South Africa 119, and India 131. In 2015, India ranked 130 with score of 0.609 and was placed in the medium human development category. Life expectancy has increased from 68 years to and average of

68.3 years—69.9 years for women and 66.9 years for men. India's expected years of schooling remains at 11.7 years while mean years of schooling increased from 5.4 to 6.3 years. The percentage of inequality in education in 2015 was 39.4 per cent or 0.324 and inequality in income 16.1 per cent or 0.512.

5.7 Human Development Report 2018 Statistical Update: Human Development Indices and Indicators

Wide inequalities in people's well-being cast a shadow on sustained human development progress.

2018 statistical update is being released to ensure consistency in reporting on key human development indices and statistics. It includes an analysis of the state of human development—snapshot of current conditions as well as long term trends in human development indicators.

With a comprehensive statistical annex, an overview of the state of development across the world, looking at the long-term trends in human development indicators across multiple dimensions and for every nation, the 2018 update highlights the considerable progress but also the persistent deprivations and disparities.

Said Achim Steiner, UNDP Administrator, "while these statistics present a stark picture in themselves, they also speak to the tragedy of millions of individuals and whose lives are affected by inequity and lost opportunities, neither of which are inevitable."

India climbed one spot to 130 out of 189 countries in the latest human development ranking released by UNDP. India's HDI value for 2017 is 0.640—an indicator of the country's remarkable achievement in lifting millions of people out of poverty.

5.8 Human Development Report-2019

Beyond income, beyond averages, beyond today: Inequalities in human development in the 21st century.

United Nations Development Programme (UNDP) which publishes the human development report, released the HDR 2019 with its focus on inequality that is shaping the 21st century. It looks beyond income and considers inequalities in health, education and climate-related shock and will look beyond averages to paint a more accurate and timely picture of the state of inequality.

The world is witnessing both convergence and divergence in human development. There have seen a marked differences between children in poor and wealthy households, and these inequalities will have lifetime consequences, especially due to the rapid technological changes which impact labour markets. Hence, UNDP's analysis of inequality to go beyond income, beyond averages and beyond today.

In every country many people have little prospects for a better future. Inequalities are prevalent. A human development approach opens new windows on inequalities—why they matter, how they manifest themselves and what to do about them—that help to create concrete action.

In today's world despite unprecedented progress against poverty, hunger and disease, many societies are not working as they should. The connecting thread is inequality.

A new generation of inequalities is opening up, around education and around technology and climate change.

These inequalities in human development are a roadblock to achieving the 2030 Agenda for Sustainable Development. And they will shape the prospects of people that may live to see the 22nd century. This report explores inequalities in human development by going beyond income, beyond averages and beyond today. This will help in framing policies that can simultaneously help nations to grow their economies, improve human development and reduce inequality.

In 2019, HDI released by UNDP on December 9, India inched up one spot to rank 129th out of 189 countries, inequality and deprivation continues to be high in the country (0.642).

This means that in the last three decades, life expectancies at birth in India increased by11.6 years and the average number of schooling years increased by 3.5 years. Per capita income increased 250 times.

Shoko Noda, UNDP India resident representative, stated that Union Government schemes on financial inclusion and universal health care would help India in achieving Sustainable Development Goals.

Conclusion

Human development index as a measure of human development, in spite of its limitations proves to be a better guide to the policy-makers. Many of its limitations have been addressed and HDI remained to be widely used tool than normally income-based indicator—GNP.

Since the early 1990s, HDI has revealed some deficiencies and to overcome, the HDI construction changed by assigning new maximum and minimum values of each three indicators.

The two indicators of 'knowledge' dimensions—the adult literacy rate and the combined gross enrolment ratio—of the earlier HDI reports has been modified in 2010 HDR by taking into account expected years of schooling and mean years of schooling. Further, instead of GDP per capita indicator to assess the standard of living, the 2010 HDR considers GNI per capita.

Table 23.2: Pre-2010 and Post-2010 HDI Construction Methodology

Dimensions	*Previous (Aggregation: AM)*			*Previous (Aggregation: GM)*		
	Indicators	*Transformation*		*Indicators*	*Transformation*	
		Minimum	*Maximum*		*Minimum*	*Maximum*
Health	Life expectancy at birth (years)	25	85	Life expectancy at birth (years)	20	83.2
Knowledge	Adult literacy rate (%)	0	100	Expected years of schooling	0	18
	Combined gross enrolment ratio (%)	0	100	Mean years of schooling	0	13.1
Standard of living	GDP per capita (PPP US $)	100	40	GNI per capita (PPP US $)	100	107.721

Source: Human Development Index (HDI): An Overview Article shared by Mahendra Kumar. https://wwe.economicsdiscussion.net

Human Development Report 2010: The real wealth of nations—Pathways to human development: This report surveys critical aspects of human development from political freedoms and empowerment to sustainability and human security and outlines a broader agenda for research and policies to respond to these challenges.

***Human Development Report 2011: Sustainability and equity—A better future for all*:** The 2011 report projects how the world's most disadvantaged people suffer the most from environment degradation, including in their immediate personal environment. The report further emphasizes the human right to a healthy environment, the importance of integrating social equity into environmental policies and the critical importance of public participation and official accountability. The report concludes with a call for bold new approaches to global development financing and environmental controls.

Human Development Report 2013: The rise of the south—Human progress in a diverse world: The 2013 report focuses on the "rise of the south" mapping the shift in global dynamics from the traditional power base in the West to newer emerging countries. This report identifies more than 40 developing countries that have done better than expected in human development in recent decades.

Human Development Report 2014: Sustaining Human Progress—Reducing vulnerabilities and building resilience: Human Development report introduces a gender development index for the first time, which measures gender development gaps among 148 countries. The report urges a threefold path: universal provision of social services, strong social protection and a return to full employment policies. All these would require a strong and active role of the state.

Human Development Report 2015: Work for Human Development: The link between work and human development are synergistic, work enhances human development. Globalizing of work and digital revolution brought about fast changes in the world of work. The benefits are not equally distributed and there are imbalances in paid and unpaid work particularly for women. Hence, creating work opportunities for both present and future generation would require moving towards sustainable work.

Human Development Report 2016: Human Development for Everyone: Human development is must for everyone. Caring for those left out, reaching them using universal policies, pursuing measures for groups with special needs and empowering those left out. Human development is about agency, self-determination and the freedom to make choices and shape outcomes.

Human Development Report 2018 statistical update: Human Development Indices and indicators: 2018 statistical update is being released to ensure consistency in reporting on key human development indices and statistics. It includes an analysis of the state of human development—snapshot of current conditions as well as long term trends in human development indicators.

Human Development Report 2019: Beyond income, beyond averages, beyond today: inequalities in human development in the 21st century: In every country many people have little prospects for a better future. Inequalities is prevalent. A human development approach opens new windows on inequalities—why they matter, how they manifest themselves and what to do about them—that help to create concrete action.

List of global reports prior to 2010:

- ***Human Development Report 2009:*** Overcoming barriers: Human mobility and development.
- ***Human Development Report* 2007/2008:** Finding climate change: human solidary in a divided world.

- ***Human Development Report 2006:*** Beyond scarcity: Power, poverty and the global water crisis.
- ***Human Development Report 2005:*** International cooperation at a crossroads: Aid, trade and security in an unequal world.
- ***Human Development Report 2004:*** Cultural liberty in today's diverse world.
- ***Human Development Report 2003:*** Millennium development goals: a compact. A compact among nations to end human poverty.
- ***Human Development Report 2002:*** Deepening democracy in fragmented world.
- ***Human Development Report 2001:*** Making new technologies work for human development.
- ***Human development report 2000:*** Human rights and human development.
- ***HDR 1999:*** Globalization with a human face.
- ***HDR 1998:*** Consumption for human development.
- ***HDR 1997:*** Human development to eradicate poverty.
- ***HDR 1996:*** Economic growth and human development.
- ***HDR1995:*** Gender and human development.
- ***HRD1994:*** New dimensions of human security.
- ***HDR 1993:*** People's participation.
- ***HDR 1992:*** Global dimension of human development.
- ***HDR 1991:*** Financing human development.
- ***HDR 1990:*** Concept and measurement of human development.

REFERENCES

Human Development Index (HDI): An Overview. Article Shared by Mahendra Kumar. Retrieved from https://www.economicsdiscussion.net/human-development-index/human-development-index-hdi-an-overview/11782

UNDP (United Nations Development Programme). 2014. *Human Development Report 2014. Sustaining Human Progress: Reducing Vulnerabilities and Building Resilience.* UNDP, New Delhi.

www.in.undp.org

www.hdr.undp.org

https://en.m.wikipedia.org

https://www.livemint.com

www.economictimes.indiatimes.com

https://en.m.wikipedia.orgswiki

https://www.businessstandard.com

SDG Knowledge hub-a project by IISD, sdg.iisd.org
HDI Our World in Data, Max Roser, 2014, revised 2019
Full methodology notes: The UNDP 2018 version
www.investopedia.com
http://hdr.undp.org/en/
https://www.linkedin.com

24
The Manpower Planning Approach

Qudsia Hafeez

> "If you are planning for one year, plant grains;
> If you are planning for ten years, plant trees;
> If you are planning for hundred years, then plant men."
>
> — *A Chinese Saying*

Introduction

Human Resources are known to be the wealth of Nation by economists. The current population of India in the year 2020 is 1,377,048,321 (Worldometer, 2020), which accounts to 17.7 per cent of the total world population, leading India with 2nd rank in the list of countries by population, following China. The median age in India is 28.4 years (Countries in the World by Population, 2020).

Apart from the quantity of human resources available in a nation, what matters most is the quality, with which it produces its output affecting the Gross National Product. Recent statistics (2020) on economy of India shows the country stands at 139th rank as world's fifth-largest economy by nominal GDP and IMF together. Further, standing at 118th rank, making India, the world's third-largest by purchasing power parity GDP by the year 2018.

The modern era of 21st century, has raised the average GDP growth from 6-7 per cent over a period of 4 years from 2014-2018, attributing India as world's fastest growing economy, surpassing China (Economy of India, 2020).

It is inevitable to note that Literacy is a key factor for socio-economic prosperity. India stands at a rank of 168th/234 globally, with female literacy of 65.46 per cent and male literacy of 82.14 per cent with a total of 74.04 per cent in the category of literacy rate as per 2011 Census of India data. As per the MHRD report on Educational Statistics released in 2018, the overall literacy rate in India is 69.1 per cent in 2014 (Literacy in India, 2020).

Socialists and Economists hold true that education is a prominent factor in deciding the nation's economic power. It is obvious that as part of fundamental human rights, basic education attainment is essential. Education has its utmost value in organizing human ability for the purpose of fulfilling every goal of National effort, which led to launch one of the rapidly growing branches of Economics, termed as Educational Economics or Economics of Education.

Adam Smith, 'the Father of Economics', asserts that the human capabilities, education, skills, talent, and training sums up to the economic value of human resources, thus by far and large is a win-win situation for any nation.

Theodore W. Shultz, an Agricultural Economist, developed the Human Capital Theory of economic development focusing on how educational investment can escalate productivity and efficiency of manpower.

In this case, economic development depends much on enhancing the potential of human resource by increasing the quantity (population) and quality (skill). In countries like Italy, Canada and USSR both quantity as well as quality needs to be tackled; whereas, in countries like India, Saudi Arabia, Africa, it is essential to focus on the quality development of human resource (Economics of Education, 2012).

An important qualitative indicator of human resource development is education and training. Hence, it is pivotal to plan education keeping in view the future demand and supply of efficient workforce. Educational planning is a solution to diverse national problems such as increasing populations, environment protection, manpower needs, science and technology related issues etc. Educational planning refers to efforts involved in planned and deliberate change brought in the system of education for achieving a common goal or identified objectives.

Educational Planning in India dates back to 1854, Wood's Despatch as the first effort on educational planning, then in 1938, when Indian National Congress appointed a National Planning Committee. During the Second World War, Planning and Development Department was set-up in 1939-40. Post-war Sargeant Report was prepared in 1944 by Central Advisory Board of Education. In 1946, Planning Advisory Board came into existence and later in 1950 Planning Commission was created to implement annual plans and five-year plans which eventually dissolved in 2014, paving way for a new institution named NITI Aayog (National Institution for Transforming India) which is a policy think tank of Government of India, to achieve sustainable development goals, targeting economic growth, infrastructure development, and industrialization *via* protecting environment, social inclusion, and empowerment of the poor. Every State also has its own Department for Planning relating to the over-all planning matters at the State Government.

Approaches to Educational Planning solve the issues of imbalances between demand and supply of education from various different perspectives of societal needs. It is an answer to the problem of Educational Development. The various approaches to Educational Planning are enlisted as follows—

(i) Social Demands Approach,
(ii) Rate of Return Approach,
(iii) Manpower Balances or Requirement Approach,
(iv) Target Setting Approach,
(v) The Linear Programming Model,
(vi) 'Intra-Educational' Extrapolation Model,
(vii) Demographic Projection Model,
(viii) Social Justice Model, and
(ix) School Mapping (Sharma, R.N., 2002).

In this chapter, we may focus on the "Manpower Balances or Requirement Approach".

Manpower Planning

Generally the term 'Manpower' in a broader sense covers the total labour force of a country, and in a narrow sense represent how raw manpower can be converted into skilled manpower after acquiring years of education and training for accelerating economic growth. This approach intends to predict future manpower needs determined by occupational categories resulting in manpower requirements which are then transformed into educational requirements. To implement this idea of manpower planning, it is required to optimally utilize the available human resources. Firstly, it is needed to assess the available bulk stock of country's workforce, then scrutinize the type of skills required to inculcate in the human resources efficiently. Indisputably, this so-called human resource development approach to educational planning emphasizes that need-based modification in educational system should be constructively planned to fulfil the country's manpower requirement (Pandey, Subhash Chandra, 2016):

- In the perspective of Gorden MacBeath, there are two stages which describe manpower planning; initially, all sectoral types and levels of employees are forecasted over a period of the plan. Finally, recruiting the right kind of skilled workforce, that meets the requirements of the organization.
- According to Vetter, the management can decide upon improving the manpower planning from its current status to the desired level. Through thorough planning only, management can lead the organization towards achieving prosperity *via* procuring accurately the number of employees required at proper time and place performing effectively.
- Stainer expresses that manpower planning is a strategy for acquiring, utilizing, enhancing, and conserving the workforce of an organization. It demonstrates the guidelines to exercise future manpower requirement.
- Wickstrom opines a progression of activities under the arena of manpower planning, such as forecasting manpower requirements econometrically over a specified time period for an industry, preparing an inventory for assessing the existing status of manpower resources and strategizing on enhancing optimum utilization, predicting future workforce related problems by analyzing the adequacy of current resources and determining its consequences both qualitatively and quantitatively, and scheduling recruitment, employment, development procedures of human resource.
- Geisler proposes that manpower planning is a process including forecasting, developing, and controlling the required human resources (Das, Nageshwar, 2018).
- Coleman describes manpower planning as a process to determine the need for future manpower and identify ways to meet these needs, for effective functioning of an organization (Chand, Smriti, n.d.).

Significance of Manpower Planning

Statistics reveal that there is a positive correlation between scarcities of education, natural resources, and low income. In such a circumstance, manpower planning is made with regard to education (Narasaiah, M.L., 2007).

Lack of appropriate planning results in low level of economic development, surplus consumption of goods, lesser savings, and vague investments. Furthermore, there would be problems of un-employment, underemployment, overemployment, and also self-employment of human resources. Thus better planning would increase the rate of savings, redress investment resulting in economic growth (Suravi Swati, 2016).

According to sociologists and political scientists, human resource development is the process of modernization catering in transformation of social and political institutions, thereby converting education into skill-intensive and need based commodity. In view of emerging technologies and occupational changes, educational institutions must raise its standards and act as harbours skill generation to get linked with the employment sector. Different economic sectors/industries may require diverse workforce comprising blue-collar, white-collar, grey-collar, and pink-collar employees. Undoubtedly, the crux of human capital development lies in the hands of humans, who should be well-equipped with necessary knowledge, attitude, skills and be motivated to organize themselves appropriately in consideration of optimizing economic power (Nagpal Mittal, 1993).

The manpower balances approach requires balancing manpower supply in a country by balancing different levels (primary, secondary, higher education) and types (general, vocational, physical, and cultural) of education thereby also targeting socio-economic development of a country. To obtain a typical estimate from this proposition; every occupation resulting from general education category, can be translated into number of educational years required to achieve the desired occupational position. Similarly, every vocation resulting from type of vocational education category can be translated into number of training years required to achieve the desired type of vocation. Considering general and vocational education time frames, the difference between the stocks of manpower needed at present and in future can be predicted and this in turn would transform in robust education and training planning (Narasaiah, M.L., 2007).

Furthermore, manpower planning is also based on the unit level and on the duration of time. Unit level considers macro-level planning at national level to effectively utilize skilled manpower for nation's human resource development; and micro-level planning at sectoral/industrial level, in providing the right people suitable to fulfil the tasks for raising economy. Whereas time duration; considers planning workforce for short-term (1-2 years), medium-term (3-5 years), and long-term (6-10 years or more).

Irrespective of being one of the many approaches for educational planning, manpower forecasting approach should not be narrowed down in its concept only to educational planning, but in a broader perspective it must be viewed as a human resource development strategy. This is because it targets both the economic and the educational sectors together. Education, Skilled Manpower, and Economic development are key factors for Human Resource Development, which are interdependent and directly proportional to each other. The higher the standard of education, the better will be the availability of skilled manpower which in turn will fuel the economic growth. This relation has been tested out statistically by the social scientists and there are positive effects felt in the society like increase in literacy rate, population control, better health and sanitation facilities, civic development, digital literacy, and increase in innovative developments in diverse fields (Suravi Swati, 2016).

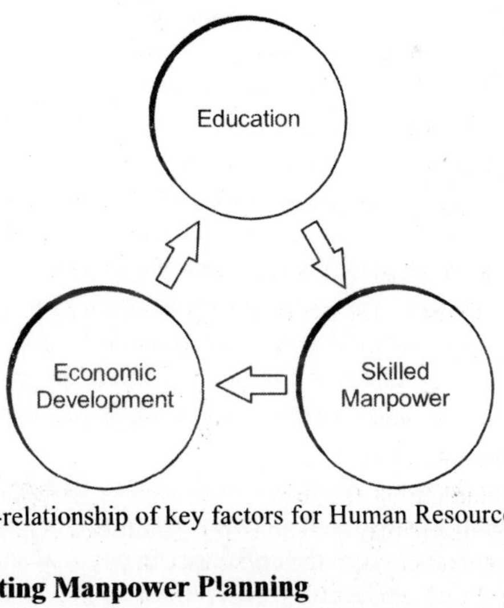

Fig. 21.1: Inter-relationship of key factors for Human Resource Development.

Factors Affecting Manpower Planning

(i) Educational Level—The higher the education level and type of

education attained by the public in a country, the higher will be the rate of return to the economy.

(ii) The Literacy Rate—Literacy rate is a strong measure of educated population in a country, the literacy rate is directly proportional to the Gross Domestic Product of the country (Narasaiah, M.L., 2007).

(iii) Ratio of Skilled Workers to Labour Force—It is the ratio of number of educated workforce such as scientists, engineers, doctors, to the number of labour force, also known as saturation ratio. It predicts the quantity of labour required by different types of sector (Nagpal Mittal, 1993).

(iv) Technical Knowledge and Skills—Today's contemporary era, has converted everything into virtual from manual. Technological explosion catapulted the economy by pulling every industrial sector under its virtual radar. Technology functioned as a catalyst for replenishing the skill sets of human workforce. This has led to a sharp competition thriving in the demand-supply of employable workforce in the knowledge economy, which impacted recruitment policies of many organizations turning away from quantity to quality skilled manpower staffing. Education in the wake of globalization has now accelerated to hone lifelong education to get updated with new technology and knowledge explosion; also resulting in increasing the number of white-collar jobs from blue-collar jobs (Suravi Swati, 2016).

(v) Economy—The economic conditions prevailing in any country is capricious and decides the prosperity of the nation, which in turn is an indicator of manpower demand and supply in the job market, and drastic changes in economic conditions resulting in occupational changeovers would bound to have ramifications in human resource development.

(vi) Legal Aspects—Every country differs in its employment rules and regulations, such as the fixed hourly-wage pay rule, monthly or annual fixed salary for employees, contract or permanent jobs, jobs in government or private sector, working hours, rotational shifts, pay cut-offs, overtime pay, eligibility conditions for appointment, promotion, voluntary withdrawal, death, and retirement affects manpower planning in future (Nagpal Mittal, 1993).

(vii) Demographic Aspects—In a country like India, where mixed-cultural diversity prevails, it is challenging to provide employment to every ethnic member given the imbalance in physical and social amenities between rural and urban areas. Nevertheless, it is indisputable that the large chunk of Indian population in this modern era will belong to the skilled manpower resulting in surplus supply outweighing the demand

(Narasaiah, M.L., 2007).

(viii) Political Aspects—Different countries have different political systems like monarchy, oligarchy, democracy, which governs the development of human resources in the country.

(ix) Government Policies—Central Government has launched many employment drives, schemes, policies either solely or in collaboration with the State Governments to provide jobs to the skilled mass, following the reservation pattern, seniority list, on merit basis, and the like.

(x) Organization—Different types of sectors, industries, enterprises, companies have their own strategies (short-term, mid-term, long-term) to pump human (part-time, full-time, contractual basis) and material (temporary, permanent, on-rent, on-lease, donations, gifts) resources in cost-effective manner to boost their net-profits. Manpower planning also helps in efficient management of four broad administrative functions, *viz.* planning, organizing, directing, and controlling of personnel (Das Nageshwar, 2018).

(xi) Motivation of Prospective Employees—Motivated employees perform better, have better human relations, work morale, and use their knowledge up to the maximum advantage than those unmotivated. Honing a skill without the motivation to achieve a task through it; is capital wastage of resources in itself. Physical and financial resources are dependent for its effective usage upon the best abilities of human resources boosting higher productivity. Driving forces such as incentives, performance appraisal, promotion, awards are important to keep the workforce motivated (Das, Nageshwar, 2018).

(xii) Uncertainties in the Type and Quality of Forecasting Information—Planning for forecasting manpower requirement, needs access to demographic, social, and economic information from a reliable and valid source. Such planning is made for six-months to a year in short-term mode or for three to five years in long-term mode. Indisputably, forecasts are subjected to uncertainties arising in the future environment of time horizons leading to changes in labour market (Mishra, R.K., 2014).

Methods of Manpower Forecasting/Requirement Approach

The basic rationale of Manpower forecasting approach is to predict the future demand for skilled manpower, which are conditional forecasts in a given economic period. It is based on the demand factor of the educated human resource; for instance, the time taken for a person to become a high school graduate is 12 years, for a college graduate it might take 16 years, 20 years to be skilled professional and further more years added if a person engages in research pursuits.

Implementing the Cobweb Model effect to this situation, it may seem that the time lag taken eventually plays a crucial role in demand and supply of the educated manpower to the market demand.

The crux of various methods for manpower requirements approach is close to the viewpoint of Gorden MacBeath, where two stages are employed in manpower planning; first a detailed analysis is made with reference to forecast the demand of manpower of all types and levels for a specified period. Next, every industry is provided with the right employees at the right place in the right time to meet the planned requirements and organizational objectives (Agabi, C.O. & Ogah, J.I., 2010).

Manpower forecasting approach can be further understood by following few methods—

(i) The Employers Opinion Method (EOM),
(ii) The Incremental Labour Output Ratios Trend Method (ILOR),
(iii) The Density Ratio Method (DRM),
(iv) The International Comparisons Method (ICM), and
(v) Parnes' Mediterranean Regional Project Method (MRPM).

(i) The Employers Opinion Method

In this method an opinion is ascertained from the employer directly as, "How many employees they intend to employ in the next few years?" The information provides the type and number of employees required in near future. Then all the requirements from all employers are added minus the estimated retirements and deaths over the next few years will result in the employees required for the intended year. This method of surveying firms and industries is mostly based on data gathered by assumptions; yet, it is likely to be employed by both developed and developing countries.

(ii) The Incremental Labour Output Ratios Trend Method

Any occupation demands skilled workforce. The input of a particular skilled labour in an occupation and the rate of increment in the output is calculated with the change occurring over a period of time based on the changes acquired in educational composition, the resultant output ratio will generally be higher than the inputs. This method calculates the future demand of labour quality with respect to the trend of education and labour output relationship. This method is well-suited for countries relying on time series data for long-term planning of the number of skilled workforce required with regard to profession, designation, and educational qualification.

(iii) The Density Ratio Method

To determine the manpower required in long-term in any economic sector, first the number of educated workers is calculated to the total number of available workforce, and then a stable ratio is derived from this calculation based on different types of labour in an industry, for instance, the ratio of doctors to nurses, engineers to technicians, using time series data over a period of time. This stable ratio is the density ratio, also called the ratio of saturation of the educated manpower of a particular sector.

(iv) The International Comparisons Method

This method is based on the assumption that different countries employ the same manpower requirement approach with respect to occupational and educational distribution. Though, a comparison is derived, from the time series data in one country being the premise for another country to forecast its manpower needs. Critics disapprove of this method as no two countries are same on demographic features, economic development, and the type of workforce requirement.

(v) Parnes Mediterranean Regional Project Method

H.S. Parnes developed this method to determine the demand for educated manpower quantitatively based on Gross National Product (GNP). The contribution made by different industries and the labour output coefficients in different industries is calculated with regard to industry labour force in each industry, labour force in each occupation, labour force with each level of education. This can be calculated in equation as—

$$P = GNP$$

Pi = Contribution to GNP from each industry ($i = 1, 2, 3, 4 \ldots n$)
Li = Labour force in industry

Lo = Labour force in each occupation

Le = Labour force with each level of education

Where,

$$P = (Pi/P)\ (Li/Pi)\ (Lo/Li)\ (Le/Lo)$$

$$P = Le/P$$

$$P \times P = Le$$

$$P^2 = Le$$

$$P = \cdot\ Le$$

This means GNP is greatly affected by the number of educated labour force (Robinson, E.A.G., Vaizey, J.E.,1966).

Several other methods are also suggested by Parnes (1962). Using the current position of workforce educational attainment by occupation, future workforce needs by occupation is predicted, later leading in identification of prospective educational needs.

Parnes suggested ***Job Analysis Method***, where educational development indexes are prepared, and each job is analyzed according to the skills acumen required by the workers such as language ability, logical reasoning, mathematical aptitude, technical knowledge, and the like; which are then converted into equivalent educational requirements for each job. But this method is difficult to implement (Cohn Elchanan, 1975).

Beckerman and Parnes (1968) proposed an alternative method called as ***Social Objectives Method***, where they assume that more educated and skilled labour force will undoubtedly promote economic growth. Hence, it is not necessary to measure manpower requirements for economic objectives. Therefore, the purpose of this method lies to identify the shortcomings/gaps in the existing educational system, with respect to specific social and educational objectives. The future needs are then made in terms of estimated population growth and their inclination towards different types and levels of education. This method would then seek to set manpower requirements and determine the expenditure incurred to obtain it at different intervals of time. The social objectives method is more favourable for educationists, as implementing it would reduce educational wastage, illiteracy, pupil-teacher ratio, and improve educational standards, increase enrolment ratios in secondary education, reconstruct more realistic educational objectives. The downside of this method is that there would be less integration between educational and economic planners.

Yet, another kind of manpower requirements approach is ***Tinbergen-Correa Model*** (1962), where current secondary and higher educational outputs are directly related to the given rates of economic growth. Tinbergen-Correa relies on simple input-output table to suggest an appropriate educational structure that would be relevant to achieve a certain rate of economic growth. Changing economic rates should then be a catalyst in modifying the desired educational structure. Frederick Harbison and Charles A. Myers (1968) criticize that shortages and surpluses in required number of individuals with secondary and higher education may hinder estimating aggregate economic production. Moreover, this model assumes that in a given period technology and productivity remains constant. It does not make any distinction between types of education, i.e. general/vocational/physical/cultural; between major economic industries, any qualitative imbalances in education system, and factors that might affect required occupations and educational qualifications.

Harold Goldstein (1958) proposed a method of manpower planning by applying past trends of growth of number of people in a specific occupation by total employment; to project this information to extrapolate the future manpower requirements. Some advanced countries had applied this method to assess the need for high-level workforce such as scientists, engineers, technocrats etc. Frederick Harbison and Charles A. Myers (1968) advocated that, despite being a useful method, it lacks practicability, because many countries may suffer from inadequate data, and if so data are available; there may be consequences arising from future relationships with respect to multiple variables, such as future demand-supply market, modification in the recruitment criteria, desired eligibility skills, socio-economic factors etc. (Nagpal Mittal, 1993).

Drawbacks of Manpower Forecasting/Requirement Approach

Manpower planning analysis is still not much in trend as it has many variants to be adopted and implemented successfully by educationists and economic development planners. As manpower planning approach attempts to forecast future demand of educated workforce, in a meantime of ten to fifteen years ahead, it is difficult to predict and analyze the changing trends of job market. Moreover, the slow growth rate of economy is a concern at large because of mal-utilization of manpower skills that are falling short to meet the demand of requisite skills in the modern day economy; which is further saddled by increasing population growth.

To tackle this problem, economists suggest a robust recruitment policy where workers salaries should be linked up with increase in productivity; thereby paving way for providing training and development of human resources to meet the demand of emerging skills. Hence, executing effective top-bottom-top approach of human resource management would help in enduring the changing economic times.

Forecasting the impact of future scientific and technological changes occurring globally; is difficult to be predicted by sociologists, educationists and economists. Despite this, there is a lacuna in estimating manpower projections contributing to economic rise, between highly trained and less trained manpower. This might be due to majority of studies assessing workforce coming from general education category rather than the vocational education. For instance, engineers belonging to blue-collar category can disturb the manpower analysis, by switching to a white-collar job of a manager, which might not require the technical education background. Therefore, it is inevitable that, there is no clear differentiation of jobs and many overlap paving way for transferability of jobs without any clearly defined educational qualification.

Further one needs to do cost-benefit analysis before investing in the workforce imparting appropriate training intending to meet the future demands. To curb the costs needed for training of the manpower later in a period; one strategy is to reform the education system early by giving more emphasis to scientific and technical education keeping in view the future demands. Education system must revive vocational, adult and lifelong education, and enhance the overall quality and quantity of education in terms of maintaining high standards, pumping qualified teaching fraternity, modern technological pedagogy, establishment of research centres, boosting enrolment, enhancing overall inputs and outputs to match employment generation capabilities (Robinson, E.A.G. & Vaizey, J.E. 1966).

It is still a complex task to convert manpower needs into educational requirements as 'years of schooling' greatly varies for different types of vocational and general education. There seems also an imbalance in demand and supply of educated manpower in the job market. Suppose, if there is a demand of scientists in the job market, there should be enough skilled manpower, say, teaching fraternity to produce that required number of scientists to meet the future demand (Cohn Elchanan, 1975).

According to Frederick Harbison and Charles A. Myers (1968) most of the countries lack in availability of accurate data on expected increases in productivity and its effect on altering occupational requirements; further, this approach relies on assumptions in predicting the demand and supply of high-profile professionals (Ahuja, Amrish Kumar, 2007).

Moreover, such forecasting also tends to get effected from socio-economic and political conditions. Hence, multi-stemmed approach in analyzing various factors affecting supply and demand must be implemented in manpower forecasting approach rather than being aloof and assessing only single prediction of expected manpower and educational needs.

India being a semi-advanced agrarian country, there exist a wide divide in social amenities available between rural and urban areas; which results in more people opting for livelihood in modern urban spots rather than in rural areas. The problems are not merely quantitative but also qualitative. Unemployment and shortage of skilled manpower certainly affects economic growth quantitatively. Due to overpopulation, unemployment does not only hit the unskilled but also the educated human resource that have attained years of education and training, rigidity in occupational composition of workforce arising due to traditional practices of recruiting methods, inadequate data relating to employee withdrawals and mobility from each occupation, further, if the acquired skills do not match the industry demands; it will result in lack of skilled manpower. Qualitative problems arise due to inefficiencies in manpower resource such as underemployment, mal-utilization, poor quality of education and training, lack of motivation and disinterest among workforce etc. (Cohn Elchanan, 1975).

Frederick Harbison and Charles A. Myers (1968) criticized that manpower productivity estimates can be quantitatively measured from industries such as manufacturing, construction, transportation, and the like, whereas, it is difficult to measure qualitative productivity outcomes from general administration, public health and services. Apart, from this in agrarian countries like India, productivity is measurable in the quantity of agricultural products produced, but the manpower requirements in agricultural field is unlikely to be assessed. But economic research shows that there is a positive association between education and productivity in agriculture. The more the literate rural population is, the more better and easier for the government to implement its various rural development policies (Ahuja, Amrish Kumar, 2007).

Other reasons mounting the drawbacks of this approach arise due to: (i) analysing only in-demand highly educated individuals, ignoring the bulk of workers with lower level of education; (ii) focusing only on the quantity of workforce rather than economic wage or price changes;

(iii) procuring data from employment department which largely comprises workforce from public sector than private sector; (iv) takes into account only formally educated resource than those informally educated or trained from various private sources; (v) assumes long-term manpower planning which could be discontinuous, distorted than considering planning short-term goals which could be more realistic; (vi) typically uses fixed relative economic price, output and labour to extrapolate future economic and manpower status; (vii) manpower forecasting approach directs attention of educational investment only in those promising economic areas whose demand and rate of return is highest, and does not consider the 'cost' factor in decision-making approach; (viii) as evident, the society is plagued with social issues, forecasting the future by employing the current statistics, leads to further disequilibrium in the data; (ix) it is also worth considering that economic factors are characterized by certain production function, where there cannot be substitution in any production factors, hence forecasting based on substitutability of production factors, results in possible inaccuracies; (x) consumption and investment components of education play a dual-hatted role, where differences between the two is inscrutable, if government involvement in education is all about financing it, then manpower forecasting approach is bound to analyze overinvestment in education (Cohn Elchanan, 1975).

Frederick Harbison and Charles A. Myers (1968) claim manpower forecasting approach, instead of performing the function of 'forecasting'; this approach would be better off for 'target-setting' the future needs (Ahuja, Amrish Kumar, 2007).

Manpower Forecasting/Requirement Approach in India

Developed nations like USSR, Turkey, Greece, Spain, Italy, Portugal, Yugoslavia and West Germany, and less developed nations like Nigeria, Tanzania, Kenya, Zambia implemented this approach; whereas India did not pay much impetus towards it (Cohn Elchanan, 1975).

Considering India as the world's second highly populated country with diverse demographic share, comprising majority of youth, it is needless to say that special attention must be focused on manpower planning to upkeep the economic growth and prosperity of the country at large. Human resource development planning is the crux of generating a diverse talent pool to maximize rate of return to the economy and avoiding any anticipated pitfalls.

Comparing 2nd rank in population to that of 168th rank in literacy rate globally (Countries in the World by Population, 2020), India needs to assess thoroughly the problems, to bridge the gaps in education and training with that of required job skills. At the national level, sectoral manpower analysis must be made to tackle various types of issues related to education and skills that are industry dependent. For instance, agricultural, industrial, service sectors need to be addressed separately to solve the issues of manpower planning (Suravi Swati, 2016).

India is progressing faster by standing at 139th rank as world's fifth-largest economy by nominal GDP and IMF, and the world's third-largest at 118th rank, by purchasing power parity GDP in the year 2018. India has also progressed faster in raising GDP growth rate to 6-7 per cent. Henceforth, economic and educational planners should work conjointly to develop the required skills in human resource that corresponds to the skills required by the industries, to further drive the nation towards economic prosperity (International Rankings of India, 2020).

Pre-independence era to few decades in post-Independence, Indian women did not had much share in the economic growth, however, in recent years, Women Empowerment has been an emerging context towards contributing in economy, where many illiterate urban and rural women are being trained to self-finance themselves in the job market, further turning them into entrepreneurs of small scale businesses/start-ups by providing micro-loans, funds from governmental and non-governmental financial bodies (Suravi Swati, 2016).

India has no dearth of talented people, but the country fails in proper channelizing their energies towards economic development. According to Ministry of External Affairs Report (2018), there are about 28 million, with 1,24,99,395 million Non-resident Indians (NRIs) and 1,55,92,357 million Persons of Indian Origin (PIOs); leading India with a global diaspora of 17.5 million (NRI & PIO, 2020). Still many more Indians are following suit. The reason for this enormous international migration is people seeking greener pastures, better facilities, better human resource management, strong economy, and quality life abroad. Prominent Indians like Satya Nadella (Microsoft CEO), Sundar Pichai (Google Inc. CEO), Nikki Haley (US Ambassador to the UN), Indra Nooyi (Pepsi Co. CEO), Leo Varadkar (PM, Ireland), Kalpana Chawla (American Astronaut), Abhijit Banerjee (American Economist & Nobel Prize winner in 2019) and many more have charted their success in international economy (20 Global Indians, 2018).

According to Amartya Sen, a distinguished economist has thrown light on the crisis in Indian education and way forward:

(i) Shortage of skilled manpower in any economic field can be solved by raising the salaries in that concerned field, hence converting it into a demanded field, which will attract more workforce. An extensive debate has taken over the low-level of salaries of teachers, which is also suffering from shortage of good teachers because of increasing growth of education system; one way to predict the outcome, suggested is to make comparison between the rises in national income per head with the levels of teacher's salary.

(ii) Education Commission (1964-66) had employed manpower estimation for service and non-service industries separately in view of Commission's enrolment programmes in higher education. For non-service area, economy was divided into a number of sectors and was based on the assumption that increase in net output in each sector is directly proportional to the employment/demand of educated manpower. For service area, certain norms were used, like teacher-pupil ratios, doctor-patient ratios, for which growth rates were analyzed.

(iii) The allocation of budget to educational expenditure, should consider the relative costs and contributions of different types of education. As unemployment of highly educated people is an expensive waste of money, this trend is expanding further with the supply of even more educated people due to the expansion of poor quality higher education.

(iv) There is a high growth rate in the University education than in primary education. As compared to developed countries, every individual receives quality primary education but Indian primary education lacks in the quality with respect to 3 Rs (read, write, and arithmetic) and quantity in terms of enrolment of children.

(v) In consideration of private and social rate of returns of education, individual makes a small part in bearing the cost of education in terms of fees, than compared to the government investing on educational expenditure. Similarly, while analyzing the benefits of education, private benefits purely rest on personal goals; whereas, social benefits in attaining educated society, to be in concurrence with the government, in increasing the highly educated populace. For instance, if a person finds it difficult to compete among the bulk of graduates to acquire a particular job, then he/she may improve his/her chances by acquiring higher education and becoming more desirable in the job market; which he/she may take over the job at a loss of other person. The losses of others in this process have to be subtracted from the gains of this person, while analyzing private and social rate of returns to education. Rate of return to education gradually declines as educational tier progresses higher. Private rate of returns are higher than social rate of returns. Further, an inadequate distinction between the two has resulted in confusion in developing educational policy.

(vi) To understand whether education had any impact on the productivity of a person, a conventional measure is to analyze the wage differences. A rise in person's salary may be attributable to the extra training or education acquired. Moreover, it is a perplexed economic situation whether job market ensures in providing such incentive irrespective of that additional educational attainment. In India, all the estimations considering rate of returns to education employs wage differential technique.

(vii) Implementing inefficient techniques of manpower planning for educational policy have paved way in overestimating the requirements of highly educated manpower, inadequate recognition of educated unemployment, overqualified appointments, and inaccuracies in productivity estimations; that has victimized the statistical data with technical errors rising from grass roots level to top organizations, *viz.* Education Commission, Planning Commission, and Union Government's Department of Labour and Employment.

(viii) In the era of unemployment, there has been a greater demand on individual to pursue higher education which is strongly encouraged by political factors, thereby shifting public policy from other important social causes towards expansion of higher education.

(ix) The allocation of public funds has gathered the attention of urban populace rather than the rural community in dire need of primary education and its relative economic return.

(x) In an agrarian nation, economists, educationists, and sociologists have collapsed in relating education to economic life of the nation. Many rural schools have been constructed, but its inefficiency is such that its vacations do not match the cultivation seasons of agricultural activity, thereby resulting in massive drop-out rate. For instance, in Uttar Pradesh, the conduct of school examinations in the month of April often coincides with the '*Rabi*' period of harvesting. The rigidity in functioning of education never eased the practical realities of the society at large.

(xi) The increasing rate of unemployment of highly educated professionals emerges from poor estimations of supply-demand, rate of returns, political pressures in implementing of public policy in expanding the higher education sector. There needs to be a shift from over-expansion to a more balanced approach of educational growth; via, accurate estimations of manpower needs, private and social profitability, considering the rural economic life inequities, focusing on practical realities rather than political liabilities, and of social diversity of the nation.

(xii) There is an urgent need for educational transformation in India with courage and determination to combat the political pressures and rise above to meet the long-term development goals of public policies; which requires best synchronization among economists, educationists, and sociologists (Mishra, R.K., 2014).

Summary

Educational planning is important for a developing nation like India, where it has to be on competitive edge on par with other developed countries in every sector. This is not just to follow blindly the footsteps of developed nations, but to foresee the opportunities and threats of future and plan accordingly the physical, human, and financial resources with regard to strengths and weaknesses of an Indian economy. Manpower forecasting approach is one of the many approaches towards educational planning. It mainly forecasts the number, type and level of manpower needed when required by the country, taking into consideration the occupational categories, and translating it into educational requirements. This method is also termed as human resource development method, because of its crux in analyzing the relationship among education, skilled manpower, and economic development. There are several socio-economic and political factors affecting this supply-demand relationship. Various techniques to attempt manpower forecasting approach are: The Employers' Opinion Method; The Incremental Labour Output Ratios Trend Method; The Density Ratio Method; The International Comparisons Method; Parnes' Mediterranean Regional Project Method. Other methods outlined by prominent economists are Job Analysis Method, Social Objectives Method, and Tinbergen-Correa Model. Despite its shortcomings, in technical errors, improper estimations, and outlook of only expected manpower and educational needs, this approach can be strongly implemented in fulfilling all socio-economic short-term plans in relation to boosting rate of returns and national income. It is also an important driving force in educational transformation preparing future ready skilled workforce. Relying only on one approach for accelerating the economic development by preparing realistic public policies, is risky and erroneous; hence for every component of the economic system to be analyzed, it is better off utilizing various approaches in collaboration, which can be amalgamated by the best efforts of economists, educationists, and sociologists.

REFERENCES

20 Global Indians: Riding the New Wave (2018). Retrieved from https://www.indiatoday.in/magazine/cover-story/story/20180430-powerful-global-indians-aborad-nikki-haley-sundar-pichai-satya-nadella-1216650-2018-04-19 on 18-04-2020

Agabi, C.O. and Ogah, J.I. (2010). "Education and Human Resource Planning In Nigeria: The Case of National Manpower Board (NMB)." *International Journal of Scientific Research in Education*, *3*(3), 152-165. Retrieved from http://www.ijsre.com/assets/vol.%2C-3_3_-agabi—ogah.pdf on 02-04-2020

Ahuja, Amrish Kumar (2007). *Economics of Education.* New Delhi: Authors Press.

Chand Smriti (n.d.). *Manpower Planning: Its Definition, Process and Affected Factors.* Retrieved from http://www.yourarticlelibrary.com/employee-management/manpower-planning-its-definition-process-and-affected-factors-hrm/27911 on 06-04-2020

Cohn Elchanan (1975). *The Economics of Education.* USA: Ballinger Publishing Company.

Countries in the World by Population (2020). Retrieved from https://www.worldometers.info/world-population/population-by-country/on 12-04-2020

Das Nageshwar (2018). *Definition, Importance, and Affected Factors of Manpower Planning.* Retrieved from https://www.ilearnlot.com/definition-importance-and-affected-factors-of-manpower-planning/49684/on 05-04-2020

Economics of Education (2012). Retrieved from http://archive.mu.ac.in/myweb_test/ma%20edu/M[1].A._EDU_ECONOMICS_OF_EDU.-Final_1_2011-12.pdf on 12-04-2020

Economy of India (2020). Retrieved from https://en.wikipedia.org/wiki/Economy_of_India on 16-04-2020

Educational Statistics at a Glance (2018). Retrieved from https://mhrd.gov.in/sites/upload_files/mhrd/files/statistics-new/ESAG-2018.pdf on 17-04-2020

International rankings of India (2020). Retrieved from https://en.wikipedia.org/wiki/International_rankings_of_India on 14-04-2020

Literacy in India (2020). Retrieved from https://en.wikipedia.org/wiki/Literacy_in_India on 16-04-2020

Nagpal Mittal (1993). *Economics of Education.* New Delhi: Anmol Publications Private Limited.

Non-resident Indian and person of Indian origin (2020). Retrieved from https://en.wikipedia.org/wiki/Non-resident_Indian_and_person_of_Indian_ origin on 15-04-2020

Narasaiah, M.L. (2007). *Education and Economic Development.* New Delhi: Discovery Publishing House. Retrieved from https://books.google.co.in/books/about/Education_and_Economic_Development.html?id=aWyOStJKXHEC&printsec=frontcover&source=kp_read_button&redir_esc=y#v=onepage&q&f=false on 12-04-2020

Pandey Chandra Subhash (2016). "An Overview of Human Resource Planning." *International Journal of Interdisciplinary and Multidisciplinary Studies*, *4*(1), 8-12. Retrieved from http://www.ijims.com/uploads/57daf1d942b7104c3eac3subs.pdf on 05-04-2020

Robinson, E.A.G., Vaizey, J.E (1966). *The Economics of Education*, U.S. & Canada: Stockton Press. Retrieved from. https://books.google.co.in/books/about/The_Economics_of_Education.html?id=lOheCwAAQBAJ&printsec=frontcover&source=kp_read_button&redir_esc=y#v=onepage&q&f=false on 12-04-2020

Sen Amartya (2014). "The Crisis in Indian Education." In R.K. Mishra (Ed.), *India: Leading Issues in Economic Development* (2nd ed., pp. 149-182). New Delhi: Academic Foundation.

Sharma, R.N. (2002). *Educational Administration, Management and Organization.* Delhi: Surjeet Publications.

Suravi Swati (2016). *Need for Human Resource Planning in India.* Retrieved from https://www.mbaskool.com/business-articles/human-resource/15840-need-for-human-resource-planning-in-india.html on 06-04-2020.

25
Role of Education in Human Capital

D. Anita

Role of Education in Human Capital

Capital is the whole thing that engrosses costs and yields fixed income over a period of time. According to H. G. Johnson's classification of capital, Education is classified as Human Capital as opposed to Social Goods, Social Capital and Intellectual Capital. Capital is man-made resources. It is a means any produced means of production, which has a money value and yields steady income. Education is human capital as opposed to Social goods, Social capital and intellectual capital. We can say that education can act as both working capital and fixed capital in the process of production. The thought was that development of education would develop the personality and also promote social attitude and social service among the people and working efficiency will be promoted. Education makes a man self-dependent as he is trained and becomes good produce and increases the productivity. Economic growth and development it gained through education. Education is an investment in the industry where the government is spending lots of money to produce skilled labour for economic prosperity of country. It means expenditure done on productive work is an investment. When expenditure is incurred on education lands, equipment buildings another expenses are an investment, the return of which is received in the form of useful, dynamic and efficient citizens who contribute to economic welfare of the county. The profitable return is in the form of dynamic self-reliant, hard working, devoted and efficient citizens who will contribute to the natural prosperity.

Marshall felt that education is "the most valuable of all capitals that is invested in human beings". He considered it "as a national investment."

The term "education" is used in its broadest sense encompassing training also. G.U. Papi lists the following ways by which education increases the productivity of labour and entrepreneurship.

Development of education and skilled manpower in the long run reduces risks and costs. On this G.U. Papi says, "It follows that, more particularly in the early stages of a country's economic development, education, rather than consumer goods, which are advantageous only to those who profit directly from them, is instrumental in increasing output in all sectors of production and creating starts for continuing progress. Nor is it by accident that all progress starts with the human element, since it is the human element that is always the originator of everything that is created and is responsible for every development of himself, his family and his country.

Investment takes place when capital goods are produced. Gross Investment is the total output of capital goods during a given period of time, usually one year. From this we can say that without education we cannot produce skilled labour for producing goods in an effective manner. Thus, education is always helpful as investment for production purpose. Education is the most valuable of all capital that is invested on human beings known as National Investment. Education, being an investment in economic terms is the capital invested in business. The expenditure on education is a sound investment for economic uplift and welfare by increasing the productive efficiency of the workers in the field of production. The capital on education once invested gives the people an opportunity to achieve a job or develop their skill in order to gain a better work. It removes poverty and raises the standard of living.

In economical terms, money is invested in a factory when there is demand for more goods. When more goods are produced, consumption increases, increased consumption done by the household gives profits to the form and the profits are reinvested to produce and service. For more production they need more human resource, as education is the only source to generate skilled labour. Human Capital Education creates the right attitude towards work and development. It creates awareness for better living.

Human capital is independent of the source of its investment. It is said that Irvine Fisher was the first person to analyze Human Capital forms in an economic perspective. Education is a form of capital formation as investment in schooling represents an income potential embodied in human beings. Human capital is one of the factors of production in an industry like the factors of land and capital. Human capital acts as both labour and an entrepreneur. It is education, which determines the vocational aim and prepares a person for a complete living.

Education as Human Capital

Education is considered as Human Capital as it unswervingly supports the quality and capability of human beings, it contributes to intellectual capital as well as, to some extent, social capital.

Education is regarded as human capital because:

- Development and formation of human capital involves costs.
- The cost of skilled human resources is incrementally to the natural product.
- Expenditure on human resources not only increases the national product but also the national wealth.

Education plays its role to bring awareness and attitudinal change among the masses. Making the masses aware if the importance of education, facilities available its utility in democratic set up of life and make a better life. Knowledgeable people can only make progress in their life up to date knowledge is necessary to make up business better and suitable for the competitive market and discharge his duties to the entire satisfaction of the concerned officers. Basic skills can be acquired through education. This complement of education is necessary pre-condition for modernization and self-reliant economy. Education is to facilitate the development of highly qualified manpower and generation of knowledge through research and development activities.

Attitude or outlook of the people may be positive or negative. Education helps in changing the attitude from unfavourable to favourable; it helps in making the social climate of the individual and society more conducive. Education socializes the individuals. Social efficiently is a must for every individual to live in the society. The formal education is given in the class or in the school and informal education, given outside the school socializes the learner.

In a model situation, research and development would be incorporated with the requirements of socio-economic policy thrusts in the country. All the ideas of Human Research Development should be applied with the help of education to increase productivity and excellence in organizations.

Factors that have an effect on human capital formation are investment in formal education, improved health, on the job training, manpower rehabilitation, migration, etc. Formal education enhances the economic value of human capital by raising the potential earning power and current asset value of human beings.

Human capital, i.e. acquisition of skills and useful knowledge, can be developed through education, job training, public health, medical facilities, nutrition, housing and social services. Improvement of human capital results in qualitative growth of manpower, of course, there is no consensus on this issue among economists. While Schultz considered quality manpower alone as human capital, J.S. Mill questioned the very concept and averred that wealth existed for people and people cannot be treated as wealth.

Human capital is the stock of habits, knowledge, social and personality attributes embodied in the ability to perform labour so as to produce economic value. Hence, education not only includes the ability to perform better using his education but also Companies can invest in human capital for example through education and training enabling improved levels of quality and production. Human capital is unique and differs from any other capital. It is needed for companies to achieve goals, develop and remain innovative.

Human capital is noticeably different from the concrete monetary capital as human capital has the capability to grow in a collective manner over a long period of time. Growth of tangible monetary capital sees ups and downs in business cycles. During the period of success, monetary capital grows at comparatively higher rate while during the period of recession and depression; there is lose pace of monetary capital. Whereas, human capital grows or develops in a ordinary rate of growth over a long period of time as the basis of human capital is dependent wholly on educational and health contribution. In the present situation, human capital is qualitatively developed by the effective inputs of education and health. The future generation is more benefited by the advanced research in the field of education and health, undertaken by the current generation. Therefore, the educational and health inputs create more productive impacts upon the future generation and the future generation becomes superior to the current generation. In other words, the productive capacity of future generation increases more than that of current generation. Therefore, rate of human capital formation in the future generation happens to be more than the rate of human capital formation in the current generation. This is the cumulative growth of human capital formation generated by superior quality of manpower in the succeeding generation as compared to the preceding generation.

In India, the rate of human capital formation has consistently increased after Independence due to qualitative improvement in each generation. In the second decade of the 21st century, the third generation of India's population is active in the workforce of India. This third generation is qualitatively the most superior human resource in India. It has developed the service sector of India with the export of financial services, software services, and tourist services with improved balance of payments. The rapid growth of the Indian economy in response to improvement in the service sector is evidence of cumulative growth of human capital in India. In the year 2019, India is said to have ranked 158 out of 195 countries (www.wikipedia.org/wiki/Human_capital).

Life Cycle of Human Capital

The growth and decline of Human Capital can be categorized under three divisions.

In this phase, calculation of opportunity cost (earning foregone) is difficult to estimate and differs considerably from region to region.

***Productive Period*:** The next three decades of Human Capital formation involve capital production resulting from education and technology. In this phase, productive analysis and cost-benefit analysis show rising trends both in production and human welfare.

Production, consumption and capital formation enable the system (economy), to help people earn means of living and also to help raise their standard of living.

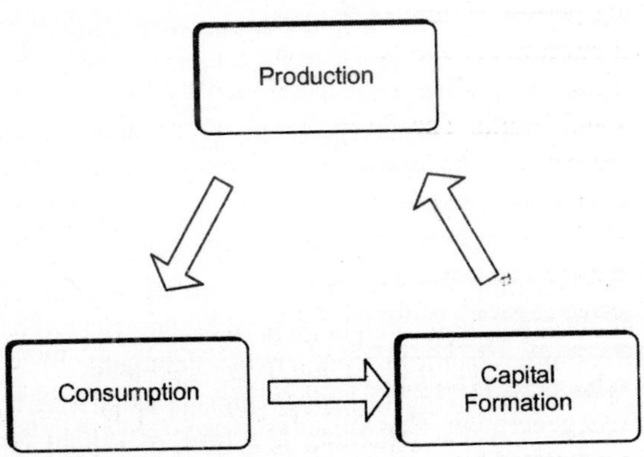

Fig. 25.1: Cycle of Human Capital.

As seen in the Fig. 25.2, various goods and services are produced in an economy. A part of this production is for immediate consumption and the rest is made available for capital formation.

Capital formation helps to raise the production potential of the economy, resulting in more production, higher consumption, and larger capital formation. Increase in capital formation leads to higher levels of consumption, investment or both. These basic economic activities combined together influence the overall growth of an economy.

Human capital theory is closely associated with the study of human resources management as found in the practice of business administration and macro-economics. American Society for Training and Development identified nine human resource areas for human resource management.

Characteristics of Human Capital

Comparatively Human Capital has a longer gestation period than non-human capital. Being an integral part of the individual Human Capital cannot be mortgaged or transferred or similar. Though several persons possess the same qualifications, their returns may vary. Being mobile, Human Capital depends on salary and status considerations.

One cannot easily calculate the depreciation of Human Capital. A UNICEF document on the State of World's Children, 1990, warns in this regard, "investment in Human Capital in the form on nutrition, basic education and health cannot be postponed. It either takes place at an appropriate age when need is present or it does not. For the young child, there is no second chance. The unemphasized tragedy of disinvestments in human capital in the eighties will be carried forward in stunted bodies and deficient education well into the twenty-first century." Social and cultural environments influence the productivity of Human Capital. Human Capital has non-economic attributes too.

Economists neglected the role of Human Capital and investment in education, for a long time. On this, Fredrcik Harison and Charles A. Myes said, "Modern economists, however, have not paid much explicit attention to human resources in economic growth as did some of the great classical economists like Smith and Marshall. Perhaps because physical capital was measurable and capital-output modern economists virtually ignored the human resources factor in economic development.

Irvine Fisher was the first to analyze Human Capital from an economic perspective. He said that schooling is a form of capital formation as investment in schooling representing in income potential embodied in human beings. In his view, educational development of man is a form of capital that is vested in human beings. An important aspect that differentiates Human Capital from Physical Capital is that the control over Human Capital is vested in the individual who embodies it. As such Human Capital is independent of the source of its investment. In this context, one has to also bear in mind a closely related concept—the intellectual or knowledge capital, which once created becomes a free good immediately in the sense that is use by a person does not reduce its part as a product of investment in human capital and an important input in the production of new physical capital through technological change. Thus, the concept of human capital involves a whole set of interacting factors that operate to produce a multiplier effect on the growth process.

Summing up the place of Human Capital in economic thought, Harbison and Myers said, "The economic analyses of investment in man which have been made recently, though representing a significant contribution to economic theory, are of little use as yet a planners, except perhaps to highlight the general importance of education and to suggest that some of the outlays for education could be considered as expenditure. It is not surprising; therefore, that the weakest sections in nearly all economic-development plans are those dealing with education, training and other aspects of development of the capacities of the peoples. And little progress is likely to be made until the processes (rather than merely the financial returns) of human resource development are analyzed with some precession and sophistication."

"In our judgement, the efforts to give greater emphasis to human resources in economic theory and the attempts to measure the contribution of education to economic growth are constructive. But the concept that humans resources development wither can or should be analyzed solely in economic terms in misleading. It is incorrect to assume that the central purpose of human resource development is to maximize man's contribution to the creation of goods and services. Nor is it realistic to measure the return on education solely in terms of increases in individual income or the income of the economy as a whole. And increases in productivity certainly should not be taken as the exclusive test of the effectiveness of human resource development. Nevertheless, as professional specialists, economists do tend to measure progress exclusively by economic criteria, even if as individual members of society they have often a much broader view of the goals of society."

Affirming that educational investments are necessary to develop human resources and to realize the indispensable socio-political-economic and cultural goals of the society, Harbison and Myers remarked. "Progress is basically the result of human effort. It takes human agents to mobilize capital, exploit natural resources, to create markets and to carry on trade. The builders of economies and elites may be revolutionary intellectuals, nationalists leaders, or members of dynamic or rising middle class. Their effectiveness as prime-movers depends not only on their own development but on the knowledge, skills, and capacities of those whom they lead as well. Thus in a very real sense, the wealth of a nation and its potential for social, economic and political growth stem from the power to develop and effectively utilize the innate capacities of people."

Economic Orders

There are three types of economic orders:

(1) Agrarian Economic Order,
(2) Trade Economy, and
(3) Industrial Economy.

Agrarian Economic Order and Education: In this order, the people are engaged in agriculture and allied occupation like dairy, cattle breeding, poultry and other minor vocations. Being a bare sustenance economy, this economic order does not need any sophisticated technology. People can do with primary education, often without formal schooling. One does not find here provision for secondary or higher educational institutions of industrial, technical or vocational education.

Education as Trade Economy: Inmade economy, production of goods is considerable whereas the supply of goods produced in the country for home consumption is meagre. Here, the trade balance is positive and the savings increase gradually. With limited hours of work in this economic order, workers have sufficient leisure time. With goods being sold in the foreign markets, people travel abroad in search of markets and these foreign travels promote the hearing of foreign languages and understanding of their geography, ways of living, needs and tales. This way national saving are increased leading to economic prosperity. In this economic order higher education of various types is necessary and therefore, more and more institutions are established for secondary, higher and specialized education for the benefit of trading community, selling agents and marketing personnel.

Education in Industrial Economy: In capitalists economy, individuals establish and manage their industries. In this economy, industries are run to derive maximum profits to the individual owners on the industries. This means the stress is on cheapest labour and cheaper raw materials to produce goods that fetch highest returns or profits.

In the Socialistic Economy, all industries including officials are nominees. The public sector controls all industrial activity and agricultural activity. In the Mixed Economy, industries and agriculture are run by individuals and the government in a cooperative spirit. In the Industrial Economy, primary, secondary and often vocational and specialized education is made free, compulsory and universal. Higher technological education is made available to those who need it, providing ample opportunities for research.

While in the capitalistic economic order only the rich have access to education in all fields, in the socialistic pattern all the children are able to get the desired education according to their needs, aptitude and capacities. In the mixed pattern, education provided to all children by both private and public institutions and agencies with the government exercising some amount of control and supervision over the private institutions.

Factors Influencing Human Capital

Harbison compares human capital formation to the process of acquiring and increasing the numbers of persons who have the skills, education and experience which are critical for the economic and political development of a country. He says, "Analysis of human capital formation is thus parallel and complementary to the study of the processes of savings and investments (in the material sense). In designing a strategy for development, one needs to consider the total stock of human capital required. It is the rate of accumulation and its commitment to (or investment in) high priority productive activities." Some of the external factors that influence human capital development include:

1. Acquisition of human resource planning, recruiting and employee socialization.
2. Developing the human resource by employee training, management development and career development.
3. Motivating by developing job design, performance evaluation, giving rewards, benefits and maintaining discipline.

4. Maintaining safety and health and maintaining employee/labour relation.

(*Source:* Adopted from Meg Isaac Sternberg, Organizational Model for Human Resource Planning"(Unpublished paper, Baltimore,1964).

Training is considered a merit good giving positive externalities. A better trained labour force provides private benefits to those trained and to firms which finance training. It also provides positive externalities in the form of higher national output arising from increased productivity and overcoming of skill shortages along with education.

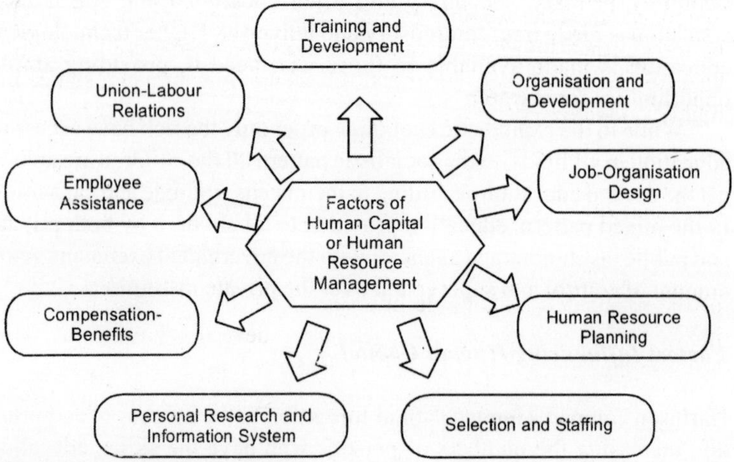

Fig. 25.2: HRM Areas Outputs.

Education as Human Capital Development

All types of production is possible only when all the factors of production are put together and they work efficiently, that is land, labour, capital and entrepreneur. "Education is definitely an asset for man". Education develops knowledge, attitudes and skills. Education promotes the quality and capability of human being. Training is considered a merit good giving positive externalities. A better trained labour force provides private benefits to those trained and to firms which finance training. It also provides positive externalities in the form of higher national output arising from increased productivity and overcoming of skill shortages.

Human capital labour-surplus countries

Development and formation of human capital has a price for it.

Labour has a cost for production. The cost of skilled human resource is higher than unskilled manpower. Increased expenditure on human resources for education will increase the national product or output and increase the national income.

Education can raise the living standard of the people and it leads to the economic growth of the country.

The concept of human capital has relatively more importance in labour-surplus countries. These countries are naturally endowed with more of labour due to high birth rate under the given climatic conditions. The surplus labour in these countries is the human resource available in more abundance than the tangible capital resource. This human resource can be transformed into human capital with effective inputs of education, health and moral values. The transformation of raw human resource into highly productive human resource with these inputs is the process of human capital formation. The problem of scarcity of tangible capital in the labour surplus countries can be resolved by accelerating the rate of human capital formation with both private and public investment in education and health sectors of their national economies. The tangible financial capital is an effective instrument of promoting economic growth of the nation. The intangible human capital, on the other hand, is an instrument of promoting comprehensive development of the nation because human capital is directly related to human development, and when there is human development, the qualitative and quantitative progress of the nation is inevitable. This importance of human capital is explicit in the changed approach of United Nations towards comparative evaluation of economic development of different nations in the world economy.

The statistical indicator of estimating human development in each nation is Human Development Index (HDI). It is the combination of "Life Expectancy Index", "Education Index" and "Income Index". The life expectancy index reveals the standard of health of the population in the country; the education index reveals the educational standard and the literacy ratio of the population; and the income index reveals the standard of living of the population. If all these indices have a rising trend over a long period of time, it is reflected in a rising trend in HDI. Human capital is measured by health, education and quality of standard of living. Therefore, the components of HDI, *viz.* Life Expectancy Index, Education Index and Income Index, are directly related to human capital formation within the nation. HDI is indicator of positive correlation between human capital formation and economic development. If HDI increases, there is a higher rate of human capital formation in response to a higher standard of education and health. Similarly, if HDI increases, per capita income of the nation also increases. Implicitly, HDI reveals that the higher is human capital formation due to good levels of health and education, the higher is the per capita income of the nation. This process of human development is the strong foundation of a continuous process of economic development of the nation for a long period of time. This significance of the concept of human capital in generating long-term economic development of the nation cannot be neglected. It is expected that the macro economic policies of all the nations are focused towards promotion of human development and subsequently economic development.

Human capital is the backbone of human development and economic development in every nation. Mahroum (2007) suggested that at the macro-level, human capital management is about three key capacities: the capacity to develop talent, the capacity to deploy talent, and the capacity to draw talent from elsewhere. Collectively, these three capacities form the backbone of any country's human capital competitiveness. Recent US research shows that geographic regions that invest in the human capital and economic advancement of immigrants who are already living in their jurisdictions help boost their short- and long-term economic growth. There is also strong evidence that organizations that possess and cultivate their human capital outperform other organizations lacking human capital (Crook, Todd, Combs, Woehr, and Ketchen, 2011).

Human resources are the capital of the country. They are the wealth of a nature. Education can only make an individual grow and develop fully.

Kothari Education Commission Report (1964—1966) highlights the role of education in human resource development in this way, "One of the major programmes in national reconstruction is the development of our human resources, and in this there can be no limit to the education to be provided." According to National Policy on Education 1986, "It should now be possible to further identify the nature wide effort in human resource development, with education playing its multifaceted role."

A rise in human capital leads to modern approach, better quality of life and higher life expectancy. It leads to more efficiency, more production and finally, leads to more economic growth. Education has to play its multifaceted role to bring awareness, providing basic skill and education with technology empower economic domain of life along with social, cultural, political life and make India self-sufficient and self-reliant dream of Gandhi, said by Prof. D.A. Ghanchi.

Human capital is an intangible asset, and it is not owned by the firm that employs it and is generally not fungible. Specifically, individuals arrive at 9 am and leave at 5 pm (in the conventional office model) taking most of their knowledge and relationships with them.

Human capital when viewed from a time perspective consumes time in one of these key activities:

Knowledge (activities involving one employee), and
Collaboration (activities involving more than 1 employee).

Processes (activities specifically focused on the knowledge and collaborative activities generated by organizational structure—such as silo impacts, internal politics etc.) and absence (annual leave, sick leave, holidays etc.).

Human capital is unique and differs from any other capital. It is needed for companies to achieve goals, develop and remain innovative. Companies can invest in human capital through education and training enabling improved levels of quality and production. Human capital theory is closely associated with the study of human resources management as found in the practice of business administration and macro-economics.

Human capital is a means of production, into which additional investment yields additional output. Human capital is substitutable, but not transferable like land, labour, or fixed capital. Becker's book entitled *Human Capital*, published in 1964, became a standard reference for many years. In this view, human capital is similar to "physical means of production", e.g. factories and machines: one can invest in human capital (*via* education, training, medical treatment) and one's outputs depend partly on the rate of return on the human capital one owns. Thus, human capital is a means of production, into which additional investment yields additional output. Human capital is substitutable, but not transferable like land, labour, or fixed capital.

Some contemporary growth theories see human capital as an important economic growth factor. Further research shows the relevance of education for the economic welfare of people. Adam Smith defined four types of fixed capital (which is characterized as that which affords a revenue or profit without circulating or changing masters). The four types were:

- Useful machines, instruments of the trade.
- Buildings as the means of procuring revenue.

- Improvements of land.
- The acquired and useful abilities of the inhabitants of the society.

The acquisition of such talents, by the maintenance of the acquirer during his education, study, or apprenticeship, always costs a real expense, which is a capital fixed and realized, as it were, in his person. The greatest improvement in the productive powers of labour, and the greater part of the skill, dexterity, and judgement with which it is anywhere directed, or applied, seem to have been the effects of the division of labour.

There is a complex relationship between the division of labour and human capital. In the 1990s, the concept of human capital was extended to include natural abilities, physical fitness and healthiness, which are crucial for an individual's success in acquiring knowledge and skills.

World Economic Forum Global Human Capital Index

Since 2012, the World Economic Forum has annually published its Global Human Capital Report, which includes the Global Human Capital Index (GHCI). In the 2017 edition, 130 countries were ranked from 0 (worst) to 100 (best) according to the quality of their investments in human capital. Norway was at the top, with 77.12. In October 2018, the World Bank published the Human Capital Index (HCI) as a measurement of economic success. The Index ranks countries according to how much is invested in education and health care for young people. The World Bank's 2019 World Development Report is on The Changing Nature of Work.

The government has raised "serious reservations" over the first Human Capital Index (HCI) compiled by the World Bank as part of the World Development Report 2019. India is ranked at 115th position in the index with its score of 0.44 on a scale of 0 to 1 coming even below the average score for South Asia. In a strongly worded statement the Finance Ministry has questioned HCI that ranked Singapore on top with a score of 0.88.

"There are serious reservations about the advisability and utility of this exercise of constructing HCI. There are major methodological weaknesses, besides substantial data gaps", Finance Ministry said. HCI, which covered 157 countries, seeks to measure the amount of human capital that a child born today can expect to attain by age 18. The index values convey the productivity of the next generation of workers, compared to a benchmark of complete standard education and full health. It has three components—survival, expected years of quality-adjusted school, and health environment.

Published at the annual meetings of the International Monetary Fund and World Bank Group in Bali Nusa Dua, Indonesia, the Human Capital Index showed that for 56 per cent of the world's population HCI score is at or below 0.50; and for 92 per cent it is at or below 0.75.

The government has rejected the findings, saying it does not reflect the key initiatives that are being taken for developing human capital in the country, such as Samagra Shiksha, Ayushman Bharat Programme, Swachh Bharat Mission, Pradhan Mantri Ujjwala Yojana, Pradhan Mantri Jandhan Yojana and the Aadhaar identification system—enabled direct cash transfer, that have improved governance and social protection.

Sustainable Development Goals (SDGs) are far from satisfactory. The two basic facets of human capital covered in the SDG—health and education highlights some of the alarming gaps in achieving the target by 2030. For instance, the SDG goal aims at reduction of under 5 mortality rates to 11 per 1000 live births by 2030 but we have reached 50 per 1000 live births—a gap of 39 per 1000 live births to be covered in the next 11 years. Further, SDG goal aims at 100 per cent immunization of children in the age group 12-23 months but we have achieved mere 62 per cent. SDG 2018 status of global mortality ratio is 130 per 1,00,000 live births and it is targeting to 70. 2018 goal states that 221 government health workers per lakh persons are at work. Drop-out rate reduction is 17 per cent, 81 per cent of school teachers are professionally qualified and 70 per cent of elementary and secondary schools with pupil ratio is less than or equal to 30.

"These initiatives are transforming human capital in India at a rapid pace and very comprehensively touching upon the lives of millions of people living in rural and tribal areas", the Finance Ministry statement said.

"The qualitative aspects of improved governance that have a strong correlation with human capital development cannot be and have not been captured by the way the HCI has been constructed", it said.

Human Capital Index Ranking (*Top 10 Countries*)

1. Singapore 0.88
2. South Korea 0.84
3. Japan 0.84
4. Hong Kong, SAR of China 0.82
5. Finland 0.81
6. Ireland 0.81
7. Australia 0.80

8. Sweden 0.80
9. Netherlands 0.80
9. Canada 0.80

Conclusion

Any kind of expenditure done on formal and non-formal education gives some benefit for teacher education. It studies about in-service education benefits. Efficient and good medical facilities are provided in order to check the Human health condition of the people in the country. Education is a precious resource to turn human resource to human capital. All expenditure done by the government on labour, mobility, information, education, health and training can increase the productive capacity of the workers, i.e. productivity due to investment on human resource by giving knowledge about balanced diet. Re-orientation programmes are given for the development of manpower.

Each and every human being may be an agriculturist, labour, engineer, doctor, the entrepreneur or any other professions are enabled to get the advantage of investment made in human capital.

REFERENCES

Bhatia and Bhatia (2001). *The Philosophical and Sociological Foundation of Education*, Doaba House.

Bhatia, K.K. and C.L. Narang. (2001). *Philosophical and Sociological bases of Education*. Ludhiana: Tandon Publication.

Dash, B.N. (2004). *Theories of Education and Education in the Emerging Indian Society*. New Delhi: Dominant Publishers and Distributors.

David, A. DeCenzo., Stephen P. Robbins (1998). *Personnel/Human Resource Management*.

Grant, S.J. (2000). *Stanlake's 'Introductory Economics'*, Pearson Education Limited.

https://economictimes.indiatimes.com/news/economy/indicators/government-questions-world-banks-human-capital-index-rank/articleshow/66172833.cms?utm_source=contentofinterest &utm_medium=text&utm_campaign=cppst

https://economictimes.indiatimes.com/

http://www.marketexpress.in/2019/02/human-capital-economic-growth-in-india.html

National Policy on Education 1986, Ministry of Human Resource Development, Government of India, New Delhi.

26

The Economic Dimension of Investment in Human Capital

Ahmad Mahmoud Ali Alghzawi

Summary

The critical importance of the human element and its potential have led economists to consider it the first productive element in economic and social development processes will not play its role without an appropriate level of education. Education is the first and most important factor influencing human capital formation, return and productivity, so the focus is on investment in education or the so-called education economics.

Countries, in all their economic systems, pay close attention to education the basis of its progress and its standard of excellence. As for the interest in education and the increase in its expenses and the demand for it, the economic outlook has increased and it has evolved considerably to become a wide field for scientific research in view of the various intellectual trends and the different approaches that have been addressed.

Most studies on education economics have attached great importance to measuring the extent of education, the contribution of education to economic growth after it has been incorporated as an essential factor of economic growth in various modern theories of growth.

The first topic: The economic dimension of investment in human capital, all branches of social sciences today are interested in the concept of human capital, because individuals, institutions and countries firmly believe that it is an important factor of security and success, and the concept of human capital is among the basic concepts in the general economic analysis. We will try to address the general concepts of human capital and investment in it and identify the most important economic theories that addressed the subject.

The First Requirement: What is Human Capital?

Human capital represents the knowledge, skills and abilities that make the human element capable to perform his duties and responsibilities in an effective and efficient manner.

Definition of Human Capital

There are many concepts and definitions given to human capital, widening and narrowing according to a vision the goal of its owner, we find that the concept of human capital in the broad sense is the totality of knowledge that acquired by individuals during their lifetime and that they take in the production of goods and services in or outside markets.

In the narrow sense, human capital is "Total investment in activities such as education, health, vocational training and training in the workplace that allow increasing worker productivity in the labour market."

There are those who know you as the totality of competencies, expertise and knowledge that individuals possess in their work positions.

It is also defined as the totality of qualifications, competencies and other characteristics of man that are of interest to economic activity.

So human capital relates primarily to the knowledge that employees have and that the organization does not have, this is what is stable within the heads of staff (De Dearlove, 1999), and is expressed by all individuals. Sveiby, one of the pioneers of thought, adds that human capital is represented in the level of education, experience, knowledge of employees, spirit of innovation, values and training in education, experience and knowledge. In short, all the contributions of researchers in this field link human capital to the total competencies, skills and knowledge possessed by an organization's employees, which have a direct impact on the achievement of the organization's objectives and Daiha.

The Basic Characteristics of Human Capital

Human capital is characterized by a set of characteristics that can be summarized in the following points:

- Human capital consists of two parts: an innate part and an acquired part.
- Knowledge and competencies are the most important compounds in human capital and can be classified accordingly in terms of

quality of knowledge, qualifications and competencies, there are two main categories:

General human capital: It arises from the acquisition of general knowledge and competencies such as knowledge reading, writing and arithmetic.

Private Human Capital: It arises from the acquisition of knowledge and competencies specific to a job or by a particular profession or by an institution itself.

- Acquisition and formation of human capital requires:

    1. Investment of financial resources.
    2. Make some time for.
    3. Make an effort for it.

- Human capital develops through employment and experience in the field of work or through training and education of all kinds.

Human capital is obsolete and needs renewal.
Human capital is concerned with the individual who acquires it.
Human capital is a major source of income.

Measuring Human Capital

The subject of measuring human capital has been the subject of many researchers of different orientations and their ideologies. This is because any measurement given to human capital is influenced by the concept that human capital takes, by way of measurement and aggregation, as well as by the purpose of using measurement.

Human capital, as intangible capital, is closely linked to knowledge (Competencies) acquired by individuals however use knowledge as a measure of human capital it faces many problems because knowledge is very different economically from other goods and services, according to researchers (Aghiow & Howitt, 2000).

Among the Most Important Obstacles We can Mention

- The framework within which human capital is formed. It includes formal education, non-education formal, and education by doing, works etc. (OCDE, 1998).

- The heterogeneous nature of human capital is, therefore, difficult to express activity, it is difficult to aggregate these characteristics for individuals to obtain the stock of human capital accumulated by a country.
- The content and nature of the knowledge acquired by human beings themselves poses a great problem because they differ from individual to individual, for example, you measure the human capital of individuals by way of testimony as is known to all, two individuals are equal in testimony and the content varies the knowledge obtained for each of them thus different economic performance of each.
- The availability of information and data used in the measurement and the accuracy, comprehensiveness, authority, etc.

For these reasons, and others, it can be said that it is difficult to reach an accurate and comprehensive measurement of human capital. One of the most important measures used in the economic literature of capital, the human can recall:

- Schooling rate.
- Literacy rate in contrast to the illiteracy rate.
- Percentage of people with a certain educational level.
- Number of university graduates.
- Number of patents.
- The average years of schooling of the active population is the most widely used measure.

Hence, human capital is an intangible asset that cannot be measured accordingly one specific variable, leading to the use of approximate variables to measure composition and products human capital.

To measure the stock of human capital in one country, the total accumulations of approximate variables depends on quantitative and qualitative investment decisions. In the calculation of indirect economic variables is a method that lacks accuracy, recognizing that it remains the method available to estimate the tangible and indirect variables.

Basic Principles of Human Capital Measurement

There are basic and guiding principles for measuring human capital:

(1) *Individuals and information are the driving force of the knowledge economy:* The human element of the most important

resource, without it, growth cannot be maintained in all areas of business, and without it you will not be able to build institution's structure, their activities, and this requires changing the cultures within them, so that they revolve around communication and methods of knowledge transfer and participation, and linking individuals quickly to technological development.

(2) *We cannot manage without data:* Most decisions made without data are not accurate, this is due to the complex work environment, which requires rapid response to emergencies, this is what it is imperative to create a database of human capital and reporting systems.

(3) *Human capital data is the foundation of every success:* The human element is the only asset able to make decisions, so their behaviours are everything happening positively and negatively.

(4) *The strength and validity of human capital measures:* The human capital scale is as inaccurate as financial metrics, due to the use of some unproven external measurements or accuracy, and everyone started adjusting to suit their needs in fixed and prolonged use.

(5) *The relationship between causes and consequences:* One of the obstacles in the qualitative measurement of human capital is belief not knowing the relationship between causes and results in this scale, because there are a lot of interferential forces that can be identified and can influence the results of measurements.

(6) *Human capital is the driving force of value-added whatever equipment or quality operations or even intellectual capital:* It cannot add any value to the enterprise, because the skill of the workers, their experience, the knowledge they possess and the degree of motivation within them that creates value added.

(7) *Success requires commitment:* Without commitment, no strategy, however strong, can succeed distinguished in all areas of business, dedication and sincerity in dealing with employees and customers all beneficiaries are the basis of excellence throughout history.

(8) *Walk for the future:* One of the most dangerous things to walk to the future with closed eyes for the results in the past, the wide open globalization market today allows everyone to compete, in addition that the dramatic change in technology makes yesterday's operations not fit today as well as free instant access to information.

(9) *The manager is the basis:* All signs indicate that personal relationships are the cornerstone of staff performance, highly qualified employees expect managers to be strengthened, guided and developed on the career path. The manager is the basis of communication and two-way and is the path that saturates employees' ambitions and desires.

(10) Preparing for the future is harder than preparing for the past more complexity, networking and much more difficulty for businesses living in an environment rapid change and volatility in all areas and at all levels.

Economic Importance of Human Capital throughout the ages, life has witnessed spectacular achievements that demonstrate the human ability to construct the enormous edifices of human civilization through the rise of the value of the human element as an economic unit and considering it as a part of the wealth of nations for the contribution of human action in the production process, and the differentiation of the productive capacity of man and its superiority over all. Other forms of wealth place human labour as the most important element of production, even in its possible circumstances (Ani, 2002).

The experience of global economic development has clearly demonstrated that qualified cadres their professional, scientific, and technical knowledge in particular, and productive and managerial expertise are among the most important elements of social reproduction that often determine the progress and prospects of the development process (Ani, 2002).

Other accounting studies have shown that labour training costs result in a significant increase in production capacity. Spending on raising the efficiency of workers and improving the methods of work performance increased the number of units produced for the same period, which reduced the total and average cost of the unit produced and gave more opportunity to make more profits (Zayed, 1997).

Researchers believe that one of the most important results of the information and technology revolution and the movement of variables global, contemporary trends in modern management are moving towards a new topic of interest more human assets than physical assets. It became the largest proportion of its assets, because the addition and maximization of physical assets comes due to the availability of human assets, and this the theme in its new dimensions is human capital (Nima, 2010).

Definition of Investment in Human Capital

Defined as a set of concepts, knowledge and information on the one hand, skills, experience and elements on the second hand, performance, trends, behaviours, ideals and values on the third hand obtained human through formal and informal education systems, which contribute to improve productivity and increase, thus the benefits of his work (Egyptian Munther Wassef, 2003).

Investment in human capital is defined as "Spending on the development of abilities, skills and talents of humans in a way that can increase their productivity" (Abdelhamid Abdel Wahed Ben Khaled, 1997).

Through these definitions, investment in human capital can be defined as the use of part of the savings of the community or individuals in developing the abilities, skills, information and behaviours of the individual with the aim of raising its production capacity and thus the total capacity of society to produce more goods and services that achieve welfare sooiety as well to prepare it to be a good citizen in its community.

The Importance of Investing in Human Capital

Human resources are one of the main measures by which the wealth of nations is measured at the top of the components of capital and assets affecting the economic and social situation of States, where the human factor and the degree of efficiency has become the decisive factor for progress.

Economists have long emphasized the importance of human resource development in achieving economic growth. In his famous book, *Wealth of Nations*, A. Smith stated that all the acquired and beneficial capabilities of other members of society are a cornerstone of the concept of fixed capital, the fact that acquiring capacity while learning costs financial expenses, yet these talents are an important part of an individual's wealth, which in turn forms a major part of the wealth of the community to which he belongs.

The Importance of Human Resources in the Economic Process

Human is a kind of precious resources, has been the use of the concept of human resources, human resources you need wise management, like any other scarce resources, and human resource management with multiple functions triple:

- Mobilization of human resources (inventory, statistics and identification of different characteristics by quantity and quality).
- Human resources development (quality upgrading through education, health, nutrition, culture, migration).
- Employment of human resources (actual utilization of investment in human capital).

Human resources development: There is an educational stock of individuals that can be measured independently of a mere number population, but not separate from man. This inventory in turn needs to be managed from its job functions previous: measurement of educational inventory, development of educational inventory, operation of educational inventory.

Reintegrating human resources management into its broader context: sustainable human development or development: The economics of education of all doctrines recognize a great recognition that man on this earth—every investment in the development, improvement and improvement of cultural quality (education, training, nutrition, health, social and cultural care, appropriate housing and clothing, democratic practice and the revitalization of scientific research to increase the identification of its nature is the best investment without condition—the success of any other investment. Agricultural, industrial or commercial in this presence..... However, this Muslim or—theoretical in the value of man and his investment is governed by the conditions without which say in the field of education and training—invalid or half of the fact and these conditions:

- Integration and coordination between school education (formal) and non-formal education and related integration and coordination between education, training and employment.
- Quality and adequacy of education and training.
- Equitable distribution of education and training.
- Accompanying and coordinating education, training and services in nutrition, health, social and economic care.
- Social justice and alleviation of disparities between social groups and classes.
- Security, political and military security and the related spread of the atmosphere of freedom.
- The growth of a new international political and economic order and the reduction of disparities between developing and

developed countries (Ahmed Mandour, Ahmed Ramadan, 1999:90).

Components of human capital: Human capital includes many different components as follows:

Working knowledge: It includes individuals who are able to sort, collect and interpret the use of accepted information and of value, and benefit. Two types of knowledge can be distinguished:

(1) *Explicit knowledge:* Which can be embodied by texts, drawings, images or symbols, it means the knowledge of an organization that is stored in physical means such as Archives, Data, Procedures, Charts, Process and Operational Standards, Forms and Documents. Individuals can within the organization accessible, used and shared with all employees through seminars, encounters, books etc. (Ishawi, 2005).

(2) *Implicit knowledge:* It is the fruit of personal experience, and can be expressed with the skills found in minds that are difficult to transfer or transfer to others.

Contemporary organizations, in their quest to be educated, must focus on continuous development of the capabilities of employees and give them some flexibility in thinking and continuing education including they are motivated and ambitious to create modern models and ways to achieve the desired results of the organization. Nor in order to remain competitive and successful, organizations must become (educational organizations) which are defined as "Organizations with the skill to create, acquire, interpret, transmit and retain knowledge" Workers' Experience: It means the level of accumulated shelf life of working individuals current and previous posts. Al-Maghrabi (2004) argues that there are many reasons in the field of expertise, it has a great impact on the individual performance in the organization, namely:

(1) Experience reduces training cost and time.

(2) Experience works as a social indicator, where the individual has learned in other organizations that work which type of behaviour is required.

(3) The quality of experience acquired by an individual is important for future promotion purposes the time served by the individual is not as strong a justification for promotion as the type of work the individual has practiced throughout his life.

Skill of Employees: It represents the abilities that are gained by training and work experience.

The capabilities lay humanitarianism as seen by Al-Mughrabi, (2004):

(1) Mental abilities, verbal, mathematical, logic and creativity.
(2) Motor ability.
(3) Mechanical ability.
(4) Creative ability includes the ability to animate, organize and group icons in new and different modes.

The most important responsibility of the management of the organization is to identify the differences in the capabilities of individuals and even trained grow their skills to the level required to perform the work.

Sources of human capital by defining human capital, Hinnawi (2006: 8) identified sources of human capital, namely:

1. *Teaching and learning through work:* Where teaching and learning through work play inseparable roles, as sources of human capital, on the one hand, what is taught at school should always be complemented by practice the process where learning through action takes its toll, and on the other hand the learning process itself develops assimilate all the important skills and knowledge that may appear independently while learning through the importance of this assimilation should not be underestimated. Indeed, many new skills originate in the market before they are analyzed, categorized and eventually incorporated into the education system.

2. *Internal Migration:* The writings of human capital provided only a few additions to wealthy migration studies, which are related to the old question of whether migrants make a profit or not as a result of migration. It has not had a great impact, because the relationship between migration and human capital as skill and knowledge has remained largely unclear.

Other sources: One source that cannot be ignored is advanced capital equipment, like this equipment plays the role of a study lab as it transfers more technological knowledge to those who do this source is very important in the developing countries represented in imported technology, if used rationally, it can be highly effective and can be used as a laboratory to train local technologists and master local technological knowledge, have this lab the more sophisticated the higher the practical content of the imported technology.

Modern Theories of Investment in Human Capital

The modern theories according to the opinions of economists, especially those who conducted field studies; all criticized the findings of previous writers on education spending. We will explain some recent contributions as follows:

(1) Fisher's Contribution

Through his study in 1994, Fisher reached the following differences in earning levels associated with the level of personal education are significant.

The level of earning associated with educational level is influenced by several factors such as social level sex, race etc.

The age of the worker and the length of work should be added to explain part of the differences in the level of gain investing in long-term education can only be rewarded after a period of time and the longer you age less human spending on education.

(2) Jurgenson and Greelishes' Contribution

They conducted a field study (Jurgenson & Grilliches, 1967), and concluded that the remaining factor was probably due to inaccuracies in measuring inputs, and that the indirect impact of advancing knowledge on economic progress did not exist.

They reject the theory of the remaining factor.

(3) Ginz's Contribution

The attitudes theory of Ginz stipulated that the school improved productivity, the individual not by the knowledge provided, but by the development of behaviour and attitudes are appreciated institutions productivity, these attitudes are compliance, obedience and acceptance of work within a regulated group sequence where everyone finds their place.

Studies have found that the impact of education expenditures on economic growth is minimal on the contrary; I found that the impact of GDP on education expenditure was very strong as output nationalism is distributed to education, health, defence etc., the more the national product, the more spending on education. Criticism of the theory of human capital: The theory of human capital was deficient in a number of aspects, including:

Assuming the perfection of the market, which is not the case either in terms of competition or compound wages.

Assuming that education raises productivity.

The inability of human capital variables (education and training) to interpret income variables in a way only partially satisfactory.

Among the criticisms of the theory of human capital is the difference in incomes by race, sex, family background and work position. It was noted that the results differed according to the different models and data used and the existence of other non-economic goals of education, which led to the emergence of other theories or interpretations of the wage differences between workers (Adnan Wadih, 2005 : 6).

Refinery Theory

This theory holds that education does not raise productivity but reveals it to the employer. Ear Education plays the role of a refinery on or within the labour market (Zwair and David, 2010: 120).

Signal Theory

This theory considers the education and training received by an individual merely as a preliminary indication of their potential future productivity. The signals enable the employer to determine the wage before his knowledge of productivity (Wadih, 7: 2007).

Competition theory for work and waiting line this theory holds that productivity is not the property of the individual but the property of the workplace and technology, education reveals the learner's ability to adapt and learn, and the employer is ready to qualify his employees to fill the necessary work (internal market), and that the employer is ready to pay fair remuneration for skill holders to retain them (the institution's training) as the worker accepts. To stay on the waiting line (unemployment) in order to get good paid work and high benefits decreases despite an excess supply of those willing to work (Zwair and David, (2010 : 121).

Labour Market Fragmentation Theories

The other counterpart to the theory of human capital and its ramifications in explaining the pay differentials between the workers' current is the 'fragmented labour market' and is based on the assumption and testing of the existence of several labour markets separate:

Independent Primary Labour Market: There is a turnover of workers in leadership frameworks.

Primary Affiliated Labour Market: There is relative uncertainty in management and production frameworks.

Secondary Labour Market: There is a turnover in less skilled labour because it is marginal.

Assuming that technology determines the business and then the characteristics of the workers required to occupy it and that each of the sections of the market rules in wages, dealing, training and characteristics of workers and in a radical development has shown that the cause of fragmentation in the market is not technology but class struggle.

Employers, and the desire of employers to divide the labour market for exploitation as the technology deepening the market fragmentation does not create that fragmentation, the theory has defined a number of problems.

The definition of sections is precisely defined and their borders are invisible and vary from one community to another (Wadih, 2007: 7).

REFERENCES

Abdulhamid Abdulwahid Bin Khalid, "Investment in a Nation", *Knowledge Magazine*, Riyadh Ministry of Education 1414 e, 2 Mohamed Said, Hani, Intellectual capital, a breakthrough contemporary management, Dar Al-Sahab for Publishing and Distribution, Cairo, 8. 200

Aghion, P., and Howitt, P, Théorie de la croissance endogène,

Aishawi, Ahmad, (2005) "Knowledge Management and Improving the Competitive Advantage of Organizations", Third International Forum on Governance of Institutions and Economics.

Ani, Taqi Abdul Salem, The economic importance of human capital and the role of education in it, Research presented to the educational symposium accompanying the Central Council of the Arab Teachers Union held 2/22/ 2002-In Algeria.

De Dearlove, (1999) *Entrepreneurial Thought—The Road to Complete Success*, Library Translation. Shaqri, Riyadh, p. 177.

Egyptian Munther Wassef, (2003), *Economics of Vocational Education and Training*, Benghazi, National Library First Edition.

Grace, Melody. (August 21, 2014) *Man built a god and cursed from his demolition*, retrieved

Hinnawi, Hamdi, (2006). *Human Capital: Theoretical Rooting and Application to Egypt*. Alexandria Book, Alexandria, Egypt.

http://www.kitabat.com, dated May 23, 2015, from the writings of Ani, Taqi Abdul Salem (2002). "The economic importance of human capital and the role of education in it", a paper presented to the educational seminar accompanying the Central Council of Teachers Union. 2/13-2/Arabs held in Algeria.

Mazerolle, F. (Trans.) (2000). *France: Les éditions Dunod,* 467-482.

Moroccan, Full. Organizational Behaviour, Concepts and Foundations of Individual and Community Behaviour in 2004 Organization, 3rd floor, Amman, Dar Al Fikr.

OCDE, L'investissement dans le capital humain: une comparison.

Zaid, Dr. Mohamed Essam El-Din, "Investment in Human Training at the Project Level," 1997, pp. 18-13, *Arab Labour Magazine*, No. 8.

Index